T0374673

THE FLETCHER JONES FOUNDATION
HUMANITIES IMPRINT

The Fletcher Jones Foundation has endowed this imprint to foster innovative and enduring scholarship in the humanities.

The publisher and the University of California Press
Foundation gratefully acknowledge the generous support
of the Fletcher Jones Foundation Imprint in Humanities.

Specworld

Specworld

Folds, Faults, and Fractures in
Embedded Creator Industries

John Thornton Caldwell

UNIVERSITY OF CALIFORNIA PRESS

University of California Press
Oakland, California

Library of Congress Cataloging-in-Publication Data

Names: Caldwell, John Thornton, 1954– author.
Title: Specworld : folds, faults, and fractures in
  embedded creator industries / John Thornton
  Caldwell.
Description: Oakland, California : University of
  California Press, [2023] | Includes bibliographical
  references and index.
Identifiers: LCCN 2022016255 | ISBN 9780520388987
  (cloth) | ISBN 9780520388970 (paperback) | ISBN
  9780520388994 (epub)
Subjects: LCSH: Mass media—Economic aspects—United
  States. | Mass media—United States—Employees.
Classification: LCC P96.E252 U62733 2023 |
  DDC 338.4/730223/0973—dc23/eng/20220531
LC record available at https://lccn.loc.gov/2022016255

31 30 29 28 27 26 25 24 23 22
10 9 8 7 6 5 4 3 2 1

Contents

Preface

Why is it there? The divide between light and darkness?
The divine presence. Dividing the conscious from the
unconscious. The future from the past. I put myself, for
this project, in a kind of psychoanalyst's presence to understand the reasons. You know, symbolically, a beam of light
coming from the right side, has a very specific meaning.
Because that means the sun is in a setting position. Symbolically, in psychoanalysis, the sun setting means the death
of the father. There is no doubt. . . . This element
(light/dark) gives to him a kind of consciousness. That
he, tragically, needs to do some kind of deep immersion
into himself. Starting a kind of self-analysis, through
his own creativity. He is trying to understand his own
journey.   (Consciousness)

—Vittorio Storaro, "Caravaggio as Cinematographer"[1]

The most important duty of the Camera Operator is to
get along with a lot of people: the Director of Photography,
the Director, the actors (particularly), the camera crew,
grip crew, electrical crew, set crew, etc. in order to work
with ALL of them. . . . At times [you] will be besieged by
questions and requests, and must be attentive and sensitive
to everyone's needs in a timely fashion. . . . One must
remain CALM, even in the midst of great
confusion.   (Confusion)

—Bill Hines, ICG, IATSE Local 600, *Setiquette*[2]

How has the job description changed? We've become
engineers. We come in, we have to figure out the entire post
workflow, everything. . . . I'm getting calls from [camera]
crews in the field about how to set up the cameras, and how
to record audio, and how to slate. . . . It's a pretty big

nightmare. We're getting all these new formats, working with multiple frame rates, with these reduced schedules, and we're the ones who have to figure it all out.   (Chaos)

—Rob Kraut, "Reality Check": MPEG union organizing meeting[3]

Understandings of film and media production diverge as widely as the vantage points taken to view them. The distinguished Vittorio Storaro's mentoring, from the top, makes cinematography a spiritual affair. By contrast, the ICG's practical bible for on-set work behavior requires camera operators stuck in-the-middle of industry to employ immense amounts of emotional labor to diplomatically hold the collective "confusion" of film crews together. Scholars have ably researched these two high- and midlevel vantage points on production. Yet what of the third? What are we to make of the professional editor raging about the chaos being rained down onto postproduction workflows by professional camera crews who must either be incompetent, inconsiderate, or both? Why not consider intratrade tensions and intercraft conflicts like these as strategic areas in production studies?

As I began my career, I had to reckon with how to put ideas into practice that had been so easy to philosophize about in art, film theory, and aesthetics—things like imagination, expression, form, countercinema. No surprise there, right? Storaro's view of production work as self-psychoanalysis proved seductive. Yet abstractions like that easily evaporate in the material world of work, where machines have a mind of their own. Tempered by how organizational routine often derails creative aspiration, I have spent my career trying to figure out the complex process whereby makers put their creative ideas into practice. I embarked on this long project early on, not through aesthetic analysis or theoretical argument but by looking at how groups of workers and firms come to manufacture artistic vision and how they form creator communities and cultures. *Specworld* results from that journey to get a better grip on how media—film, video, and digital—are made. The book offers a detailed framework for analyzing routine, often-overlooked, behavioral interactions and connective tissues that link film forms (aesthetics) and film industries (organizations). To take on this challenge, the chapters ahead examine what I term *embedded* subproduction systems. Many technical crafts may seem delimited, unexceptional, and free-standing, yet their work is never autonomous. The very ways each craft is embedded, stressed, and managed feeds into a much larger transmedia industry, whose boundaries continue to shape-shift profitably in the twenty-first century.

Even as these shape-shifting multimedia industries challenge us to analyze and describe them more accurately, their new industrial behaviors also provoke and unsettle our research methods. They challenge the traditional ways we study industries. *Specworld* explores whether there may be other effective ways to access, conceptualize, and understand the industry. I have tried to consider alternative forms of analysis that go beyond film studies' traditional impulse to extract and isolate clean parts (films, a studio, a national cinema) or exceptional cases (auteurs, canons, movements) to analyze. Instead, *Specworld* imagines and employs what I intend as a more dimensional or tectonic approach to cinema and media studies (CMS). The reader will note that the book integrates production research methods that travel in-between the theory- and text-driven humanities and the empiricism of sociology and ethnography. Because I am suspicious of clean part-to-whole assumptions in traditional film studies, my research highlights and engages production's messier connective behaviors, treating industry as a routine-driven "complex system" comprising many embedded levels and morphing sectors that perpetually interact and contend with each other, usually out of the public eye. But since unexceptional complexity in large systems frustrates attempts at systematic research, finding ways to meaningfully delimit the evidence we analyze is necessary. As such, *Specworld* proposes that one initial key to effective research involves locating and framing an embedded production system's fault lines and stress behaviors.

Locating and researching industry's conflicted stressors, faults, and rifts forces two divergent ways of thinking, two uneasy neighbors, to speak to each other as a way to make better sense of film and television. Research for the book meant cross-examining the conflict between media specificities and broader industrial systems. Whether something is distinctive or systemic in film and other media remains an unavoidable, foundational question in media studies and forces us to account for and justify the conception of scale in our scholarship and criticism. I have danced around this question for some time, wondering whether a higher or wider view (of the general industry system) might help explain human-size production work on the ground or screen (in specific forms). And

FIGURE 0.1. Futurism lands in coal country (dueling prototypes for media preemption). Drawing: © 2021, by J. Caldwell.

vice-versa. Uneasy with bounded, self-evident categories in film studies (director, genre, scene, style, fans), I have been nagged by thoughts about whether it might be possible to add usefully to these categories in any way—whether we might make cinema and media studies more inhabited, more dimensional. My specifics-vs.-systems double bind may follow from conflicting metaphors I have dragged with me from childhood.

A quarter mile from my childhood home, in a rural town of twelve hundred in the early 1960s, we played and swam in the open-pit "strip-mines." These were deeply scarred clay and coal canyons cut by massive "draglines" that the soft-coal industry had recently left behind. This is what mountain-top removal looked like in regions without mountains, once filled with rainwater. Long before I learned from the scholarly class in my twenties that this landscape was "apocalyptic" and "dystopian," I guessed that these scarred canyons—and the geological sense of time disrupted by quick-and-dirty extraction—were probably needed to sustain our town's economy and the local way of life (fig. 0.1).

By 1965, however, a competing model of time, scale, and thinking simultaneously landed in a university town eight miles to the west. It, too, was preemptive but in a conceptual rather than geological way. In the very same years that we swam in the open coal pits, I was taken in by the geodesic domes, by calls for "anticipatory design," and by the happenings and the buzz around them that Buckminster Fuller brought to his professorial appointment in the town next door.[4] Yet it was not until I started studying social media entertainment production and the digital media "ecosystems" in this millennium that these competing models of time/scale and thinking from childhood a half-century ago came back to me in retrospect. Open-pit strip-mining functions as a form of brute physical preemption. It evacuates wealth in a way that forestalls many other possible outcomes.

Industrial extraction like this greatly simplifies the future in real time by materially eliminating any possibility of an alternative cultural afterworld on these lands. Strip-mining also serves as an apt prototype for today's preemption of cultural expression. The new online media platforms now oddly emulate the soft-coal strip-mine, probably unaware of how well it currently fits as a prototype for their endless digital data mining of both consumers and creative media workers. Soft-coal strip-mining and online data mining both function as efficient scorched-earth customer service policies gifted by industry to their respective locals (fig. 0.2).

The contrast was stark. During the same historical period, Buckminster Fuller's "anticipatory design" enterprise served unwittingly as a poignant prototype for a different kind of futurism and industrial behavior. An intellectual missionary, Fuller promoted innovative math-based conjecturing in "design science" as a strategy to solve real-world problems. By the 1960s the world was in trouble: obsolescence threatened, and survival required solutions. Fuller's futurism, distilled from an amalgam of scientific insights, resonated generationally. He talked optimistically of "synergetics" (reciprocities understood via "geometric thinking"), "precession" (how motion systems influence other motion systems), and presupposed human progress based on rational "co-evolutionary design accommodations in nature."[5] Fuller's future-making gospel wooed designers and engineers, in part because he insisted that solutions must be "industrially realizable." Yet this Fullerian futurist scheme behaved in practice more like a "theory of everything"—long on totalizing speculation, short on things actually, and industrially, "realizable."

Many years later, I came to sense the ghost of Fuller in a wide range of "anticipatory" corporate media theorizing behaviors and preemptions: "vaporware" in the dotcom run-up, "rebranding" in the postnetwork

FIGURE 0.2. The Anticipatory Industrial Complex. The ghost of Buckminster Fuller on a keynote stage at Slush Helsinki tech confab, where the future is visualized via big data analytics. Helsinki, Finland. Photos: © 2017, by J. Caldwell.

era, "viral marketing" in the age of "convergence."[6] I described such things in those later studies as "critical industrial practice" and "industrial reflexivity" (i.e., forms of "recursive" feedback that media industries use to make sense of themselves during times of disruption and change). Yet I now see them as far more extensive "get-out-in-front" business

FIGURE 0.3. A VR demo/workshop at the DGA, Los Angeles, CA. Deep recursive feedback builds an industrially imagined future. Many production technologies crowdsource their development to creative workers who provide feedback at the beta stage. Photo: © 2015, by J. Caldwell.

practices. Beyond any media technology or content, the industrial conjecture attached to them about the future—directed at the trades, personnel, and stockholders—operates as forms of cognitive and cultural preemption. Trade conjecture functions alongside financial speculation. Both team-up as market-preemption strategies employed to forestall alternative futures imagined by competitors, and both play out on the very same online platforms that strip-mine, surveil, and data-mine users and aspirational creators. Such acts pose as benign behaviors in a helpful (but proprietary) "ecosystem." In this de facto premarket for "sharing" media content, online media platforms employ both behaviors—strip-mining and anticipatory design spec-talk—as a means to solicit, enable, and manage online aspirational labor. Clearly, anticipatory expression is something the industry now capably manages and monetizes. This challenges scholars to unpack the scheme, not just via content or personality but as creative labor, as work (fig. 03).

The face-off I have just described raises questions about just how instrumental futurism and (data) strip-mining now are in the media production industries. On the one hand, strip-mining and data mining underline but elide the future by prioritizing the present. On the other, as prescriptions, Fuller's anticipatory design activities in the 1960s and today's online maker/influencer culture (featured in my fieldwork and case studies in chapters 4, 6, and 8) both evoke an evangelical ethos. This is because both Fuller and YouTuber paradigms sought/seek adherents by promoting personal idea-sharing and voluntary disclosure in public; they both sanction creative speculation as sharing but not labor; and they both normalize endless deferrals of professional payoff. Most important, they both legitimize and reify aspiration as an end in itself, as something ostensibly distinct from mundane matters of economic necessity (like production).

Interestingly, we once thought of all the ideals and imaginative behaviors I have just outlined as inseparable from "art" and "art making." Speculative creation has long been a voluntary predicament chosen and willingly adopted by often self-marginalized art makers. The difference now, however, is that this cultural repertoire of preemptive behavior is normalized inside immense proprietary, technical platforms that efficiently monetize all that artistic speculation and creative expression in veiled ways. This churn of disclosure inside cloaked extractive digital economies—even when couched as collective brainstorming—is not unlike soft-coal strip-mining. Yet this twenty-first-century cultural version of creator strip-mining now unfolds on a transnational platform scale far more vast than the coal mines I swam in. I want to understand how that scale matters (fig. 04).

GEN-Z CHALLENGE

If the odd partnership between Fuller's futurism and open-pit mining anchored my early views of film/video production, an experience fifty years later challenged my assumptions about production in a different way and provoked the fieldwork described in chapters 4, 6, and 8. My engagement with a new generation of aspiring film and media creators, that is, encouraged me to rethink *where* media production might now actually be located. For sixteen years I taught college-level film and media production, but since 1998 I've focused mostly on film and media research. Because of a staffing shortage in 2015 and 2016, I was asked to chair our undergraduate production programs. This return to production education was an eye-opener on a lot of levels. Our faculty admissions committee reviewed twenty-four hundred applications (in

FIGURE 0.4. Preproduction imagining (IP strip-mining) never ends in "specworld." Script and development documents publicized in 2020, years after Spike Lee's 1989 *Do the Right Thing*. *Left:* Script fragments from Universal via *Entertainment Weekly*. *Right:* Netflix 2020 marketing for Martin Scorsese's 2019 *The Irishman* included a bound coffee-table book with this obsessively marked-up script page proving genius auteurship and linking him to all "Netflix Original" creators. Promotional fragments (from studio marketing swag) in composite photo. Illustrations: © 2020, by J. Caldwell.

order to admit fifteen freshman and fifteen junior transfers per year). Once our review got that number down to two hundred, I began to see patterns emerging with which I was unfamiliar: many film school applicants had highly trafficked YouTube channels; several had huge fan bases (of one hundred thousand or more subscribers); a number had already showcased their work on the professional film festival circuit; several hyped their corporate sponsorships; several already had deals with "Maker Studios," now owned by corporate giant Disney.

What planet had I just naively returned to? The planet's surface was unrecognizable, and not just because all this hyperproduction involved social media and digital technologies in the commercial online space. This world of adolescent media-making I glimpsed also appeared completely corporatized. And so a bit unnerving. This was a far cry from the "outsider" borderlands that earnest "alternative media-makers" like me once self-righteously plowed through—where we identified ourselves (as a badge of honor) as independents or "indies."

Because I've done production culture research for the past two decades, I rationalized: these twenty-four hundred applicants, adolescent millennials, might serve as my new research sample or data set. After all, I'd been studying older below-the-line professional film workers in LA for many years. That task had begun to feel like studying the decline and fall of the Roman Empire, given that the Hollywood I observed behaved as an unstable world defined by outsourcing, runaway production, ageism, technical obsolescence, and dust-filled equipment rental houses stacked to the ceiling with unwanted no-longer-state-of-the-art gear. Given the unanticipated challenge of working with Gen-Z creators, I embraced the opportunity to interview our fifty finalists to find out, in person, "why" applicants who've already been to Sundance or SXSW as sixteen- or seventeen-year-olds, featured by Maker Studios, with commercial sponsorship and merchandizing deals, would even want to go to "film school" anymore? This question nagged me, since many of our MFA graduates over the past decade (in the hypercompetitive production market that everyone faces) would die to go to Sundance, to have sponsorship and merchandizing deals like these, or to contract with Disney. These are no small accomplishments, even to early career filmmakers and older professionals.

Working with the incoming class over the year both confirmed and undercut many of my hunches: here were eighteen- and nineteen-year-olds that spoke confidently about media branding, content repurposing, even film aesthetics. This left me with two nagging questions. First, where does the forming of this de facto pre-college-film-school—that is, the front-loading of film/media production training to the adolescent preuniversity years—leave university *production* training and the traditional "film school"? Second, where does the new preuniversity education in film concepts and aesthetics—a broad, preemptive strategy in the commercial online space—leave university film and media *studies* departments? The skill sets millennials and Gen-Zers now bring from their adolescence into universities on admission—both in theory and production—are dramatically different from what they were ten or twenty years ago. Should film and media studies departments acknowledge this and respond in some comparably dramatic way? Should "film schools" retool their practical approaches to production in any way, to better engage with the realities of the digital online space in which these creator trends occur? (fig. 0.5).

I have tried to drill more deeply into these questions in the last several years, and I will return to some practical responses and suggestions

FIGURE 0.5. Old film studios try to partner with adolescent influencers at the online "creator" convention VidCon. Such pro-with-aspirant courting triggers the "who's-repping-whom" confusion and tortured production pedagogy featured in the comparative fieldwork case studies in chapters 4, 6, and 8. Photo: © 2017, by J. Caldwell.

throughout this book. To answer these questions means backing away from the maker-disruptor-influencer buzz a bit in order to get a more institutional, bird's-eye view of the digital online space, as well as the content-and-creator pipeline that feeds into it. Part of the problem is that we may simply be too close to the flash and too enamored with the suspect terminology that tech companies have invented to "helpfully" frame this whole enterprise for those trying to make sense of it.

Can we ask alternative questions of this online enterprise that the online enterprise itself does not ask—or want to have asked? Such as: what are the foundations for new forms of digital and online production? Might we as analysts and educators develop (or greatly update) an aesthetics or poetics of production to explain it? Such questions might not matter to external corporate funders of digital research, but they should matter to the humanities and film schools. In short: do we need to "retool" our media and film schools to better prepare for the world our graduates now enter?

Why rethink how we study and write about production? Uneasy bed-fellows by habit, producers and scholars share a history of ambivalence toward each other, if not mutual disciplinary contempt. Yet producers and scholars alike now marvel as the industrial ground of media is digitally pulled out from under us all. It is worth noting that at the same time, the scholarly ground of media research has also radically shape-shifted. A range of new production studies and innovative media industries researchers are capably questioning, deconstructing, and mapping the world of Netflix, Google, Amazon, and social media as either a transnational groundswell or a complex-culture sinkhole.[7] Revisionist production cultural researchers have also pushed the field and its methods forcefully into the geographic, economic, cultural, and ideological blind spots of earlier industry scholars.[8] Yet even as production studies keeps its radar locked on the manic digital wave, I have wondered if anything fundamental and more independent (even if less sexy) might have been lost as corporate funders and governments now bring media industries research into the research-funding mainstream as blueprints for national cultural policy and economic growth. This trend is especially acute in sectors (unlike my own) where scholarly media industries research closely aligns with and feeds sanctioned governmental or national "creative industries" policies.

The labor economics of below-the-line workers has long sustained my interest and anxieties about both university-industry linkages and my scholarly discipline. At the same time, several decades working as a film school and university professor have also periodically forced me to rearticulate the rationales for both the industrial production enterprise as a whole and the value and utility of how we study media. Even as the political right now habitually targets professors as "intellectual elites," film schools and universities still serve as ground zero for culture arming and cinematic-standards vigilance. In some ways university film schools act as buffer zones for the reproduction of knowledge and for efforts to understand how media works and why media culture is significant or problematic. Rethinking how we produce media art, how we think about media, and how we teach both of those things matters. I hope that this book—which treats embedding, speculation, and aspiration as industrial practices—will add to our foundational understandings of these larger questions.

CREATOR ASPIRATION AS A SYSTEM

The twenty-first-century media industries treat and handle aspiration as a form of managerial capital. Far beyond personal vision, aspiration is collective, decentralized, monetizable. My scientific colleagues on research review boards often employed *aspirational* dismissively. They used the term to devalue well-meaning but failed attempts by rising scholars in the physical or social sciences to find and confirm convincing correlations or harder causalities. My colleagues in film and art schools, by contrast, aligned the term with long-standing tropes of culturally sanctioned selfishness: creative intuition, signature ambition, personal vision. Imagine, however, that aspiration is instrumental, transactional, administrative. Imagine how real-world cultural institutions manage and draw from the wave of disaggregated personal aspirations surging around them. Imagine aspiration as a complex industrial system, as I do in this book. These alternative frameworks make certain contexts unavoidable. They require the analyst to describe the bureaucracies of creative labor and screen content-making as forms of administrative production. Shifting our vantage in these ways raises immediate questions about how the industry reproduces itself, through knowledge about itself. Shifting also challenges us to explain how the system solicits, mentors, and develops emerging creators. *Specworld* aims to unpack the logics of creator aspiration as cultural and managerial schemes that our creative economies critically value.

Similarly to business schools, film schools and trade worlds push norms and creator conventions to make production one thing. They do this to form and sustain coherent, rule-governed enterprises. Local conditions, however, necessarily create many deviations in these trade-induced norms. Production studies describe those deviations. Production research treats those deviations not as isolated exceptions but as bared cultural nerves that industry's larger neural networks animate and trigger. Rather than quickly leap as scholars from production's local deviations to, say, broad political-economic structures, production culture research can be maddeningly incremental. It makes scholars patiently aggregate insights from fieldwork. It requires them to build any generalizations outward, from specific observations, slowly, recursively over time.

As such, we can appraise production studies on their ability to describe adjoining interests, trace-out the thick connections of local practice, and unpack the many industrial layers that embed and stress the local creative workers in question. Unpacking, disembedding, and contact-tracing like this are not methods we normally associate with the correlations and causalities that much research seeks. Yet those are precisely the methods I used to research *Specworld*. Recurring problems involving scope pushed me to those ways of working and thinking. One factor: media production has *never* been one thing. There is no standardized filmmaker, director, studio, maker, influencer, or creator. There are only iterations of each—distribution and trade norming to the contrary. To the thousands of versions of production under way globally since the mid-twentieth century, online social media creator platforms now add an even greater challenge. Scholars, that is, face literally millions of possible production variants across the worldwide online space. This scale makes generalizing definitively about production now seem like a fool's errand. It makes scholarship suspect if we do not meaningfully acknowledge production's endlessly mutating local iterations and the limits of our evidence.

These realities—especially scope and localism—troubled research for this book. My response was to find ways to frame production research in more manageable ways. Industry's hyperflexibility means that the standard ethnographic tropes for the local (a stable village or production shop-floor from which to observe) are no longer tenable. I observed or participated, instead, in a series of two dozen professional production workshops (across the crafts, mostly in the LA area) and international trade gatherings (film festivals, conventions, and markets) over a decade as my field sites. This necessarily limits what I will say in these pages to (a) Hollywood and its aspirational feeder systems and (b) the paraindustry intermediaries that host intertrade negotiating and partnering. As such, this book cannot be about some universal form of physical production work.

Instead, I have written a far narrower ethnography of trade workshopping and the social construction of production—rather than provided any definitive account of timeless production principles or transportable core values in production. Nor can the chapters ahead ever pretend to be about "all" YouTubers, influencers or creators, or to describe "all" emerging production workers in Hollywood. Rather, the chapters ahead describe only (1) the Gen-Z makers I talked to and participated with at VidCon and in social media creator workshops in

California from 2016 to 2019; (2) the aspiring and emerging below-the-line workers being trade-mentored by IATSE, ATAS, MPEG, CDG, ASC, and ADG around Hollywood that I observed or interviewed from 2011 to 2020; and (3) the trade gatherings and material infrastructures I observed and photographically documented at Paramount, Raleigh, Sundance, CBS, the Prix Italia, Helsinki, Cinecittà, Barrandov, and Babelsberg studios from 2010 to 2019 (the photos and illustrations featured in this book are drawn from this third register).

The decade covering my intermittent fieldwork further constrains not just my evidence but also any theoretical generalizations I can make from that evidence. I started my study as research on *contemporary* production. Yet since finishing my draft in early 2020, I've become acutely aware that *Specworld* may be better understood as a *historical* project. Since I finished my fieldwork and writing, the global pandemic shutdown, the collapse of theatrical exhibition, Hollywood's various MeToo/Times-Up/Black-Lives-Matter reckonings, and industry's disruptive transition to platform streaming all require further caveats about historical scope. In retrospect, by unpacking tensions between HBO/A-list and YouTuber pedagogies, *Specworld* may primarily reckon with production during YouTube's fleeting golden age before 2020. The creator industries in the following pages, that is, are pre-COVID and pre-TikTok. This period roughly starts with the growing public attention given the YouTube/Google/VidCon synergies, including Disney's acquisition of Maker Studios in 2014 (when the studios and HBO still dominated critical attention). The period ends with the growing eclipse of YouTube by TikTok and the failure of the Internet Creators Guild (ICG) in 2019 (even as Netflix and Amazon dominated the studios in premium content exhibition and revenues). In effect, those historical moments necessarily bracket the fieldwork described in the chapters that follow. Despite those caveats about limited historical scope, however, I am struck by how many of the supposed core production "fundamentals" outlined in chapters 4, 6, and 8 have actually become more extreme and acute in professional rhetoric, rather than less so, in the age of disinformation and accelerated TikTok content.

One takeaway from these combinations of observations? The acute gap apparent between the big-budget discourses (and A-list modes of production) and low-budget pedagogy (the ways trade "experts" mentor precarious aspirant creative workers lower down the food chain on "how-to-succeed" professionally) confirmed one hunch I held when I started research: aspirational labor stirs up production profitably at nearly every level of the caste-stratified production industry. I wanted to understand how industry engaged profitably and mainstreamed those aspirants in ways that at times acted beneficial, exploitative, or self-defeating.

Specworld's restrictive focus on socioprofessional expressions (production pedagogy, trade mentoring, and workshopping) also builds a networked "localism" that differs significantly from the geographic localism that anchors the fieldwork employed by Vicki Mayer (Louisiana), Eva Novrup Redvall (Copenhagen), Kristen Warner (LA), Petr Szczepanik (Prague), and James Fleury (Burbank/LA) in their definitive production ethnographies.[9] My observations, furthermore, took place in institutional "contact zones" by design, which meant that I was witnessing collective rituals and negotiations, interfirm arm-twisting, and partnering give-and-take. As a result, in those sites I could not simply transcribe clean principles about content creation or describe stable truths about production. Instead, I had to better describe the flux, the haggling, partnering, throw-downs, and exploratory chatter that produced negotiated norms within those contact zones.

The reader will find no critique or judgment against either the aspirant social media creators or the precarious preprofessional and early career production workers that I describe in the pages that follow. Far from it. Instead, I directly indict industry's predatory dealing with those creators, alongside industry's conflicted, contradictory production pedagogies, which aspirant creators often struggle to make sense of. Industry's predation makes career longevity difficult if not unsustainable for creators. Its warring pedagogies and doublespeak create impossible labor expectations for many aspirants and entry-level workers. As a career educator, I have been troubled by the long odds and human predicament faced by anyone who wants to create onscreen media. I began *Production Culture* (2008) when I found companies that had to give their overworked twenty-five-to-thirty-five-year-old VFX workers mid-career "sabbaticals" in the late 1990s to physically survive their workstation "masters" and 24/7 "digital sweatshops." Years later, I started *Specworld* after viewing scores of online "down-in-flames" "quitting-my-channel" videos by angry teen and postadolescent makers/influencers who raged that their fickle or perverse giant platform "hosts" had cruelly demonetized them, making it impossible to continue toward careers in production.

It seemed like one thing to ask how career-threatening pressures trapped twenty- and thirtysomething creative pros in the late twentieth century. It felt like an entirely different matter to discern how and why aspiring twenty-first-century adolescent creators in the social-media sharing era would rail against similar stress-inducing precarities. Over the years, in an academic setting, I responded to both dark prospects by trying to rebalance our curriculum's listing ship. Several missing areas, I argued, might better serve and equip our creator students for the industries they would actually enter. In particular, we needed to add courses (*especially* for artists) that covered intellectual property history, production and creative labor history, media law, and political-economic analysis of media. These perspectives could bolster media art-making, I reasoned, even as electives to the core production curriculum (which traditionally emphasized form, narrative structure, technical practice, and aesthetics). None of the twenty-first-century workshops, the how-to sites, and the MCNs of today's online platform world that I studied for this book employ the nonscreen ways of analyzing that I pushed for back then. Yet those nonscreen problems remain critical in most sectors of screen production today.

The de facto new pre–film school I researched for *Specworld* behaves instead like a managerial MBA program on neoliberal crack aimed at adolescents. Its platform mentoring casts a vast and harsh economistic spotlight that online creators must dance under (and measure themselves against). Although I initially intended this book as a scholarly guide for media industries researchers, I also trust it addresses, even if only in small ways, the aspiring or emerging creator's human predicament. That is, I hope this book can add at least some perspective for those working to create and upload new content on media platforms today. If one looks past influencer mythologizing, celebrity branding, and crossover star windfalls, the platform world can be reasonably regarded by many more other creators as alternately disheartening or crazy-making. I think that wider conflicted creator predicament matters. Production doublespeak anchors that predicament—doublespeak that can trip up rising creators who want screencentric rather than economistic careers in film and media production.

Abbreviations

AC	assistant cameraperson
ACE	American Cinema Editors
AD	assistant director
ADG	Art Directors Guild
AIC	Autori Italiani Cinema (Italian Society of Cinematographers)
AMPAS	Academy of Motion Picture Arts and Sciences
ASC	American Society of Cinematographers
ATAS	Academy of Television Arts and Sciences
AVID	AVID Technology Inc.
CAA	Creative Artists Agency
CDC	Centers for Disease Control and Prevention
CDG	Costume Designers Guild
CMS	Cinema and Media Studies
DGA	Directors Guild of America
DIY	do-it-yourself
DP	director of photography
DSW	Design Showcase West (Los Angeles)
FCC	Federal Communications Commission

FCP	Final Cut Pro
FIND	Film Independent (Los Angeles)
FTC	Federal Trade Commission
GUI	graphical user interface
IATSE	International Alliance of Theatrical Stage Employees
ICG	Internet Creators Guild; International Cinematographers Guild
IFP	Independent Feature Project (renamed the Gotham Film and Media Institute in 2021)
ILM	Industrial Light & Magic
IP	intellectual property; internet protocol
IPO	initial public offering
IRB	Institutional Review Board
LBO	leveraged buyout
MCN	multichannel network
MEP	Media Ecology Project
MOU	memorandum of understanding
MPEG	Motion Picture Editors Guild
NIH	National Institutes of Health
PA	production assistant
PGA	Producers Guild of America
RED	RED Digital Cinema
SAG	Screen Actors Guild
SME	social media entertainment
SOC	Society of Operating Cameramen
SXSW	South by Southwest Film Festival
UGC	user-generated content
UI	user interface
UTA	United Talent Agency
UX	user experience
VACT	value-adding career task
VC	venture capitalist
VES	Visual Effects Society

VFX	visual effects
VR	virtual reality
WGA	Writers Guild of America
WGC	worker-generated content
WHO	World Health Organization

1

Ethics?

Stress, Rifts, and Bad Behavior

When you search Unruly Agency the first thing you see is
about women empowerment. . . .

    These guys are basically pimps. . . .

    [They] are pretty bloodthirsty and money hungry [and]
treat their talent as objects. They most definitely don't have
your best interests in mind. . . .

—Blowback by coerced online creators and content removal
    specialists against "cash-grabbing" Unruly and Behave "talent
    agencies"[1]

We seldom think of artistic accomplishment through the lens of bad
behavior. We pay less attention to the industrial infrastructure that
facilitates managerial harm or enables untoward acting-out, even as it
produces media content. Instead, we continue to pose media aesthetics
as largely disconnected from ethics per se. Large commercial industries,
however, sorely complicate our habit of segregating the individual production of creative work from collective questions about right and
wrong, power and domination. Several contentious controversies in the
film and TV industries that recently became reform movements—
MeToo, OscarsSoWhite, TimesUp, Black Lives Matter, the 2021
Golden Globes racial diversity takedown—suggest just how short-
sighted (or lazy) our neat critical distinctions between artistry and domination may be. How can the victims that MeToo and TimesUp advo-
cated for be understood as outcomes of standard business practices, as
logical (even if unintended) industrial productions?

    I undertook this book because I wanted to better understand film and
media production workers as communities interacting and contending

with each other. I was much more interested in long-standing norms and routines used offscreen to find intertrade advantage or consensus than in short-lived celebrity controversies about racial or sexual harassment of the sort in which the tabloids excel. Yet in trying to map how film and media production are embedded within a complex industrial ecosystem, I repeatedly ran into stress points, faults, and rifts that appeared to function as logical parts of corporate and industrial advancement. As a result, I came to understand the structural stresses in contact zones between embedded production groups as viable routes for researching the industrial production system as a whole. Finally, while I was finishing this manuscript during the COVID-19 pandemic, an immense amount of racial pushback and cultural vitriol in the political sphere churned within film and television as well. As such, I now approach the tabloid manic news cycles differently: as symptoms, as surface flags connected to longer-term trade fault lines. They often serve as warning signs connected to deeper structural stresses, like precarity, that I had been studying for several decades.[2]

My nagging sense that bad behavior and ethical minefields might naturally result from routine industrial practice may be a by-product of the way ethical problems frame the very research methods that my UCLA doctoral students and I employ in fieldwork. In ethnographic research the ethnographer is inseparably linked to the problem of protecting human subjects. The scholar's professional protocols are established to ensure the ethical protections of informants in the field. Yet this sole focus on the *scholar's* ethic makes little sense when we research large corporate organizations. There, the power imbalance between the researcher and researched is flipped; the tables are turned, so that the researcher is more legally at risk than the research subject (the corporation). The reasons for this risk asymmetry are many.

Outside funding, national policies requiring supportive partnerships between academics and creative industries, and lock-tight legal constraints in the proprietary digital media platform era all complicate the role of ethics in production culture studies. Patrick Vonderau's recent critique of the absence of ethical considerations in "media industry studies" offers a compelling analysis.[3] His indictment—"Do ethics matter?"—strikes me not just as a shot across the bow of the maturing media industries field. The critique also gives me a chance to briefly reflect on and question my own journey in the field. How and in what ways are my work and the methods I propose in the chapters ahead "ethical"? I take this question as an opportunity for retrospection—a chance to unpack

FIGURE 1.1. Stressed fault line: labor blowback in the film industry. The worldwide shift to outsourced, subsidized, and flexible "offshore" production labor triggered industry crises in many dominant film and media production centers. Here, workers and activists "occupy" Italy's legendary national "Cinecittà" film studios outside Rome to protest its downsizing and partial commercial redevelopment. Photos: Cinecittà, Italy. © 2012, by J. Caldwell.

how and why ethics informs my approach in this book to researching stressors in embedded production systems (fig. 1.1).

Even if my students hope to research production tools, trade texts, or media markets, I require that they complete the "protection of human subjects protocols" and IRB (Institutional Research Board) workshops in my graduate foundation "Cultures of Production" seminar at UCLA. I view this requirement as an instructive, and at times necessary, reset. This especially holds for graduate students trained in the arts and humanities, like myself. Why had many *human*ities fields somehow never deemed such *human* ethical protections important enough to the discipline to be required in those fields?

Fieldwork opened up one troubling void in IRB protocols that still nags me. Twenty-first-century media companies necessarily dwarf me (and my doctoral researchers) in terms of economic clout, institutional leverage, and the sheer size of their legal divisions. In a potentially litigious "stare-down" over information or disclosure, I am clearly the "human subject" at risk—*not* my corporate "research subjects." How do university review boards protect professors from giant multinationals that may not like independent views of their corporate brands or criticisms published by researchers? Should corporations be able to censor independent scholar-ship with threats and excessive lawyering in this way?

Unfortunately, university IRB offices have never been able to provide me with a parallel request: a "protection of human *researcher*" protocols or workshops. My university seems uninterested or blind to the very acute legal and ethical *asymmetry* that defines most media industries research encounters. This institutional indifference toward protecting human *professors* from the corporations they write about or critique may be sustained by the deep positivist tradition that establishes how research-able information is defined in the physical and social sciences. There, data is deemed neutral (not socially constructed a priori). In effect, data is bracketed off categorically from the scholar's professional standards and protocols meant to oversee and protect that collected data.

Early on in a research project, I remind my hesitant or anxious stu-dents to "remember that the marketing or publicity staffer that you have contacted (or been shunted off to by the creative workers you actu-ally want to talk to) is employed precisely to get company information out. At least initially, you represent a possible route to achieve that company's disclosure goal. So learn to factor in what you think *they* want with what *you* need as you negotiate for access. You might not get what you want, but your haggling will likely tell much about what is going on there, even if you don't get the data you initially asked for. Analyze and treat that haggling not as secondary, or as flak, but as fun-damental to your production research."

Unlike the text-based humanities, anthropologists have been tangling with the muddy politics of slippery research encounters for some time. They have developed various ways to address the ethics of how knowl-edge is coproduced by ethnographers and informants. Many of these fieldwork strategies require "reflexivity" on the part of the ethnographer. Vonderau makes a persuasive case that reflexivity (self-reflection, -disclosure, and -critique) reveals how a researcher's knowledge is "produced" and how it can provide a viable and preferable alternative to simply falling back on (or deferring to) a scholar's "professional" protocols. After all, IRBs can be deployed (and then buried). IRB checklisting can easily cloak problematic ways that project researchers may have captured industry knowledge in the first place.

While I have not written separately about ethics in my earlier media industries or production studies, my practical decisions about how to research have likely been guided by a moral framework that I developed much earlier in life. I hope to briefly sketch out here three themes that recur in decisions I have made about what in production I choose to study and how. These themes are even more basic and less clinical than the IRB checklist of topics and protections. All three target fundamental media industrial and production workplace behaviors that (somehow) mostly pass as legitimate in the professional world. These suspect but normalized production standards include *industrial deception* (lying), *industrial intimidation* (coercion and bullying), and *industrial extraction* (stealing, under another name).

My argument here is that the production culture practices I focus on interest me in part because they express or involve a range of unethical industry fundamentals. These suspect tactics and postures are arguably pernicious because they are normalized through otherwise innocuous-looking everyday working interactions and trade reporting. Beyond my *primary* research task of describing complex embedded production systems more accurately, I believe that a *secondary* goal is inseparable from it. Specifically, I presuppose that sound critical cultural analysis of production can also meaningfully unpack unethical normalizing and legitimation habits. Production culture research on system stressors can add ethical dimensions to the insights organizational sociology and political economics achieve in their analyses (fig. 1.2).

Production studies are often effective because they are good at clear-eyed observation and close, "thick" description. Research subjects and human informants necessarily complicate that descriptive dimension. Yet as research objectives, the researcher's descriptive mission and ethical obligations are not mutually exclusive. Stated differently: when students ask me why I take on the research that I do, I've come to confess in retrospect that, frankly, I must have chosen to study things that make me angry. I do not like liars, bullies, or thieves. Never have. Whether in production work or academia. The complex industries that I study seem

FIGURE 1.2. Artisanal work as behavioral ideal. Here, lighting grip "shapes" illumination on a soundstage. Production texts and trade books largely treat the soundstage as a creator cocoon cut off from suspect bureaucratic practices. From cinematography workshop directed by DP Bill McDonald. Photo: © 2009, by J. Caldwell.

to have mainstreamed and justified several suspect dispositions—deception, coercion, and extraction. Such things are often normalized as benign and sanctioned as managerial realities in production. This presupposes that they are parts of some odd professional skill set, things to be accepted "if you want to make it in the industry." I address each of these three normalized dispositions in turn.

INDUSTRIAL DECEPTION (DISINFORMATION)

I have caught more grief from my "inverse credibility law," which I originally put forth in *Production Culture,* than from just about anything else in that book. I stated there that the value of information often diminishes as the scholar ascends in the media industrial hierarchy in search of information. Thus the formula: More Authority = Less Veracity at the executive level; and Less Authority = More Authenticity at the worker level. My personal experience of industry's food chain informed that principle. Producers and management-types always seemed to get the better of me in discussions, or they offered little more than their publicity machines had already advertised online or in the trades. I reasoned that what higher-ups said casually to me must also have already been masterfully "scripted" from talking points in their branding or business plans. My interviews or panels with professionals on media matters, therefore, actually served as stages for a kind of stealth marketing-art-of-disclosure by insiders. I reasoned that their staying on point so authentically, in the ways they answered my questions, probably also contributed and added value to the respective media business and creative successes those same individuals had achieved.

I recognize the inverse credibility law as one factor that justified shifting my research focus away from higher-ups and auteurs to below-the-line workers, who are normally anonymous. I offered "standpoint theory" to bolster this shift in view. This framework builds on the idea that persons at the bottom of a complex system often have more accurate understandings of the system as a whole than persons at the top. While I still consider that standpoint logic sound, I confess here that I also intended the inverse credibility law at the time as an academic provocation, as well. I reasoned that scholars, myself included, are usually so grateful to have been given access to any higher-level in the industry that we/I bend over backward to reframe their words positively. Regardless of our misgivings.

I want to double down here on the insight that industrial information is usually less cloaked by vested corporate interests if you can access it below or *outside* management's official bureaucratic sphere. In reality, spin, misinformation, and disinformation go far beyond what a high-up says in an interview. Arguably, industrial deception is a widely sanctioned premise across industry in both high and low production sectors. Standard managerial tactics for deception that industry normalizes include spin, dissembling, integrated product sponsorship, viral marketing, public-relations fixer interventions, unacknowledged intraconglomerate cross-promotions, countermarketing and disinformation campaigns, and trade-show keynotes.

Think about the many ways that companies say one thing when they mean something else, or when they simply want fans or the press *not* to look at some rift, trend, or problem area in the firm. Token "diversity initiatives," "third-rail" marketing campaigns, publicity firms, back-channel social media sharing, fan initiatives, meet-and-greets, and industry's various professional associations and shadow academies can all kick into gear when internal problems are disclosed publicly—or

FIGURE 1.3. Studio flack buffers dissent. Here, a picketing VFX worker in Hollywood protests coercive international tax subsidies, which spur LA studios' "runaway production" and union-busting (labor strategies that are celebrated both by nearby executives and producers elsewhere in the world). Photo: © 2015, by J. Caldwell.

when they are leaked or hacked. As a result, beware of the launch of sunny "overly ethical" corporate initiatives. Yet even as they misdirect, they offer valuable sites for critical production research. By overselling a progressive social initiative, a company often inadvertently flags a site or industrial practice that is necessarily less sunny than the misdirection initiatives launched to cover it in public.

Trade behaviors that steer perception by dissembling or disinformation can frustrate scholarly attempts at "direct" empirical observation, objective description, documentation of industry, or statistical quantification. Some "objective" quantitative methods—like randomized sampling to create a representative data set—become absurd measures in the context of industrial disinformation. Publishing conclusions from a data set consisting of *planted* information, for example, can reduce the scholar's role to a mere mouthpiece for a firm's proprietary talking points. I argue that industrial dissembling usually requires research methods that go beyond the statistical analysis of a randomized data set. These alternatives can include considerable further *textual deconstruction* by the scholar via the textual analysis of deep trade artifacts (EPKs, demos, clip-reels); embedded discourse analysis (planted trade stories or industry news cycles); Geertzian interpretation (behind-the-scenes looks, explanations, or "mentoring" of the researcher by a craft master or industry "expert"); or ritual analysis from symbolic anthropology (to unpack affiliate meetings, upfronts, or executive internship programs). Industrial deception is precisely why deep textual deconstruction can be so crucial as a foundation or prerequisite for industry disembedding research of the sort this book features (fig. 1.3).

INDUSTRIAL COERCION (BULLYING AND INTIMIDATION)

I learned a great deal when I worked for a television art director in my first significant job after college. The backroom file cabinets we had that were stuffed with mountains of photographic visuals and style references awed me. This working research archive was far more comprehensive than comparable files I had seen in university settings. But I also quickly ran into work behaviors with which I was completely unfamiliar. I had never in my life seen so much periodic dormant-then-vitriolic anger and loud intermittent acting-out in the workplace. Let alone as part of a creative work process. I realized these behavioral habits might say more about my own rural thin skin than about creativity or other forms of masculine insecurity. Yet I also noted that our group did indeed make *collective* progress, meet deadlines, and succeed. This impressive success came in spite of (or maybe because of?) the vocal venting and short-term catharsis that made it all, apparently, possible.

OK, I reasoned, production's rage-caste system somehow works. I was uncomfortable with the culture shock in my initially unsettled reaction. I thought at the time that film and television in Los Angeles must in some way sanction emotional behaviors that agriculture or construction would never tolerate in the Midwest. Hollywood's variant of collective work, that is, must be distinctive. But appropriate? I puzzled over that question. This contention unfolded four decades before the "MeToo" movement fractured and exposed the once neatly laminated facade of many Hollywood companies. Eventually, the public reckoning of #MeToo and #OscarsSoWhite exposed deep systemic rifts and power fault lines in the long-embedded work layers of major and minor firms alike (table 1.1).

A range of standard managerial practices likely facilitate and normalize conditions that perpetuate intimidation and coercion. As the chapters ahead will show, these include inordinately long employment periods as personal assistants, the use of unpaid interns for necessary work, endless "creative" outsourcing, cease-and-desist actions, takedown orders for "fair-use" indie docs, paying-your-dues rationales to salve long-suffering and underpaid underlings, and coercive end-title and credit politics for contract workers. These production *norms* all represent ethical minefields with industrial downsides that effective production research can highlight.

If chosen as a research topic, industrial intimidation arrangements actually provide scholars with ample sites or locations for production study. Mid- and lower-level companies and subfirms offer scholars more varied forms of access than the big "go-to" firms with Hollywood A-listers offer "at the top." These sub- and paraindustry research sites can include unregulated business and creative management offices, suppliers and support firms, nonunion shoots, runaway productions, blind but parallel VFX contracting, union-busting campaigns, and the study of localized cultural politics ingrained in below-the-line work standards. At the same time, such topics and sites force production studies to shift from or deemphasize the deconstruction of deep trade texts in order to add research methods more appropriate for human subjects and paraindustrial spaces. These methods might include oral histories, participant observation, standpoint theory interviews, emotional labor studies, sociologies of consensus and hegemony, and labor precarity

TABLE 1.1   ONE ETHICAL COMPASS FOR PRODUCTION CULTURE RESEARCH

Normalized industry practice	Standard managerial tactics	Research sites and locations	Disembedding methods
Industrial deception (lying)	Spin, dissembling, viral and integrated marketing, **PR** fixers, cross-promotions, countermarketing, disinformation, trade-show keynotes	Marketing departments, publicity, diversity initiatives, back-channel social media info, fan confabs, links to cultural nonprofits, shadow academies	Deep trade textual analysis, embedded discourse analysis, Geertzian symbolic anthropology, follow-the-money to find interfirm logic
Industrial coercion (bullying)	Personal assistanting, unpaid internships, outsourcing, cease-and-desist actions, takedown orders, paying-your-dues mythologies, coercive end-title and credit politics	Unregulated creative management offices, nonunion shoots, runaway production, parallel FX contracts, union busting, below-the-line work habits	Oral histories, participant observation, standpoint theory, emotional labor studies, sociologies of consensus & hegemony, precarity labor research, fracture research
Industrial extraction (stealing)	Online platform analytics, soft-capital erasures, symbolic capital exchange, indie's pretesting task, aspirant's fan burden, for-profit film schools, influencer how-to workshops	Fake contests, entrant-funded film festivals, pitchfests, cobranding opportunities, oversupply of intermediary wannabes, showrunner-absent writers rooms, off-the-clock work expectations	Political economy, surveillance capitalism, platform studies, media ecosystem studies, organizational sociology, breaching experiments, prioritizing union negotiating in research

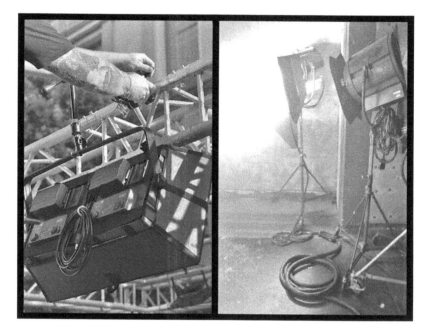

FIGURE 1.4. Media industry research without human subjects can veer into research overly deferent to corporate intentions and to the myth that everything researched in industry was indeed intended or designed by management. Scholars should avoid creating analytic echo chambers that amplify managerial utopias. Industry's cultural trade expressions naturalize and embed human labor inside managerial norms that can be ethically problematic. *Left:* Rigging lights at Paramount Studios. *Right:* Tools should matter to media industry researchers. Photos: © 2011 and 2017, by J. Caldwell.

research. As the chapters ahead show, such qualitative research methods often prove more sensitive to the rifts and complexities that exist within occluded faults and fractures.

Bullying in production is so commonplace that "how-to-make-it" books in screenwriting and production often feel like a user's guide to S&M boot camp. Some justify masochism as part of the skill set that rising screenwriters need:

> Life can be shockingly tough. Sometimes we take a real blow. Fate sneaks up and steals something from us. . . . Accept that there is no off switch for stress in our bodies. But you can live with it, wear it down, mold it, take charge of it, use it. . . . More good things about stress. . . . Stress can give you the gift of insight. It can make you more poetic, more aware of the human condition; it is a dark gift, but a gift nevertheless. (Pen Densham, "A Filmmaker's 'Positive' Thoughts on Stress")

Suffer on, good creator soldier! This same vocational cheerleader account indicts industrial masochism's flip side—industry's sadism— largely by conspicuous omission. Specifically, it does so by *not* acknowledging the extent of bad behavior by bad actors who (by implications) would trigger and then revel in creating stress among their employees or contacts. If "how-to" production books normalize overlord perpetrators of industry stress, then production culture research can indeed have a mitigating role in at least outing the bullies or documenting the bullying conventions. Such research can also call to attention a necessary question: what corporate rationality can this systemic and managerial sadism possibly bring to profitable media production? (fig. 1.4).

INDUSTRIAL EXTRACTION (STEALING)

Like soft-coal strip-mining, extraction economies now surround production in the online platform era. Explicit accusations of stealing often generate little attention in the world of skeptical professionals. This general disregard may be pervasive because so much *self-justification* and *volunteerism* drive aspirational and underemployed specwork and social media creation. Victim narratives only occasionally show up in the professional trade space (since most creative workers want "to work in this town again"). While career-burnout videos made by twenty-two-year-old YouTubers are indeed a genre, they don't dominate rankings. Instead, the platform system promotes a countervailing manic fortitude among makers (never-stop-uploading), underscoring it as a key to both successful content creation and Gen-Z "authenticity." Platform pedagogy provides aspiring creators with endless reasons to give content away. This is why I prefer the structural term *extraction* rather than *theft* as a term to describe this third unethical foundation in media industries practice that researchers can harvest.

This book's case studies of aspiring maker/influencer creators offer a glimpse at the automated ways that social media creator platforms like YouTube, Vimeo, and Patreon manage, harvest, and monetize the aspirational surge of young content creators. Chapters 4 and 8 examine how professional production normalizes ostensibly collective "insourcing," "credit-jumping," and "you-share-we-take" arrangements to keep the production pipeline humming. In addition to these automated extraction behaviors (which are now driven by online platform analytics), there are many other tacit, implicit, and de facto extraction dynamics at work. Examples that depend on leveraging symbolic capital or employing soft-capital budgeting include pressuring aspirant creators to predevelop and deliver a packageable fan base to the platform or studio; expecting indie filmmakers to pay for the pretesting of their spec project at festivals and cultural venues; and culling aspirants produced by the predatory economies of for-profit film schools, getting-an-agent workshops, and influencer how-to confabs.

Industry does not just extract surplus economic value in these ways from creative workers. It legitimizes the taking by employing a range of symbolic cultural rituals and by marshaling the industrial reflexivities that production culture research excels at unpacking. This book will feature many examples of extractive schemes that industry uses to *culturally normalize* theft: fake script contests, entrant-funded film festivals, pitchfests led by mid- or low-level "experts," cobranding merchandizing opportunities, showrunner-absent writers rooms, and the perpetual oversupply of unqualified wannabe agents, intermediaries, and reps. All of these industrial cultural schemes make draining money from the independent creator community and underemployed professionals seem productive and to-be-expected.

Researching this third element of my ethical compass for production studies challenges CMS scholars to integrate research methodologies that go beyond either close textual analysis or closely observed ethnography. For production scholars, these adaptive lenses (methods and frameworks that are more sensitive to the *structures and infrastructures* of extraction) include political economy, surveillance capitalism studies, platform research, media ecosystem studies, organizational sociology, the text-finance scaffolding research of deWaard, and the breaching experiments of Vonderau and his Spotify research colleagues.

A package of such methods is not just suitable for researching online aspirant creators in the media "platform" era either. We also need to adapt those methods, and expand our research tool kit so that they are able to unpack the ethics of high-budget production, as well. In high production, for example, recent managerial "innovations" that changed the creative workflow can trigger rifts in the once stabilized fault lines that hold writers and studios in productive tension. Consider the acutely divergent definitions of creativity between screenwriters and producers in the following trade account. This pitched battle was triggered in the trades by studio executives who proudly celebrated the collective "tel-evisioning" of film (bureaucratic creativity) as innovative in massive blockbusters and feature franchises like Marvel's *Spider-Man* and Hasbro/Paramount's *Transformers:* "There is such reciprocity between TV and movies now, that we're borrowing this from TV. . . . The whole process of the story room was really delightful, and we are seeing it more in movies as this moves toward serialized storytelling. . . . *We're trying to beg borrow and steal from the best of them,* and gathered a group of folks interested in developing and broadening this franchise."[4]

Studios create an ethical swamp when they brag about internally crowdsourcing feature-film scripts through grateful staff-sharing. Remarkably, the producers do not even try to hide, deny, or bury their writer-demeaning management "innovation" in this published trade account of their new form of creativity. This, after all, has been normalized as the Michael Bay era of vulgar auteurism. Yet the angry pushback from actual creators and "real" screenwriters against this studio—for publicly bragging about its enlightened harvesting of script ideas from staff—was immediate and unequivocal:

> Wonder what the WGA will say about this? Does the writer of the script get credit for the [*sic*] all the work that's been "fleshed-out" by other writers? (Hmm)[5]

> No legitimate, established writer should take part in this nonsense. This is why these movies are unintelligent messes to watch. They are assembled from the half-baked ideas of these group-think jerk off sessions. This is a scheme hatched up by studios to cut costs and take people's ideas and . . . credit bonuses. . . . This is why these movies make no sense and have no structural, stylistic or tonal integrity. They are just assembled from everyone's half-thought-through spare parts. (YUP)

> Jeez this is grim. Millions of dollars that could have been spent on original stories about people instead of loud, frenzied chicken-fried crap that you can't see, hear or understand. . . . This sheltered workshop for hacks . . . (Loathe Transformers)

> None of the writers of the comic books or the old animated TV episodes will get any credit from this room. They will be able to lift whatever stories they want and they won't have to share credit with the original writers. This is criminal and the WGA should slam them for doing this. . . . Those humans deserve to be credited and compensated by this overpaid room. (Optimus Prime)

To add insult to injury, executive apologists for the Paramount film "writers room" in question actually echoed the soft-coal strip-mining metaphor with which I began this book. To justify the brilliance of their industrial extraction scheme without shame, Goldsman explained wistfully: "It just felt like such fertile ground and a rich environment for storytelling, and there has already been thoughtful work done before any of us came into the room. *We will be innovative miners, and we will have fun* and get to do what we imagined this was all about when we were kids." To which another less-joy-filled "Wga Writer" retorted cynically: "Fuck us all. Really. Great job Hollywood. Fantastic."[6]

Accounts of habitual speculation-work throughout this book suggest and underscore the necessity of a darker flip side in production's economic system; that is, the wide-ranging scope of specwork only makes sense if media industries employ an analogous big-volume system to harvest both content and aspirants. An institutional structure approximating the same scale is needed to effectively redeem speculation work and gifted content ideas. This preemptive media alliance often applies—in different ways—both to hopeful "outsider" online creator aspirants and to precariously employed "insider" creative professionals.

The immersive, exploratory approach to qualitative research I favor employs evidence gathering, inductive theory-building, and multimodal analysis. This approach allows for fits and starts and readjustments during research and an openness to fold-in new information and factor unpredictable insights from constantly looking across intersecting or adjacent embedded production sectors. This approach may suggest that I've invested more in building a foundation of insights and recurring research principles than in highlighting research ethics. Yet I would like to think that my production culture research also follows the "situative, recursive, and grounded" ethics proposed by Vonderau: "Production studies follows a *situative approach* to ethics, making ethical judgment integral to a process of grounded theorizing. . . . While the positivist tradition often bases *ethical rigor* on rigid procedure and replicability, rigor in this more qualitatively oriented area stems precisely from reflexivity. Here, 'good' research practice is marked by ethical revisionings and the need for researchers to be recursive in their thinking and actions, making ethics an engaging dialogue and negotiation with multiple stakeholders."[7]

By identifying parts of production industries as unethical and systemic, and by adapting methods to highlight, analyze, and mitigate those unethical practices, I may have flipped the conventional roles presupposed in one important academic protocol. That is, the research I push for in this book may position production scholars as a kind of uninvited but de facto IRB that monitors media industry (rather than an IRB that oversees the scholars). Yes, protection of human subjects is central to our research, but this applies equally as much to our goal of *seeking out, isolating, and outing regressive industrial managerial practices.* Research ethics do not just apply to necessary technical matters (like protecting the data scholars may have extracted or sources they may have anonymized). One outcome of greater reflexivity is that researchers may serve unintentionally as industry's uninvited (and maybe unwanted) ethics-warning IRB.

Industrial disinformation, coercion, and theft are more than abstract ideas. They play out in workplace business behaviors and predatory relationships. More than, say, economic "markets" or strategic "synergies" or "creative economies," all three dispositions (deception, coercion, extraction) necessarily involve embodied, experienced, and affective dimensions. Each stress can be located at the interpersonal level of the human subject in production. Each acts on and impacts people. Earlier ethical critical judgments in film studies against industry from Marxism, situationism, or apparatus theory often allowed scholars to sequester inside the safe abstractions of, say, "base-superstructure," "society-of-the-spectacle," or "fetishism." These schemes behaved as theoretical ethics, with little need for or interest in fieldwork or actual human subjects. I would argue that predatory and coercive behaviors are far more difficult to theorize-away as general predicaments. The fact that deception, coercion, and theft play out in small creator groups challenges scholars to come-clean, critically, about their own position on the human subjects they study. Production culture study makes the human predicament unavoidable in analysis. Media industries are not industries without the people that make up and animate them. Their condition or duress should matter more in scholarship.

Keeping "culture" in media industry studies makes ethics unavoidable. This is because industry's cultural expressions facilitate, operationalize, and normalize systemic deception, coercion, bullying, and stealing. You want to counter predation and coercion as you research structures and institutional systems? Then deconstruct the cultural fabric that industry weaves to normalize these behaviors as acceptable in production firms and trade groups. See how those stressors work at the level of the individual worker. Or the team. Or the crew. Or dig up and closely map production's online back-channel chatter—leaks, hacks, and snark that often capably rip open and expose deep managerial ethical fault lines.

Apart from the detailed credits and book's appendix, which describe my sources and fieldwork sites, I have not added extra discussion of where the recordings, transcripts, and photos for this book came from or why they might be problematic or why I might be sued. I hope, instead, to have answered Vonderau's challenge but by turning the table in a different direction: by underscoring why ethical critique is an almost unavoidable consequence of embedded production culture research. Far from being a "soft" or "symbolic" "expression" emanating from industry, or hovering and obscuring it, culture provides industry with a formidable array of managerial control instruments. Culture gives industry fundamental in-the-trenches tools to enact and justify industry's unethical behaviors. Making culture managerial also somehow makes precarity seem desirable as a defining element of film and media creativity.

To better understand the industrial structures and systems that enable industry's three unethical interactions featured in this chapter, the field of production studies would benefit by rethinking some of the general framing paradigms that we traditionally employ for analysis in cinema and media studies (CMS). The next chapter does just that. It introduces and outlines a three-part model for describing and understanding industrial stressors and fault lines as sites for systematic research.

Framework

Spec, Folds, Leaks

"It's sad because I worked really hard every day putting the hours in, but they haven't paid me," he said. . . . He was once posting as many as 100 videos per day.

—Joseph Melles, quoted in Rodriguez and Bursztynsky, "Snap Creators"[1]

Discerning why industry normalizes excessive self-disclosure as a collective good for the same workers whom the industry treats badly is challenging. In what universe, for example, does voluntarily scripting, shooting, creating, and giving away one hundred new video productions every day (just to create the *possibility* of getting paid) make any sense? How could twenty-first-century film schools even teach this new three-thousand-new-videos-per-month "formula for success" in production? More generally, how does unpaid and uncredited creative brainstorming in public (say, the 24/7 uploading of expressive content on social media by company underlings) relate to the management practices of the major studios and giant tech platforms that mine and harvest the unmoored brainstorming that results? Here, I introduce the book's concepts and general argument that a deep and unfortunate synergy exists between wide-ranging speculation behaviors (on production's expressive "creator" side) and folding and rift behaviors (on production's stressed, managerial "industry" side).

These two sides represent less of a pitched battle between autonomous, opposing skill sets than a kind of ideological yin and yang, a double bind that many production workers face at the same time. I define industry's "Spec" side as the sectors that promote short-term, unpaid, voluntary IP disclosure among emerging and rising creators. By contrast, the industry's "Fold/Rift" side involves longer-term, underpaid, financially overleveraged work among professional workers. In terms of volition, the Spec side gushes with *voluntary disclosures* about production that scholars can analyze, albeit with caution. The Fold/Rift side offers *involuntary disclosures* about production that scholars can meaningfully target and research, in different ways. Although film studies has long exceled at explaining film's imaginative practices on the creative side, and political economy ably describes media's market behaviors on the managerial side, this book employs both frameworks together in comparative analysis. In general terms the book asks, What kind of functional rationality and benefit do these strange bedfellows (specwork vs. folds-rifts) bring to the twenty-first-century production industry as a whole?

This proposed link between speculation and rifts begs two practical questions. Given the arguably dark synergy I have just described—a system-wide predicament in the production industry—why and how should we actually study or research it? Having introduced twenty-first-century media production in my preface from the broader perspective of a conflict between futurism (ideation) and creator mining (monetization), I delineate in this chapter a more precise three-part integrated model for analysis, a framework of basic categories within which the rest of the book's research is organized and can be understood. I want to argue in this chapter for the benefits of utilizing this tripartite model in media industry research.

This model for integrated analysis builds on some basic definitions that can help us productively triangulate among (1) speculation or specwork (expressive practices like pitching, piloting, brainstorming, script coverage by unpaid interns, and for-fee table-reads); (2) folding (industrial stressing, labor conflict, trade rhetoric, negotiated and unnegotiated consent); and (3) fractures and rifts (unintended or unwanted disclosures, leaks, and hacks of proprietary information). The book as a whole is informed by and its chapters organized into these three broad parts and categorical distinctions. Each of these larger unit categories in the book (speculation, folds, fractures) features both an explanatory chapter (context and theory) and a fieldwork chapter (a case study). Each case-study chapter elaborates the explanatory chapter that precedes it, describing and explaining a narrower site of practice from fieldwork (production pedagogy, online creation, industry-aspirant partnerships). My hope is that these paired ethnographic case sites exemplify the sometimes illogical interactions of the three broader industry behaviors (speculating, folding, fracturing).

Why try to research expressive creator behaviors alongside trade rhetoric and labor conflict as an analytical package? Why, furthermore, try to understand and explain such things within a unified model or integrated scheme for analysis? Corporations have long frustrated outsider attempts to connect-the-dots of industry's less-marketable inner workings. Faced with that habitual disposition, I designed and undertook this project over a decade through grounded, theory-building production research.[2] Grounded research is by definition inductive. It deliberately rejects, in early stages of fieldwork, a priori attempts to prematurely lock down a final research question. Instead, the research *process* itself, by design, generates the final research *question*. The following section describes how my tactical attempts evolved to make greater conceptual sense of the dynamic evidence in front of me, as it unfolded. I turn now to detail that incremental theory-building process. *Specworld*'s three-part model emerged over time, as odd connections, parallels, and oppositions became clearer in evidence and fieldwork. I offer the framework as an alternative way to explain the sometimes odd logic and order underneath what might on the surface look like disruptive, disorderly, or disorganized behaviors in contemporary media production.

A wide range of industry practices observed in fieldwork raised questions about whether some wider logic of economic preemption (not just future-speak) might be at work in the system as a whole. For example, far beyond an aspiring writer's pitch or outsider's spec-script, the process of brainstorming imagined worlds is built into the bureaucratic DNA of vast, traditional industry enterprises like the RAI/Turin Prix-Italia, and Studio Cinecittà, Italy (fig. 2.1). Epic set-designs shadowed program buyers at the TV market in Italy's Turin and cultivated the sense that buyers speculating about TV's next profitable trends constituted the primary task of the collective event. By contrast, Cinecittà studios responded to the disruptive digital era not just by launching its own "Digital Factory" but by opening an immersive space that bathed visitors' imaginations with future prospects enabled by both the studio's heavy filming infrastructure and its long history of proven cultural distinction. The once carefully managed and *orderly* salaried specwork that defined Cinecittà's producing and art departments now seem largely disconnected from upstarts in the *disorderly* digital era, where creators "give-it-away-for-free" on social media, YouTube, and elsewhere.

Yet the ways today's digital platforms induce and showcase premature creator expression dwarfs the disciplined assembly-line specwork long managed at Prix-Italia and Cinecittà. On social media, influencers and creators are taught to lead with their IP in public, to share their best ideas until it hurts. Rather than told to guard their best ideas, or manage

FIGURE 2.1. Brainstorming imagined worlds is built into the DNA of long-standing production enterprises like the RAI/Turin Prix-Italia *(left)* and Studio Cinecittà *(right)*, Italy. Photos: © 2012, by J. Caldwell.

their scarcity, aspirational Gen-Z and millennial makers are advised and incentivized to churn their best IP out in order to build public brands through social networks (fig. 2.2). This sunny advice and mentoring from large media companies, traditional creative agencies, and firms like Shopify presupposes that paid sponsorships and "cobranding opportunities" will grow alongside the emerging creator's increasingly networked and thus successful brand.

Of course, MBA management and start-up schemes have long valued corporate getting-out-in-front strategies like Shopify's. This commitment challenged me to articulate how corporate entrepreneurialism relates to specworld's adjacent impulse—the promotion of creative speculative expression in public. In one way, economics is fundamental to the definition of specwork, in either low or high settings. *Specwork*, that is, can be defined simply as expressive work undertaken "freely" to increase the odds that the expresser will score some greater or more profitable cultural or career goal in the future. Questions about the way money may link corporate get-out-in-front strategies and individual speculation seemed to go beyond the issue of an individual's free labor. Did all the enabling workshops and therapeutic mentoring of YouTuber

FIGURE 2.2. To YouTube creators: "Lead with your IP in Public!" *Top:* Preemptive corporate system for IP-harvesting of aspirants. Online merchandizer Shopify incentivizes adolescent influencers and YouTube creators to share their IP up front, and stop worrying about monetizing their uploaded content until after they have been discovered as influencers. Media trade pavilion, Anaheim, CA. © 2017, by J. Caldwell. *Below:* Diversified conglomerates can counterbalance costly big-IP of feature film and premium television with cheaper small-IP. Studio Babelsberg is highly dependent on traditional professional craft labor while the adjacent UFA conglomerate employs numerous network tiers that excel at branding and the less risky "reformatting" (of reality TV, etc.). Germany. Photos: © 2016, by J. Caldwell.

and film school aspirants I observed actually involve lowering corporate financial risk in some way at the production industry's supply-chain front end?

Managerial reconnaissance of aspirant creators (to scout, categorize, and cull as many free ideas and creator candidates as possible), I reasoned, might help firms resolve capital deficits and stabilize media companies facing unruly market changes. This would give preemptive partnering with aspirants a risk-mitigating logic since the current media platform model enables firms to vigorously and cost-effectively content-mine and creator-mine the platform's upload churn. The fieldwork with social media creators described in chapters 4, 6, and 8 suggested as much. Yet few informants I talked to shared my growing suspicion about content mining and predation. For me, such managerial stealth scouting among aspiring online creators might more accurately be understood as nonconsensual, low-cost "R&D." Most YouTubers, more so than me, seemed locked in on a sunnier view of social media as a Gen-Z El Dorado; that is, they believed that their distinctive personalities would allow them to create and upload something unique that would (eventually) virally trend as content bait to be monetized.

Studying creative speculation may make sense partly because we already have a long history of focusing on the concepts involved: expression, creativity, foresight, personal vision, and innovation. Arts and humanities scholars are well-versed in researching the artifacts of specwork—sketches, inspiring incidents, first drafts, storyboards, test scenes—that point to or somehow prove those personality-based philosophical ideals. Scholars have long sought vision in production's upstream. This was traditionally called "development" and "preproduction," clean phases controlled by the director (in film) and producer (in television). Figure 2.3 provides one example. As they anticipate and prepare for forthcoming shooting days, auteur John Ford and Henry Fonda ponder the results of tests and filmed dailies midstream during the shooting of *Grapes of Wrath* (Fox, 1939). Studios often exposed and publicized preproduction (as well as midstream quality checks and prep like Ford's) during a film's later distribution. In the digital media platform era, by contrast, a paradigm of "semipublic brainstorming" would better describe online production's preemptive phase. This is because very little actual physical production is required. This makes *preproduction* seem like an archaic term.

Yet this conversion from traditional preproduction to real-time brainstorming as online production's main stage still leaves one preliminary question: why should we research either of those things, systemically,

FIGURE 2.3. Preparing for what's next: Traditional production's upstream and midstream. Publicity photo: 20th Century Fox. Courtesy of the Margaret Herrick Library, Academy of Motion Picture Arts and Sciences.

through the lens of stressed folds and fractures? For starters, scholars of film and media often find that those industries are often anchored or closed off by prepositioned interpretive armor. Most national cinemas, like Italy's, come packaged with their own self-interpretations, schemes often anchored into their museums, archives, and academies (fig. 2.4). These hardened industrial hermeneutics (which are often locked into an auteur pantheon or official film canon) can frustrate anyone pushing for more unorthodox empirical observations. They can also frustrate scholars at industry's front door seeking to ask independent research questions counter to the industry's own. Unintended rifts, fractures, and backdoor access, by contrast, often give scholars room for unofficial, independent, or less sanctioned counterquestions in research.

Recognizing these complications, *Specworld* explores ways to research film and media production as an ecosystem or "complex system." I have long defined and researched media ecosystems not with the wistful biological overtones of harmonious self-regulating worlds;

FIGURE 2.4. For scholars, film and media industries are often closed-off by prepositioned interpretive armor (culturally anchored by film canons, academies, and auteur pantheons). Photo: Museo nazional del Cinema, Turin, Italy. Photo: © 2011, by J. Caldwell.

rather, I take seriously the first term *(complexity)* in the ecological conception of such systems. In part, this means researching production as a *hierarchical,* industrially systemic mess. This working concept is far from dismissive. I do not employ it to mean that industry is merely chaotic, convoluted, or dysfunctional. Rather, as the next section introduces, I repeatedly ask practical questions about what functional order or systematic patterns we can discern within messy embedded systems made up of many adjoining sectors and many different moving parts.[3] I hope, that is, to describe industry's connective tissues in order to place the unexceptional, contingent, habitual, subaltern, and routine as squarely at the center of our media industries research as the distinctive cases that our CMS field is already well-versed in explaining.

SPECULATING (ORDERLY AND DISORDERLY)

Why connect industry's creative impulses (speculation) with its managerial and bureaucratic practices (folding, monetization) in an integrated model? One reason is that both creator-talk and management-speak often habitually code-switch between disordering-and-then-ordering rhetoric and tactics. Creator-types and CEOs alike, that is, sell the trade public and investors on "disruption" (disordering). At the same time, they sell how-to books on ways to corral and "leverage" (reorder) the creative or bureaucratic churn that results. This conflicted utopian thinking in companies creates prospects for corporate brainstorming that must (eventually) be assembly-lined to find Fordist market efficiencies. This industrial doublespeak challenges media industries researchers to articulate the extent to which they themselves seek out and research order or disorder in media industry systems.[4]

This odd marriage between conceptual (disruption) and managerial (ordering) schemes circulates in both scholarly venues and industry trades. The split is very apparent, for example, in the disconnects often made between celebrations of frictionless creative speculation in fan studies and the media trades, on the one hand; and the vast stressed labor sectors of film/TV production that produce fan bait, on the other. *Specworld* tries to unpack those disconnects. It asks how industry's showcasing of creative-idea sharing (commonly spun as "outside-the-box" innovative "disruption") relates to a parallel activity: the routine ways industry habitually buries its subworlds of outsourced and networked production labor. I am especially interested in the way industry monetizes and *mutes* the very stressed labor sectors on which creative brainstorming and content development still largely depend. This book tries to square the industry's outside-the-box myths about IP creation with its habitual inside-the-box schemes for hiding, normalizing, and managing disorganized (aka "flexible") creative labor.

Online creation has triggered an immense surge, not just in fickle, distracted viewers/users but also in the amount, diversity, and force of aspirational creative labor. This surge functions to create far more than just an oversupply of new candidates from which an opportunistic industry can now clinically select "winners." Historically, Hollywood couched this sweepstakes ethos in trade rhetoric about finding the industry's "next" important writer, director, producer, or "discovery." Industry's smart money now increasingly accepts that it must manage and develop this unruly new aspirational force—to discipline and monetize it in efficient ways—without appearing to exploit or destroy those who make it up. In the media-platform era, converting aspirational volatility into bureaucratic efficiencies—bringing rationality to the unpredictable supply chain—lies at the heart of making profitable media.[5]

After starting my research on production's new and expanding upstream, I was surprised by the extent to which preemptive creative labor (specwork) often involved seasoned professionals. Specwork, that is, is not just a predicament restricted to desperate online aspirants or the underemployed. Consider the following backstory explanation of unpaid creative prework by a seasoned film professional. Her account provides a cogent example of the often elaborate investment of time ("80 hrs.") and money ("a lot") put into unpaid speculation work by *three* established professionals (a union costume designer, costumer, and music supervisor) just to land a single job on one Quentin Tarantino production:

> *Arianne Phillips, CDG.* I'd been told that [he] had someone else in mind. . . . So on this film I thought "I can't just go in and talk my way into this job. I have to really make an effort." . . . So I hired a costumer . . . and [we] worked for about 80 hours on a presentation [before my pitch]. Which was based on the script that I had read. Unfortunately, when I read it, I couldn't have my phone, or a pen or paper [with me]. So I had to absorb it. . . . I just went from there, and I got all of this detail. . . . So I made a visual-chronological collage. A book of reference. . . . I also made an "epilogue" for the end [of the film] which was a separate book. And then I [thought] . . . "Oh, well, I'm going to put some Brylcreem in there" (because he mentioned Brylcreem) and I'm going to find a vintage pair of sun glasses. I made it an experience. . . . A director (on *Hateful 8*) told me "make it as experiential as possible." So I [told] a friend of mine . . . a music supervisor [that] the core of our script is KHJ radio, which kind of takes you through the movie. So we created a CD of [that] music. So I sent the book, in a box, with big letters, I said "listen to this music while you are reading this book." I did a playlist of top music from February to August of 1969. And then I put in a vintage Hawaiian shirt that I knew would fit him. . . . (laughter) . . . I had heard that he was going to hire someone that he'd worked with before. So just take that as a lesson . . . you have to go the extra mile. . . . And I'm really glad I did. I had to spend a lot of money on it . . . And by the way, I had most of my research for the first two weeks done.[6]

This explanation by a single professional worker about how she was hired for a key job on a feature film illustrates some of the central themes of this book. This includes the pervasiveness of unsolicited artistic idea-gifting, the competitive oversupply of qualified labor, the role of self-financed speculation work, aspiration as a professional skill set, trade-and-barter labor economies, and back-channel negotiations between embedded but distinct production cultures. Phillips's creative "productions" before the "real" production began were considerable and included a rich variety of original "deep texts": a chronological visual collage, a "look-book" for design reference, a handmade "epilogue book," a period-specific mix-tape/CD with playlist, a tube of Brylcreem, and a vintage Hawaiian shirt in a DIY gift box. Effective exchange of these preemptive nonscreen artworks can bring managerial value as well. They can make the complex rhizome of production workers and crafts temporarily cohere as a "team" for the fleeting duration of a single film shoot.[7]

Media industries now attend closely to what might once have been associated with "talent scouting" or "development." Now such activities often posture as "cobranding opportunities," "influencer sponsorships," or "relationship marketing." The need to find and extract viable new content candidates and creator candidates from the online surge has spurred companies to find ways to achieve managerial rationality over the irrationalities of largely unaffiliated, aspirational creative labor. By seeking to monetize this cultural expression, many firms acknowledge social media as an informal frontloaded, preemptive phase of film and television. This creates a protracted prestage for harvesting online production that is, arguably, far more amorphous and ubiquitous than what we once simplistically and neatly delineated as "preproduction," "packaging," or "development." The new preemptive industry strategies "to get out in front" of content trends, technology shifts, and market risks should matter to production research. When industry jumps the gun in this way—by relocating attention to focus on where creativity takes place in the online era—it also complicates some trusty categories that guided my earlier production culture research. In retrospect, I may have benefited in my earlier studies by conflating "old media" or "legacy media" with the "physical production" phase. In those projects, even though production was already noticeably slipping on the digital precipice, I benefited by grappling with a neater creator-world, something simply called "film and television."[8] The prestage of preproduction in the online era is now far more vast.

This corporate relocation of the source for creator candidates has consequences. No longer just an irrelevant oversupply of outside "wannabes" trying to break into the prestige film/TV centers, aspirants, entrants, and the underemployed now form integral parts of the industry's cultural supply chain. Even if kept at arm's length, aspirants help make up industry's "labor workflow." Public for-fee pitchfests provide but one example of industry's preemptive engagement with and monitoring of its cultural supply chain (fig. 2.5). Mimicking the traditional ("completed") film festival scene, public "screenwriting festivals" promote (preemptive) speculation-work from an ever-larger creative aspirational workforce. Aspirational labor on social media platforms

Under the Knife/Cutting Edge
by Shonda Rhimes

THE WORLD:

Training to be a surgeon is like no other job.

After 4 years of college and 4 years of med school,   if you're
smart enough and tough enough to be accepted into a surgical
residency, you have seven more years of training to go. 7 more
years at the bottom of the surgical food chain.   7 more years as
a grunt, as a soldier. You work at a crazed pace -- 60 hours on,
18 hours off.   You make $28,000 a year. You rarely see your non-
doctor friends, you refrigerator never has any food, you can't
remember the last time you had a date or got your hair cut. You're
sleep-deprived, nutrition deprived, you smoke too much, drink too
much caffeine and when you get those 18 hours off, you either sleep
your life away or you party far to hard -- desperate to get squeeze
a week's worth of living into one day. You eat, sleep and breathe

---

A GAME OF THRONES

George R.R. Martin

October 1993

Each of the conflicts presents a major threat of my imaginary
realm, the Seven Kingdoms, and to the lives of the principal
characters.

The first threat grows from the enmity between the great houses
of Lannister and Stark as it plays out in a cycle of plot,
counterplot, ambition, murder, and revenge, with the iron throne
of the Seven Kingdoms the ultimate prize. This will form the
backbone of the first volume of the trilogy, A Game of Thrones.

PITCHFEST

FIGURE 2.5. Long tradition of incremental drafting of script treatments (inside studios) now joined by preemptive "pitchfests" (outside studios). Photos *(top):* Opening new story-worlds, first, in "treatment" for *Grey's Anatomy* TV series, © Shonda Rhimes; then, in synopsis for *A Game of Thrones*, © George R. R. Martin. Sources: Larry Edmunds Bookshop, Los Angeles. Photo *(lower):* Offscreen still frame of Pitchfest promo from London Screenwriters Festival. Photo of displays: © 2018, by J. Caldwell.

FIGURE 2.6. (Speculating) parts make up industry's (identity) whole. A loading dock for the below-the-line night shift at a film/video production stage. "Hollywood" as a constructed, collectively willed affinity. Hollywood, CA. Photo: © 2011, by J. Caldwell.

also functions as research, providing data with predictive value, which film and TV can leverage as fungible capital. As such, the new studios and networks must find ways to systematize and industrialize aspirational cultures once seen, and thus largely dismissed, as unruly and unmanageable. Industry traditionally wrote off such aspirants as amateurs to keep out via high barriers to professional entry. No longer. Industry now engages aspirant creators as a vast focus group for predictive research.

One persistent industry posture over the years nagged me, motivating me to employ the integrated framework outlined in this chapter. That is, I have tried to make sense of production's creative work as film and television have gotten even more diverse, splintered, outsourced, and "flexible." Despite the fact that most firms are materially disaggregated from each other, thousands of subcompanies and small contractors now form the imagined "industry." But this same splintered world of microfirms persists under a unifying drumbeat from the last century: that they are somehow all part of "the" industry. Every disaggregated sector within production's complex system seems to contribute to this collective public aspiration, posing as an aggregated, unified industry (fig. 2.6). Firms may value this preemptive unifying cultural chatter because "flexible" industries force their subunits to constantly reassert and legitimize their identities if they ever hope to successfully affiliate and partner. This institutionally splintered but symbolically unitary paradox informs the analytical framework in this chapter. While many scholars locate reflexivity at the top of industry (in official studio or network marketing of "finished" media products), I look for recurring patterns of reflexivity in lowlier production worlds. Subfirms there ceaselessly cycle between disaggregation and partnering in symbolic gestures of willed affinity with something bigger.

FOLDING (EMBEDDING, ORDERLY CONSENT, AND DISRUPTIVE PUSHBACK)

The second category or tier in my analytical model, the behavioral or collective flip side of speculation, is something I term "folding." Stated simply, folding describes the industrial efforts and interactions needed to form working, serial-production partnerships. Contractual and coproduction partnerships are functional alliances that are often difficult to forge and temporary. Since flexibility via outsourcing now largely defines production, folding refers to the difficult work of turning small-scale individual specworkers into a profitable larger-scale collective enterprise. Folding is often triggered by partnering efforts between neighboring crafts, subcontracting competitors, union and nonunion crews, above-the-line executives and precarious below-the-line workers, and in-house staff coexisting with runaway labor.

The corporate pursuit of more orderly, manageable pipelines for both new screen ideas and new creative personnel, described above, can stir up industry's less glamorous structural complications and labor stresses. Industrializing specwork often pressures firms to resolve structural frictions that stress the systems on which the specwork they seek depends.[9] As such, folding often flags itself to scholars through acute or contentious intertrade cultural expressions. The dissonance and intensity of cultural expression in trade sectors often corresponds directly to the degree of difficulty of the bureaucratic work it takes to coalition-build the fleeting partnerships now needed for media productions. After a project-specific partnership, producers and firms must move on quickly to their next coalition-building production challenge.

As with specwork, researchers can find orderly and disorderly versions of folding. Depending on the differences bridged, and the cultural trade work required, folding can produce lasting rifts or quieter consent behaviors. Industry hypes outside-the-box IP sharing as a frictionless key to

FIGURE 2.7. Forging a temporary embedded alliance to marshal premium screen content (fleeting production partnerships between soft creator capital and hardened infrastructure). Cinecittà Studios backlot, sets for HBO's *Rome*, Italy. © 2012, by J. Caldwell

cutting-edge cultural disruption and innovation. Yet it seldom admits the ways that it cloaks the friction-heavy shadow world of production labor that props up and enables spec sharing. Making sense of production's disordering stressors in this stubborn labor flip side means grappling with how and why production must first be understood via its frictions within a complex embedded system. That is, workers speculate inside of specific production subcultures, which themselves are embedded within other production units or firms that constrain those creator subcultures.

Analyzing folds, therefore, requires scholars to first describe how a given production entity is embedded within the industry sectors that host and sustain it. Big-budget A-list transnational coproductions like the miniseries *Rome*, for example, exemplify successful, orderly folds (fig. 2.7). For the series, HBO forged an alliance between the many initially disaggregated entities of labor, firms, infrastructure, and financing so that the production could cohere as an orderly partnership of integrated parts. *Rome*'s heavy footprint on Italian back lots and Cinecittà soundstages publicly symbolized the success of this coproduction fold, even as it gave scholars evidence of collective, negotiated consent. Yet this A-list series alliance proved fleeting and ephemeral once the series

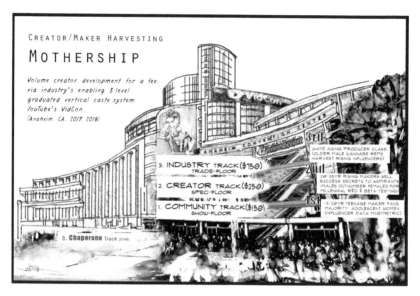

FIGURE 2.8. Creator harvesting mothership. VidCon trade convention embeds and folds together three distinct online production cultures. The event postures as a benign host tasked with facilitating low-to-high crossovers and profitable future-careers for aspiring creators. Drawing: © 2021, by J. Caldwell.

wrapped, and its human and material resources disaggregated again back into their underutilized industrial norm.

Film, television, and online content creation can feel shape-shifting and slippery when scholars attempt to put them under a microscope. Just as they complicate viewer and maker experience, those media no longer exist within finite frames or discrete distribution windows that scholars can study. Even a short time of observation in the field quickly reveals that any one type of media production is rarely isolated from other forms of production. In fact, production routinely signals that it is inseparable from other economic, labor, and cultural systems in a variety of ways. These multiple systems invariably overlap, shadow, feed, alter, monetize, or manage the specific production practice that the researcher initially sets out to study. Consider two examples of layered *embedding* when industry folds and congeals different production cultures within a common industrial space.

If scholars want to study (a) new online social media creators, for example, then they'll also have to account for cohorts of adjacent cloaked personnel embedded with them (fig. 2.8). These suitors would include (b) the old media talent agencies that capably harvest aspiring creators and (c) the legacy ad agency departments in the game that package the necessary sponsorship and merchandizing deals that online influencers depend on. Influencers, talent agents, and ad agencies all employ different trade conventions. They pose distinctively in their own trade sectors, and each of these largely different groups makes media differently from the other. Yet here—via temporary social media partnerships formed in intertrade contact zones and trade shows—the sectors are knotted strategically together. Trying to describe or feature any one production group (like online influencers) in scholarship should entail describing the group's position within the embedded system as a whole. Specifically, what cross-strata, cross-cultural working predicament do the makers being studied have to contend with to create?

The task of describing the embedded system that hosts one's research subject applies not just to unorthodox schemes (like influencers/creators colliding with Hollywood agents at VidCon) but also to conventional work groups. Scholars might want to research, say, (a) traditional camera crews. If so, they would be wise to examine the cinematographers' relevant, integrated "side-worlds" as well. These side-worlds would include (b) the equipment companies that network and incentivize crew specialists; (c) the history of any formal union rules (if unionized) or pay deals involved (if nonunion); (d) the informal reciprocity and trade-and-barter arrangements that allow crew members to work overtime, or for less pay; (e) the "paraindustry" players, the metaproducers; and, finally (f) the ancillary subcompanies that charge crewmembers for necessary on-the-side workshops, sizzle reals, demos, and social media presence far from the crew set in question. How can we best disaggregate or study embedded labor/business/trade knots like these? To answer this question, the book's concluding chapter explores research methods to appraise alternative ways of framing production scholarship as disembedding research.

Embedding is only one unavoidable problem that production researchers need to address up front. Another kind of intermixing can also obscure our attempts to isolate a clean object for research—something I try to unpack as an *identity-knot* problem. This describes the multiple simultaneous identities that even single subjects or informants often embody— even if or as they work inside of what may initially look like a distinct job description. Take, for example, a scholar who wants to research postproduction. What should or could their scholarship make of the fact that almost everyone in the studied post facility also likely has some other "off-hours" creative activity or media aspiration on the side? Some assistant editors are writing spec scripts, others seeking pitch meetings, others shopping their own "indie" no-budget side projects intended for Sundance or SXSW. I would argue that "multitasking" is not the best way to describe this directors-in-the-closet passing-as-editors. Identity "passing" can also be performed by aspiring creators whose day jobs list them as "technicians" and "below-the-line" workers. Passing poses often involve asymmetry, in that such individuals have not yet achieved the status of formal "hyphenate-careers" (such as "writer/producer"). Their competing, parallel identities may be imbalanced, tied to different career stages in each vocational trajectory. One's creator ID may still be aspirant-to-emerging, while their parallel technician ID may be journeyman-who-has-made-it).

Consider how the following filmmaker's personal identity knot complicates the official digital technology fold his corporate employer *thinks* they are embedding and hiring him for:

> *David Gauch, Digital Interaction Designer.* Like many filmmakers, you're looking for all of these mini-breaks to compound. I have to get stuff out there on the side. And hopefully that will compound. As people see it. So it's just doing it on your own time. With no money. A lot of the stuff I'm doing, I need a little bit of funding because it's got the technology. You just have to make it. And try to get it out there. (David Gauch, interview by author, UCLA, April 7, 2016)

Since many rising creators, like Gauch, invest more into their aspirational identities "on the side" than their official day jobs (here a tech firm), why don't scholars follow their lead and focus there, on the side? That is, why not focus on where their subject's emotional and psychological labor is actually invested—which is often outside of the "day job" identity title they may have in some media firm bureaucracy?

Even if one's industry status mashes-up provisional or asymmetrical identities (i.e., midcareer technician who writes scripts aimed at directing), we need to find ways to reckon with multicareer knots like these in analysis. Identity knotting and vocational passing pervade twenty-first-century production labor. This holds, in large measure, because of the serial nature of on/off employment. What do all of the creative side projects and parallel sub and creator metaworlds that the researcher will run into have to do with the initial primary research subject (say, the editing or camera crewing that was targeted as the researcher's main focus)? How do these secondary production career identities impact the same person's primary production career identity? Such side-worlds are not insignificant or unrelated. Ethnographic production culture research needs to acknowledge and take the interactions between an individual worker's hybrid or parallel identities seriously. They do impact and alter each other, even if they appear asymmetrical.

Another factor that can disrupt an employer's orderly fold (or a scholar's attempt to cleanly nail down a subject's identity) is the widespread threat or practice of underpaid assistants "jumping ship" to a competing firm. Consider how one agency staffer pretends to happily "become their boss" in the interview below. He suggests that assistants of one sort or another arguably run Hollywood as the faces, extensions, or avatars of those bosses. But since the very success of agency assistants depends on parallel, midlevel networking across competing firms, assistants and junior executives simultaneously create the socioprofessional conditions that will allow them to eventually "jump ship" to another firm. In the following agency case, it allows Masukawa to jump to another, preferred career in something different (screenwriting):

> *Michael Masukawa, Piller/Segan Junior Development Executive.* When you work for an agent you work for his 30 clients as well. So . . . some people want to [eventually] be writers, so you work for a TV Lit agent. So you get to talk to—get to know—all of these writers he works for. So, when the client's show gets turned into a series, you're the first one to know—if they need a writer's assistant. So there's a lot of access from agencies to the people who run shows. Just because your boss is dealing with all of these shows across town, at ABC, NBC, Fox and everywhere, you are [also] dealing with these other assistants at other companies that you would probably rather be working at You get to know others. Have drinks. Maybe 3 months later, you say, "I'm leaving my job at an agency" [to get a position at his firm]. At an agency, you meet a lot of people. You see how things work. (Michael Masukawa, interview by author, UCLA, April 7, 2016)

NDAs usually take care of disloyalty and IP issues. Yet the nagging sense that most employees (whose firms initially fold them via consent) are always looking to jump ship (to a rival firm for more money) creates trust issues and some corporate instability.[10]

To what extent should these three interactions and tensions between production subsystems—caused by either embedding, or identity-knots, or ship-jumping—become factors in the production scholar's research? This book assumes that film, television, and media production comprise complex subsystems that are nested within other larger complex production systems, which themselves are embedded in other host systems. As a result, production researchers need to take the relations and interactions between and across these embedded strata and systems seriously. In fact, I argue throughout this book that it is precisely the interfaces,

FIGURE 2.9. The aspirant creator's low-to-high crossover conundrum. The invitation: "you give." The end-use: "we take." Images: Offscreen still frames from *Life in a Day* promo and solicitation video, Scott Free Productions and YouTube.

fissures, and fault lines between embedded subsystems—not anything we've bracketed off or defined as distinctive or exceptional—that provide the most productive sites for production culture research.

Having acknowledged these complications for ethnographers, here I want to introduce and contrast one example of an unremarkable industry fold with one example of a stressed fold. The latter case exemplifies a highly researchable rift precisely because of the trade disruption involved. That stressed fold differs from the orderly embedding inherent in, say, new technology days or summits. Many unions, guilds, and trade associations often host such confabs to enable their stable of film workers to collectively ponder how new equipment might expand their menu of artistic options in production. Such consensus-building gatherings can also be understood as courting rituals between the artisans and various equipment companies, who always seek greater control of production trends.

New technologies don't just evolve or develop but are brokered in production culture trade gatherings like these through collective rituals of prototyping, beta-testing, and market stare-downs (between competitors) via concept demos. Selling filmmakers on a new look often betrays a tech firm's vested hope in some preemptive technology. Trade demos are bets that a firm's new IP will serve as a linchpin giving them greater market share. Such gatherings feel routine, as collective tactics to fold pros into adopting new gear. Yet these interactions mostly behaved as refereed sales pitches, with pro user musings, at least as I observed and studied the interactions.

In contrast to such consensus-building tech days staged by a trade group, a stressed fold arguably provides a richer opportunity for systematic industry research. One advantage is that stressed folds are less scripted than consensual partnering. One example: a contentious MPEG union-organizing meeting in Hollywood I observed in 2011 betrayed little of the refereeing and scripting that I observed at the well-behaved 2015 DGA tech event. Agitation defined the MPEG organizing event from the start. I summarized the event in my fieldnotes using a recurring trope the editors employed when they complained of "too many cooks in their kitchen." Unlike controlled, refereed trade courting, TV editing's uncontrolled industry-wide shift from recording on digital tape to filming on digital drives and cards spurred an acute trade rift between embedded production cultures that industry researchers could isolate, trace, and study as a boundable, frameable phenomenon.

Consider the chaos that ensued for twenty-first-century video editors as they faced immense changes from two fronts. First, the *genre* "Reality TV" greatly changed TV's shooting ratios on location. Then the *technological shift* in cameras from durable film/tape to digital drives/ cards exponentially increased the amount of footage that editors had to wade and cull through in post:

> *Rob Kraut, MPEG.* We come in, we have to figure out the entire post workflow, everything. . . . It's a pretty big nightmare. We're getting all of these new formats. . . . [And] every step of the way is painful with these reduced schedules. . . . What happened to [one assistant per editor]? Remember that? . . . Now it's [me and twelve guys] all running at the same time. That's been the biggest thing for us assistant editors. The [workload is] exponentially growing and we're cutting back on the people we have. (Rob Kraut, MPEG, "Reality Check" union organizing meeting, Hollywood, CA, August 30, 2011)

Simultaneous changes in both genre *and* technology thus dramatically disrupted the several technical crafts that once peacefully coexisted alongside each other. Such intertrade peace only lasts as long as each embedded, adjacent craft shares the same understanding of a common, managed workflow. The move to camera cards spurred videographers to greatly overshoot, producing mountains of digital "footage" beyond what any editor could possibly look through. Multiple competing codecs also created chaos in job descriptions, labor jurisdiction battles, and arguments over control of the knowledge that once defined once-stable—but no longer discrete—job classifications.

I embraced this collective predicament and confrontation during fieldwork as a research opportunity, since the MPEG interaction offered a coherent ground zero for analysis. That is, it provided a way I could locate and trace out actual points of contact and conflict between non-union and union editors, camera operators, engineers, producers, assistants, specific shows, and the union organizers who were trying to ride herd on the tech change that triggered system chaos in the first place. They interacted precisely because they had stressed and conflicted (but purposive rather than random or disinterested) labor relationships. By contrast, it was far more difficult to find honest raving or acting-out at the well-behaved DGA confab.

I favor looking for and analyzing stress points in folds on the verge of breaking, even though the acute prosecutorial fractures detailed in the next section may provide the scholar with cleaner, more comprehensive access points for research. Examples of in-progress rifts within highly stressed attempted folds show how intensifying contradictions can stress and push a consensual fold toward a breaking point. This often results in contentious, publicly outed disclosure. The first on-the-verge fold involved a production group that launched by hyping its ability to enable two-way online partnerships. Yet the group ended up creating a "partnership" that mostly benefited one side of the equation. In 2010, the trades lauded the hybrid online video/feature documentary *Life in a Day* as an "innovative" commercial content-producing strategy. The project was produced by Ridley Scott, Scott Free Films, and YouTube. Those "producers" solicited, culled, and reaggregated huge amounts of uploaded user-generated content of others. *Life in a Day*'s marketing promised to undercut "old media" and to open up the floodgates to "outsiders," the marginal, anonymous, and subaltern. One YouTube video posted by the Hollywood producers underscored the high-volume basis of their democratic invitation to aspirants to make pro media. Their direct solicitation to lowly online prod-users intoned: "Most important to us. You can upload as much as you'd like. Don't hold back. Although YouTube will stop it after 10 minutes." Keep giving us more! In addition, aspiring filmmakers were warned to remove their own names and website URLs in uploads to the pros so that the resulting feature documentary could be distributed and named instead for the A-list auteurs and corporate brands that oversaw the harvesting process (see fig. 2.9).

With these solicitations for volume uploads, this project functioned less like an exercise in resistant culture media democracy than it did an online vacuum cleaner loudly sucking up vast amounts of free video content. The supposed "democratic" Aspirant(giving) + Industry(taking) logic underscored how pernicious cross-promotional partnerships can be. Industry heavyweights YouTube, Scott Free Films, director Kevin MacDonald, and producer Ridley Scott all added value and profits to their established respective corporate brands. Yet they achieved this precisely because they intentionally and overtly *anonymized* their thousands of video-fragment-submitting online aspirant creators. This initiative was staged as a celebration of "partnering" through the emancipatory, democratizing wonders of digital media. Yet this collectivism mantra mostly pervaded *Life in a Day*'s top-down marketing rhetoric and overseers.[11]

New platforms also often risk rifts when they oversell their extractive economies to creators as enabling, as win-win reciprocities. Platforms sell aspiring creators, for instance, on "personal brand-building" rather than on their need to make and control traditional, bounded forms of distributable indie "content" (films or videos). This shift from content-to-brand, within extractive digital economies, requires much less upfront equity and risk from studios and media corporations. Those hosts sell and justify "you-give" schemes to aspirants as enabling "partnerships." The core production goal of an edgy persona that "trends" (rather than distributable screen content) encourages individual aspirants to shoulder most of their resulting self-development costs. Those aspirant creators that survive the extractive partnerships that result are told to do so by mastering hyper self-management. Chapter 8 focuses in more detail on these asymmetries of creator risk as "overleveraged" partnerships. Such rifts often downsize and end aspirant careers just like hedge funds intentionally gut and bankrupt overleveraged firms for profit.[12]

FRACTURING (DISORDERLY AND DISRUPTIVE)

Looking closely at how industry folds its ill-fitting parts into a working whole requires better descriptions of collective consent. Such studies require detailing how and why industry incentivizes workers and sub-firms to temporarily fall into line. Yet, obviously, many (perhaps most) partnering efforts eventually end or fail. Instead of analyzing consent for some successful partnering scheme, fieldwork often runs into the opposite: splintered relations, financing failures, failed pilots, derailed coproductions, finger-pointing, and self-justifications in the trades. The depth and intensity of this trade dissonance often points to the third dimension in my model for analysis: rifts and fractures.

I take fractures to be folds that have snapped or failed, spewing an inordinate amount of conflicted often snarky self-reflexive trade discourse into the public. Humanities scholars have long marveled at the film and media industry's "intertextuality," even though such things are usually just marketing mechanisms for *intentional* cross-promotions in synergy-seeking business plans. Yet a whole range of highly contentious interfirm and intersector snark and trolling is also triggered during rifts and fractures. These serve an institutional logic that extends well beyond the well-behaved cross-promotional intertext. Fractures and rifts offer ideal opportunities for production researchers precisely because they are *unintended* by the system as a whole.

One apt example of a researchable fracture, triggered by an economic crisis, was the strike and picket line at Cinecittà Studios in 2012. This protest was staged ostensibly to protest encroaching real estate development by the studio owner at the nation's historic film production site. Italian production workers, suspicious that this real estate diversion contributed to runaway production and declines in local and national film production economy, staged a lengthy occupation in front of the Cinecittà studio walls and offices. At the same time, production workers flooded social media and the surrounding area with agit-prop media in attempts to publicize the workers' "side of the story" (fig. 2.10).

Chapter 7 includes more specific examples of legal and financial hacks and fractures that we can systematically study precisely because they surface in public as *acute* trade rifts. The 2017 Sony studio hack provides a dramatic example of an unwanted fracture that disgorged mountains of internal material for analysis. Such info (including the exposure of many additional interdepartmental conflicts embedded inside the well-oiled studio machine) would otherwise not be accessible to researchers. Of course, using someone else's hack for research creates its own ethical problems for the scholar.

Rifts leak or crack incessantly through the well-manicured surfaces of Hollywood and its global competitors. A spate of four researchable fractures, for example, appeared in public over a few short weeks in 2021. All involved speculators and their discontents. First, AT&T threw in its Warner Media conglomeration towel by selling off its large, poorly producing, Hollywood assets to Discovery. The trades mocked AT&T's hubris for thinking it could ever bring "corporate culture" in

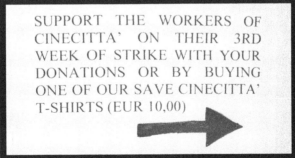

FIGURE 2.10. Industry fracture flagged by unrefereed back-channel SOS and agit-prop. Image: Handmade signs and drawings taped alongside graffiti on wall next to film studio entrance. Photo: Cinecittà, Italy. © 2012, by J. Caldwell.

to discipline the Hollywood culture of its now divorced production arm. Wisdom on the street was that traditional management (outside of showbiz) is simply never prepared to tolerate the long-term financial speculation, high risk, and excessively deferred profits that film and television production have long required.[13] Just as Seagrams, GE, and AOL had gone down in flames before it, AT&T never understood the economics of its high-end specworld. Jim Cramer gloated about the failure on CNBC, and studio historians and political economists had yet another case study to add to their files. Yet the AT&T fracture may matter more to Wall-Street investors than to scholars.

In the same month, a controversial rift at major creative agency International Creative Management (ICM Partners) completely derailed the company's once-lauded multiyear diversity and inclusion initiatives. Since 2017, ICM had conspicuously celebrated its progressive management practices in response to the #MeToo, #TimesUp, and #OscarsSoWhite critiques of systemic harassment in Hollywood. ICM offered numeric and visual proof to the press of its diversity overhaul with photographs of its smiling, diverse staffers. ICM's proud oversell of its new diversity proved intolerable to many of the minority trainees and assistants used in its dog-and-pony diversity show. Thirty current and former employers stated that "the company tolerated a hostile work environment, where women of color were subjected to harassment, bullying and other inappropriate conduct."[14] I cite this because the exposé is far more than grist for celebrity news. The 2021 ICM debacle is merely the latest of many surface cracks exposing the deep, systemic forms of harassment and subjugation in film and television firms systematically researched by scholars such as Erin Hill, Vicki Mayer, Miranda Banks, and Kristen Warner. The industrial structures of harassment—not the celebrity ICM agents personally embarrassed by the public leaks—would make ICM's blood-in-the-water a good starting point for systematic research on deeper institutional issues.

A few weeks later, the press exposed another researchable industry fracture that dramatized the very issues of predation and appropriation that my YouTuber case studies in chapters 4, 6, and 8 describe. In virally trending #BlackTikTokStrike, Black choreographers accused white influencers of stealing and profiting from the choreographed dance moves first developed by young black choreographers. Exhibits A for the strike were seventeen-year-old Charli D'Amelio, a white performer with one hundred million TikTok followers, and highly successful twenty-year-old white TikTok star Addison Rae. Both had appropriated and profited from dance moves created by Black artists. Making matters worse, NBC's Tonight Show invited white D'Amelio to showcase "her" moves, which were originally created by fourteen-year-old African American Jalailah Harmon. The #BlackTikTokStrikers' initial threat was to refuse to choreograph Megan The Stallion's latest drop. Yet the strike's deeper target was the deep-seated whiteness that seemed structurally embedded both into the social media platform and into the white media corporations (like NBC-Universal) that routinely glean from and cover pop culture. As with the ICM rift, the personalities (Megan The Stallion or D'Amelio) may be less interesting for production studies research than the persistent racialized systems that facilitated the appropriation of Black artists for white artist profits. Ethnographic scholars aiming to research this current production rift would find that CMS scholarship by Aymar Christian, Bambi Haggins, Beretta Smith-Shomade, Dan Bernardi, and Ellen Scott provide solid historical grounding. Much as the "overleveraging" study in chapter 8 argues, legal scholar Madhavi Sunder insists that aspirant creators must look beyond outrage at individual culpability and learn to engage with copyright law to stop this latest reiteration of *systemic* white-from-Black racial appropriation.[15]

A final example of an acute rift came through a perverse form of specwork. In April 2021, a Hollywood actor swindled two hundred investors out of $690 million in a Ponzi scheme based on "financing" new feature films "for HBO and Netflix." How did Zachary Horwitz convince so many to "invest" in his spec movie ideas? He confidently offered monied Hollywood wannabes shares in a large slate of his "sure-shot" feature films. His trick? Horwitz simply employed and mastered the standard pitching rituals and development behaviors taught in any "How to Produce 101" classes at hundreds of workshops, colleges, and film schools. His artistry, though, was not to actually make the feature films but to persuade those to whom he pitched to pay up because Horwitz "believed" passionately in his personal vision of winning box-office prospects. Horwitz sold promissory notes to each investor (amassing more than 2/3 of a billion dollars). When he had to start repaying them their returns, he paid the old investors with new investor money. How did Horwitz's crime differ from the standard pitching and speculating BS that defines Hollywood's ethos? Horwitz—an actor—was apparently just better than most aspiring or emerging producers in performing the pitch to close the deal. Horwitz would be a poster child for the "fake it until you make it" ethos that MFA producing students have tried to sell me on over the years. As a means to climb the industry ladder, Horwitz's spec flew faster and more efficiently than physical production. Unfortunately, for Horwitz, federal prosecutors and Securities and Exchange lawyers had other ideas. Fortunately, for scholars (as chapter 7 will elaborate), litigation and prosecutions provide highly researchable entry points for wider system research. This is largely because court fractures force the release of a paper trail of connectable documents and traceable human subjects that tie embedded industrial layers and sectors together.

Production labor conflict also often triggers pitched battles in social media through back-channel worker metatexts that scholars can map and unpack in research. This range of unauthorized, often anonymous, back-channel screen missives includes social media and videos intended to disrupt or troll some trade or industrial status quo. One labor-rift genre might be termed worker-generated snark. These are online videos produced in off-hours and anonymously, often by bitter below-the-line media workers.[16] Viewing these snark videos forces viewers and researchers to better understand the causes and bases for creative labor standpoint theory.[17] That is, they provide a glimpse of how the overall system is viewed from below, by embedded workers. By this I refer to the barely contained resentment (and sometimes rage) about work conditions expressed publicly by stressed production workers. The term *precariat* aptly describes these increasingly alienated workers within the creative industries.[18] Consider the nasty interchange in one online snark video.

A contentious drama unfolds below between an increasingly underemployed veteran Steadicam operator and a low-ball bidding film school wannabe. This trolling text suggests how the production industry works, not from the top but from the embedded middle layers:

> *Professional Filmmaker.* So what are you doing to get work?
>
> *Newcomer.* I'm going to call all the DPs in the union directory. To let them know that I'm a Steadicam operator. I'm also applying for every job on Craig's list. So I'll be working a lot, very soon. I'm going to offer super low rates. And undercut everybody else, so I'll be the "go-to" Steadicam guy. I just got an email from a producer who wants me on his next Rap video.
>
> *Professional Filmmaker.* . . . What's the rate?
>
> *Newcomer.* He offered me $100 a day. But I got him up to $125 because I'm a savvy negotiator.
>
> *Professional Filmmaker.* Yes. You obviously are. You know. It's brainless dipshit fuckheads like you who are screwing everybody else in the Steadicam industry. And shitting all over our beloved craft. ("StedicamProShredsWannabe," https://youtu.be/1KaXOdLPWiU) (fig. 2.11)

FIGURE 2.11. Steadicam professional shreds pretentious job-destroying Steadicam wannabe. Animation apps like "Xtra Normal" allow production workers to anonymously tear into each other. Images: Offscreen still frames from "StedicamProShredsWannabe," YouTube video, https://youtu.be/1KaXOdLPWiU.

This online worker-generated snark lacks subtlety and restraint. Yet such back-channel missives offer rich perspectives about how media industries actually feel to workers on the ground.[19] They can also provide specific insights into economic and labor conditions for specific creative workers, low theory about new tech, and, occasionally, damning critiques of the industry as a whole. Macroscopic political economies, corporate disclosures, and even access to media executives do not provide scholars with the same kind and intensity of insights when we actually consider the critical standpoints of the largely invisible below-the-line workers that remain crucial to any production. Online social media gives such workers anonymous back channels to rage, vent, and critique difficult or regressive conditions. This unsanctioned anonymity makes them both compelling and useful for researchers, especially given the likelihood that the snark-critic on a production back channel would lose work or be fired if they were outed, named, or identified. The stakes are high.

Worker-generated snark and hacker texts can also betray a darker and more cryptic vision of the interorganizational struggle buried within production (that one would never find in an official "making-of"). The sobering moral lesson in much hack and snark: collective media production work involves contentious cynicism of those both above and below one on the Darwinian creative-labor "food chain." Worker snark can be understood as cautionary tales. The stressed professional cinematographer cited above taunts a pretentious film school grad who is looking to underbid him and steal the work of the pro. The pro responds cynically: "I can give you a number to my scrap metal guy. He buys used garbage rigs [like yours] for good-rates, and recycles them for better use. It might come in handy in one year when you and your cousin are quitting the business. And moving back to whatever b_ _t-f_ _k town you came from." Such video tirades often serve as direct, intraindustry threats to competing workers or aspirants.[20]

Agitated back-channel trolling by below-the-line workers on social media is not the only metamedia scholars can use to zero in on embedded stress points. Sometimes, acute intraindustry conflict among above-the-line creatives will spill over and muddy the viewer's primary onscreen content as well. This can occur when a network's multiyear leverage over showrunners and writers rooms falter. In such cases, the trades and social media often provide scholars with blood-in-the-water evidence of deeper institutional rifts that do not need to be anonymized like the below-the-line craft snark. Oblique social media communications and ad hoc negotiating surround many primary onscreen texts and include a snark genre I term slash-and-burn creator snark. Executive producer Kurt Sutter of *Sons of Anarchy* (F/X 2008–14) stirred up the industry by tweeting personal critiques and jealousies about unjustified network favoritism given Matthew Weiner, executive producer of *Madmen* (AMC 2007–15). Sutter's tweets betrayed the impact Weiner's negotiations had on the budgets—and thus the textual production values—of three other series and an entire network. Sutter's tweets hit AMC by announcing to the trade world why he signed with F/X instead of AMC: "closed my deal for 3 more years on SOA. no headlines, no pushed schedule, no stealing from paul. thank you FX and 20th for your generosity."[21]

ScreenRant explained Sutter's take on Weiner's negotiations with AMC as "negotiations that reportedly put the future of *Breaking Bad* [AMC 2008–13] in question, as well as led to budget cuts for *The Walking Dead* [AMC 2010–20]. It's been reported that one of the main reasons why Frank Darabont was fired from *The Walking Dead* was because he was continuously fighting with the network over their reduced budget for season 2." The trade's metacommentary exposed ugly internal negotiations among shows, as well as social media trolling by A-list creators. This social media snark and commentary flagged researchers to look more closely at the stressors and rifts in a specific industrial battle between AMC and F/X on a deeper internetwork level.[22]

WHY INDUSTRIAL TECTONICS TO EXPLAIN FLUID CREATIVITY? (CAPITAL AND CINEMA STUDIES)

Specworld's tectonic three-tier framework for analyzing industry's systemic stresses might raise a basic question for the reader. Why, specifically, seek out connective frictions and study stress interactions in a book supposedly about sunnier aesthetic speculation scenarios like creating, expression, and envisioning in film? Stated simply, CMS needs analytic terms more sensitive to complex systemic behaviors, descriptive terms that go beyond cultural distinctions and bracketed-off critical exceptions. Genre, style, auteur, cinema, movement, national cinema, even resistant readings, while immensely productive paradigms for the field, all largely work by showcasing how their exemplars are somehow *unlike* the system as a whole. Production tectonics simply provides more conceptual room for scholars to describe the connections and infrastructures that coexist and enable the exceptions and exemplars. Which CMS is already well-versed at explaining.

Beyond this conceptual challenge—of adding system-terms to our field's already well-developed part-terms—there are more practical reasons for arguing for greater attention to the ways creators are embedded. In some ways, researching stressors in trade interfaces (caused by industrial embedding and folding) could give production studies more practical precision in locating and handling evidence. One foundational task in research involves describing the sort of evidence the scholar will study and articulating how much of that evidence will be included in the research "sample." As chapter 9 will discuss in more detail, a sample is a subset of evidence or info representing some larger population of data. Determining the sample of evidence to research depends on making an argument that credibly justifies the method used to select and limit the data. Establishing this data-framing justification means answering a question: which narrower subparts of something bigger and more complicated (in our case the media production industry) will you select for analysis?

Although often conflated with statistical methods, answering the sampling question, while challenging, must also be addressed in *both* qualitative and quantitative work. This is because it is impractical to study every unit of a larger, complicated phenomenon. Certainly it is impossible in systems as complex as film and television. Yet overgeneralizing from too small a data set remains one methodology minefield researchers should avoid. One way to steer clear of the reductive data-sample trap has been to employ complex systems theory (referenced earlier). This paradigm has roots in both ecological biology and information science. Influenced by this tradition, some CMS scholars have shifted from narrow conceptions of texts, directors, and genres in order to research "media ecologies."[23] Others in the "digital humanities" have embraced algorithms to analyze culture via "big data." They aggregate large amounts of info, then look for patterns in large textual or cinematic databases. I am arguing for an alternative to the *distant analysis* that this emerging big data–mining in the humanities offers and promotes.

Instead, I am proposing a method that acknowledges the largeness of complex industrial systems even as it eschews distant readings in order to employ *close analysis* to understand large systems. Specifically, analyzing interface stress points in embedded production systems, as *Specworld* proposes, allows CMS scholars a different kind of precision in locating and systematically mapping actual (or operational) links between human subjects, firms, projects, and texts. By focusing each production research project on specific, operational stress points, folds, faults, and rifts, the research methods I draw on employ alternative methodologies. These include "contact-tracing" methodologies (used in public health and epidemiology) and "chain-referral sampling" (used in anthropology). Both parallels better fit and open up the system behaviors of cultural industries. Chain-referral and contact-tracing methods reject out-of-hand the requirement for sample randomness as a benchmark for calculating probability. As a qualitative researcher, I also reject the allied premise from social science that research should be "predictive." The relationships evident in the production industry's folds, rifts, and stress points are *purposive* (not *random*) by design. This purposiveness enables us to analyze and *describe actual interactive relations* and *network flows* (not static predictive statistical probabilities). The final chapter of *Specworld* will return to explore other practical questions and methods for undertaking disembedding and fracture research on production.

Chapter 3 turns to elaborating how production both *rationalizes* and *industrializes* what might otherwise be conceived as industrially untethered: the creator's freewheeling ideal of speculative innovation. To address this, I consider the economic and bureaucratic schemes used to anchor and manage specwork. My goal is to show how creative speculation is embedded (sometimes problematically) within at least three adjacent and competing managerial regimes: craftworld, brandworld, and specworld. Unpacking these competing schemes provides a clearer picture of how the prescriptive tropes that the trades celebrate (e.g., creative disruption, prescient foresight, cutting-edge innovation) are in fact the products of a much heavier and slower industrial footprint.

Depending on one's perspective, chapter 3 will offer a picture of either a profitable, sustaining codependency between self-focused creators and system-focused industrializers or an asymmetrical predatory deal with the devil—on the one side, the weightless emotional labor and cultural gratifications of free specwork; on the other side, the inertial administrative drag needed to manage outsourced labor, aggregate complex coproductions, and mine and monetize content. The specter of a dark synergy may follow, since industry's specwork codependency is likely unsustainable long-term, at least for most individual aspirants, emerging makers, an underemployed pros.

3

Regimes

Craftworld, Brandworld, Specworld

The social media giant [Snapchat] minted a new class of
millionaires, changing hundreds of lives.
—Rodriguez and Bursztynsky, "Snap Creators"

Speculative expression does not just change or disrupt physical or technical aspects of film and media production. It often normalizes for
workers in advance certain economic worldviews and not others. It
incentivizes creative labor to think and accept certain ways of working
and not others. Reflexive trade talk about media markets culturally
legitimizes those production markets by making the working conditions
inside them seem natural. This may help industry gain advantage by
getting out in front of alternative ways of thinking about work that
might otherwise be disruptive or suspect. To set up the ethnographic
observations about the maker/influencer production case studies in
chapters 4, 6, and 8, this chapter steps back to offer a wider-view of
how creative labor is programmed and managed.

The three managerial frameworks presented in this chapter provide a
wider foundational perspective on the broader industrial systems that
embed speculation and the institutional logics that keep production cultures provisionally embedded together and cooperative.[1] The framework here compares and contrasts production practices within three
specific political-economic spheres: craftworld, brandworld, and specworld. This comparative mapping demonstrates that it is important to
place any local production practice within the marketing and economic
logic of the institutions that oversee those different production sectors.
To do so, this chapter draws on macrolevel political-economic analysis
to describe the implementation schemes by which specific production

cultures are embedded together. Even as this complex systems analysis employs macrolevel political economic perspectives, I begin, as I often do, with an observed human interaction.

In the heady air of an MIT Transmedia conference, the *"aca-pro" audience* voiced appreciation as the futurist digital media consultant speaking onstage bragged about how *nonhierarchical innovation hot spots* like the one he'd created in his boutique company were poised to make old, conservative approaches to film and television production obsolete. Like dinosaurs and "Detroit," he argued, no tears would be shed for the death of lazy, inefficient "old media" film/TV production professionals—who, like the auto industry, had lived long past their prime. The unequivocal message from the digital disruptor was good riddance. Another panelist, an edgy new media branding consultant, teased out some of his own recent viral marketing and stealth stunts that had successfully created "buzz" while costing the client little money. One of his stealth stunts involved triggering the LAPD, law-enforcement helicopters, and public first-responders to hover around a fake emergency. News coverage of this fake "media event" indeed spilled onto the marketer's covert goal: greater notoriety for a transmedia start-up in Hollywood. Again, the MIT audience knowingly giggled at the sophisticated ironies in tricking tax-supported public infrastructure to unknowingly provide the "free" heavy marketing muscle required to launch a bit of edgy new IP (fig. 3.1).

No one, however, discussed the political-economic or ethical downsides that this stunt buzz-making involved. Who were these bemused digital people, both the aca-pro panelists and conference attendees, I wondered? How were they paid, and by whom, and for what, exactly? Cultural geography might provide the answers. Most of the visionaries gathered at MIT were from New York or Boston (not Detroit or Los Angeles). That is, they hailed from northeastern cities where creative workers apparently no longer need or want to be paid or to have benefits—pay and benefits like the film/TV/auto workers out West, mired as they supposedly were in the outdated heavy-industry quagmires that have apparently entombed them.

And why was I at this conference, given that the celebrated viral marketing "innovations" and free labor being worshipfully gossiped about here by digital disruptors would horrify the fieldwork informants that I had been talking to: professional cinematographers, editors, directors, and grips? Of course, like some of the panelists, I myself had been publishing on "convergence media," "repurposing," and programming through

FIGURE 3.1. Nonhierarchical innovation hotspots gloss over class and labor issues. Like the "aca-pro" marketers-as-conceptual artists/poseurs at the MIT Transmedia conference, keynotes at Slush Helsinki marveled at their own abilities to hack the "real world" but rarely acknowledged inextricable issues of privilege and economic power. Photos: © 2017, by J. Caldwell.

"content migration" for some time. But my understanding of these current new media practices now seemed—from the perspective of Cambridge— to have come from some distant planet rather than from the clean, ethics-free, and wage-free world being celebrated at MIT.

Then it hit me. My conference trip to Cambridge involved time-travel; I'd fallen back thirty years into art school, and these capitalist marketing executives had become the new avant-garde: conceptual artists, performance artists, street artists, and provocateurs. But unlike their 1960s and 1970s predecessors from the art world, these new social media conceptual artists were now handsomely paid for their faux outsiderness, unruly marketing innovations, snark, and boundary-crossing provocations. This financial recognition of disruptors came arm-in-arm with acclaim for bored and studied public disinterest of the disruptors in matters of wages, benefits, or job security. If transmedia and viral marketing and branding consultants were now the new "conceptual artists" of the twenty-first century, then my research must be clinging to dying professional communities defined by something more archaic and suspect: "craft." This lower creator caste, often treated and othered by scholars as antithetical to disruptive innovation, was a foil for actual creatives (fig. 3.2).

Based on this encounter, I'd like to begin this chapter with three simple and very basic questions before taking on and unpacking the three terms in my chapter subtitle. First, why does TV labor matter to media aesthetics or TV studies? Second, how can or should we study it, given widespread and disruptive recent changes in media and technology? And finally, given those same disruptions, *where* does TV production actually exist anymore? That is, where and *how do we locate production* meaningfully before we can research it in the digital era? These questions are particularly acute in the American media sectors within which I operate. Locating production there is frustrated by an institutional sea-change: government regulation and funding has withered; neoliberal economics dictates trade-thinking; traditional producing arrangements no longer dominate; and online crowdsourcing (via Kick-Starter, Indiegogo, or Patreon) has become a legitimate option even for the unapologetic higher-level industry professionals who increasingly slum online.

The last of my three preceding questions actually complicates the first two, so I'd like to start with it. Two possible answers have been offered to the question of where production is located—one by economic geographer Allen Scott and media scholar Michael Curtin; the other by media political economist Toby Miller and his coauthors.[2] Targeting Hollywood, both sides rebuffed the common clichés about production—that "it is a state of mind"—but did so in very different ways. Curtin's and Scott's research on "media capital" and infrastructure resource "agglomeration" undercut the ephemerality state-of-mind cliché. Their accounts detail why certain film and television material nexus points survive as geographical centers despite the clear economic advantages that might be gained by moving somewhere else, away from media "centers" (fig. 3.3). Miller and his coauthors, by contrast, disrupt the lie that geographic inertia or exceptionalism anchors production geographically in any way. They argue instead that the real phenomenon for production research today can be found in what they term the "new international cultural division of labor" (or NICL). NICL presupposes that media can migrate or shape-shift in response to rapid economic change. It contends that an economic force in globalization splinters labor and disperses the physical sites for production.

FIGURE 3.2. Spectech preimagined the DGA way. Specworld feeds off the fact that media production is never stable or static but is always in-the-process of becoming. In the courting negotiation *(top)* a new VR tech company invites Guild members to imagine a VR tool's uses by embedding its multiscreen monitor into exhibit/demo tableau surrounded by the DGA's own directorcentric photo iconography. Another tech demo *(bottom)* promotes new proprietary 3D computer scanners and 3D printers for props and production design at the same new-tech day. In effect the higher DGA acts as a benign overseer and gatekeeper that sanctions even the slowly changing journeyman tools of below-the-line crafts. Photos: Directors Guild of America, Los Angeles, CA. © 2015, by J. Caldwell.

FIGURE 3.3. Production's centering agglomerations. Paraindustrial synergies among production entities go far beyond the official film production centers. Following Curtin and Scott, centers like the Czech Barrandov Studio provide not just material infrastructure but also an institutional and cultural gravity that attracts and sustains all sorts of adjacent secondary and tertiary firms and makers. Photos: Barrandov Studio overview and public entrances. © 2016, by J. Caldwell.

Whereas Scott and Curtin examine the regional anchoring of production and Miller the global dispersion and splintering of production through runaway production, my research leads me to suggest a third alternative. That is, our quandary about where production is located may result from our failure to recognize that a widely dispersed conceptualizing process may be as central to the core of television/media production today as the industrial and material production of series, formats, and network programming once was. Those traditional "physical" features once garnered the lion's share of attention from critics and media scholars. I am suggesting here that hybrid forms of creative-economic speculation now systematically animate media production. Speculation—or "specwork"—has become a fundamental part even of the complex mainstream economies of TV. Figuring out how to manage specwork within the deregulated creative labor "herd" helps provide rationality for TV industries as they seek to master (and eventually monetize) their new, unruly creative labor pipelines.[3] These labor pipelines proliferate within the "remix" and "gift economies" that aspiring creators leverage from their skill sets mastered in social media.

In saying this, I am not reverting to Scott's and Miller's target— Hollywood or media as "a state of mind" cliché. Instead, the dispersed conceptualizing process I am targeting is as much a professional result and defining property of contemporary media labor as are the onscreen series that TV labor officially produces. TV is more than just the end product of TV production labor. I take television labor to include anticipatory practices as well—to include the endless prototyping, brainstorming, workshopping, ad-hoc viral repackaging, and vocational spinning that precede and follow the shows for which TV companies officially take credit. Significantly, anticipatory specwork adds economic value to TV shows, even if TV producers and executives ignore it. I am especially sensitive to Mayer and Stahl's critiques of labor "erasures."[4] Both *Televisuality* and *Production Culture* presupposed that paying greater attention, even in aesthetic studies, to the cultural functions and institutional logics of physical production and creative workers was essential.[5]

Over the past two decades, I have recognized that an entirely different work activity surrounds and infuses physical production, one based on constant, recurrent cognitive speculation about imagined, experiential, onscreen worlds of one sort or another. To clarify: I am not talking about the construction of "imagined narrative worlds" driven by fans in "transmedia franchises" of the sort Henry Jenkins has postulated.[6] I am, rather, talking about the commercial "labor" of habitual and calculated speculation now found in workaday, frequently unremarkable, television job-sites (fig. 3.4).

Significantly, specwork can be found in both below-the-line and above-the-line production sectors. This means that imagined-world conjecturing functions increasingly as part of lowly, run-of-the-mill trade practice. Notably, this anticipatory production work is *not* owned or triggered exclusively by the "creatives," executives, and producers. Rather, it can be found and plays a role in many lowlier technical crafts,

FIGURE 3.4. Preseeing is believing (and trying out). In this gendered trade meeting scene, production technicians evaluate a demoed green-screen product. Creator-buyers are asked to imagine some future production by staging young women as image fodder, a foretelling of their own creative efforts. Creatasphere, Burbank, CA. Photo: © 2015, by J. Caldwell.

as well. My specwork focus may seem to reject the exceptionalism we normally assign or reserve for the creative higher-ups in TV—the show-runner, producer, director, or executive. Yet I am only proposing that we need to add to what we research in the executive suites. Arguing that we augment managerial showcasing by taking seriously the rich terrain of cultural conjecture and anticipatory expression that now make up the below-the-line worker's skill set, as well. Such things function as an integral part of the bigger system we think of as "television." Specwork is both workmanlike and ubiquitous rather than unique in any way. As such, it challenges media studies to rethink the parameters and bounda-ries it habitually assumes in CMS, in general, and in production labor research, in particular.

The shift toward habitual speculation as a form of creative work on the microlevel is linked to bigger changes in the macroscopic market predica-ment and thus transnational goals of many production companies, stu-dios, and networks. Specifically, success in media markets today depends less and less on the fabrication of a durable distributable entertainment object—which historically became the basis for television's core project of owning shows and syndicating series. In this old picture-locked system, we thought that a production was over when we finalized or "locked" picture and soundtrack, then timed (or color-corrected) and archived a stable program master, which allowed us to sell copies and versions in markets for distribution to buyers. Now the notion that our program masters are never done, always prone to change, goes well beyond the traditional alterations—remixing, recutting, dubbing—required for international distribution. Producers now know, upfront, that it is even possible (via corporate contracts as yet unknown) to completely recreate interior scenes onscreen through the digital imposition of new product placements, online links, and integrated sponsorship within preexisting narratives. And this directly impacts creative decisions creators make on the set. Digital makes masters completely malleable, reworkable, remakeable, endlessly.

These changes are not completely novel. We have always trimmed scenes for breaks to intercut ads, converted NTSC to PAL standards, panned-and-scanned or letter-boxed, and altered program masters for foreign languages when needed. What was once secondary is now primary, however. That is, masters are now malleable not just at the level of plot or episode, but at the level of the pixel. This means that even effects layers "inside" of fictional narratives and dramatic scenes can now be tweaked during distribution, as well. The growing presumption of an endlessly malleable program master means that the entire process of television production can be imagined as postproduction's anticipatory task, with the potential for (and goal of) an endless, lucrative, life on the "back end" of a project. Proliferating digital technologies means that most forms of production can be understood as functions of postproduction—where the cognitive work of preproduction speculation on the "front end" has ramped up to keep pace with the digital production's repurposing's task on the "back end."

Issues of intellectual property help stimulate these changes. Rather than produce the durable syndicatable object (a film or TV episode), the company's primary goal, specwork enterprises now obsess on the creation of potentially endless malleable and self-replicating IP (intellectual property). For clarity's sake, we can further distinguish (especially within the same corporations) between "big" self-replicating IP (the blockbuster or high concept), and "small" self-replicating IP (reality TV, and the unexceptional online consumer interactions that go with it). As we will discover, there is often a strategic economic relationship between "big IP" and "small IP" in the transnational multimedia conglomerates. That is, such diversified corporations now need vast amounts of the cheaper, reality-based, small-IP in order to pay for their expensive big-IP blockbuster and prestige cinematic needs. We need to think beyond specific tactics of content migration or repurposing to consider this broader intraconglomerate dynamic that embeds them. That is, spreadable speculation now animates and monetizes production well before—and well after—the series or episode in question.[7] This temporal spreading of pre- and postspeculation is precisely why specwork has aligned so well with transmedia production, industry-fan interactions, and viral marketing, which mirror it.

I am arguing that we examine recurring interactions between two systems. Specifically, that specwork provides the broad conditions that facilitate linkages and synergies between the malleable digital "material" and technologies of TV production, on the one hand, and current corporate management strategies aimed at developing malleable and self-replicating IP, on the other (which ideally suits corporate reformatting, franchising, branding, transmedia). Before mapping out the fuller range and logic of specwork, it is well worth considering something more provisional—that is, how specwork fits within the rapidly changing industrial and economic landscape. We can usefully unpack the broader mediascape that embeds specwork by further comparing "craftworld" and "brandworld" to "specworld."

CRAFTWORLD, BRANDWORLD

The studio, the TV network, the director—such neat, clean, and expedient categories for cinema and media studies research. Yet these categories are not innate, self-evident, unproblematic, or clearly bounded. The question of labor complicates the place and utility of each category in media production's paraindustrial root system or "rhizome."[8] Rapid changes in how creative work is done and marketed provide one key to mapping the "nodes" of the studio, network, and director within a networked paraindustrial system. Productive recent attempts to generalize about "digital labor" or "creative labor in the digital era" tend to overlook the fact that we are almost always dealing with blended labor systems in contemporary film/television—even within the same institutions (studio, network, director).

Presuming that digital technologies have cleanly eliminated "old media" labor in the "new media" overgeneralizes and disregards how old media labor somehow keeps adapting to new media technologies even as many new media entrants enter and disrupt the resulting blended media

FIGURE 3.5. Collectively operationalizing prevision. Cinematographer Vilmos Zsigmond, ASC, oversees the lighting and smoke effects on a set, while crew members rig the lights to achieve his desired look. Even technical crafts like these require crew members to share in tactical imaginative speculation in order to grasp a DP's prevision. Kodak Cinematographer-in-Residence Workshop, directed by DP Bill McDonald, Los Angeles, CA. Photos: © 2009, by J. Caldwell.

labor field. As such, media scholars are stuck with the difficult task of explaining how the same current screen form or genre might result from very different or contradictory work arrangements or organizational partnerships. This predicament—*one result, many causes*—muddies the water for anyone hoping to systematically research/isolate industrial factors that cause, trigger, or fuel a cultural screen form (fig. 3.5).

Head-scratching by others over my previous production studies suggests that I may have been researching from a largely craft-labor orientation, while others have leapt ahead to focus on narrow new creative entrant perspectives as somehow more symptomatic of contemporary media/culture as a whole. Many in the transmedia and online industries seem less interested in the physical work or labor economics of professional screen-workers than in the conceptual artistry of the newcomers from marketing-and-art. Digital innovators currently seem to be displacing the older-style craft labor in trade consciousness. Of course, this *innovation-vs.-craft split* may seem logical or commonsensical. Corporate sponsorship and academic politics—when married—make innovation bias a conspicuous goal worth pursuing in scholarly media studies (and perhaps in corporate digital media development, as well).

The innovation-vs.-craft bias applies not just to gaffers but to screenwriters as well, who are constantly told to choose between writing spec-scripts or clones of writers room prototypes. Compared to the precarity of the off-the-lot feature *film* spec writer, for example, the collective nature of the writing and the business of *TV* rewards stability-seeking continuity habits. Longer-term assignments are enabled by the demonstrated craft of the writer, which TV incentivizes by offering more predictable paychecks than does film. Yet some WGA mentors question how business has reduced spec originality by incentivizing writers to become merely unoriginal clones of the often absent showrunners:

> Let me jump over to the WGA. We had our townhall meeting last year, and the room was packed with quality, working writers. And the question was asked: "how many of you all are working?" And there were quite a few hands raised. And then the question came: "how many of you have original work, so that if your network came to you today and asked, hey we would like to consider you for development, do you have work ready?" Three people raised their hand, and I was one of them. And that's the thing. People aren't writing if they are writing for other people's show. They are not writing original content. So that's the problem. So, no. Some of them aren't ready. Or they're mimicking the voice of their show runner so closely that their voices are not distinct. That's happening too. I don't want to name names, but there are strong show runners who have trained up writers to sound like them. And that's the problem. "Who needs you if we have the original. (Michelle Amor, WGA, "Breaking into the Industry" panel, UCLA, Feb. 3, 2020)

The conventionalized stability-seeking habits I continue to run into, on a wide-scale in film/TV industries, have been simplistically linked—by both scholarly transmedia theorists and corporate start-ups—to the culturally outdated, the technically obsolete, and the industrially dead. Critical theorists and entrepreneurs (once considered strange bedfellows) treat continuities as leaden, as intellectual/economic cul-de-sacs. This crafterasure, based on an attention-seeking disruption formula or metric, is short-sighted. As an alternative to this antithesis, I suggest that blended labor systems—enmeshed in different economic conditions—more aptly describes the new norm in production—blended systems that might be best understood according to the three-part model that scholars, investors, and producers alike must now constantly negotiate. By finding ways to hybridize the craftworld, the brandworld, the specworld (fig. 3.6).

Craftworld

Production studies would benefit by addressing one preliminary question before theorizing broadly about contemporary film and television in the

FIGURE 3.6. Craft: Humanities' Kryptonite. Lockstep workflow displaces effusive idea-sharing in craftworld. Prepwork, rather than specworld idea-sharing, rules traditional, mainstream film production. *Top:* Lighting crew waits in staging area by curb before rigging a shooting location. *Bottom:* A teamster driver waits to unload his lighting gear at film location in downtown Los Angeles. In the humanities, industry's unionized "craft" (inertia)-vs.-"creative" (innovation) split often means that CMS scholars overresearch the "creative" above-the-line side while ignoring the lower, more modest inertial "technician" side of creator cultures. Photos: © 2016, by J. Caldwell.

TABLE 3.1   THREE CONTESTED LABOR REGIMES

	Craftworld	Brandworld	Specworld
Physical production	Agglomerated, centralized	Outsourced, regionalized	Disaggregated, dispersed
Labor protocol	Wage labor	Licensing	Symbolic pay, microfinancing
Aesthetic goal	Durable syndication artifact	Flexible reformatting	Brainstorming, sharing, growing social network
Production process	Building content, plantation farming	Concept-iteration, sharecropping	Gleaning, scavenging, crowdsourcing
Key	Engineering scarcity	Marketing scarcity	Excessive disclosure, abundance
Instigators, enforcers	Guilds and unions	Contract and IP lawyers	Online platforms, paraindustry, film schools
Examples	Studio feature films, premium programming	Reality TV, high-concept series	UGC, YouTube, Kickstarter, TikTok

digital era: to what extent does "physical production" matter anymore? As the first of the three dominant labor modes in the blended labor systems we now face, the "craftworld" still generates considerable value by enabling "quality" physical production. Yet many executives/producers discount this value-adding metric as crucial, since physical production can always take place somewhere else, for less money—in their minds.

The characteristics of the traditional craftworld are familiar. Production there usually takes place in urban centers with dense agglomerations of skilled workers, physical resources, and paraindustrial feeder organizations. As Allen Scott and Michael Curtin both demonstrate, this geographic resource-massing (of infrastructure, finance, and creative labor) creates resilient media industrial synergies and helps keep film/TV corporations from decentralizing, from moving away casually.[9] Craft workers in these regional centers often use unions and guilds to negotiate hourly or daily wage labor. They also tend to work collectively to build content in concentrated or adjacent physical spaces, in close proximity to support firms. Organized labor is largely uninterested in distribution and actively hostile to harvesting content from outsiders elsewhere (fig. 3.7).

FIGURE 3.7. Spec's classical factory workflow. Before today's public free-for-all sharing of creator speculation, traditional national feature film industries made specwork a clinical, incremental part of a paid factorylike production workflow. *Top:* Art directors appraise paintings and drawings of numerous scene designs and mock-ups of proposed sets long before the sets from those spec artifacts are actually built. Display with photos on legacy of design at Barrandov Studios, Czech Republic. Photo of studio's public display: © 2016, by J. Caldwell. *Bottom:* Directors often try rigidly to precontrol mise-en-scène by locking it down via detailed storyboards, as art director William Cameron Menzies is doing. Drawing of Menzies drawing storyboards: © 2021, by J. Caldwell.

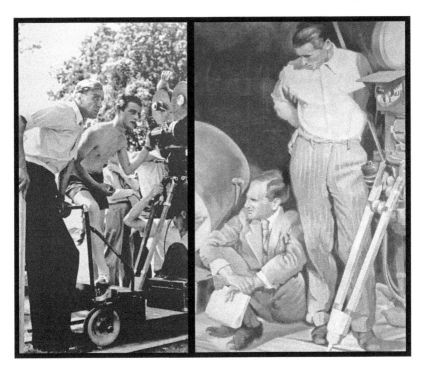

FIGURE 3.8. Continuity and stable homosocial relationships anchored traditional craftworld. *Left:* Director and DP set up a shot. *Right:* Wall-mounted oil painting of director and cinematographer during filming pause. Photo and painting from Barrandov Studios. Photo of public display of painting and publicity still, 2016, by J. Caldwell.

This craftworld labor scheme, associated with larger budgeted studio films and national networks, still aims to produce film and TV as durable artifacts that can be controlled and monetized through sequential distribution windows. Media corporations persist in partnering with craft labor, since this guarantees a high level of quality and predictability in production. The key to this first labor regime, the craftworld, is scarcity. Unions and guilds manage and police scarcities in labor (through high barriers to entry) on the input boundaries, at the very same time that studios market and police scarcity, by controlling access to screen content (via exclusive exhibition rights) on the output boundaries (fig. 3.8).

Brandworld

A second labor regime threatens but coexists with the first: the "brandworld." This world—obsessed with engineering corporate psychological signatures capable of animating long-term "interpersonal" synergies with fans—now dominates the warring blended-labor systems economically. This may be because the brandworld allows for considerable transnational flexibility on both production's front end (the craftworld sector that feeds "high-concept" blockbuster films) and production's back end (the specworld sector that monetizes user-generated content to promote reality TV). An ecumenical, counterintuitive logic tied to IP drives the brandworld. That is, as blockbuster budgets go higher and higher for fewer and fewer feature films, considerably more cheap screen content must be produced within the same corporate conglomerate to sustain it, buffer the risks, prop it up, and cover the conglomerate's high-stakes feature bets. Brandworld economics, that is, require fairly wide-ranging complementary screen practices, ensuring that a studio's repertoire will be diverse. It might include expensive high-concept features, transnational coproductions, and franchises on the big stage alongside cheaper, ubiquitous forms like reality TV, licensing, reformatting, merchandizing, and product placement, scattered across endless unremarkable side-stages and affiliated firms. This is why contemporary screen content is best understood within the mixed conglomerate economics that I have detailed elsewhere.[10]

Like the craftworld, the brandworld cultivates and manages scarcity but in different ways. Unions and craft associations cultivate labor scarcity by establishing high barriers to "professional" entry and by standardizing proprietary high technologies. By contrast, branding executives largely ignore traditional, restrictive labor arrangements in favor of harvesting the results of effective (and effusive) conceptual R&D. That is, rather than limiting the physical supply of expert labor or high-end technologies, the brandworld initiates, stimulates, and then manages the scarcity of the conceptual supply of screen ideas that can be policed and monetized through affiliation, contract, and litigation. If IATSE locals and studios agree to coexist in the craftworld as "signatories," then transnational conglomerates and regional broadcasters agree to coexist in the brandworld as "licensor-licensees" through the haggling of IP lawyers.

The craftworld assumes a win-win for both labor and management by constricting content pipelines and monetizing costlier production values. Brandworld thinking, by contrast, presupposes a financial win-win for IP-rights holders and IP-rights licensees—but simply disregards (sometimes cynically) where the production labor for the system of exhibition/broadcast comes from. The craftworld prizes durable screen content; the brandworld pursues a regionalized, quasi-indigenized vari-

FIGURE 3.9. Two ways to industrialize specwork. *Left:* Storyboard artist previsualizing producer's speculative vision of cartoon shorts on Hanna-Barbera's animation assembly line. Los Angeles, CA. Photo: Courtesy of UCLA Library Digital Collections. *Right:* Sharecropping on Poverty Row. Artistic innovation from economic precarity's deep prehistory includes LA's postwar "Poverty Row" studios, which produced cheaper industrials and theatrical shorts. With meager budgets, a few of these firms— like Mark VII Productions *(above, right)* and Jerry Fairbanks Productions *(below, right)*—helped establish "deficit financing" and "syndication" as ways to "sharecrop" risk with the majors. Photos: Courtesy UCLA Library Digital Collections and *(bottom right)* advertising flyer from Jerry Fairbanks, Inc. Collection of the author.

ant of a common IP experience. The brandworld looks agnostic and open to all possible creative labor solutions, and this is why it is so threatening to organized creative, professional, production labor. Brandworld does not just stand as an alternative to craft or technical expertise. It actively works—by circumventing labor scarcity—to change the relatively rigid conditions on which production workers once maintained their value (fig. 3.9).

One of the dark advancements of nineteenth-century American agriculture was that the South shifted from slavery as a dominant mode of capitalist production to its shadow world—a profitable, more user-friendly looking labor arrangement—to achieve the same ends: sharecropping. If film and television's craftworld can be likened to a "plantation system," where trained labor is "kept on the farm" but offered some level of protection, then the brandworld can be likened to production "sharecropping," where employees give away protections in exchange for a small share of an unpredictable revenue stream and a life of permanent insecurity. Most creative labor in the transnational brandworld today—including labor involved in first-run syndicated TV reformatting—can be understood as profitable forms of sharecropping, arrangements that give film and television today a great deal of fluidity, insecurity, and impermanence. This follows from the fact that IP can travel quickly and replant itself in any country that wishes to partner in a format or high concept, while specialized craft labor is seen as inertial and leaden, a personnel anchor that undercuts quick profits.

Well below the unionized feature-film world, consider the collective conflict caused by the sharecropping, deunionizing expansion of reality TV. Conglomerates that market low-cost reality TV (cheap, repurposeable IP)—instead of high-concept blockbuster franchises—place great stresses on a once-stable unionized craft labor system:

> [Editor B]. "Not to be attacking someone's else [sic] profession, but . . . one way to find the money in the budget for going union is to basically get rid of story producers. You don't need story producers doing string outs because you give the editors time to look through all the footage. I've worked on shows [that use editors] like that, and it works fine. It takes [nominally] longer, like maybe a day and a half at the most.

> [Editor F]. That's not the reality of what's happening because the power shifted over to story years ago. Editors used to be king. That ended a decade ago.

> [Editor K (Charlie Kramer)]. My show's violating that right now. We are annoyed by it . . . because we're seeing story producers doing string outs. . . . The reality of it is that they are taking away jobs from AEs [assistant editors], so either we need to *make* them AEs and have them join our guild as story editors, somehow, which goes back to . . . new classifications or . . . That's [not] going to happen right away. That's something that we're going to be talking about more and more. Or? We just "flip" [unionize] the show and get our people in there."

> ("Reality Check": Motion Picture Editors Guild union organizing meeting, Hollywood, CA, August 30, 2011)

Licensing a TV "format" to different regions around the world allows national media industries to individuate and trot out indigenous versions of the licensed IP. Brazil and China, for example, get to promote inexpensive shows that look Brazilian and Chinese to their audiences, while the Dutch or British corporate brand owner gets to monetize multiple indigenized variants of their format IP. The reformatted shows travel more quickly than distributed and dubbed shows. Yet the new cheap formats often collapse and confuse job distinctions. Those threats are not lost on professional post workers, as the editors above push back against the producers, accusing nonunion "story producers" of taking over their editing jobs and benefits.

Specworld

The third labor regime in the blended system is the "specworld." From an agrarian design precedent, it can be understood not as an industrial plantation (like the craftworld), or production sharecropping (like the brandworld), but as an agricultural process mimicking an early and late-autumn ritual that unfolds after the primary crops have been harvested: content gleaning and scavenging. Some online practices today feel exactly like scavenging: the creation of incongruent mash-ups, filk music, and fan-vids in particular. A question arises, however: how can this world of fans and free user-generated content be viewed economically as a labor regime? Various scholars have noted how online users add value to corporations by inadvertently feeding rich marketing and demographic info the proprietary corporations that give them "free" access. I am not focusing here on that form of "free" consumer labor. Rather, *specworld* refers to vast, new cultural arenas in which professional participants and production aspirants alike are expected to produce creative works "on-spec." Screenwriters have known a fairly benign form of this term for decades. "On spec" in television jargon meant writing and submitting entire teleplays as "calling cards" intended to win over executives or producers—even though spec scripts were never expected to generate near-term revenues.[11] The real goal of the television spec script? To show producers and executives that writers seeking work have the chops and skills to write professionally— but on some show, series, film, or project of the studio or network other than the one listed in the title of the spec script. In television trade logic, ideally, spec scripts open doors and get potential partners to start brainstorming imagined narratives, series, or relationships.

A diverse range of workaday precreation habits now populate industry's specworld. Consider the following examples of unacknowledged but de facto previsioning by low-level workers:

- A vast underclass of low-paid "readers" writes up "script coverage" on every one of hundreds of screenplays submitted to the studio each month. This now obligatory narrative preanalysis essentially culls, preselects, and cognitively projects an idealized imagined narrative for quick comprehension in the minds of producers, agents, and network executives. Essentially the studio's ultimate onscreen narratives and scenes are preimagined and thus preproduced by underlings (this ad hoc process of calculated imaginative projection by *underling preproducers* transforms features into collectively-imagined narrative aggregates).

- A personal assistant to an overbooked executive habitually employs a cultural caste system, to prioritize which agents/ producers get development meetings, thus acting as an unintended, underpaid story-element gatekeeper for the select stories eventually told in series episodes. As Erin Hill has shown, no one sees clerical staff gatekeepers as preemptive, de facto story editors, but, industrially, they function that way.[12]

- A filmmaker asks the crew on a low/no-budget feature production to bring their own gear in exchange for "points" from distribution income. The newcomer director implicitly "pays" his more experienced AC/recordist/gaffer with greater license to fill gaps and stylize scenes. The film gets a "festival release," no crew member gets distribution income, but the director leverages this improv-first-feature-as-calling-card to raise real money for a second film.

- The star showrunner of a "blockbuster TV" series rarely sets foot in his "writers room," where a dozen staffers and uncredited writers assistants all contribute story elements. Yet press and fans alike hail the narrative as the *absentee showrunner's creation.*

- Using the new Red digital camera, and file-based recording, a director vastly overshoots each scene for a prime-time episode. Unable to view all the dailies owing to this high shooting ratio, the director depends on his/her editor to pull the best takes, but there aren't enough hours in the postproduction week to even view all the footage from the overshooting. This forces the editor to defer to lowly assistant editors, minimum-wage loggers, and undermotivated PA's to informally preselect (thus preimagine) the eventual narrative world, just to meet deadlines. Final screen content? Cobbled in part from *prestory fatigue culling.*

- An American studio enjoins a cross-cultural negotiator to break down the proposed narrative of a planned feature film in China. As Aynne Kokas observed, this matchmaker/bureaucrat spends considerable effort speculating, pretelling, and projecting the imagined story world in order to (1) convince Chinese censors to imagine the scenes as benign; (2) convince Chinese governmental overseers that even the scenes with American actors are in some way authentically Chinese, thus justifying the claim that this should be "counted" not as an "American" coproduction but as a privileged "domestic" Chinese film (giving it huge advantages in theaters under the Chinese quota system); and (3) convince Chinese venture capitalists that the narrative will fill theater seats across China.[13] At the same time, other producers from the same studio make the very opposite arguments elsewhere—speculating that the unmade narrative will resonate with American audiences as an American film. The result: contradictory *two-faced transnational specwork,* out of both sides of a studio's mouth.

These examples describe various deep, integral, and often unrecognized ways that acts of narrative speculation (and unacknowledged coauthorship) emerge from diverse forms of relatively low-level industrial work. All of these practices seem ad hoc yet somehow make speculation or brainstorming core tasks in media. The final example—the fragmented "imaginative work" needed to get a Chinese-US transnational feature going—even shows how delegated imaginative speculators can align neatly with uneasy capitalist bedfellows: the binational "economic speculators" that finance a film.

While conventional film/TV production ("old media") has adapted and cloaked specwork for the streaming era in these ways, high-tech start-ups ("new media") have long touted horizontal idea-sharing (in the workplace) as an explicit part of innovative business planning. Whether wooing or competing against Hollywood, high-tech start-ups hype the trope of horizontal, peer-to-peer sharing (see this conceit in HBO's *Silicon Valley*). Yet this pose often creates a problem: the highly complex technical challenges that start-ups face require highly specialized skill sets that go well beyond the utopia of collective sharing:

CALDWELL. *Does your company use hierarchical management (like traditional film/TV), or is it open to idea-sharing from workers?*
DAVID GAUCH, INTERACTION DESIGNER. It is horizontal. Stuff blends. You know everybody speaks up. If we are on a call to someone like DirectTV, they want everybody [to be able to speak]. If I have something to say, they want me to speak up. So it's definitely like: if you have a good idea, and you have a solution, they praise that. A creative solution in data-thinking. And so it is very horizontal in *that* sense. But it is also kind of segmented: developers, UI [user-interface] designers; UX [user-experience] designers. There's a project manager and leads. So there are [still] all of these titles. (Interview by author, UCLA, April 7, 2016)

As Gauch suggests, writing computer code or programming in high-tech firms requires the same kind of deep, difficult, and narrow expertise that cinematography does in the craftworld. Yet the lateral brainstorming once reserved for the TV writers room is now often performed or acted out more widely, often, as here, in front of specworld firms' paying clients (DirectTV).

Yet long before the twenty-first-century industry feigned both tech start-ups and TV writers rooms as (temporarily) collective and nonhierarchical, the low-budget mid-twentieth-century industry assembly-lined specwork via lateral "team" story sessions in preproduction. The economic logic behind the convention? Overprepare so you can undershoot. Drawings (fig. 3.10) show group story sessions pegged to storyboards during preproduction at Jerry Fairbanks Productions. Austere budgets and meager shooting days (first for theatrical shorts in the 1940s and then for syndicated TV in the 1950s) required small, lower-caste companies to nail down imaginative tasks (and any possible improvisation) in rigorous cost-efficient ways.

Unfortunately, as these examples suggest, "on spec" ceased being the exception—limited to screenwriters—a while back, and now it arguably orients the industry as a whole. Vast amounts of creative work in film and television (outside of screenwriting, that is) are produced and circulated as unpaid speculative demonstrations of artistic competence or as blueprints of imagined worlds. As I have documented elsewhere, specwork includes many self-financed "festival films" (which "pretest" the value of indie directors and concepts before studios have to risk any of their own capital); short films (aka "calling card films"); serial pitching protocols at work; ceremonial public pitchfests staged at television

FIGURE 3.10. The overprepare-to-undershoot bare-bones business plan. Group story sessions pegged to storyboards during preproduction turned prevision into bread-and-butter collective work at Jerry Fairbanks Productions (a Poverty Row studio). Drawings from archive documents: © 2011, by J. Caldwell.

trade gatherings; film production competitions, company "brainstorm-ing" sessions, conference panels, how-to sessions, and "how'd they do that?" demos and websites. Specwork once applied largely to the des-perate and less qualified, trying to "break into" the business. The rea-soning? Who would be stupid enough to give their professional craft-work or writing away for free?

Given the extent of these practices, specwork pervades media produc-tion both outside and inside even professional film production and net-work television. In effect, even pros now often "give it away for free," in hopes of stiffing the considerable competition and winning new work—their own "guaranteed" WGA or guild rates be damned! Professionals who give their work away for free typically defend this practice based on heightened barriers to entry. To succeed, that is, you can't just verbally "pitch" a new show idea to an executive anymore. You are pressured to present additional prototyping materials—"tape" or "video" of sample scenes or a beta-tested "web series"—to demonstrate, dramatize, or preenact your proposed production. And of course, all these ancillary media forms must be self-financed by the spec-artist. Much of moving-image production, therefore, actually takes place well before the director calls "action" on day one of any official shoot.

The spread of specwork feels inevitable, especially to many fatalistic indies trying to score deals within deregulated media markets. Such media sectors discourage long-term affiliations and deal entitlements. Yet while indies, angling to be discovered, learn ever more sophisticated ways to "give it away for free," the emerging companies of the brandworld have learned increasingly to move away from internal development of IP in order to master what I would term external specwork harvesting.

In this corporate IP harvesting system, a screenwriter increasingly cannot expect to get paid the Guild rate to write a treatment without occasionally facing pressure to write successive screenplay drafts—without pay or acknowledgment. In essence, such writers are implicitly blackmailed and expected (or have learned how) to "sweeten the deal" with executives by agreeing to write-up and submit full (and sometimes multiple) drafts, as well, for gratis—or for some hoped-for downstream payoff. In some ways TV series pilots have always been speculative, performing as a brief test run that allows producers, networks, and audience to interactively speculate on whether the show will succeed as a series. Yet even the practice of producing series pilots has shifted increasingly to the financeless logic of the specworld. These days, you can't just independently produce your own "pilot," as desperate as that might seem; you may also have to agree to fully self-finance the first half-dozen or dozen episodes of the proposed season, as well, to win the network deal for the whole package.

The genius of industry's blended labor systems comes in the ways that industry deploys quasi-cultural institutions to allow the brand-world to interface, harvest, and monetize the labor of the specworld. Such spaces function like refereed contact zones and include nonprofits, NGOs, and advocates (i.e., IFP/FilmLA) that keep the film/TV precariat on life-support through enabling exercises involving group speculation. Such interface sites also function as cost-effective (sometimes bargain basement) IP markets. The slippage here between career and economics works so well because such zones simultaneously promote themselves as therapeutic sites for specworker career-development.

If filmmakers/producers once risked little by "sticking their necks out" by sharing creative ideas with a few key, well-placed individuals, they did so just to solicit potential, lucrative long-term relationships. Now they have to keep their necks out and exposed for months, willing to eat the considerable losses that come from making professional media with no real or immediate promise of outside revenue. Studios and net-works once provided money up front to close a deal with a creator. Yet the many lesser networks and basic cable channels now increasingly appear to "greenlight" deals without actually paying even seasoned producers for them. This alternative allows studios and networks to wait on the sidelines to "pick-up" only the films, pilots, and series that survive preliminary or initial runs—that is, series that have not already "crashed-and-burned." Specworld can be a pathetic and ugly world, indeed, and not just for the hopeful "users" and unpaid "prosumers" gifting videos across the globe via YouTube and Vimeo, hoping against extremely long-odds that they will be "discovered."[14]

In short, the specworld off-loads or, better, "preloads" more and more of the responsibility for actually producing/financing screen content onto the shoulders of the makers. Out of this process emerges an odd align-ment: even film and TV professionals increasingly bear an uncanny resem-blance to the younger, desperate aspirants who hope to take their jobs.

PRODUCTION CULTURE AS SPECWORK

A broader question remains: how and why do these three interpenetrating labor regimes spur media industries to build paraindustrial cultural buffers to survive? What kinds of specific cultural practices (chatter, written and

TABLE 3.2   CULTURAL PRACTICES OF THE THREE PARAINDUSTRIAL REGIMES

	Craftworld	Brandworld	Specworld
Cultural chatter	Self-legitimation, boundary-policing, gatekeeping entrants	Cross-promotion, inside-dealing, fake buzz, insider "leaks"	Sharing, self-promotion, hyperdisclosure, sponsor wooing, self-analytics
Cultural expressions	Pro blog and creator social media presence, clip-reels, WGC, snark	EPKs, showrunner Twitterverse, value-adding online sites	Demo films, spec-scripts, spec-series, vanity festival showcases, data-selfies
Cultural labor, habits and rituals	Open houses, tech demos, bake-offs, migratory crew orgs	Industry summits, trade conventions, TCAs, season upfronts	Pitchfests, trade-&-barter, shootouts, soft capital, market auditioning

visual expression, artifact-making, habits and rituals) do these competing labor arrangements ramp-up in ways that the "old" industries did not? My argument: moments of industrial contestation and change greatly accelerate the amount of paraindustrial cultural expression, chatter, and specwork. In some ways, this is a pitched battle. As table 3.2 suggests, each regime employs and engages culture differently. The threatened craftworld, for example, favors "self-legitimation" strategies, boundary-policing of amateurs, and the rigid control of entrants via high barriers to entry. Its cultural expressions (online, offline, in-person) cultivate "professionalization," and the careful maintenance of socioprofessional communities. Even so, preoccupation with technical "experts," masters, and mentors keeps even the social media and trade rituals of the craftworld closer to a quaint, almost predigital scale (open-houses, bake-offs, how-tos).

Brandworld does not need to act out culturally using the same ostensibly nonpartisan, helpful, and pedagogical methods that craftworld employs. This is partly because brands do not need to sustain the socioprofessional human communities that craft traditions require. Yet brandworld has to do considerably more of a different kind of cultural work to bring rationality to its worldwide licensing, reformatting, high-concept, and franchising schemes. Success in the brandworld can mean mastering cross-promotion between the conglomerate's platforms, the systematic leaking of "insider" info, the development of incestuous relations with the "trade" media, or the creation of fake buzz. While this cultural chatter once gushed forth via the press junket and the EPK, the showrunner "Twitterverse" is perhaps the most effective tangible expression of current brandworld chatter.

The cultural chatter strategies of specworld are well known from social media, such as Twitter, TikTok, and Facebook: sharing, self-promotion, networking, and bartering. Socioprofessional cultural expressions on those platforms include worker-generated content (WGC) that mirrors user-generated content (UGC); stealth stunts and staged online "scenes" aimed at "hailing" the attention of higher-ups; circulating demos to facilitate one's "discovery"; subscribing or friending for lateral movement across job classifications; and social media posting to build migratory crew networks. Professionals have learned specworld postures—trade rationalizations, spin, hype, and dissembling—partly from online social media practices. These combine with a range of indigenous sharing traditions normalized within their own long craft histories.

SELF-DEFEATING LABOR TACTICS

I undertook this research partly because so many frustrated individuals that I talk to misperceive the very labor regimes they aspire to or operate in. Film school students think that they are mastering the craftworld (unaware that it is maintained by creative labor's scarcity practices), even though the same film students' file sharing, mash-ups, and online UGC gifting destroy the very scarcity-policed craft conditions under-which they might once have made incomes in film or television. My nineteen-year-old film students usually get depressed when I point this out. By contrast, marginal producers glibly invoke their supposed Hollywood IDs, even while pitching and self-financing pilots according to the new deficit tactics of the brandworld. The aggregate downward budget-spiral this creates spurs runaway production—thus destroying the very high-end craftworld the same producers will desperately need if they ever hope to achieve industry "insider" or big-screen distinction. Alternately, below-the-line IATSE editors and above-the-line WGA members justify their "off-the-books" nonunion specwork as what they need to do to get more work or "pay the bills." This wistful posture is likely reinforced and legitimized by social-media-sharing practices they've learned and adopted from the specworld. Sadly, this freely given surplus-work undercuts peers, taking more work (and thus screen time) away from others, further increasing craftworld precarity.

Finally, earnest unemployed and outsider aspirants (adept at social media from the specworld but living far from physical production centers) send up-front money, entrance fees, registration fees, and retainers to agents who are not agents, managers and talent scouts who are not managers and talent scouts, film festivals that are not film festivals, "master classes" that do not master anything, student loan mills posing as "film schools," "industry insiders" who are not insiders of anything, and "exclusive" online short film "showcases" that no one from the industry ever bothers to watch. In large measure, this collective aspirational surge—the aggregated resources and capital from ubiquitous film or TV aspirational cultures so vast that the sun never sets on their worldwide borders—is what feeds the paraindustrial beast and the industry it presumes to support. In these final cases, the misrecognition of the specworld labor regime by those struggling within it alters both of the other two regimes but in very different ways. First, proliferating specwork destroys craftworld scarcity even as it feeds huge amounts of new ideas into the brandworld, which large corporate conglomerates efficiently strip-mine.

Yet even seasoned pros, not just aspirants, learn to vigilantly appraise how much individual control, and how much of the network's shared ideas or creative "team's" brainstorming, they should incorporate. For some, the problem of when to "take" and "give notes" (instructions about how to revise a script) amped up as writers moved from film to TV. This resulted, in part, because proliferation of personnel in studio and network management almost guarantees that too many cooks are stirring the story pot. One screenwriter coaches other writers on how to adopt passive-aggression as a creator stance, implying that it provides one way for a writer to save her soul:

> If you take notes from everyone, you'll end up with a Petri dish. I would push back in any way that is nice and professional. . . . Don't react immediately. You might have some people on your team where their notes aren't that helpful. Their fixes aren't that helpful. Maybe the big note is. But their actual solutions never work. You're going to have to learn to silence that person in your head, to do the right thing. . . . But it's up to you if you have to take them. They don't have to know if you do or not. You have to answer to network a bit. But Just don't get behind anything you can't get behind. That you can't put your name on. (Felischa Marye, WGA, "Breaking into the Industry" panel, UCLA, Feb. 3, 2020)

Specworld does not just entail consensual strip-mining; it provides many examples of subtle resistance. This includes how widely teamed-up (among note-givers) a screenwriter allows her speculation work to

FIGURE 3.11. High production A-listers camp out in lower-caste Specworld (Lynch and Herzog). *Left:* Offscreen image of transcendent back-channel "film school" advertisement (from David Lynch MFA in Screenwriting ad). *Right:* Offscreen image of *IndieWire* front page offering "contact" with avatar/director Werner Herzog via AI. May 22, 2016. © 2016, by *IndieWire.*

become. Whereas Marye likens this tension between a writer's vision and outsiders' notes to the bacterial mold of a "Petri dish," I will propose (see chapters 7 and 8) that such a conflict provides a systematic "fault line" that can be productively researched by scholars.

With so much to lose, and so much at stake between these three competing labor regimes, professional workers, aspirants, and scholars alike face complex alternatives in the dense paraindustrial buffer. Navigating that buffer—which is now inseparable from industry proper—requires considerable awareness and adroitness. This predicament means that the culture and specwork of production are now as much a part of a worker's skill set as the physical competencies of production craft once were.

Finally, media conglomerates are not the only ones navigating the three regimes. Some successful firms and high-end pros also complicate the rules for aspiring and emerging workers. Why would film director A-listers like David Lynch or Werner Herzog, for example, camp out in specworld (fig. 3.11)? With his screenwriting courses focused on

"Transcendental Meditation" (TM) rather than actual instruction or in-person residency, Lynch (left) offers his "nonresident" MFA "Film School" to aspirants struggling to make it in the specworld. Meanwhile, auteur Werner Herzog (right) offers aspirants "contact" with his avatar (an AI-substitute for busy Herzog) for mentoring. Apparently successful A-listers need avatars and lots of interns to handle the new back-channel messaging tasks that their slumming among aspirants in specworld now requires.

SPECWORK, PROTOTYPES, PRETESTING, PILOTS (BRAND AND FRANCHISE FODDER)

I research speculation work because corporate/professional apologists for free/gifted labor provoke my long-standing interests in production's cultural politics, industrial aesthetics, the logic of multimedia branding, and industrial reflexivity.[15] Those concerns resonate with many current labor practices: the spec-script, the pitch aesthetic, the professional craft-worker's Meta (née Facebook) network, the technician's how-to demo, the underemployed editor's clip reel, the disgruntled crewmember's theoretical deconstruction of executives, the creative producer's fan-pandering Twitterverse, and the endless proliferation of reps, agents, middlemen, "contact men," and handlers. Such mediators and facilitators complicate the paraindustry, yet they also provide scholars with many new opportunities and sites for paraindustrial research.

In some ways, the pilot is no longer just a preliminary artifact setting up more durable or primary forms of lasting screen content. Rather, the pilot now arguably defines all film and television production. Or said differently: *all film/TV productions are pilots,* or now ideally function as pilots, in the broad sense of the term. This is because most films and shows (even yearlong series) merely stand in as prototypes for a bigger corporate goal. They create the possibility of endless, systematic iterations of the very same readaptable concept. This posturing in turn heightens the prospects that a corporation will be able to endlessly monetize some proprietary IP. Facing markets where most films and series ultimately "fail," the logic is clear: endless speculation, conceptual pretesting, workshopping, and "piloting" provide time-tested ways that brands or franchises can minimize risk and succeed. Such is the specworld. The fact that much of both the material burden and justification for spec, prototyping, pretesting, and piloting has been financially off-loaded onto workers means the labor will continue to persist as a nagging, but important, complication in media studies. This hybrid industrial system means that front-loaded prototyping and pre-testing matter, even in a worker's "off-the-clock" vocational toolkit and career plan.

4

Case

Warring Creator Pedagogies (The Aspirant's Crossover Dilemma)

Don't let perfection be the enemy of being done!

—Theorist Media expert to YouTube creators, VidCon Anaheim, 2017

Just have a set-up that you can come in, sit-down, and shoot. Just quickly crank-out content.

—VideoCreators.TV expert to YouTube creators, VidCon Anaheim, 2017

Production workers teach and theorize about production alongside their primary task of making screen media. This chapter frames such industrial "emic" theorizing about production as platform pedagogy and as forms of culture-building. Far beyond university film schools, professional organizations (ASC, ACE, CDG, WGA, IATSE, etc.) and paraindustry groups (IFP, FIND, AMPAS, ATAS, etc.) manage and reinforce what is taught and theorized in most industry sectors, field sites, and contact zones. Ethnographic scholars will almost surely run into this interworker talk and critical assertions about production even when they try to get beyond it for an unfiltered view of actual production work. As such, I hope to underscore how industrial mentoring is integral to actual media work and to examine how and why what is being taught about production (in the field) might be undergoing rapid, stressed change.

This chapter and the two other case study chapters that follow (chaps. 6 and 8) compare and contrast warring creator pedagogies in two different (but oddly connected) production sectors. The first sector involves vast amounts of low-budget aspirational online production and field sites where makers create and upload to a mediascape that self-brands as their host "platform." YouTube, Patreon, Vimeo, GoFundMe, Maker Studios, and MCNs were studied online and in person, via workshops, how-to resources, creator manuals, maker conventions, trade shows, equipment demos, and meet-and-greets. The media often treat this sector (made up of YouTubers, online makers, and influencers) as much larger and antithetical to the high production values and screen content of Hollywood. As shorthand, in the pages ahead, I reference this as low-production culture based on the practices that pervade it: micro- or no-budget productions, hyperactive online uploading, low barriers to entry, tangential monetization, and gift-like distribution behaviors via "free" social media sharing. The cultural pose of this "low" creator world remains conflicted, however, since its production pedagogy simultaneously mimics but also rejects out of hand the practices and values of "pro" or "high production" that many associate with Hollywood and other major national feature film industries. The reasons for the pedagogical double bind in trade rhetoric that aspirant creators face on tech platforms deserve exploring.

In this chapter professional or high production provides the contrasting sector for comparative research. The explanations quoted in these case study chapters from both nonunion managerial figures and unionized professional creators mark out career boundaries and cultural expectations for prestige production. The prestige paradigm evokes "Hollywood" and now HBO, Amazon, and Netflix Originals. This "high" production culture is characterized by big-budget productions, methodical workflows and pacing, crews with vast numbers of creative workers, specializations with high barriers to entry, meticulously integrated subunits, and business plans built around disciplined, long-term monetization.

These ambitious norms for high-production pros largely clash with the effusive, low-end "how-to-succeed" basics that online platforms and their workshops "teach" to desperate aspirant creators. This managerial-scheming-as-art mode that platforms teach aspirants troubles many aspiring online makers who struggle to advance up to "real" careers as film/media creators. The double bind that aspirant creators face over what is supposedly fundamental to production is the basis for calling this chapter an ethnography of warring creator pedagogies. At a minimum, the mashing-up of high and low poetics unsettles many aspirant creators trying to bootstrap new careers in film/TV. I was particularly keen to understand how this double bind in high-vs.-low pedagogy might sustain an irresolvable media-art-making predicament, one that helps fuel the vast extractive economies of online platforms.

Humanities scholars since Aristotle have employed "poetics" as a framework to explore the basic, constituent categories that constitute an art form, literature, or cultural practice. So invoking an archaic philosophical term like *poetics* in a case study in this book (which is otherwise informed by fieldwork) may seem like an odd gambit. Yet I employ poetics here not to establish universal or timeless principles underlying film/video form or aesthetic structures. Rather, by listening closely to public pedagogy and corporate discourses about production, I hope to sketch out the parameters of what might be called an industrial poetics of production. Film and media production aesthetics and poetics are, at least initially, unavoidably approached as social constructions.

As such, I approach production poetics in this chapter as an ethnographic question and framework, not as a philosophical inquiry about immutable elements of screen-making and form. Specifically, in the case study of industrial speculation that follows, I ask how two very different production sectors—aspirant online makers and established legacy professionals—relate to each other in the ways they explain and theorize what they believe to be the fundamentals constituting online media production today. The three fieldwork chapters follow an incremental logic and arc. In this chapter I detail how makers are told and incentivized to expect a distinctive bodily experience of production as they create. Trade experts indirectly mentor aspirants that the artistry of low and high production should feel different to makers as they create. Chapter 6 will shift away from these supposed embodied or *phenomenological* core elements of "successful" production values in order to unpack the *managerial systems* that ideally oversee the twenty-first-century online maker's creative process. I argue there that industry's promotion of those subsequent administrative "basics" can be understood as the "televisioning" of low production. I chose this analogy because aspirant pedagogies now promote odd bureaucratic basics that go well beyond the boundaries of traditional poetics or core creative principles.

In fieldwork for this case study I tried to understand how millennial and Gen-Z film students and media production aspirants reflect on and explain what the basic constituent categories of film media are. That question is timely given the bold claims about social media disruption and radical innovation that have spread widely, spurred by new digital technologies, platforms, and markets. Many millennial and Gen-Z makers and influencers already speak confidently about the nuances and complexities of digital media creation. They carry these specific maker experiences with them as a kind of hard-earned self-ethnographic apparatus. As "natives" of this vast (but low-end) online production culture, creators and makers ostensibly know digital's schemes in a useful deep-and-narrow sense. This familiarity arms influencers and self-styled YouTube insiders with the sort of complex data set that ethnographers normally seek out in the field from "informants." Yet, from my interactions, online makers seldom connect these local specific experiences about media-making with larger philosophical, ethical, and moral histories and questions.[1]

Given the wide diversity of what passes for moving-image making now, is it possible to theorize about production, that is, to offer broadly applicable generalizable propositions about what constitutes the basics of film and media production? Attempting this would presuppose that production is one thing, a coherent phenomenon, or a stable category. Apart from whether or not there is an airtight necessary and sufficient scholarly definition that describes the core of production, one that can be intellectually justified and widely applied in critical scholarship, there clearly is a social and cultural tendency to *talk* about and posture production as a knowable, self-evident entity. Professionals regularly talk this way. In trade gatherings (like the NAB/Las Vegas, the TV Upfronts/ New York, the Berlinale Film Market, and Slush Helsinki), professionals generalize all the time about "production this" and "production that," about where production comes from and where it is going.

It is this version of production as a socioprofessional discourse—a rhetorical trade convention that constantly makes production one thing, a tactical trade assertion, a reduction—that interests me. In this chapter, I want to tackle the observable declarations and gestures that cultivate the notion of film media as a self-evident field (albeit one established by convention, consensus, and collective- or self-interest). The social construction of production functions for industry as an organizing myth or ideal, something created and pursued through socioprofessional interactions.[2]

I try to unpack these issues in the pages that follow based on the comparative analysis of five bodies of evidence gathered from localized qualitative fieldwork. These include (1) ethnographic observation, conversations, and transcripts from low-budget online makers and creators (including the weeklong VidCon convention in Anaheim in 2017 and 2019, cosponsored by YouTube and Google); (2) teaching and supervising film students in my role as professor (1998–2020) and vice-chair of undergraduate studies in the film school (2015–16) at UCLA; (3) master-class workshops with production designers at Design Showcase West/LA in June 2016 and June 2017 (the first featuring intertrade

Chapter 4

remarks by Quentin Tarantino, the second a master class in art directing led by Deborah Riley, who was responsible for production design in
Game of Thrones); (4) a series of yearly Kodak cinematographer residencies and workshops with ASC and Local 600 DP's at UCLA (from
2008 to 2015) organized by DP Bill McDonald; and (5) a series of networking, "how-to," and "behind-the-scenes" events with screenwriters
(WGA) and costume designers (CDG) in Los Angeles in winter and
spring 2020.

STRANGE BEDFELLOWS OR CREATOR SUPPLY CHAIN?

Many YouTubers unabashedly celebrate that they create on pop culture's
center stage, while justifying it as their primary career goal. Yet many others offer conflicted personal explanations about whether YouTube is "just
a stepping stone" that will allow them to advance to higher-level professional film/TV work. In many ways—at least in refereed contact zones
like VidCon and SponCon—high makers and low act like uneasy neighbors, anxious about whether they are like or unlike their "other," from
the higher or lower caste. Generally, "higher" production treats or disregards low-making as amateurish or "just" marketing—something, for
example, suitable for rewarding HBO fan production, or a tactic seeking
synergies in a space loaded with willing-to-partner "influencers." This de
facto dismissiveness by "professional" filmmakers of "aspirants" may follow from the generally sorry economics of the lower-maker world. There,
as one weary online maker remarked to me—despite the millions of views
and likes possible, and the crossover influencer exceptions celebrated by
Entertainment Weekly—"no viewer is ever going to pay you."[3]
    Yet, as if to convince themselves of an eventual payoff, the Gen-Zers
in low production repeat a collective mantra that suggests eventual
advantage over "old media." As one maker explained: "Now, the generation of YouTubers here are the first generation to grow up with
YouTube as their primary [career] aspiration."[4] This cynical "who
cares anymore about Hollywood" mantra from successful YouTubers
sometimes comes from the naive view that old media labor and success
are *easier* to get and keep than YouTube revenues. Consider how one
emerging online creator folded this odd view into his strategies for success: "If [online producing] doesn't work out, I'll go and work in the
film industry."[5] Translation: "Hey, Hollywood is always there for me
to simply fall back on, even if YouTube/influencer stardom ultimately
fails me." In the face of the disregard many pros have for YouTube,

these maker comments suggest that any dismissiveness is two-way. Conflicted posturing or ignorance may explain both sides of the high-vs.-low stare-down. If we look beyond generational and economic differences, many low makers personally identify with and aspire to careers in high or big-screen production.[6] This is the subset of makers/influencers that face the crossover dilemma researched here.

These online maker comments suggest that some logical link bridges the two creator worlds. This connection may hold because the trope of YouTubers "making it" in Hollywood pervades popular culture. In the popular press, Lilly Singh and Issa Rae became Exhibits A for that crossover trajectory, a status proven by the way their visibility spiked in celebrity media. Issa Rae's YouTube webisode showcase *The Misadventures of Awkward Black Girl* enabled Rae to adapt the character and to create and star in the subsequent HBO comedy *Insecure*. NBC premiered Singh's *A Little Late* in September 2019.[7] Aymar Jean Christian explains the extent of the online creator-to-Hollywood feeder connection in crossovers like these in his definitive study *Open TV: Innovation beyond Hollywood and the Rise of Web Television*.[8] The book is based on more than one hundred perceptive interviews with creators like Rae and Singh who work in the online space. Christian states, "I don't think I interviewed one person who said they rejected Hollywood completely and would never participate."[9] This crossover logic strikes me as a functional template for creative work employed by Christian's informants—not just an index of aspiration.

Christian locates the friction between the two worlds in the personnel that protect the crossover points: "The leading networks and production companies, from casting to writing, will look at someone who's done digital work, but they don't view digital work as equally credible to mainstream work. . . . If your goal is to make it into legacy media, I recommend people just make content that's recognizable to legacy media." So, despite the practical needs of my own informants to affirm their respective YouTube, TikTok, Twitter online systems as legitimate vocational ends in themselves (when they are on them), online makers also learn to make and keep at the ready crossover arguments about the value and logic of their personal fit in the higher-production world, as well.

I would like to add to Christian's take on the high-and-low connection by considering a different kind of evidence beyond influencer interviews per se: the oblique (and often costly) instruction and mentoring by creator platforms and third-parties that promise to professionalize aspirant creators. Before unpacking the core elements in those "how-to" and

FIGURE 4.1. "Film School RIP" (killing-off cinema aesthetics) is sold to aspirants as a key to success as a screen content creator. The aspirants crossover dilemma? Low creators who want to graduate to high production pay for mentoring and workshopping that actually guts the skill set needed to transition to big-screen careers. Photo from VidCon career workshop, Anaheim, CA. © 2017, by J. Caldwell.

"making it" mentoring packages aimed at aspirants, I want to reckon with four preliminary assumptions often used to distinguish high creators from influencer-creators: cultural edginess, structural footprint, scope of skill set, and labor of expression.

First, creators in social media (aka makers, influencers) are often instructed to reject traditional film/media aesthetics. Their celebrated social media "disruptions" pivot on the notion that Gen-Zers occupy an edgier conceptual and cultural vanguard than old media creators. Aspiring disruptors presuppose that the old thinking of "film school" from the legacy era is obsolete. The online creator workshop on how-to-make-it I observed in 2017 started with bold visuals celebrating the death of film schools ("RIP") (fig. 4.1). Even so, this same workshop (like the conflicted YouTube ecosystem in general) simultaneously sold the attending aspirants on the contradictory notion that film/TV production careers are indeed a viable (or possible) future professional option.

FIGURE 4.2. Industrial footprint vs. personality. *Left:* Big-budget film production's heavy-industry branding. Photo: Courtesy of UCLA Library Digital Collections. *Right:* Low-budget aspirational, Gen-Z "MakerWorld": onscreen still frames and intertitles from online "Maker Studios" promo and recruiting video. Los Angeles, CA. 2016.

A second truism commonly used to distinguish high and low production involves infrastructure. It assumes that online creation is personality-based while legacy production requires a heavy industrial footprint. Countless marketing making-ofs celebrate heavy-industry Hollywood by referencing its iconic studio infrastructure. This material footprint somehow reaffirms Hollywood as a stable meritocracy adept at finding and allowing only exceptional creators to rise to the top. By contrast, online multichannel networks (MCNs) like Maker Studios (fig. 4.2) promote their expansive social network of influencers as a young demographic El Dorado for marketers and merchandizers. This personality-vs.-material footprint distinction rings true in many respects. Yet such posturing also serves as calculated misdirection, since the actual technical and material infrastructure required by Google/YouTube/Facebook dwarfs Hollywood's.

Third, both the press and trades often presuppose that creator-influencers (at least initially) are both self-made and responsible for all of the technical aspects required for production. YouTube pedagogy echoes a mantra that the creator has sole oversight for all technical aspects of online production (whether they want it or not!). By contrast, actual commercial and corporate digital media companies must employ cadres of narrow technical specialists for the firm to profit, with restricted areas of expertise. One early career production artisan (a jack-of-all-trades pondering whether he should specialize) says, "I do know some coding and I'm definitely not an engineer. Right now I'm just trying to learn. How to build these spaces. How to think about them. Right now I am focusing on these corporate companies. But in the future, I'd like to be something like an 'interaction director,' like a 'film director' . . . creating a different kind of story paradigm."[10]

Entry-level jobs like this one place many new and rising employees in a highly conflicted posture. They need to master a technical specialization to stay employed even as they carry a longer-term burden to somehow make these tasks lead to a career overseeing the entire process. The digital media worker above likens his graduation from narrow coding specialist to eventually becoming an overseer, "a film director." For many no-budget online makers lacking resources, however, multitasking is simply a necessary practical curse. They literally do everything in a production. For the successful career director who has graduated from specialization in a firm, however, seeking a wider skill set may make him/her more effective in overseeing the many narrow specialists needed below.

A fourth and final common trope for the high/low question involves physicality, the difference between creating through bodily work or immaterial expression. Scholars rarely consider phenomenological aspects of media labor in cinema theory or aesthetics. The comparative analysis from fieldwork in this chapter explores whether core differences exist between the experience of work in traditional filmmaking or television production and the embodied experiences promoted and normalized by platforms for aspirational online makers/influencers. The convention-driven ways filmmakers are instructed to work—by their respective trades, in how-to venues, and platforms—impacts the eventual form their content takes onscreen. Not unlike the big-budget production design workshop and HBO-ethos detailed next, for example, classical era Fox Studios tacitly publicized earthmoving as a metaphor for DP Greg Toland's and director John Ford's epic geographical and logistical ambitions in the studio's *Grapes of Wrath* (fig. 4.3).

My CMS work is guided by the basic anthropological distinction between "emic" perspectives (articulated by fieldwork informants and production communities) and "etic" theories (brought to analyses by

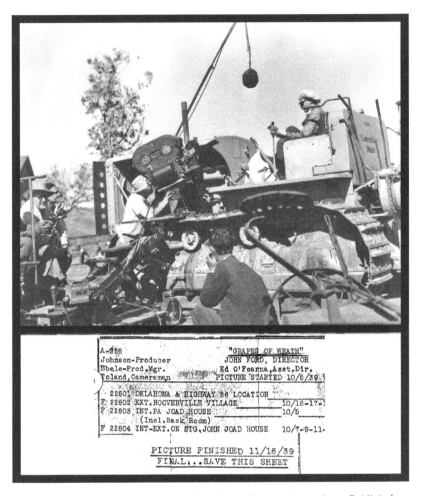

FIGURE 4.3. The embodied experience of production for creative workers. Publicity/ promo photo: 1939, 20th Century–Fox Studios. Courtesy of the Margaret Herrick Library, Academy of Motion Picture Arts and Sciences.

scholarly outsiders, analysts, and observers). On the emic perspective for the study that follows, a skeptic might question my initial research premise—that is, question whether YouTubers/makers now even care about advancing to the higher-production-values world. After all, very few Gen-Zers ever watch the academy awards live on TV any more, and most consume media online or on handheld devices. So before getting to the core poetics categories being taught and workshopped, I want to acknowledge one final preliminary question: to what degree do online aspirant creators and big-budget pros themselves even assert that they are connected or related to each other?

I begin with a conversation from fieldwork to offer some emic perspectives. A public argument I observed among five successful YouTube producers about their prospects for career crossovers between the two worlds unfolded as follows:

Phil Ranta. Is the dream still to go to Hollywood?

Thomas Ridgewell. Lots of creators still see [YouTube] as a stepping stone.

Benji Travis. [But it's changed] Being a Youtuber is now a number 1 profession.

Joe Penna. It's a completely different skill set, to make a forty-two minute documentary feature film.

Megan Batoon. People on YouTube are artists. . . . But I would never say "no" to a [TV] show![11]

Faced with the question of whether YouTube is a "pipeline to Hollywood," these video creators differed about whether they wanted careers that advanced to film/TV. Yet the fact that rising YouTube creators engaged the high-low pipeline question so publicly underscores how important the question is (even without answers) within this creator world.

The next section drills down through trade discourses in several production settings and workshops, including both high and low venues. In addition to the YouTube and VidCon workshops already discussed, these sites included an MPEG union organizing meeting in Los Angeles for editors, a costume designers' (CDG) panel discussion, and a master class in production design by Deborah Riley. After discussing new speed pressures in post, I pivot to Riley as she gives a master class to graduate and professional designers on the making of *Game of Thrones* from an art department perspective. My goal in sifting through and comparing workshop rhetoric (hierarchical) and interactions (lateral) was to try to isolate and pin down the type of basic categories that a study of poetics traditionally entailed. I begin with trade rhetoric about five specific maker/influencer practices—core values, as it were—to further explore the extent of the high-vs.-low connections. The production pedagogies I observed normalized all five of these embodied phenomena as linked to screen-media-making. Professionals mentor makers and early career creative workers that they will need to get on top of these de facto capacities if they hope to begin or advance through careers in production.

Speed, Velocity

High production values typically require good financing, large budgets, and methodical pacing. This high resource bar can easily halt the making-it hopes and long-shot aspirations of online creators. Such outsiders are often taught to work much more quickly, or they are left to do so out of necessity. Yet far from these two extremes, speed has long reigned as a management problem in a wide range of productions. Between the two poles lies an extensive midlevel industrial purgatory of commercial production that lacks both the ample budgets and extended calendars of high production and the imperatives about frantic work speed faced by aspirants in low-production. Producers have long-pressured some middlebrow, moderately-budgeted television genres (like unscripted reality TV) to achieve a manic speed and velocity not unlike online makers. This is because the ad-supported TV format has spurred an exponential increase in the number of recorded videoclips that editors need to wade through to meet impossibly short postproduction schedules. Many working editors are cynical about producers who act clueless about math (and reality). This is evident in editors' gallows-humor descriptions of the soul-crushing numbers of digital clips they must wade through in shorter and shorter time frames:

> [They tell us:] It's going to be great. It's easier. There's no tapes. . . . The first day they handed me 18 hundred clips, [800] gigabytes of these things, and they weren't labeled or anything! It was just "Roll 1" [but] it was a thousand clips! . . . Then, "Roll 2." Here's another one. No time code! . . . We had to bring [all] this stuff in. . . . Technology's changing so much. It's exponentially growing. I don't know how many times I've had a producer . . . or a coordinator come in . . . and they'll try to tell you [about] this technical workflow that *you* are going to do. It's like . . . [their plan] has nothing to do with [reality]. I might as well . . . be sitting with a hand-cranked camera. . . . They don't have a clue. They think that by going tapeless, they're going to save time and money. (Rob Kraut, MPEG, "Reality Check" union organizing meeting, Hollywood, CA, August 30, 2011)

Successful social media creators are far more likely to land first jobs in this kind of midlevel industrial purgatory than in the prestige ranks of A-list studios or HBO series. So, manic work speed will likely still be required in their vocational skill set, even if they eventually get entry-level paychecks in "real" TV production.

A-listers can be unequivocal in emphasizing how pacing distinguishes their premium production values (high maker poetics) from either middlebrow TV or no-budget aspirant makers (low maker poetics). In a

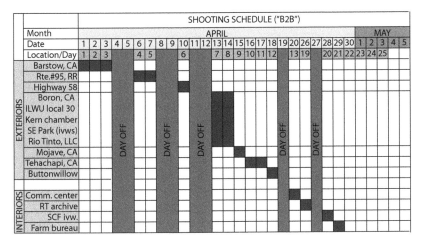

FIGURE 4.4. *Verso (top):* Deborah Riley *(right)*, production designer on HBO's *Game of Thrones*, prepares to give a master class on the making of the series from an art department perspective. Costume designer Deborah Landis *(left)* hosts the workshop at Design Showcase West. *Verso (bottom):* High-production design shows off its lumbering pace via physical model- and set-building, which are excessively scheduled, methodical, calculated. *Recto:* Generic production/shooting schedule, which (unlike social media creating) disaggregates and then rations scenes over an extended calendar of workdays. Photos of publicly displayed production personnel and images, Design Showcase West, Los Angeles, CA. © 2017, by J. Caldwell.

workshop for early career designers in training, *Game of Thrones* production designer Deborah Riley's lessons foregrounded the incremental, methodical pacing of physical production as a key to quality production values. With shot-by-shot deconstructions of series segments for her mentees, she extolled the virtues of plodding inertia: "to create the cave of the 3-eyed Raven . . . [we used] 20 Tons of soil. Twenty tons of rock were brought into the studio."[12] This attention to the impact of material mass onscreen directly constrained work speed, helping to give the series its methodical pacing (fig. 4.4).

The handmade labor needed to assemble the many parts of the *GoT* sets required preemptively planned, methodical pacing. The explanation in one demonstration: "So what happens is all of the wired tents are laid on their sides, and the drapes department makes the tents themselves, but in an abandoned quarry in some terrible conditions." Riley underscores that this materiality and handwork harks back to the speed of preindustrial labor, as if that strenuous toil guarantees onscreen media quality. "So the interior was completed, and the plasterers excelled [*sic*] themselves again. . . . The plasterers had achieved a whole new aesthetic for the show. The English crews are renowned for their plaster, and I absolutely understand why" As the series' HBO seasons progressed, physical mass and solidity became conspicuous in the imagery. Material heft was thus marketed along with the narrative and became part of the *Game of Thrones* brand, part of the IP. Both onscreen and off, HBO marketed how the laborious physical heft of their sets required immense skill among their digital compositors, who had to integrate those massive sets into seamless scenes with digital precision using green screens.

Methodical leaden inertia, however, is far from the norm in production discourse. While A-listers justify the deliberate protracted pace of the preindustrial manual labor they employ, low-production pedagogy endlessly pressures wannabe producers to do just the opposite. Online social media "experts" explain why makers need to greatly ramp up the speed of their productions if they ever want to have careers or to survive financially in the online digital space. Tom Greenwood-Mears, Head of Events at Endemol-Shine UK, explains to aspirants the kind of project-pacing norm most valued in his new online creator clients: "I make a new video every single day. Try to be creative. Make a video every single day."[13] In like manner, Matt Gielen, CEO of Little-Monster Media Co., explains that a hyperpace is needed to even be *recognized* by the YouTube recommendation algorithm: "Frequency of uploads is more important than ever. You need at least 3+ uploads per week" to avoid the "YouTube Death Spiral."[14]

Other "veterans" and "experts" ponder ways to "hack" and "beat" the YouTube algorithm by artificially speeding up their videos: "I have 5 channels and 3 daily uploads (minimum). There is a 24hr. decay rate, like clockwork. Why? Because there is less value compared to newer content. It's the first 24hrs that matters most."[15] What is the underlying lesson intended for aspirant creators "shared" by these YouTube successes and third-party mentoring firms? Work fast, don't take breaks between episodes, and upload your "new" content frantically. The moral: failing to script and finish one's creative uploads with adrenalin will simply make you disappear from the platform's recognition radar and cause the derailing of your career (fig. 4.5).

These self-identified YouTube "insiders" promote a mode of speed production to aspirant creators as a creator hack. Notably, this newly idolized *creator velocity* also spills over and ramps up the pace and diegetic timing within the video's *screen content* and frame, as well. As one "successful"

FIGURE 4.5. Aspirants are bombarded with software shortcuts to achieve manic work speed. *Top:* Public signage and beta users. Adobe collapses low-makers' production workflow into singular time bursts ("Shoot. Edit. Share."—all at the same time!). To spike influencer/creator mania, trade groups remind anxious online makers that they're *competing* against "400 hours" of "new" video uploaded "every minute." *Bottom:* Public display at VidCon by Monster taunting aspirants about the upload volume with which their competition will now overwhelm them. Anaheim, CA. Photos of public displays: © 2017, by J. Caldwell.

creator intones: "If I make a beautiful 20min. video . . . nobody cares. They say 'this is boring.' So I cut it down to 1 minute."[16] "Video velocity is crucial. . . . The best is a 5–8 minute viewer duration . . . [with faster] editing and pacing."[17] Even the software companies now inculcate hyper-velocity in aspirant content creation. Adobe enables its newer users to collapse the entire process (pre, production, post, distribution) into one frantic singularity (see fig. 4.5, upper). Monster Media reminds its mentees that their competitors are uploading four hundred hours of competing content every minute, 24/7 (see fig. 4.5, lower). Anxiety attacks and ulcers may thus be taken as benchmarks for creativity in this sector.[18]

Other experts sell mentees on producing early and quickly—instead of worrying about quality—since aspirant creators who hope to master production can only learn from the *mistakes* in their early uploads.[19] In this way, while costly high production must solve mistakes *before* finalizing production or distribution, low production does just the opposite. That is, online creator workshops actually *promote mistake-making* as a simultaneous, inevitable part of the production and public distribution process. In the value-added learning curve of low-production aspirants, the social media platforms teach a hyperactive finish-and-upload pace as the key performance metric needed to grow their channel.

The hypervelocity mode being preached in online low-production trade pedagogy also underscores, by contrast, the relatively plodding quality of high-budget production. Certainly, a great deal of collective, preindustrial hand labor is needed to embed the kinds of visual production value that HBO wants onscreen for *Game of Thrones* or that Netflix seeks for *Medici*. By contrast, promoting hyperactive production uploads as a requirement for aspirants in social media's low production, makes online production align more with ADHD behavior than Fordism. This speed requirement also diverts or deflects viewer attention from the visual quality of the well-designed screen to the performer or influencer's presence. The plodding, premium high-creator metric of *hours-per-year* for HBO, Amazon Prime, or Netflix programming differs dramatically from the collapsed low-maker metric of *minutes-per-day* for YouTube programming. Velocity is repeatedly underscored as the linchpin and ephemeral consolation prize for underresourced aspirants.

If in these ways creator velocity has somehow become a de facto core principle for aspiring and rising media producers, such a goal cannot be attained without drastically reducing what production has traditionally included. Consider the following primer from a VidCon workshop, which was based on an analysis of the most successful YouTube creators: "Sustainable content is efficient. Being able to make content on time and on budget is key to sustainability. A format that takes too much time or costs too much money adds so much unnecessary stress to the creators. Sometimes less is really more. . . . A great example of efficiency [is] because the show: (1) Can make multiple episodes at a time. (2) Is on a single set. (3) Doesn't have intensive post-production. (4) Is based on simple, easy to achieve, concepts."[20] Each of these four meager pillars of aspirant production make media-making manic, creating efficient shortcuts to get content done and uploaded in daily clockworked regularity.

Joining Adobe in collapsing the long, sequential production workflow into an abrupt singularity of "live" everything, maker/influencer trade *Videomaker* pulls the plug even further on preparation, urging online creators to get rid of planning and preproduction entirely (fig. 4.6). By hard-selling its aspirant creators to get rid of *both* preproduction and postproduction (at least if they want to succeed) maker pedagogy doesn't just shortcut the temporal duration of filmmaking. It shortcuts complexity, screenwriting, production planning, previsualization, and editorial, as well. Reducing film aesthetics to questions of creator velocity points toward a second, related core difference between high- and low-production pedagogies: scale. It, too, vexes aspirants, who eventually hope to "cross over" to big-screen careers.

Scale (High Transnational Reach vs. Low Slop Tech Primers)

Producers now face considerable pressure to develop content that is repurposable and transmedial. The industry trades also presuppose that content production today benefits by being transnational or transgeographic. This entails working toward production design based on some spatially networked or geographic logic, something I will call "scale" or "reach." Like creator speed, differences in scale mark one of the most dramatic formal differences between high production and low production. Riley explains to her mentees the narrative space she is building: "You know, the *Game of Thrones* universe exists in many different kingdoms. . . . The main job of the art department is to make sure that all of those kingdoms are distinct from each other. And when they work within the show, the audience accepts them as being real" Press-kits and production staff second this principle and proudly wear their mastery of global logistics on their sleeves. "The producers and I sit down and work out what is assumed to be a location shoot . . . which might happen in Northern Ireland, Croatia, Spain or Iceland. Or, which will be a stage build, housed in our studios in Northern Ireland" (fig. 4.7).

The language Riley uses to describe the physical circumstances of the shoot reads at times like a vacation travelogue: "I had two main references for the House of Faces. The first one was the Allora Caves in India, which is the world's largest rock hut monastery and also a World Heritage site. And the second reference was the Temple of the 10,000 Buddhas, which I photographed many years earlier in Hong Kong" Riley's mentoring to underlings includes an undertone emphasizing the travel required in high production: "All of the drawings were completed

FIGURE 4.6. "Who needs preproduction?" *Top:* Aspiring YouTubers (many of whom want eventual big-screen careers) are told that production planning is for suckers and that nonstop creator output creates the efficiencies needed for success. *Bottom:* The influencer-creator's holy grail: only one idea allowed per video production. Aspirant-producer "how-to-succeed" video instructs creators to eliminate complexity in content (to "think like a media company"), promoting a count-the-content approach to simplify the creator task. Photo: Public visual displays by Epipheo, Anaheim, CA. © 2017, by J. Caldwell.

FIGURE 4.7. High-production creator Deborah Riley leverages transnational reach in shop-floor talk. Her design master class morphs into a transnational making-of travelogue, which underscores both the crew's artistic inspirations and its geographic challenges. *Game of Thrones* weaves globe-crossing geographic pretense into the fabric of its design and storytelling to build premium marquee status. Image components from HBO marketing combined in publicly displayed video screens. Design Showcase West, Los Angeles. CA. Photographs of displays: © 2017, by J. Caldwell.

in Belfast, and then it was built in Croatia. . . . The exterior of the (Dash Kalleen) temple was built out of Almyra/Almeria in Spain. We had a practice building it in Belfast, and so it went out to Spain in kit form. And came together very quickly" These production tropes linking vast global locations also echo off the set, throughout the series' marketing and promotional surround. HBO online marketing winks to viewers that it made a high-end travelogue, on the side, for one of the series' host countries, Croatia. Their selling of this transnational scale proved to be productive fan-bait. Travel agencies organized *GoT* tours. *GoT* shooting locations are theme-parked for visitors. Investigative *GoT* fans create and match their own frames on social media, into diptychs with "actual" *GoT* shooting locations that they post on social media. Epic scale tied to the series look provides imaginative real estate and reach that transmedia feeds on.

In stark contrast, an odd kind of antiscale monism anchors pedagogy in the world of lowly online makers. Matthew Patrick of Theorist Media clarifies the arms-length ideals apparently needed for content acquisition in these unequivocal terms: "Each piece of content must have a single objective."[21] Other VidCon experts reinforce this hyperreductive screen content "mono" rule as necessary based on the supposed media specificities that constrain any online video that makers upload. Creator Benji Travis elaborates: "What works on YouTube gives people headaches on TV. I can't imagine making anything long enough for TV."[22] Time and space collapse here in VidCon's aggregating primer for online success. Nicole Sweeney's "Crash Course" summary to her paying aspirants echoed the same cautionary lesson about physical production for her mentees: *"Don't let perfection be the enemy of being done."*[23] That is, to be successful, rising YouTubers do not need to worry about achieving excellent visual/sound quality in screen content.

Other YouTube "successes" provide mentees with their own nuts-and-bolts guides to the scaled-down collapsed-space ideal promoted widely in social media platform pedagogy. Instead of A-list transgeographic scale, fee-charging experts persuade online makers to think about the creative efficiencies of *chair-scale* video content. The underlying mantra in various workshops I observed was that creators need to find ways to just "sit down and shoot." Consider one example of this instruction for online creative success to "just quickly crank out content": "Maybe also consider cutting back on the production side of your video. . . . So for example, I just have a place here that is set up. But just have a setup that you can come and sit down and shoot. You don't have to set up lights and cameras and microphones and backdrops and everything over and over again. Figure out a system you can put in place that makes it easier for you to just quickly crank out content (snap, snap, snap)."[24]

I had a hard time wrapping my head around these primers suggesting that sloppy artistry and hasty tech serve as keys to online creator success. Especially since tactical haste and sloppiness were being taught in trade gatherings and venues otherwise devoted to "how to scale up your brand" and "how to be discovered by Hollywood." These lofty aims— alongside the simultaneous promotion of slop quality content—can only exacerbate the structural double bind that crossover aspirants face.

Although the aggregating video primer just cited implicitly taught small-scale production sloppiness, it quickly undercut that notion. That is, it warned makers they will *eventually* need to attract some wider recognition if they hope to make it. To go wide, to go big-screen, makers need to move beyond a "throw-some-equipment-into-the-basement-and-shoot" aesthetic. Faced with that pressure, spatial scale creeps back into low-maker logic. Creator Tim Schmoyer offers another secret to success. He describes a higher, secondary level of interaction that can help the aspirant (eventually) expand scale: "I gave a behind-the-scenes tour for my patrons, a total behind-the-scenes tour. Thanks to all of you on Patreon for supporting that. Link to that."[25] This gambit underscores another truism online creators face: to make money in a world of free content, creators must figure out ways to add economic "tiering" to the otherwise "free" maker experiences they offer. In this example, tiering means charging added fees for "special services" such as behind-the-scenes video tours of the maker's space. At the higher tier motivated fans and Patreon supporters are able to see featured "extras."[26]

Size (Geological, Material Weight and Industrial Mass)

Physical size, not just spatial or geographic scale, matters in both low- and high-production poetics, albeit in very different ways. Consultants incentivize online makers' to travel light, to quickly build interpersonal networks that can grow them into their goal of microcelebrity status. Bigger-budget productions, however, can credit their industrial size infrastructure as an index of their success as premium content. Massive shipyards and oceanic oil rigs provided this kind of prediegetic size and foundation for *GoT*. Riley explains: "The Titanic Studios in Belfast [is where the] *Titanic* was built . . . between 1909 and 1911. Highland and Wolf, the famous shipbuilders, still own much of the surrounding land, although they repair oil rigs now, not build ships. . . . The big building in the back is where White Star Ships used to paint their big cruise ships."[27] *GoT*'s online marketing mirrored its designer's shoptalk by showing how the series was built on a massive geological and industrial foundation, which included the Belfast shipyards as soundstages.

Beyond the epic shipyards and oil rigs being shown off by the designer, *Game of Thrones* gained much of its diegetic force from leveraging even larger geological masses. "These lava formations were enormous, but because of logistics, the scene was returned to Belfast and built inside of an abandoned quarry. . . . We painted the gravel black in order to create those beaches in Iceland."[28] Riley likens *GoT* to geological sites that are large enough to be seen from satellites. At other points, the production sought to forge the perception of a *seamless* geological continuum and locations that melded the earth, buildings, and video frame: "I was very inspired by the stone buildings on the banks of the Ganges River in the religious city of Varanasi, where the steps rise straight out of the water." This *geologic seamlessness* aligned well with another art department impulse: making "props" part of the architectural materiality: "I thought it very important that the faces we displayed in the Hall of Faces not be like books in a library or objects in an art gallery but that they'd be so vast in number that the very fabric of the building house those faces of the dead."[29]

The series showcased its size and mass this way, by integrating props into the building materials and by making its design inseparable from its geology. The production also spurred a phenomenological sense by soliciting a visceral embodied identification in viewers. Riley provides the historical rationale for one key scene: "The body pile was the most important thing for the art department to conquer. . . . As early as 1415 . . . both sides had to climb over the (walls of) dead in order to keep fighting. This concept aimed to show the scale of that body pile. . . . At three thousand pounds per dead horse, production were very keen for us to work out what we would need as we progressed through different stages of the body pile."[30] *GoT* thus congeals even once-living human masses into a gooey amalgam of horizon-blocking earth, corpses, and mud (fig. 4.8).

Although prestige production can build its screen epics from geological mass and shipyard scale, low-production aspirants must often produce content at the physical scale of a suburban home basement. The DIY spatial aesthetic of makers and vloggers often underscores this sense of retooled domestic space. Just as this cramped quasi-intimate low-maker infrastructure greatly differs from the size of *GoT*'s vast quarries, the equipment needed and hyped in online aspirant-creators also poses as miniscule. YouTube coaching sites often feature some iteration of the Spartan advice: "the best equipment is the equipment you [actually] have." This great-with-few-resources mantra abounded among online makers at both VidCon 2017 and 2019. Unsurprisingly, this rationalization is tied to the typical online maker's economic predicament. As one expert cautioned younger aspirant creators: "Expensive equipment is a blackhole."[31] Travel light.

Another "veteran" online content creator explains how the new digital screen aesthetics is founded on the principle that the viewer will forgive the creator for sloppy haste and "mistakes":

> If you are doing a lot of highly produced stuff, with a lot of takes, a lot of camera angles and cuts and stuff . . . you've already seen me leave in a few of my mistakes . . . or, maybe instead of doing lots of cuts, just do one take. *Instead of doing all of these camera angles, just [tell yourself] do "one take, a vlog style, and that's all I have time for today." Your audience is probably*

FIGURE 4.8. Relative mass is in the eye of the beholder. *Top:* Pleased deconstruction by art director of massive, multiton human "body pile" made for those killed onscreen in *GoT.* Publicly displayed video screen from HBO how-to design workshop. © 2017, by J. Caldwell. *Bottom:* Patreon how-to video promotes meager geographic scale of single human maker-space: a suburban home basement as a maker's "soundstage." This format-appropriate alternative for low production contrasts unapologetically with high production's epic reach. Offscreen still frame from Patreon/YouTube streaming promo.

very forgiving. . . . The goal is to spend less time editing, setting up, tearing down, cutting cameras together, everything. Just find ways to streamline your process.[32]

In this online veteran's mentoring, technical haste is not just acknowledged; it is explicitly sanctioned. Adopting this light-footprint-enabled sloppiness as a YouTuber's production ideal, a norm, may make some sense. After all, the bunkered, just-make-it-quickly-then-move-on aesthetic often emerges from a cramped, basement-size domestic space that is all too familiar in the modest world of YouTuber. Most surprising to me was that this disavowal of production heft and equipment materiality was promoted alongside a somehow intertwined theory of audience "forgiveness." Over and against the A-lister's invocation of *physical* mass as an index of production quality arises the aspirant, who is mentored to accept the miniscule mistake-triggered *metaphysics* of viewer forgiveness.

Specwork vs. Prepwork (in Low and High Production)

A fourth core concept implicit in the production's warring rhetorics pivots around the issue and question of preparation. Preparation is highly relevant to the problem of speculative labor. Two broad significantly different types of oddly linked preemptive labor, in fact, can be usefully distinguished in production: prepwork and specwork. Here I want to examine how speculation specifically plays out in A-list vs. YouTube production cultures. As introduced, "specwork" was adapted from the word *spec-script*—a screenplay written without pay to prove that an aspiring writer has the chops to succeed as a professional. This chapter expands "specwork" to include all of those forms of creative labor that are not credited or paid for but that are nevertheless requirements for work in film and media. More than just unpaid or free work, specwork frequently functions vocationally as a "calling-card" sample or "proof-of-concept." Specwork can also involve "thinking-out-loud" during production—committee conjecture in the collective TV "writers room" being a clear example.

A lot of preproduction work, however, is neither preemptive nor freely taken. To begin thinking about how the mainstream industrializes specwork into material prepwork, consider the work and analytical process used by award-winning film costume designer Mark Bridges. Like most costume designers, Bridges's career involves mastering materials and visualizations in preparation for a shoot. The incremental approval process in preproduction and production for this craft requires handling fabrics, drawings, and the creation of stylebooks for shared reference. Yet even in the high-end, feature-film-production culture in which Bridges works, the manic velocity from digital apps and Dropbox now encroaches on the craft's conventional ways of physically envisioning things:

> I'm pretty analog. It's a craft that I learned 35 years ago. I've been doing it all of my life. And I want to feel the fabric. I want to draw with a pencil. I want to find a great book that has the right pictures. And then xerox them! You know I've been working in Hollywood since 1989. And I've noticed, now, that people will send you an email, and then, you know, they're done with it. They're like: "I SENT you that thing." "OK, I missed it. I'm sorry." (Costume designer Mark Bridges [CDG], "Sketch to Screen" panel, Copley Center for the Study of Costume Design, UCLA, Feb. 8, 2020)

Unlike the ephemeral excess and digital clutter of cloud storage, pencils, paper, and fabrics force clarity, are holdable, and thus allow actionable collective appraisals from the gathered team (designers, costumers, art directors, directors, and producers). Bridges's proven formula (to feel, to hold, to previsualize) underscores that prepwork is an administrative form of specwork central to unionized, adequately budgeted production.

With big budgets and greater financial risk, high-production design compartmentalizes specwork into a regimented linear sequence, which is overseen through a series of organizing documents and reference artifacts. Design trainees learn that *Game of Thrones* "all starts with an *outline,* at the very start of the season," which allows the key department heads to collectively brainstorm with the producers and plan out each episode of the season to come.[33] The outline, furthermore, is far more than a schematic of story. It also functions like a negotiating table for the principals in the group, proposing incremental episode parts that can be locked into an agreed-upon sequence during preproduction. Once finalized, this outline is followed by more prepwork, the "*shooting schedule,*" which projects "first, in what order the producers expect the sets to be built and then how many days they expect each set to shoot for. This gives us some idea of where the money will be spent."[34] Narrative theorists have focused much attention on how films and audiences partner to create "imagined worlds" or "story-worlds." But the job of imagining (reimagining and reiterating) story-worlds is not only a responsibility of the writer, fan, or director. It is also an obligatory visual-management task for technical crews in the workaday preproduction phase of high-end projects as well (fig. 4.9).

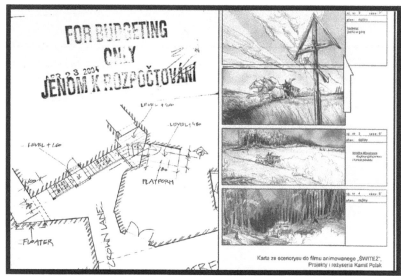

FIGURE 4.9. Administrative prepwork in the Czech national film studio vs. aspirant specwork. Specwork includes more than just the expressive imaginings of individual artists. *Top:* Czech storyboards, blueprints, budgets, and outlines all function as incremental, bureaucratic legal charters in an industrial assembly line. From public displays, Barrandov Studios, Czech Republic, 2016, J. Caldwell. *Bottom:* Screen*writers* are now told they *also* need to shoot sizzle reel of script *before* anyone will read their script. Offscreen still frame by J. Caldwell from *Emerging Screenwriters* online ad.

Production design also regularly relies on forms of *visual or art historical reference.* Riley explained that "when I was thinking about the Marin Royal Hall, I began [by] looking at Frank Lloyd Wright in his Mayan revival period." She also noted that the massive tent camps in the North country took "images of the evacuation of Dunkirk for inspiration, as well as . . . historical references to tent cities made by refugees." Art directors use what I would term prospective archaeology (archival, analytic research) to generate (i.e., to speculate or project on) their plans for ostensibly "new" images for the series. After debating these visual references and style options, the design department aims to get the producers to sign off on a third form of specwork document: the *approved concept art*. Once this concept art is locked down in preproduction, the art department can proceed with the physical construction of sets.[35]

Finally, this chain of preapprovals precedes the making of a fourth key bit of preparatory work. That is, after the sets are built but before the shooting begins, production personnel often make then appraise a "lighting test." DPs, director, and camera units are not alone in appraising the lighting test. The final look of the production design can be only fully gauged by production designers after the sets are built and the lights rigged and tested. For example, lighting tests and reference photographs taken for them can also spur late-stage changes in the design or color scheme of the constructed sets. As such, they provide a final opportunity for department heads to double check and confirm their intended results before shooting begins. Personnel employ this chain of speculative prepwork in preproduction to confirm that all systems are go (fig. 4.10).

The regimented, lockstep approval of visual speculation work just described has been central in traditional preproduction for high-end projects. This is because appropriately budgeted legacy media production typically involves segregated craft specialization, a lengthy preproduction phase, and, often, unionized crews aggregating a large number of very narrow areas of expertise.[36] Coordinating all these narrow specialists requires a lot of cross-department appraisal and confirmation. This raises questions about the type and extent of prepwork required by high vs. low modes of production. High-end production relies on *incremental* stages of speculative prepwork that provide proof-of-concept benchmarks. This lockstep process entails a linear sequence of approvals, before executives will "sign off." The high costs and time-intensive physical preparation work that material crafts require (owing to both contract and trade habit) make a managed, incremental process of consent necessary.

By contrast, lower- or no-budget online maker projects are characteristically light on prepwork but heavy on specwork. For example, YouTuber consultants sometimes mentor aspirant creators to bring-forward their behind-the-scenes speculation onto the screen itself. This supposedly provides viewers with a better, more popular form of primary onscreen content. In such cases, brainstorming about production (i.e., talk about what the featured makers/influencers are trying to do) often becomes both the channel's primary content and a ticket to greater

FIGURE 4.10. Concept art approvals. Preproduction labor in high production is far less ephemeral than it is for aspiring online influencer-creators. This photo depicts two forms of concrete artifacts that bureaucratically control and regulate preproduction in HBO's *Game of Thrones:* (1) the architectural/art historical reference (a Frank Lloyd Wright interior); (2 and 3) examples of "concept art" that must be signed off on by producers and the art department before the big-budget production can proceed. Photograph: Public display illustrations from master class, Design Showcase West, Los Angeles, CA. © 2017, by J. Caldwell.

monetization. As a result, many YouTube channels have no discernable "backstage." One example of this make-your-spec-your-primary-content is online producer Curly Valasquez's approach to successful maker content that is both fast on its feet and improvisational. His workshop pitch to mentees for live improv: "five Latinos playing off of each other on camera."[37]

By favoring onscreen improv over costly physical prepwork, aspirant creators may be logically following the meager economics of low production. One "expert" online creator explains the premise of cutting preproduction preparation to up-and-comers: "First, at the start, don't expect to make any money."[38] After coming to grips with her adage about the meager prospects for making any money, the consultant cheerleads online makers to work fast and freely. This worry-about-money-later premise drives platform advice that aspirants must make proof-of-concept production before their goal of a "real production" can ever get off the ground.[39] These workshops-for-success basically describe and sanction the use of specwork as an aspirant creator's primary content. Even for screenwriters—who are told to augment their scripts by producing "sample scenes" and "sizzle reels"—screenwriting (by itself) is now apparently an insufficient career skill.

In general, low production's bare-bones labor economics devalue the physical dimension of craftwork. One human resource expert justifies these lowered no-need-for-craft-expertise expectations to rising YouTubers: "We never hired people who were qualified; just people who were hungry."[40] This platitude that "hunger" counts more than skills or qualifications works well in a room full of very young online makers and influencers. Yet the human resource myth that finding passionate newcomers is the secret to growing an online company also mirrors in some ways the mainstream industry's favored forms of labor exploitation (including unpaid internships and low-paid PA positions for hungry newcomers).

Not surprisingly, the need for online producers to eventually make money after they've "paid their dues" begins to push down the percentage and value of specwork and push up the value of worktime devoted to more traditional forms of prepwork. So success eventually requires more prepwork and less specwork, even among rising YouTubers. One expert, in a how-to panel entitled "Transitioning Your Channel into a Full-Time Business," brings a tough-love approach to any trainees who think "making it" is going to be easy. He lays out the mutually exclusive terms: "The amateur needs inspiration. The professional needs discipline."[41]

This push toward greater efficiency is sold to online aspirants as a key to success and greater revenues. Yet the imagined career advancement for aspirants being promised in this workshop here will also likely require additional training in the more traditional crafts of higher modes of production. One successful online producer mentors less successful makers by warning that the key to halting underperforming content requires rebooting their shooting methods so that they can emulate the factorylike workflows of *legacy* film and TV. His lesson to young creators outlines elementary steps toward achieving the discontinuous shooting and production scheduling typical not of cinema but of old-style TV:

> Shoot all of your videos in batch. . . . Instead of sitting down multiple times a week and shooting and editing, just sit down once. Draft ideas for all of your content for the month. Then sit down and shoot all of them for the month in front of the camera. Then set down and edit all of them. So rather than taking a couple of hours throughout the week, just consider taking a day or two and so that you can just crank them all out. So that you can upload all of those videos.[42]

In general, higher-budget film/TV values regiment specwork administered within a clearly demarcated preproduction phase. By contrast, low production's meager resources pressure YouTubers to skip preproduction entirely. Aspiring or emerging online maker-creators, however, may discover that the onscreen spec-improv used to launch their channel eventually has career limits. If aspirants ever want to "scale-up" and monetize their IP, genre, or web-show concept in order to cross over and make it in "real" film or TV, they will likely have to study (and eventually master) the hard-earned skills found in traditional preproduction prepwork. This traditionally included compartmentalized specwork (e.g., outlines, treatments, draft scripts, storyboards, concept art, shooting schedules, itemized budgets, lighting tests) managed within a linear, sequential workflow (writing, producing, production design, set-building, etc.). A range of online sites and videos mentor aspirant creators to learn these preproduction tasks. This creates an odd double bind. Even as experts warn YouTubers to accelerate their new video upload pace (which incentivizes improv and intangible specwork), their doublespeak warns the same frantic YouTubers to simultaneously emulate traditional film/TV workflows (which value planning and tangible prepwork) (fig. 4.11).

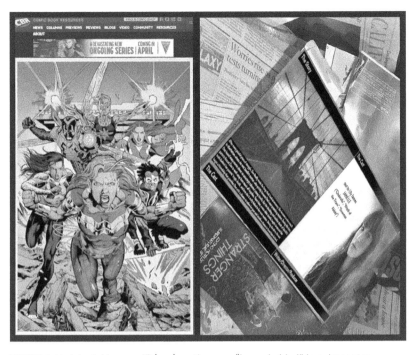

FIGURE 4.11. Adaptable spec IP (pro) vs. the spec "leave-behind" in a dumpster (aspirant). *Left:* A comic book series created as preemptive media-IP prototype for future transmedia franchise, created by veteran screenwriter/producer Felicia Henderson, WGA. *Right:* Photo of discarded office materials, including an anonymous aspiring filmmaker's "leave-behind" found in trash can. Photos: © 2020, by J. Caldwell.

Scarcity (Managing, Ensuring, and Monetizing Scarcity)

A fifth core pedagogical concern percolating through production's rhetoric today involves scarcity. How scarcity is managed or ignored may serve most to distinguish underresourced from overresourced creator worlds. This could be because scarcity has a formidable impact on economic outcomes for producers. Scarcity can provide economic leverage that applies to both prestigious high production and low production alike. Even in the streaming age of content excess, high-production franchises maintain their economic value by engineering scarcity of access to the franchise in some form. Netflix, Amazon Prime, and HBO do this to viewers via "premium" tiering, subscriptions, and the excessively protracted release over time of both series episodes and seasons. In effect, the prestige posture of waiting-for-seasons functions as a way to "ration experience." This calculated content rationing undercuts the perception of media excess signified by talk of "always-on" binge viewing and "on-demand" content. High production's rationing or holding-back impulse is also exemplified in the ways that producers preemptively distribute plot-points across successive weeks, months, and even years of an internationally coproduced premium series. I understand the *GoT* series story outline described earlier as an industrially *managed-scarcity-calendar* because HBO employs it to temporally ration the series and seasons to audiences.[43]

This high-production content rationing (maintaining scarcity) seems antithetical to the ubiquitous always-available low-production content found on the YouTube platform. In the latter, online makers radically disregard scarcity and are rewarded for pursuing the "360-degree" excessive personal disclosure popularized in social media. Platform pedagogy promotes *giving-it-away-for-free* habits as a key media creator strategy for making it. One production coach promotes the excessive social-sharing surround as a key to online production success: "Use it as an opportunity to push people to follow you on your other social profiles, maybe Instagram, or Snapchat, or maybe your Facebook page. Or whatever the case may be. Where it is easier for you to interact, and you are doing that more naturally throughout the week anyway."[44]

Content sharing can work like distribution scarcity Kryptonite. YouTube's antiscarcity economic logic is unequivocal: don't hold back; overproduce, overupload, overdistribute, and overmarket. VidCon made YouTube stars Rhett and Link's hit series *Good Mythical Morning* its keynote event, based on the following bold antiscarcity benchmarks for profitability: "1,500 Episodes. 12 Million Subscribers. 3.7 Billion Views."[45] The not-so-subtle lesson for eventual success: flood the platform with your quickly made and effusively shared content; then figure out how to add (and monetize) some form of scarcity later.

Yet this need for effusive disclosure in pushing one's personal content out to side platforms becomes problematic when the online maker eventually tries to make money from their once-free content. Many makers of free online media now argue that crowdsourcing and patronage will be the keys to eventual monetization and thus, hopefully, to monied careers. Crowdsourced funding and online patronage services also mentor YouTubers to establish graded levels of distinction for access. This gambit essentially restricts access to the creator's best content, which is locked into their online presence via a hierarchy of different price points. For example, Kickstarter teaches makers to commoditize their online content by creat-

FIGURE 4.12. The aspirant's new online business "two-step": crowdsource and disintermediate to grow (by giving content away for free); then abruptly reintermediate and "tier" via fan exclusives ("studio tours," gated content, and "behind-the-scenes" specials) to monetize content and build creator brand. Images: Offscreen still frames from Patreon.com promo and MovieMaker.com.

ing a reward-system for viewer-fans. Upfront contributions to a maker's production budget, for example, earn a fan a DVD, a signed photograph, a prop from the crowdfunded shoot. In effect, strict management of scarcity for the maker's content underscores and exploits a wide range of emotional investments in an emerging creator's subscriber or fan base.

This scheme acts like a new online business two-step (fig. 4.12). That is, aspirant creators are first told to crowdsource and disintermediate to

grow (by giving away content for free). Then they are mentored to reintermediate and tier their content via fan exclusives and premiums (via
studio tours and behind-the-scenes specials).

This scarcity-hierarchy (free content for the less motivated followers,
premium content for hyperfans) inflects another successful new form of
maker financing: Patreon. Invoking earlier forms of arts patronage (à la
the Medicis and the Borges and their subsidized artists), Patreon has
signed tens of thousands of aspiring, emerging makers and YouTubers
to receive support through online microfinancing. As with Kickstarter
and Indiegogo, Patreon works by making initially free or easier access
to an artist a kind of "gateway" consumption habit. More exclusive
access, however—through behind-the-scenes video tours, meet-and-
greets, and merch—requires more economic buy-in from each "sup-
porter" or donor in the microfinancing network.

In essence, the need to monetize for survival eventually constrains the
excessive sharing and free content gifting that first launched these social
media creators. It forces aspiring makers to eventually create and manage
a hierarchy of restrictions for access to their created content. Even though
low and high production differ in many ways, the ever-present pressures
of financing and profit mean that some form of scarcity must *eventually*
enter the picture in either production culture. Higher-budgeted prestige
projects build scarcity into their controlled "new seasons" and "window-
ing" or distribution business model. Yet even no-budget online creators
must eventually learn to invent and manage scarcity midstream. That is,
after launching their channel as a "start-up" via uploads-of-free-content,
they must subsequently learn to master scarcity as a self-management
scheme. This holds if they hope to eventually have profitable crossover
careers.

Trade talk and workshopping suggest that the five conceptual frameworks considered in this chapter (speed/velocity, scale/reach, size/mass,
specwork/prepwork, and scarcity/excess) are somehow fundamental for
both high and low twenty-first-century media creators. I initially likened this task of isolating such core principles as paralleling the goal of
traditional "poetics" (to discern the basic constituent parts of any artform). Yet I treat this core as de facto. The binary differences surrounding these five basics are not fundamental or innate to film- and media-
making. They are instead "rhetorical" and therefore socially constructed
within the two competing trade worlds.

THE ASPIRANT'S CROSSOVER DILEMMA

Why try to unpack the industrial construction of production fundamentals in this way? Stated simply, the trade mentoring, workshops, and pedagogy described in this chapter work to legitimize and normalize very specific ways of working. This package of norms for creating intensifies the stresses, contradictions, and precarities that creative labor must now expect to endure in production. Think about the secondary, embodied qualities that follow from the core principles: creator velocity, technical haste, distracted multitasking, self-defeating sharing, manic work speed. These experiential dimensions operate more like ADHD symptoms than professional or artistic guidelines. If not suspect, together they constitute career expectations that will be unsustainable for aspiring and rising creators over the long haul.

Ironically, this doublespeak, these self-defeating norms were once closely associated with innovation strategies in the arts (speculative imagination, previsualization, prototyping, pitching, and brainstorming). In online creator production, by contrast, such things behave more like institutional and economic bureaucracies than aesthetic principles. Industry's connective dimensions show themselves in the ways prepwork morphed into specwork, in the ways uploading excess displaced scarcity management for content distribution (and incomes), and in the ways platform pedagogy (aimed at aspirant online creators) collapses preproduction and postproduction into a singular improvisational unity. All of these tactics are sold to aspirants as creator "best practices" and as keys to success. Examining such claims (and practices) can clarify how production subgroups are embedded and why that embedding may seem legitimate and normal. The next two chapters shift our attention from spec labor embedding to examine the stressed, incentivized, or conflicted "folding" of labor groups that would not otherwise consent to partnering (coercive or not).

This doublespeak, therefore, represents the "aspirant's crossover dilemma." Platform worlds mentor talented young creators who may want big-screen film production careers not in quality screen-focused production aesthetic basics but in their antithesis. They promote instead frenzied antiaesthetic basics, which platforms nevertheless misleadingly (or simplistically) sell to aspirants as "keys to career success." As the televisioning chapter ahead details, aspirants seek out costly workshops and bureaucratic "influencer" schemes from social media that effectively undercut anyone pursuing bigger-screen professional goals. Aspirants trying to graduate from social media, that is, pay for administrative crossover means that necessarily do not lead to cinematic ends. But the doublespeak involved—between big-screen aspirations and how to get there—arguably creates better vocational candidates for careers in broadcasting and streaming management. This stark clash between "influencer" basics and "creator" basics sustains a predicament for young screencentric creators. Those contradictions between the online platform's requirement for bureaucratic expedience and the film industry's investment in production value often imbue the uploaded expressive work of aspirant creators with anxious, self-conflicted irresolution.

Folding

Stress Aesthetics, Compliance, Deprivation Pay

Reservoir Dogs was released in 1992. Four years before that
I was a clerk in a video store. . . . When I was in that store . . .
thinking about making films . . . renting films . . . (laughter),
I knew I was going to be a director. Everybody heard me say
that. I don't think anyone quite believed it. Some of you
might have heard that story. It's a little apocryphal. . . . The
"Sword of Damocles" . . .

—Quentin Tarantino addressing production designers at UCLA,
    June 4, 2016

In mentoring production and costume designers about his personal path-
to-success, Quentin Tarantino alluded to archaic biblical texts to explain
an early career anxiety that had conflicted him. He recalled that even as a
then-wannabe director, he had been tormented by one question: how
could he find production professionals "good enough" to help him survive and build out his personal cinematic vision? He further characterized
this anxiety about depending on other workers to "make it" as the "sword
of Damocles hanging over my head." Tarantino underscored his anxiety
about whether other pros had enough talent by repeating his mythic
Damocletian sword metaphor four times over fourteen minutes. I thought
this workshopping gambit odd. Why tell this tale just to share info across
professional job categories? And why call it "apocryphal"? What purpose
could this intercraft self-mythologizing via an oft-told Genesis tale (an
above-the-line "creative" speaking to below-the-line "workers") serve the
design craftworkers listening or the industry as a whole (fig. 5.1)?

Bruno Latour's and Howard Becker's sociological model for studying "shop-floor practice" was a formative influence in my production

FIGURE 5.1. Director gets all "apocryphal" in his production design workshopping with rising pros. Documentary drawing from DSW workshop, Los Angeles, CA. © 2016, by J. Caldwell.

culture thinking.[1] As a focus for qualitative fieldwork, the industrial overtones of a physical, findable "shop floor" may be comforting for scholars looking to find the self-evident boundaries of a walled-off location of work, a stable arena for the evidence they collect.[2] Yet the idea of a shop floor for online creation in the social media era will likely frustrate scholars. This is especially true for any scholars hoping to wall-off a clean "site" for research where some distinctive type of digital production takes place. Where is the online shop floor for digital makers/influencers? How do we find it? How do we identify justifiable parameters and boundaries for that room/space?

Answering these basic method questions about the extent, location, and geography of Hollywood's "shop floor" makes dealing with industry's explanatory discourses and communication back channels unavoidable. Why? We can only initially know about online production's physical or digital footprint via the unending hail of claims that online creators and industry make about where it is, how it works, and what it means. Physical production does indeed exist, but we usually engage and locate it via the rich array of back-channel messaging that issues from it.

How does industry theorize? How, specifically, does it think out loud? The industry speculates reliably on sets, in union halls, in the trades, and in public. Those assertions and exchanges of knowledge can help us formulate research questions that get closer to the organizational and cultural politics that grease the skids of any production. If production practices are indeed embedded within different production cultures, and these strata can fold, fracture, work together, or realign, then we need to pay closer attention to analyzing precisely how the interstrata or intertrade communication that spurs a fold or consensus takes place.

WHERE *IS* SHOP-FLOOR PRACTICE? BORDERS, CONTACT ZONES, AND FOLDING

When industry allowed me arm's-length interactions in my early research, I treated these not as failures to get "inside" the "real" industry but as loaded cultural contact zones—as sites that were arguably more ethnographically significant than industry's ostensible centers. Reason? Contact zones are culturally charged precisely because they are so habitually managed by trade convention and routine corporate business practice. This means that semiaccessible contact zones (trade shows, union meetings, technical demos, how-to panels, summits, Q&A's, bake-offs, shoot-outs, speed-dating) involve overproduced disclosures by industry, whereas industry's inaccessible inside centers (network boardrooms, A-list creative agencies, studio executive offices, financing meetings, deal meetings) ensure underproduced disclosures and subsequent, related misdirection via publicity. As such, studying contact zones cannot be reduced to relaying some truth mouthed by the industry there. It means researching how culture is overproduced in the very collision of interests that create that contact.

Precisely because the trade informants I observed lower down the food chain often gushed about conditions in production with less second-guessing and self-censoring, I had much richer material to work from, to distill, to parse out, to shake down. In addition, these trade disclosures, as I looked on, were often made obliquely to others (fellow-workers, potential clients, colleagues, customers). These oblique disclosures provided much more context in my attempts to understand the critical logic of production's shop-floor practice. Contact zones were also loaded with suggestions about how and why parties with different interests chose to partner, chose to pull in the same direction.

I reasoned at the time that my contact zone approach in production culture fit within a complex systems framework. Yet in retrospect, the contact-zone model may still have been too reductive. This is because finding a "site" for contact either presupposes a static map of a Hollywood island bounded by a vast outside societal surround, or it assumes a linear-flow model, in which the scholar or critic moves through a contact "gate," from industry "outsides" to "insides" and back again. Neither this linear-entry model nor the static-island paradigm seems to fully express how complex embedded systems work.

Both paradigms—the fixed borderlines presupposed by industry islands and the contact gates needed to process industry entrants—fail to exemplify two key dimensions of complex systems: first, that such systems are "emergent" (producing unanticipated behaviors that cannot be predicted by the system's initial parts); second, that such systems are "hierarchical" (a defining characteristic of complex ecosystems). I puzzled over how I could adequately research those unanticipated emergent behaviors in production (like abrupt changes in long-standing tradition) while factoring in the system's hierarchical dimensions.

This book argues that something more dynamic takes place in these industrial contact zones and borderlines than just interaction—something I will term *folding,* a process I will unpack in this chapter.[3] In the material world, folding is easily recognized in deformations of the sedimentary layers that geologists examine. That geological variant of folding does resonate with the "embedding" model I am using in this book. But I am mostly adopting the term from computer programming. In that field, folding (also termed compressing, reducing, aggregating) describes how a higher-order function in software hides the code of a much more complex data structure underneath. Yet it does so in a way and with keys built-in that allow the program to recreate the code on command, when needed. This "when needed" or "on command" ability allows the software or system to recursively reprocess constituent parts that repeatedly make and unmake the fold.[4]

The Windows and MacOS user interfaces offer basic long-standing examples of successfully programmed and folded operating systems. Their screen interfaces are both simple looking (on the surface) but immensely folded (underneath). Ideally, their screens' interface design seems logical enough that many users deem using it intuitive. Yet things can only be elegantly simple and self-evident on the surface if the sophisticated folding by programmers succeeds at segmenting, hiding, and subordinating the much more highly complicated code underneath. For computer programmers, this results in code that can be endlessly folded and unfolded seamlessly, without user awareness. I study serially employed film and TV work and workers who are invisible most of the time but occasionally are not. They labor in an industry that makes

FIGURE 5.2. Chain of command normalizes folds. The creator system's industrial embedding and interacting dimensions go well beyond the overt, linear Director→DP→Dolly Grip chain of command evident in the above new-tech camera demo and workshop. Photo: Melnitz soundstage, UCLA. © 2014, by J. Caldwell.

them systematically appear and disappear in a way that evokes folding. I want to understand why and how this folding and refolding became normalized as a production business practice in part because while folding code is "painless" for the computer code, creative labor folding is embodied and can involve considerably more stress (fig. 5.2).

Most of the time, stable industries like film and television betray neither their hierarchical stresses nor acute disclosures of unsanctioned information. The static, walled-in symbolism of the conventional soundstage and studio lot can short-circuit critical awareness of either the emergent or hierarchical dimensions that those buildings cloak. This deeply embeds those dimensions within the system. Yet production's interacting dimensions, layers of consent, and industrial embedding go well beyond the overt Director→DP→Dolly Grip chain of command evident in the new-tech camera demo and workshop depicted in figure 5.2.

If stable industries house and normalize their folds, where might scholars begin research? Cases where stable chains of command are broken offer scholars opportunities to find and unpack system folds.

FIGURE 5.3. One way to locate folds: rogue antimarketing. Here nonunion VES picketers protest antilabor studio moves and tax-funded film subsidies that allow US transnational production companies to outsource FX work to other countries. Photo: Hollywood, CA. © 2015, by J. Caldwell.

Unsanctioned disclosures during labor conflicts, for example, provide scholars with one way to pinpoint and start contact-tracing a fold. Figure 5.3 shows nonunion VES picketers protesting antiunion studio moves and tax-funded film subsidies that allow US transnational production companies to outsource FX work in other countries.

I have tried over the last two decades to make sense of the vast network of anonymous, remotely outsourced workers, and the endless types of subcompanies, and subspecializations that now make up what I term contemporary production's paraindustries. Tangling with these paraindustrial firms and their shadow academies in the trades pushed me to ask a question: how do these vast and different shadow practices cohere in something as big and as ostensibly unified as "the" film and television industry? It clearly takes a lot of trade chatter and cultural expression to transform something as fundamentally splintered as film and television production into something as unified, solid, and singular as "the industry."

The very cultural and discursive overselling of media as bounded and locatable gave away the lie of industry as unitary. In tackling this question (why workers rhetorically affirm unity in the face of splintering and labor disaggregation), I noted among other things that collective consent behaviors were a common trait among the shadow workers and paraindustries at which I was looking. These disaggregated workers largely affirmed the rightness of the system as a whole. The old standby Marxist explanations—that capital exploits and erases this kind of "alienated" labor to extract its "surplus" value for profit—didn't seem to fully explain the overdetermined consent by workers that I witnessed.

By consent, I mean the willingness and the ways that the film and TV workers to whom I talked justified, defended, and rationalized the system as a whole. These affirming theories often became justifications for the workers' own precarity, aspiration, or perpetual serial underemployment. Most workers, that is, were voluntary believers in the system, not "dupes" taken-in by it. Early on, I considered simply explaining this talk as a version of Gramsci's "hegemony" (the process by which subordinates misperceive the interests of those dominating them as their own). Yet I have tried not to predetermine or steer fieldwork in this direction or to simply collect evidence to illustrate the general theory.

Think about how two very different anecdotes from production normalize worker experiences despite severe industrial hierarchy. Both offer prime examples of how strategic emotional labor can be on creative projects. The first—something I term *method crewing*—seems benign, visionary even. Filming never offers a clean starting point that leads in a straight line to an onscreen end product. Workers are themselves preproduced, through recursive feedback, which they process before and during production. Often, this preproduction of the worker is unintended, latent, or unacknowledged. At other times, directors employ emotional labor to indulge the crew in calculated collective self-reflection:

> The other surprises were what an unusually special set Quentin runs, unlike anything I have ever seen. There are no cel [*sic*] phones, no (video monitors). During prep he had [film] screenings for cast and crew. Where he shows . . . he owns the new Beverly Cinema, on Beverly, and where they are still showing on the weekends, but he was specifically showing movies screened in Los

Angeles between 1968 and 1971. And the first one I went to I thought there would be a few people. But it was completely jammed. . . . We shot on film, and we had projected dailies. And when were the last times anyone had that? And if you remember, at least when I worked on films with dailies early in my career, that it was only for department heads and you were lucky if you were invited. He would invite everybody to the dailies, so that the assistants and craft service and everyone was there. (Costume designer Arianne Phillips [CDG], "Sketch to Screen" panel, Copley Center for the Study of Costume Design, UCLA, Feb. 8, 2020)

Phillips describes here the behavior modification ritual her director employed (below-the-line workers screening dailies) to steer production crew thinking. This ritual (of shared, conceptual, reflection on style and culture) parallels and complements the crew's actual physical work on-set. It is only "off-the-clock" in the narrow sense of the term. This use of group cinephilia as team-building ritual also oddly evokes one gold standard in actor performance: "method acting." Without citing Stanis-lavski, Tarantino adapts a method approach for his below-the-line tech-nical workers. Here—to normalize the many folds in his production hier-archy all the way down to "craft services"—Tarantino rewards complete emotional identification with the filmmaker's personal vision of 1970s cinema. In channeling worker identification, this managerial approach (the calculated alignment of disparate crew views into the singular vision of the director) might be better termed "method crewing."

Whereas the costume designer Phillips justifies the team-building exercise in a way that affirms the masculine emotional work of the auteur's vision, a staffer at a creative agency describes a pervasive form of women's emotional labor normalized in production. One interview underscores the ways de facto female avatars manage folds through gendered emotional labor: "Essentially, you are the face of the boss. . . . It's a lot of just thinking about social cues. Thinking about how to make everybody sort of happy. You have to keep the boss happy. But also to keep the clients happy. And to keep all of the assistants you are manag-ing happy. And it's just about managing all of that."[5] This is CAA not daycare. Considerable emotional labor from women is often employed to cut the executive patriarchy the slack it wants to remain flexible and decisive, as the young executive assistant here indicates. Yet the gen-dered workplace buffer that results may also give media patriarchs a tactical DMZ to vent, "act-out," and "behave badly" when needed. From a "MeToo" perspective, this system incentivizes underlings to try to master their performances as office surrogates to protect their (sometimes abusive or self-destructive) bosses. Production offices seldom exhibit the Disney-like "happiest place on earth" ethos that even loyal but abused worker-avatars sometimes accept or justify.

Given explanations like these, I wondered what else was normalizing this system beyond either personal rationales or managerial anecdote. To study collective and emergent forces means shifting the lens we use to look at the effusive, changing rhetoric and discourse of a trade. This shift affirmed my belief that production studies gains by keeping "culture" squarely in its "industries" sights. Cultural frameworks provide nuance in the analyses of collective consent behaviors, compliance, and the partnering politics that help define production's subfirms and contract workers. Rather than reduce them to background chatter or accept them as direct explanations, the discourses and embedded texts issuing from compliance can be approached as cultural problems. Such expressions can reveal far more about the embedded system than merely how media content is made. Because industry so adeptly congeals its trade identities into provisionally unified enterprises, scholars would do well not to segregate physical production per se from production culture that surrounds and comments on it.

TYPES OF FOLD BEHAVIORS

Before turning to more acutely stressed folds, I survey four general types of work-world behaviors that involve cooperating, consenting, and partnering. These cultural rituals and expressions include crew idea-sharing, hive building, disintermediation, and workshopping.

Crew Idea-Sharing

Unlike top-down managerial interventions (i.e., Tarantino's method-crewing) habitual work interactions aimed at lateral team-building can contribute to folds. These interactions between crafts or across subsectors might include, say, the human interplay between an equipment consultant and an editor (both seeking a competitive tech advantage) or a trade publisher and a featured creator trendsetter (seeking public exposure). Institutional negotiations take place regularly, both on sets and in intertrade contact zones, where production groups interact to negotiate consensus. I consider this haggling to pull in the same direction as trade folding (a dynamic impacting the system as a whole). More than simply meetings or adjacent interests, folds involve negotiations,

FIGURE 5.4. The DP's speculating craft. Even if it is posed as collective or reciprocal, effective idea-sharing within the crew "team" (*if* solicited) means feeding the higher-up with ways to make the director's vision more singular. John Bailey, ASC, explains the deferential diplomacy that rising cinematographers need to master. Photos of John Bailey, ASC, in Kodak UCLA Cinematographer-in-Residence Workshop, directed by DP Bill McDonald. © 2010, by J. Caldwell.

interactions that unintentionally or by design manage or oversee emerging work behaviors. One side effect is that as folding manages emergent behavior it can reaffirm some existing hierarchy in the complex embedded production system as a whole.

Even if crews act collectively as teams, complex embedded hierarchies drive much of the sharing, give-and-take behaviors within the team. Conventional film production systems place the director, regardless of personal disposition, into a self-focusing position. Cinematographers who do not grasp this interprofessional hierarchy well enough, or do not master the other-centered diplomacy it requires, likely have less success than some DPs like John Bailey, ASC (fig. 5.4). Bailey works to persuade aspirant mentees that even ostensibly reciprocal interactions implicitly need to focus on ways to meet the needs of the higher-up:

> Just how do you go in as a cinematographer and meet with the director . . .?" [As a cinematographer] you have to pitch it [to the director] in a certain way. "Oh, great script. I really loved it. This scene was terrific." No. You need to have some understanding, obviously not fleshed out the way I'm trying to [say], but something. You just have to evaluate the situation: Where's the opening? Because directors don't want to know about you. They want to know about their movie and what you're going to bring to their movie. You just have to be able to evaluate the situation, how much of an opening is there, when will the opening happen. You really need to key off what they have to say, and some directors will have almost nothing. They'll immediately engage you. (John Bailey, ASC, Kodak

Cinematographer-in-Residence Workshop #2, directed by DP Bill McDonald, UCLA, April 19, 2010)

Constant, incremental pitching between embedded personnel is scattered necessarily throughout production's craft-labor infrastructure. Filmmakers often leverage interactions by asserting that the meeting is a win-win and reciprocal—despite the fact that the whole point is to enable the higher-ups to mine, take, or apply ideas from subordinates, as needed. For the crew, staged reciprocity is an act to be performed well. One effect of a fold is that one or the other of the interacting parties change or conform to the interests they collectively represent.

Hive Building (Third Parties)

Unlike the crew interactions described above, the fate of production equipment companies—like Red, AVID, Adobe, and GoPro—rests largely on how big they can grow their respective user bases among filmmakers, including postproduction workers. Just ask defunct Panavision what happens to companies that do not prioritize expanding their network of loyal production workers. Yet this always-expand imperative forces these third-party tech companies to constantly dance around a contradiction built into the corporate technical ecosystem paradigm. Specifically, they must resolve conflicting needs to (a) expand by monetizing a "closed" equipment ecosystem (all users locked inside of the brand) even as (b) they consider whether to add new young creators and other third-party firms to the collective and thus scale-up the Red or GoPro user "hive."

Panavision did not grow its intentionally closed ecosystem enough (i.e., you could not own their gear and, if you rented it, were forced to use Panavision's lenses and accessories). This eventually led to hive-collapse among the brand's pro user group (and repeated debt restructurings to avoid bankruptcy). Upstarts Red and GoPro took different approaches to build out loyalty in their tech hives. Figure 5.5 shows GoPro representatives lending every item in their extensive equipment inventory (all the "bells and whistles") to film students in Los Angeles. The firm made this "not-for-profit" in-kind donation to fund a two-day "GoPro" "Shootout" and "Film Festival" for the students. In effect they actively folded new users into their hive through an inclusive distinction-awarding cultural ritual. That is, GoPro enacted corporate altruism and cultural patronage (rather than marketing) to expand its reach among young, early adopters. For more than three decades, AVID

FIGURE 5.5. Altruistic culture-acting to manage a closed-vs.-open tech hive. Here GoPro intermediaries donate every item in their equipment inventory (all the "bells and whistles") for a two-day "GoPro" "Shootout" and "Film Festival" for film students in Los Angeles. Photos: © 2017, by J. Caldwell.

and Adobe have also danced around the problem of how to fold in enough third-party "synergies" to grow profitably without losing control of their hives to invasive third-party species (as defunct Media100 and CMX did) (fig. 5.5).

Replacing Intermediaries

Intermediates (reps, managers, agents, MCNs, Instagram, LinkedIn, etc.) can play a role in folding a previously disaggregated group of craft specialists into a cohesive aggregate (a creative team, a package) during a shoot. One payoff for rising filmmakers who eventually make it to jobs in mainstream, unionized production is that their intermediaries and mode of representation tend to stabilize. Representation becomes less about Facebook or LinkedIn than about Local 600. The IATSE contracts governing one sound mixer (fig. 5.6, right) in effect lock down the union local as his official intermediary. Yet this unionized representation also reduces the mixer's identity into below-the-line "worker" (albeit one who is adequately paid). This stable system operates in stark contrast to the maker/influencer world we will encounter in chapters 6 and 8, where

FIGURE 5.6. Human contact can intermediate the drag inherent in crew conventions. *Left:* A VR camera rig is demoed to film directors at the Directors Guild of America, Los Angeles, CA. *Right:* Craft unions minimize intermediaries to manage folds. Union sound mixer on location film shoot, Los Angeles, CA. Photos: © 2015 and 2020, by J. Caldwell.

platforms fuel a manic disintermediation-to-reintermediation process. Creative agencies (like CAA and UTA), that is, in the free-for-all of the platform era, prowl and harvest widely to find promising aspirants. The goal: to reintermediate rising social media-makers as potential above-the-line "creators." These exceptional, trending winners should stand out from the vast majority of online makers who continue to work for free or for minimal revenues on YouTube (fig. 5.6).

Workshopping (as Crowdsourced Self-Hacks)

A final example, which will be detailed in chapter 6, involves trade-show workshops, where desperate YouTube creators pay premium fees to learn how to "hack" the fickle YouTube/Google algorithm that is supposed to "discover" them. Why is this mythical algorithm so important? Because the success of all TikTok creators and YouTubers depends on their prompt discovery by the platform. That, in turn, depends on how well or quickly a creator's newly uploaded video creations and channels are discovered, seen, liked, and followed by viewers. Google constantly changes the criteria used in its YouTube algorithm without ever telling or explaining the change to its millions of creators-users (otherwise known as their "partners"). Why is the existence of this contact zone workshop between creator and platform odd? Rather than simply explaining to YouTuber registrants how and why the platform changed its algorithm, "helpful" YouTube hosts offer revenue-generating "workshops" led by supposed outside "experts" who claim—through triangulation or trial and error—to have cracked the code of the platform's new algorithm. The workshop demo, purchased via a "registration fee," promises to help creators grasp the rapidly changing secrets to having their uploads discovered and followed by others. The stakes are very high, since everyone in the room knows that the shape-shifting algorithm is precisely the career-making or career-ending benchmark they will need to master. Mastering it promises to trigger sponsorship, more revenue, and merchandizing deals for creators. Based on this platform pedagogy, vast numbers of creators change the way they make videos as they in turn try to periodically hack the YouTube search system that hosts them.

What function does this folding fulfill? The aspiring creators in the staged-hack in effect serve as YouTube's experimental subjects, surveilled by the platform. These informal, de facto "red-teams" (consultants mentoring aspirants in "how-to-succeed" workshops) provides preemptive behavioral evidence that allows the platform to advance and continue altering its algorithm even further. The process is endless. The beauty of the arrangement for the platform? YouTube gets its experimental lab rats (workshop participants) to pay YouTube to serve as unwitting volunteers. This poses workshoppers as consenting to be surveilled as experimental data inputs. This folding—staged as a workshop between ostensible ecosystem partners—does not just function as a form of "self-hacking" for the platform; it is also a veiled but lucrative R&D ritual that allows the platform to continuously modify its search algorithm with richer insights donated from the system's most motivated users. Edgy aesthetic talk by the online video creators in the workshops I observed cloaked the experimental data the participants provided the platform. Such consent behaviors normalize the ostensibly symbiotic (but clearly asymmetrical) relationship that favors the host to proceed as a "partnership."

ANCHORING FOLDS (INERTIAS THAT RESIST AND STABILIZE CHANGE)

The examples of system folding provided thus far suggest one proposition about embedded production systems: changes in socioprofessional behavior and collective consent triggered in contact zones and folds often result from a clash of stabilizing or "inertial" industrial forces (or interests) and disruptive "aspirational" labor pressures (or interests). This tension is not entirely unrelated to the continuity-vs.-change paradigm that Bordwell, Thompson, and Staiger located in classical Hollywood's "mode-of-production" and that Tom Schatz outlined in Hollywood's film "genres."[6] The dramatic difference, however, is that the "inertial-vs.-aspirational" logic of industrial folding described in this book is not enabled by Fordist physical-economic infrastructure reminiscent of the "classical era" (soundstages, labs, unions, long-term contracts, vertical integration). It seems spurred, rather, by highly malleable post-Fordist cultural-economic behaviors (social media, gig work, extreme outsourcing, transmedia, labor disorganization, vertical disintegration–platform reintegration).

I liken the continuity-vs.-change problem in production research to "border studies" in other fields. So much of contemporary film/TV production now takes place outside of traditional studio/network infrastructure that any fair account of those industries must also pay attention to the vast amounts of subordinate labor, ideas, candidates, technologies, intermediaries, finance, and facilitators that now circulate mostly in industry's borderlands. After all, the industry has long recruited from these peripheral aspirational and feeder sectors to do business. Those on production's borders come from a diverse range of professional and economic contexts. Border crossers range from newcomers and the underemployed, to trainees and interns, to serial careerists, to workers seeking hyphenate careers. Historical change has come to film and TV in part because of the steady stream of these newcomers, who always carry the potential to destabilize the way things have long been done by the old guard. To clarify how change has been sought and resisted in folds, I will describe four examples of inertial resistance to change: human contact, geographical anchoring, creator craft metrics, and sunk costs (gear and labor).

Human contact. New firms often stage face-to-face events to woo and steer entrenched labor groups in their direction. In these, new proprietary technical innovators can employ the human touch in socioprofessional settings to earn and fold consent across established, embedded labor sectors. At one of these new tech days, a third-party firm demos a new camera rig (modeled by an anthropoid/cyborg) to film directors at the Directors Guild of America, Los Angeles (see fig. 5.6, left).

Geographic anchoring. Socioprofessional wooing by adjacent technology firms may explain one side of the system's binary (diplomatic

FIGURE 5.7. Geographic centers anchor, stabilize, and manage folds. *Top:* Subfirm MIZ "Innovation Center" adjacent to historic German Babelsberg media agglomeration. *Bottom:* Promo for hi-tech movie set construction at Barrandov Studios solicits producers and lesser partner firms who need help with industrial heavy lifting. Photos: Potsdam and Prague. © 2016, by J. Caldwell.

arm-twisting for gradual change), but what of the other force, the "inertial" (stabilizing or resistant) side within a fold? Geographic resources (not just labor agreements and traditional production markets) can also provide inertia capable of managing frictions or securing a fold. Located in one large and historic German Babelsberg media agglomeration, subfirm MIZ (fig. 5.7, top) acts out its brand as an "Innovation Center" alongside old-style "film" and "TV" industries. This brings positive spillover effects to the agglomeration. Alternatively, Barrandov Studios (fig. 5.7, lower) employs a visual ad to promote its hi-tech movie-set-construction capacity. The goal: to solicit lesser firms outside the studio to lease, coproduce, or partner with the studio, since border firms typically lack the considerable material resources that Barrandov has and that are needed for heavy lifting in the production industry. These "agglomerations" (Scott) or "centers" of "media capital" (Curtin) persist over time because their anchoring footprints facilitate all kinds of controlled synergies and manageable innovation among firms.

Creator craft metrics. Beyond the anchoring infrastructure of soundstages, labs, and top-down studio management, established professional groups also bring frictions that resist change. Personnel with vested interests in a stable production system zealously guard against change and work hard to fold newcomers into conventionalized creator practice. It is worth considering, for example, the preemptive ways that careers are frontloaded and managed to see how this inertia-vs.-aspiration tension plays out. Media industries are creatures of habit, whose journeymen seek rationality and predictability. This attracts a creator world where artistic production is habitual and often explained or treated by practitioners as natural law. For example, screenwriters (plus script coaches and professional mentors) often succeed to the extent that they have internalized a factorylike metric behind all film storytelling. For them, successful scripts should always exemplify this governing metric:

> Structurally, in features, they hit certain plot points. You've got the "hook." The "inciting incident." You've got the 10-minute point. At 17-minutes you've got the "central questions established." At 30-minutes, at the end of "act one," you're heading out of the "old world" into the "new." At the 45-minute point is the first step toward meeting the "central question" goal. At "mid-point" there's a reversal. Then there's a "false-ending" around 75 pages. Then a little poignant point. That's how all movies are structured. Roughly. They're off on these page counts only a very small amount of time. When you are seeing [a film] in a theater with a stop-watch, you can mark the "central question," you can mark these things." And that is tremendous. Everybody thinks: "that makes all movies the same." No. It's an amazing map to help you write toward these plot points. (Kelly Fullerton, WGA, TV writer/producer, interview by author, UCLA, April 7, 2016)

The strict page-number rule here acts like a collective inertial guidance system, one that helps fold writers into lockstep with the complex system as a whole. Executives often say they are looking for imaginative personal "vision" in writers and for projects "from the heart." Yet the community of aspiring and rising professionals has capably reverse-engineered Hollywood's quasi-factorylike metric—that industry actually wants—into a formula. This compliance (writers who internalize then replicate industry's story metric) enables agents and executives to

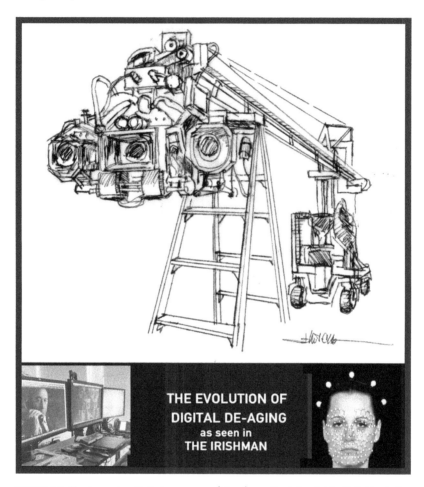

THE EVOLUTION OF
DIGITAL DE-AGING
as seen in
THE IRISHMAN

FIGURE 5.8. Hardware inertia helps manage (close) creative labor folds. Outsider indie software pushes-back to counter big-screen habits and open up labor folds. *Top:* Drawing of expensive camera rig used on Martin Scorsese's *The Irishman. Bottom:* Offscreen stills from *The Irishman* "making-of." © 2020, by J. Caldwell.

simplistically behave and claim the opposite. Executives, that is, often disavow formula, at least in public, claiming they know "intuitively" and "spontaneously" how to "pick winners" from an oversupply of pitches and scripts. Many in production deemphasize how internalized aesthetic formulas provide a rational metric (a convention-based inertia) that studios can more efficiently identify and take to the bank.

Sunk costs (gear and labor). The rigid page-location inertia in the writer's craft just cited is conceptual. But other forms of inertia are material and tied to the material tools that filmmakers use. In 2019 on the feature *The Irishman,* Netflix, Scorsese, and ILM went to extreme ends to jury-rig a Rube Goldberg multilens camera crane that could "de-age" its A-list actors (fig. 5.8). Netflix flaunted this lumbering camera-FX platform as an artistic milestone, as engineering performance art. Marketing sold the heavy gear-based-art featured as a viable alternative to cheaper, less skilled software tricks. The studio postured the crane as a guarantor of big-screen values since it required traditional Hollywood soundstages and camera crews.

Yet not long after the trades praised Scorsese's lumbering homage to heavy big-screen cinema equipment in the streaming era, upstart trade sites like "No Film School" mocked Scorsese's and Netflix's A-list industrial pretentions, lauding, instead, an anti-Hollywood alternative by a digital DIY insurgent.[7] In this take-the-big-boys-down-a-notch essay, a wise-guy indie FX artist demoed a "better" quality homemade version of the same Scorsese scenes on YouTube using cheap software. Using a side-by-side, shot-by-shot comparison, No Film School demonstrated why the home version was superior to Scorsese's. Some creators (Netflix/Scorsese) use traditional hardware to resist or stay on top of historical change. This effectively folds crews into line who aim to work on big-budget shoots. In this odd case, the crew used heavy archaic tools to achieve lightweight digital effects. At the same time, aspirational outsiders—also seeking trade support and recognition—employed widely available software to break yet another of Hollywood's heavy-handed attempts to fold labor into long-standing workday habit.

INCENTIVES TO FOLD (STRESS AESTHETICS AND SYMBOLIC PAYROLL SYSTEMS)

We fall into line in production, we partner despite bad behavior, we disregard inequity not just because producers incentivize us to do so. Our philosophies of craft also feed into our compliance as workers. We normalize our folding in the ways we self-justify precarious creative labor as a worthy pursuit. Social media creators often rationalize their stress to showcase their aspirational creativity. Yet stress is more than an anxiety disorder stimulating makers and influencers to create and innovate. In fact, stress aesthetics has a deep history and can be understood as a well-practiced, industrially justified employment scheme. Creator stressing is a form of folding that comes with a considerable, problematic history.

Stress schemes in production predate social media platforms by many decades, and this bureaucratic prehistory still speaks volumes about the conflicted labor climate that aspirants and online professionals alike now face.[8] Why is this creative labor system so resilient and persistent? Why and how do production workers accept it as normal?

The working conditions and production cultures of Hollywood are tightly and interactively woven together with film and television working conditions in many other parts of the world. In *Production Culture,* I argued that the de facto mission of Hollywood production's "race to the bottom" in the new millennium and the age of user-generated content has been "to acquire content for little or nothing and to get everyone to work for free."[9] Consider how this mantra resonates with the following disclosure by an Indian production worker, who describes current working conditions for VFX "artists" in South Asia. A vast, endless trainee assembly line helps global film and media production firms bid low and win contracts:

> There is a disturbing trend in India for the past couple years . . . where VFX artists are forced to work for "experience" or "goodwill" . . . in "apprentice" or "training" positions. These apprenticeships usually last for a period ranging between 3–9 months and are generally unpaid. Some companies at the end of the term of these apprenticeships cut loose the interns stating reasons of "insufficient quality" or the more popular "We just don't have any projects going on right now . . . We'll call you." OR They might consider extending your training to an extra three months or more, if you choose to remain unpaid for the duration. . . . You will have to repeat the whole process when you join another studio, because experience certificates and references are non-existent here (unless the studio exec is your close personal friend/relation). It appears that cheap labor isn't good enough, now the labor is required to be free . . . the end result being that the companies, get an almost inexhaustible pool of FREE Labor, allowing them to turn essentially a profit without Cost of production overhead in terms of labor.[10]

According to this VFX artist, the explicit offer here is "Congratulations. You can apprentice at our transnational VFX firm as long as you cover all costs, including your salary."

When unpaid production workers (or their families) are required to cover all their living expenses, they are in effect subsidizing their corporate employers for the "privilege" of working for them for free. This odd self-subsidizing labor scheme guarantees that production work—in Hollywood, Europe, or anywhere, for that matter—will continue to migrate endlessly across national borders in attempts to find new pools of lower-cost labor aspirants. What sort of production worker can compete or bid against this sort of implicit indentured servitude? Notably, the high-tech professional who wrote the prescient account quoted above, lamenting his company's shift from "cheap" labor to "free" (or self-subsidized) labor, works in India for the transnational media firm Prime Focus. Prime Focus distributes and harvests creative work transnationally. It does this by segmenting and delegating various components of its larger big-budget VFX projects (conceptual art, design, animation, texture mapping, rendering, etc.) across the company's network of international operations, from its headquarters in London and Los Angeles.[11]

Transnational media companies do not limit their new de facto "no pay for creative work" policy to a few locales either; indeed, the exploitation practices described above take place in various parts of the world.[12] Nor are these no-pay-for-work policies invisible. Far from it. The notion that many filmmakers and working pros often work for free is so commonplace that production trades publish features that teach their readers how to compete in a market where competitors are willing to freely give-away their corporate productions (for some imagined, possible future consideration). The scheme echoes in headline stories entitled: "How to Compete with Filmmakers Who Work for Free." Videomaker lays out the logic that charging for work is hard but makes sense in the long term: "That doesn't mean you shouldn't be compensated for you time and skill. . . . Fear of losing a client can make it tempting at times to cut your rates or even waive your fee to woo a client. Sadly, that won't keep you in business. This article aims to give you some strategies to help you compete with free."[13] Yet in urging its indie production readership to find ways to actually charge money for their creative work, the proposed package of work habits feels like an exception that proves a nonpaying norm. Interestingly, the trade column cites as a badge of honor that the author himself has worked for free. This gives the pros who mentor aspiring workers on career success the metaphysical aura of a Twelve-Step facilitator.

While a political-economic critique of corporate conglomeration certainly fits the bleak transnational scenario outlined above, I want to push beyond such a macrocritique in order to understand the local conditions and cultural scenarios that enable, facilitate, and legitimize our increasing shift to blackmailed or unpaid creative work. Knowing that such work practices are bad fails to explain why they persist. Closely mining the local work practices and cultural economies that prop these schemes up reveals a great deal about something more counterintuitive:

how and why participants in these exploitative environments facilitate and fuel their own economic self-exploitation.

Three broad-based interrelated circumstances normalize the habit of creating and working professionally for free: first, the perpetuation of underfunding and deprivation conditions as commonplace in production conditions; second, the pervasive rationalization of "stress aesthetics" to demonstrate exceptionalism, a posture adopted to justify production deprivation within difficult circumstances; and third, the shift from financial payroll systems to complex cultural and symbolic payroll systems (something I refer to as "deprivation pay" and "compensatory production"). These well-oiled pay schemes effectively prop up and give substance and credibility to claims that stressed conditions somehow facilitate artistically recognizable outcomes. This chapter attempts to map such trends across three connected levels: the industrial, the cultural, and the economic.

Industrially and internationally, deprivation and stress are ever present in production owing to either claims or realities of underfunding. Even beyond DIY, "low-budget," or "no-budget" filmmaking, blockbuster films regularly exceed their budgets and run deficits, making trade accounts of on-set activities sometimes read like corporate soap operas or fighting pits. Culturally, production communities respond to this industrial condition in various ways. Some accept stressed conditions without labor resistance or critical metacommentary. Workers in other sectors critique stressed conditions through paratextual metacommentary or anonymous online worker pushback. Still other groups conspicuously rationalize and justify production stress in public. For apologists, stress need not be a debility but can serve as a profitable catalyst for, or badge underscoring, production innovation. In the section that follows, I survey industry's justifications for stress and examine how those rationales connect meager production economics with screen aesthetics. Much attention has been directed toward "precarious" creative labor in recent years. Yet much less attention has been directed toward the cultural apparatus that props up these conditions. What, specifically, are the symbolic "pay" schemes that rationalize stress aesthetics as a profitable "value-added" economic condition? That is the focus in the remainder of this chapter.

Industry Conditions and Cultural Justifications (Normalizing Rationales)

Beyond the high-end Indian VFX work described above, mainstream Hollywood and European transnational coproductions also make excuses for the stressed conditions of production. This is justified by blaming stiff market competition, technical obsolescence, or the low bidding needed to attract transnational films or series to shoot or edit in one's home country. Yet these mainstream apologists share some counterintuitive affinities with various supposedly more "independent" or "local" contemporary film production practices in both Europe and the Americas. These odd-couple affinities come in ironic parallels with the suffering, "against-all-odds" rhetoric of various "countercinemas," including Espinosa's "imperfect cinema" championed in Third World filmmaking, the manifesto-based Dogme 95 movement in Denmark, and its extension, the "Advance Party" film production initiative in Scotland.[14] Mette Hjort has shown how and why Dogme 95 and the Advance Party have succeeded or failed by converting and individuating their "vows of chastity" and "small cinema" aesthetic principles into global marketing initiatives.[15] But Hjort also finds production constraints fundamental to the artistic success of many "small-nations cinemas."

Petr Szczepanik explains, in practical terms, that production stress was the norm and unexceptional for many European cinemas, "from their beginnings and especially after the coming-of-sound when studio rentals sky-rocketed." To illustrate, he underscores that "the average studio shooting of a feature film in Czechoslovakia in the 1930s lasted only 8–10 days (imagine how many shots they did per day)!"[16] Many of my American fieldwork informants complain of alienation in the face of similar deprivation strategies and stressful constraints on creativity in mainstream "professional" production worlds today. Yet others, from "lower-caste" US production genres (infomercials, reality videos, and soft-core production), simply acknowledge low budgets with resignation. To them, shortcuts on low-budget projects are predictable and inevitable. Some filmmakers argue that innovation results from breaking the rules, which is an almost obligatory part of most underfunded documentaries and reality TV formats.[17]

No director or editor ever seems to have enough time or money to finish a film or series properly in those formats. Some retrospective explanations by craft pros create a picture of managed, forced sloppiness in the earlier career years. This anecdotal posture of deprivation, early career suffering, and dues paying, however, also helps workers to legitimize their craft's long struggle to achieve institutional and cultural recognition. Above the widespread industrial malaise, however, some producers and firms market their production austerity to the trades not just as an index of profitability but as a marker of cultural distinction, as well. This latter practice—the promotion of "stress aesthetics" as a way to fuel innovative screen content—lies at the heart of my research in this chapter. I will return to a more general appraisal of the institutional and cultural implications of stress aesthetics in media production.

In *Behind the Screen*, I detailed a first level in the stress scheme: the industrial conditions that normalize the idea that production deprivation is commonplace.[18] That chapter focused specifically on how digital technologies and computerized efficiency and speed in postproduction have also ramped up the pace of filming and work speed on a set. As long as production's workflow was tied to 35 mm film, DPs and directors advanced their careers by mastering low shooting ratios using fewer shots. This efficiency allowed for formulaic coverage on the set and predictable cutting in post. Computerized AVIDs and then FCP systems, however, allowed the same-size team of editors to view, process, and manage far greater amounts of raw footage. Many traditional Moviola, Steenbeck, and KEM film editors simply could not manage material of this new scale and complexity. Producers, directors, and viewers get more art for their buck, but economic pressures to create ever more screen content using fewer shooting days and dollars also stress creative professionals in acute ways.

Classical aesthetics focused on artistic expression and its end product, the artwork that creator expression produced. By contrast, stress aesthetics reverses this direction of art "production." In effect, stress is the product of artmaking, an embodied pathology in the production artist rather than something left over in the officially finished media artwork onscreen. Consider the direct connection one pro editor makes between accelerating work speed and physical illness:

> I was going to say mental. More than anything . . . the stress level's [*sic*] just increased. . . . Compressing schedules, wanting you to do stuff in crazy amounts of time, very little turnaround, things like that. You get so stressed out, [I know] people just getting sick from working. It's not just the physical . . . [it's] mental stress, blood pressure's going up. One assistant editor . . . He stopped. He had an ulcer—no kidding, this big around. And his thyroid was all messed up and everything. . . . I don't even recognize him now. (Rob Kraut, MPEG, "Reality Check" union organizing meeting, Hollywood, CA, August 30, 2011).

Adding circumstantial evidence suggesting bodies sickened from stress and work speed goes well beyond American television. This includes prominently displayed signage right outside the gates of Barrandov Film Studios of a medical clinic advertisement offering crews physical therapy (fig. 5.9).

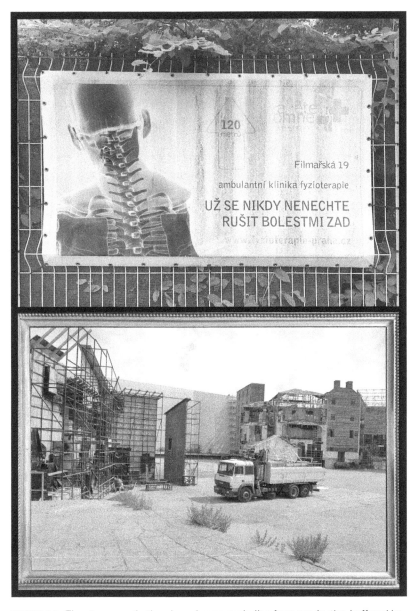

FIGURE 5.9. The stress aesthetics yin and yang: maladies from production buffered by displays of cultural distinction. *Top:* A medical clinic advertisement offering physical therapy, displayed prominently right outside the gates of Barrandov Film Studios, Prague, Czech Republic. © 2016, by J. Caldwell. *Bottom:* The cultural patina of transient work at an Italian flagship studio in decline. Migratory, come-and-go production work is often "paid" and justified via art talk used as self-identifiers of cultural distinction. Cinecittà empty back lot, Rome, Italy. © 2012, by J. Caldwell.

A generational divide also informs the extent to which production workers seem to self-justify and legitimize stress. Whereas the MPEG editor above expressed a midcareer view, the Videomaker trade urging indies to "stop working for free" was directed at twentysomething indies who often wear a sleepless 24/7 ethos on their sleeves as a caffeinated badge of vanguard artistry. Veteran editors like this next one, however, often overtly invoke production stresses in terms of anxieties about their aging lives, in which illness, child-rearing, lack of health care, or psychological breakdowns might be deal-breakers. This shifting status of generational apologetics suggests that "stress aesthetics" is a flexible posture—something that workers can adapt as a vigorous floating signifier:

> When I first got into this business, I never thought that I'd have a retirement, a pension. . . . You're freelancing. My mom would always be like, Where's your healthcare? Where's your this? Where's your that? I don't know. . . . This industry . . . really started around 10, 11 years ago when it was like "Reality TV, reality TV!" So everyone was just like, why do I need healthcare? Why do I need retirement? I'll just pay for it myself. And now, we're aging. . . . I have kids, and everyone's realizing that, I'm old. . . . . Realizing, in reality, what's my future? Because you watch producers or you watch your showrunner who makes 50k an episode. They don't have to worry about their retirement. . . . And you look at yourself. You're like, how long can I do this? How long until I have a breakdown? Or if I get sick what happens? What happens? When can you retire? (Anthony Carbone, MPEG, "Reality Check" union organizing meeting, Hollywood, CA, August 30, 2011)

Beyond accelerated work speed, producers and executives have also exploited blurred and collapsed workflows to realize the economic benefits of stress aesthetics.[19] Traditional workflows between production and postproduction involved a linear, serial sequence of discrete tasks and progress benchmarks. Shooting followed set-building and lighting, logging followed recording or filming, fine-cutting followed rough-cutting, effects were added late in post, etc. Digital confused this orderly sequencing by allowing post activities to bleed into earlier production phases. Even as production activities seeped into traditional postproduction environments. Some budget-tightening producers responded to the resulting "too-many-cooks-in-the-kitchen" labor redundancies in the below-the-line crafts by cutting out one or more of the competing craftworker functions.[20] Nasty intercraft conflict often ensued.

Finally, digital technologies create greater industry pressures for expanded work-scope, sometimes understood as greater production multitasking. As postproduction and effects work shrank to computer "workstation" scale, and digital filming and dailies morphed into data management, individuals using today's new equipment face a set of options unheard of under the old labor agreements. As they have always done, unions continue their push to segregate and distribute tasks among postproduction workers, so that rough-cutters cut, sound designers do sound, effects artists make effects, timers time, and online editors finish program masters.[21] Yet, recently, a countervailing force has pushed back. Hardware and software companies have loaded each computer workstation and software package with a mind-numbing assortment of options and once-segregated tasks.[22]

While Lars von Trier's Dogme 95 deprivation-celebrating manifesto quickly found devotees and disciples among like-minded European film-makers, film school students everywhere, and underfunded film aspirants struggling to break into the transnational film scene, the celebration of deprivation proved a much tougher sell to established below-the-line workers in the American industrial context. In Hollywood, as one might expect, a large gap exists between the theorists and apologists of stress aesthetics at the top of the production food chain (producers, directors, DPs, and department heads, few of whom posture like Von Trier) and the craftspersons that work for them. One of the best examples that reveals a fuller, darker, countervailing picture of the outcomes and implications of stress aesthetics was the "12 On/12 Off" job safety campaign being waged throughout the industry in Los Angeles early in the new millennium by below-the-line workers.[23] Other worker blowback underscored the physical risks from equipment that workers and operators face and complained that producers exacerbated such risks through the accelerated work speed inherent in stressful production environments.

In *Production Culture,* I examined a second level of stress aesthetics: cultural justifications that rationalize labor deprivation. This included the tendency of various managers and producers to voluntarily cut budgets and shooting days even when they have bigger budgets and longer shooting schedules at their disposal.[24] One A-list TV creator confessed that he voluntarily sped up work on his filmed series and mocked the stale results of lazy, big-budget features.[25] Not unlike Dogme 95 and the Advance Party, even Hollywood A-listers often cultivate the sense that the best work takes place "outside" the sluggish big-screen studio factories, where stressed production somehow logically leads to artistic breakthroughs, awards, and critical distinction.

One perverse example of these top-tier self-justifications is what I would term the paradigm for an "A-list bootcamp for underlings."

Consider how one rising pro I interviewed employs and justifies a *Hunger Games* ethos to describe acquiring the Hollywood career skill set:

> One of my bosses was really rough on me. He would throw me into the fire, and then yell at me if things went wrong. He would not tell me what to do. I had to figure it out myself. And if I did it wrong, that's when I'd get burned. And if I did it right, then I did it right. OK. Cool. And that was a great way to learn. He had worked for one of the founders of CAA. He was old. And very "old school." I had to work for him whether it was on paper, or writing coverage. What they expected in the 70s is different than what they expect today. . . . I literally worked inside of my bosses' office. Whereas every assistant usually sits outside at their desks. He literally stood over my shoulder, at a standing desk. (Amanda Lie, TV talent coordinator, interview by author, UCLA, April 7, 2016)

Even powerhouse agencies in mainstream Hollywood, that is, make stress a benchmark in professional development for any wannabes or underlings who hope to rise in their marquee system.

This basic narrative premise—that frantic working, inadequate pay, and long hours are "the mother of invention"—circulates broadly among both mainstream and independent production personnel. Music video production and independent, no-budget documentary regularly serve as the job sites in which successful artists first learn this secret to stress as artistry. Yet aesthetic talk and cultural rationalizations by themselves at this second level—no matter how concerted or determined—cannot justify and prop up the bleak physical conditions of production indefinitely. A bigger, deeper cultural-economic system at a third, or higher, level must return some real or tangible gratifications to self-subjugated creative workers. It is to this third level—the symbolic and cultural—that my analysis now turns.

Deprivation Pay (Symbolic Payroll Systems That Prop Up Stress Aesthetics)

This section examines another scheme that incentivizes and normalizes folds: deprivation pay. This refers to decentralized incentive schemes for workers consisting largely of soft-capital, labor exchanges that pass largely under the radar of studio and network accountants. The substitution of social, reputational, and cultural capital for real money helps answer a nagging question I have had from the start of my research: if the labor of film and television production is as alienating and stressful as many professionals claim, then why do those same workers continue to grow in number and flood the mediascape with vast amounts of new content, much of it impressively realized? After all, no one is holding a gun to their heads, forcing alienated production artists to work long hours against their will. Answering this question requires rethinking what media economics may mean and forces on us another question: how are these workers actually "paid" in forms other than economic capital (traditionally thought of as hourly wages, overtime, contracted fees, health benefits, retirement accounts, etc.)?

Here is where one of the more interesting distinctions between Dogme 95 deprivation and Hollywood deprivation plays out. As I hope to show in the section that follows, commercial recognition stands as the ultimate public payoff for the Dogme 95 art-as-deprivation model. By contrast, artistic recognition stands as the ultimate, largely private payoff for Hollywood's economic deprivation model. In the Euro model from the start, production austerity poses as self-conscious artistic capital (the best of alternatives, quality cinema). Yet this posture can be subsequently converted to commercial capital if branded and marketed effectively.

In the American model, by comparison, frantic work poses as a logistical cul-de-sac and economic imperative (the worst of alternatives and production conditions), but this hopelessness can be converted into artistic capital if workers tirelessly accept such conditions and willingly "team" with management. Another way of saying this is that utopianism is institutionally prebuilt into the Dogme 95 deprivation model from the start. By contrast, utopian aspirations appear as the unlikely by-product presupposed by tireless suffering in the dystopia of the Hollywood deprivation model. Interestingly, "long-odds" probabilities rule both forms of production asceticism. First, the Euro-Dogme variant frames itself as a collective long shot (a local or national cinema concocted around a transportable cultural auteur). By contrast, the Hollywood variant appears as a vocational long shot for individual workers. This is because their precarious, nontransportable careers involve rote lip service to craft authorship, an affirmation that is often overwhelmed by the collective industrial grind that workers experience.

In my research I categorize the production schemes described in the following section as forms of "compensatory production," a term I have adapted from Mark Andrejevic's concept of "compensatory consumption."[26] Unlike the "don't worry, be happy" ethos in "creative industries," apologists like Richard Florida and scholars like Andrejevic and Nicholas Carr ask questions about the relative alienation that occurs when consumers become hybrid "prosumers" or "prod-users" between production and consumption in a corporate social medias-cape.[27] For some time, my research has focused on the flip side of this question: what happens when film/media professionals from the other side (the industry) slide into the same technosocial quagmire that mixes production and consumption?[28] Although the film/media workers I interviewed would never self-identify as "prosumers," they do increasingly interact and overlap with prosumer turf (through social media, Twitter, underemployment, the obliteration of work and leisure distinctions, constant reskilling, etc.).

In the next section, I will sketch out the parameters of compensatory production—the systematic ways that cultural distinction is disbursed as surrogate pay forms to professionals—by describing what might be called the invisible or "erased artistic economies of production." With this I take a modest systems approach to understanding how the socio-professional conventions, reflexive cultural expressions, and habitual routines of production work have become de facto valuable parts of film and television production's labor payment system. A range of general economic and labor practices and incentives form the "symbolic payroll system" that I am postulating here. All of these factors are allied in that they provide surplus resources to productions that producers and executives never acknowledge as economic resources. I examine a more complete list of these cultural practices in more detail elsewhere, but I want to highlight several features of the symbolic payroll economy here, since it functions to mitigate and culturally buffer the experiential downsides of stress aesthetics.[29]

The symbolic payroll system I am describing must be understood in the context of the unabated oversupply of qualified labor and aspirants seeking to enter and gain work in the film and television industries. This competitive labor condition now accurately describes and characterizes production cultures in India, London, and Toronto as much as it does Hollywood. Such an oversupply does not just pressure successful practitioners to lower wages and bids in order to win contract work. This vast, anxious worker pool has also fueled the development of a comparably huge film/TV metaindustry or "shadow industry" adept at financially mining the zealous, overcrowded aspirant pool. I regularly joke that there are more people making livings writing "how-to" books on screenwriting and "making it" in Los Angeles than there are professional screenwriters actually making it. There are more "experts" selling desperate aspirants on production-related products (services, events, publications, memberships, workshops, DVDs) promising to "reveal" the hidden aesthetic and technological tricks of new digital production tools than professionals actually making respectable incomes using those same tools. Although lots of money changes hands, little is actually produced in this shadow industry—other than endless, churning critical and theoretical reflections on the nature of technologies, breakthrough performance, how to get representation, or how to create stylish, Sundance-capable first features with "no budgets."

What is the apparent law of this shadow industry? As the availability of creative work drops, the symbolism and talk about creative work increases. After all, workers with job security have little need to justify or constantly theorize in public about what they are doing and why or to claim that they are artists or "authors." Yet underemployed workers and unemployed aspirants are stuck with the unenviable task of constantly convincing others about how and why they are artists, why their skills are exceptional even though they are not working, why they bring creative distinction and deserve employment. Without actual work, that is, the well-oiled shadow industry stimulates—for a fee—the vast aspirant pool to master rhetorical justifications, imaginary productions, and personal authorial "brands." More than just crude hustling and self-promotion, vocational artistic self-crediting lies at the heart of this now-obligatory rule, that everyone in production should develop a "personal brand" to survive (fig. 5.10).

Although aspirants and the underemployed struggle in these ways to assign themselves credit in order to make it out of Hollywood's "shadow industry" into the "real industry," even successful overemployed or overworked professionals must now increasingly bankroll cultural capital by claiming artistic credit as well. Specifically, the practice of contract labor and outsourcing FX and CGI work to nonunion digital and postproduction "boutiques" has changed the traditional balance between craftwork and the rhetorical justifications that work in these sectors is artistic. Many CGI, animation, and FX artists and editors have accepted high daily rates as a consequence of working within transnational Hollywood's nonunion "off-worlds." These "boutiques" are increasingly viewed as "sweatshops," as I have detailed elsewhere, in part because there are few protections about long working hours and stressful conditions.[30] Because this huge nonunion workforce is largely invisible, sequestered away in scores of subcontracting firms, those same firms have resorted to a range of innovative management initiatives that constantly intend to counter anonymity and alienation by underscoring that these workers are "artists" and not "laborers."

FIGURE 5.10. Forget your day job: every task now an artistic contest. High-risk media markets overdistribute cultural and artistic distinction in order to pay or compensate for the actual failure rate and low financial return that most creators experience. This places a premium on hierarchical ranking schemes. *Left:* At international media/tech convention "Slush Helsinki," one hundred finalists are chosen and ranked from thousands of attendees to pitch their IP on the main "Founder Stage" to find "winners." Helsinki, Finland. © 2017, by J. Caldwell. *Right:* The new Gen-Z order: "all-in." Media firms tell creator-aspirants that the key to success is to go all-in, to subsidize their "daydreams" instead of finding "day jobs." VidCon 2017, Anaheim, CA. © 2017, by J. Caldwell.

This tension between day-job utility and hungry-creator status applies to creatives, as well. Writing scripts and projects "on the side" is commonplace, even though those creations must be worked on during surplus "personal" time. To justify the resources allocated to accomplish side projects, some screenwriters that I interviewed employ a binary that balances the rhetoric of "art-talk" (being "hungry," being self-motivated, having "vision") over and against the day-job economistic logic that favors utility:

Q. *Which would you recommend? Is it better to have a nonindustry "day job" while writing or a parallel industry day job—while you write and wait to be discovered?*

A. You just have to be extra vigilant [if you have an industry day job] about getting your writing in. If you are self-motivated, and you can get in there on the weekends and keep up with your writers group, you lose nothing by having an amazing job. But you have to be hungry as a writer. Hungry if you are a creative person. (Kelly Fullerton, WGA, TV writer/producer, interview by author, Los Angeles, April 7, 2016).

This truism is widely recognized. The considerable time and resources needed to survive long-enough to make-it as a real creator—that is, to move on from being just an employee or factory writer—are your responsibility.

If early career survival must be self-subsidized in these ways, managerial artistic rituals provide a kind of symbolic payment intended to convince the firm's work "talent" to stay "on the team." These forms of symbolic payment and cultural credit include free time on firm workstations to "experiment," contests between workers to produce nonsponsored spec projects, minifilm festivals and shootouts, and sabbatical leaves to allow "burned-out" twenty-six-year-old digital workers to rediscover their inner vision as artists.[31] Much as antiunion Disney symbolically offered his mid-twentieth-century workers "artist" status in exchange for low pay in the classical era, contemporary outsourced subcontractors cultivate their often amply paid but overworked employees as "authentic" noncommercial artists defined by personal vision. The apparent management logic in this stressed sector: the more anonymous the work being churned out, the more essential it is to "pay" workers for their alienating overtime with the marks and individual distinctions of artistry and authorship. In this cultural "overtime" scheme, payment in "authorial capital" substitutes for or augments payroll in economic capital.

In these configurations, communal corporate attributions of artistry and cultural significance compensate for the underpayment schemes inherent in stress aesthetics. Other below-the-line labor practices involve personal self-crediting of artistry and cultural significance. Self-attribution and self-crediting both function as potential forms of symbolic or cultural capital. Consider in this regard the corollary dynamic that percolates with even more anxiety and futility to the lowest rung in the production food chain. Cadres of "video loggers" in reality TV now labor invisibly in windowless off-world bunkers for one of TV's cheapest, and thus most lucrative (for management), genres. Unlike their entry-level historical predecessors in the industry (nonpaid interns and low-paid PAs), reality tape loggers will likely never rise out of these actual sweatshops and "make it" in the industry, even after many years of work. By contrast, at least entry-level PAs on sets traditionally worked in physical proximity to "real" producers and directors. Thus, they could potentially learn the trade by observation and, if successful and lucky enough to be recognized or anointed by a mentor, embark on an industry career themselves.

Reality video loggers have neither the close physical proximity allowed PAs nor any connection with legitimate "insiders." Yet, true to form, the resolute physical isolation and alienation of reality tape loggers does not stop these college grads and just-off-the-bus aspirants from writing "spec" scripts, plotting to make no-budget features, and attending costly how-to-make-it workshops in Hollywood's largely symbolic and virtual shadow industry. Perhaps as a form of compensating survival therapy, vocational hopelessness and dead-end industry sectors like this are, in fact, fertile breeding grounds that spur the often-desperate development—and public performance—of personal artistic self-crediting. Exercises in virtual or imagined artistic credit of this sort—a form of therapeutic semiotic compensation—may be necessary for psychological survival among Hollywood's "untouchables" in the lowest caste of the industry: loggers in reality TV production.

Four other industrial conditions help spur cultural assertions of artistic creditworthiness, and these can all be usefully understood under the broader framework of production's invisible economies. Without question, the budget numbers and math reported in the trades about the costs of a production seldom represent reality. And this factor goes beyond the phrase "Hollywood accounting," which cynically presupposes the habitual ways that studios hide and charge their long-term (non-project-specific) infrastructure costs in the guise of line-item costs on project-specific production budgets. I refer here to all the unnamed forms of "social capital" (value from social networks, organization, and interpersonal relations) and "cultural capital" (value from marks of cultural distinction, class origins, and educational pedigree) that producers leverage (away from their workers) to make a film or television series economically viable today. Executives, producers, and their accountants never quantify these aggregated invisible social and cultural economies in public, nor do they admit they exist—yet they do.

Barter-and-trade labor practices provide one form of invisible capital to a wide range of productions. Because of the overpopulated and desperate job market, and the importance of cultivating informal hiring networks, many workers volunteer or donate their work or expertise to productions that have the potential (1) to give them higher marks of cultural distinction (such as a low-budget art feature intended for Sundance, or a social issue documentary with award potential); or (2) to implicitly require the recipients of their donated labor to reciprocate by giving production labor or expertise back to themselves (thus preemptively obligating the recipient to future "payback"). Both the "shadow industry" described earlier and the "real industry" are flooded by "spec" projects (written or produced without funding) and free labor (given to indie projects, sometimes in exchange for food and credits or to simply add to one's CV or filmography). Studio and network accountants do not ever convert this value—derived from social relations and cultural interactions—into economic capital, even though social and cultural capital clearly allows producers to achieve higher levels of production value. Another work-world practice, "dues paying," also produces excess value that can be gleaned and used to enhance production. The career premise behind it: grovel and suffer endlessly now for the chance to score big later. Deferred gratification, therefore, is not just a psychodynamic characteristic of certain viewers (such as first-generation immigrant parents or those within communities informed by the "Protestant work ethic"). Deferred gratification among production workers also provides lots of worker capital to mainstream producers who monetize it even if they do not have to pay for it.

Informal or latent off-book funders represent another type of leverageable social capital in the invisible production economy. Tens of thousands of individual aspirants in Los Angeles, from their twenties through middle age, are able to survive and pursue deferred career gratification only because they are secretly supported by unacknowledged patrons. Beyond "trust funders," and "kept" individuals, this category includes the adult children of wishful parents, stage mothers (and fathers), and the partners of girlfriends, boyfriends, and working spouses. The very availability of this large labor force to production companies results from the ubiquitous infusion of unacknowledged off-book social capital that production accounts never formally itemize. Another variant of production's invisible economies and symbolic payroll system comes in the form of erased familial capital, where privilege is frequently embedded in production budgets, not always with camouflage, as a result of nepotism.[32]

These various economic and sociocultural practices all suggest that the below-the-line (BTL) work sector functions figuratively as a kind of "BTL artistic credit brokerage." Following this paradigm, producers pursue affiliations and "value" (economic capital) by leveraging (1) cultural capital (marks of individual distinction, crediting, and scarcity) and (2) social capital (informal networks based on patronage, payback, and the reciprocal "gifting" of labor). This "tactical" world of microartistic economics can also be usefully seen in the context of the broader system in which it works, that is, as a countervailing set of actions that undercut and fight back against the incessant blurring and strategic erasure by above-the-line executives of individual artistic below-the-line contributions, credit, or craft signatures in the system as a whole.

Even the collective psychodynamics of a production crew—whether on a soundstage, on location, or in postproduction—can be understood as part of this "substitute" microeconomic artistic payroll system. For example, everyone on a set and in a production firm believes they are working way below their "skill set" and at unfair wage levels. Lots of NYU alums and Harvard grads, for example, are "still getting coffee" and working as poorly paid assistants long after their career road maps projected they would be moving up. This results in pervasive forms of individual dissatisfaction and resentment—which in turn creates an undercurrent of often unspoken adversarial pressures during a production. Like flack, these tactical artistic crediting/discrediting pressures can covertly obscure or undercut upper-level control schemes and top-down authorial fantasies. In the microeconomic terms of my model, these tactical worker credit/discredit schemes can either add (as a positive externality) or subtract (as a negative externality) economic value to or from the production enterprise as a whole.

THE BIGGER PICTURE? (EXPLOITATION, ALIENATION, AND THE CONTROL SOCIETY)

For every once-employed production worker who complains today that Hollywood majors are outsourcing work transnationally to cheap sweatshops that make their entering employees pay the employers for the privilege of working,[33] there is a higher-level industry figure that tries to justify the practice. Accordingly, management uses the symbolic payroll system to fold and calm down the agitated production worker herd by convincing them that agitation, confrontation, and stress are not only the historical norm but also the very key to film and television's artistic accomplishment: "Artistic activity is totally ruthless. Everything is sacrificed to get the shot. Or making the picture. Or making a point."[34] Churning underneath this top-down labor-aesthetic argument, however, is a vast labor pool of outsourced workers who vigorously reject the prescriptive nature of stress aesthetics. Recent examples of this push-back include the Visual Effects Society (VES), which publicly announced its earnest but wishful "VES Bill of Rights" in earshot of the studios and networks that continue to contract and arguably "exploit" them. These posted demands include "[the right to] an appropriate and certifiable credit" and "[the right to] show their work after the project is commercially released for the purpose of securing more work."

This desperate fatalism about not being credited pervades postproduction as well. One professional TV editor describes seeing how his role and cultural status shifted in post from that of an "architect" to that of a "carpenter":

> The one big difference in how the job has changed. In the early days of The Real World, I got a nice [end-title] credit. [I was sort of considered the] director of the show [after we got into post]. At that point, I was highly respected as an architect. Today, I feel like I'm a carpenter. My credit is squeezed out into a cloud with [a bunch of other people]. I know exactly what you're saying about not having any authorship over [what you're cutting]. But I don't even recognize it when I see it on television half the time. Those are real issues. But this idea of [going union], it's a very complicated thing, and there's a lot of ambivalence from guys like me that you're going to have to [overcome]. Because I don't want to put my job at risk. (Comments from Editor "F" at MPEG's "Reality Check" union organizing meeting, Hollywood, CA, August 30, 2011)

A sense of collective resignation answers the disappearing artistic credits in both network production and the subcompanies that feed them.

By no logic or measure whatsoever can either of these modest claimed VES "rights" (an onscreen credit and a complementary personal video copy) be viewed as unreasonable requests from a creative worker! Yet, amazingly, American studios and networks currently refuse to grant either of these symbolic rights as a rule to the highly skilled, profitable, and proven VES workers they currently "hire" by contract. The fact that so many workers are still willing to rationalize their stress predicament as long as they are eventually "paid" overtime with some kind of symbolic form of capital (comparable to a meager onscreen credit and clips for a personal demo reel) proves that the industry's symbolic payroll system is still very much intact. Such an incentive system provides the perverse terms under which anonymity, underpayment, and stress are daily exchanged and justified in recognition of artistic attribution, symbolic credit, and cultural capital.

Shifting from macroeconomic speculation about media industries to fieldwork within the local craft communities that actually produce the texts that we puzzle over makes one thing perfectly clear: artistic crediting and (substitute) cultural payment schemes are fundamental, systematized parts of the embedded industry as a whole. In practice, such arrangements and symbolic attributions help fold and buffer the excesses, mitigate the problems, and legitimize the management schemes that fuel stress aesthetics today. I began by questioning whether the stress aesthetic practices evident in my Hollywood production fieldwork are transportable or comparable to deprivation and stress-aesthetic practices in other parts of the world—in India, Denmark, and Scotland. Although the explanations and rationales for deprivation and compensatory production may differ geographically, as discussed above, intense pressure to produce innovatively with ever-lower budgets and smaller crews is a growing transnational trend. The COVID-19 pandemic has made this race to the bottom even more acute.

To facilitate this small-budget/crew trend, production workers in various parts of the world are paid in symbolic and cultural credit precisely because they are underpaid in financial or "real" capital. While I described this as an outgrowth of "hive-sourcing" and "outsourcing," something Carr characterizes as "unsourcing" or "sharecropping," others justify it as a helpful mutual exploitation akin to the value one adds to oneself through "business socializing" in other settings.[35] In concluding this chapter, I will consider the more general question of whether the "leveling down" I have described is fundamentally alienating and exploitative.

Whether or not the aspiration/deprivation/displacement cycle involved in stress aesthetics is good depends on the stakeholder asking that question. Regardless, it seems increasingly true that ostensibly "good" and "bad" versions of "stress aesthetics" exist simultaneously, not just in the United States but in Denmark, Scotland, and India as well—since outsourcing, deprivation, and stressing are displacing older film/TV professionals in those contexts, as well. While some see this optimistically, as "leveling up," other media scholars like Vicki Mayer and Matt Stahl characterize the current "erasure" of labor in the digital era as fundamentally alienating and exploitative.[36]

Critical scholars are not alone in critiquing specwork. Blowback against spec now comes from many who have been both victims and participants—in part because even professionals face solicitations (contests, festivals, competitions) worldwide, asking them to submit unpaid creative specwork to scam creative contests and film festivals. An online countertracking site called "Specwatch" calls out and warns aspirants and rising artists about work-stealing bottom-feeder companies who promise cultural recognition as pay for creative work but never deliver on any of those promises.[37] Fiona Graham states that "Specwatch, an anonymous collective, monitors design competitions, flagging contests where, they claim, no award was made, and instances where the winning design was plagiarized. . . . When professional networking site LinkedIn started suggesting that people listed as translators might like to help with a crowdsourced project to translate the site, 'because it's fun,' the fallout from professionals resulted in the setting up of a LinkedIn group protesting the move."[38]

My own North American fieldwork on precarious below-the-line production cultures, compensatory production, artistic payroll schemes, and off-the-job online worker-generated content strongly evokes Deleuze's theorization of the "control society." Deleuze underscores two fundamental changes in the shift away from the "disciplinary society" (which was based on confinement) to "control" (a society based on looser forms of responsive management): first, lifelong education involving constant monitoring, and, second, ubiquitous "instant communication."[39] The cultural and artistic payroll schemes, industrial reflexivity, and compensatory production outlined above fit Deleuze's first trait of endless adult self-education and monitoring. The "industrial promotional surround" and the online social media blowback and "worker-generated snark" (WGS, as opposed to UGC, or "user-generated content"), which I have researched elsewhere, align closely with Deleuze's second control trait: instant communication.[40]

Thus, both industrial practices—and the apparent overabundance of what Deleuze would dismiss as "meaningless" production-worker expression in the mediascape—seem to support the control theory. Ulises Mejias explicates Deleuze's focus on the vulnerabilities of instant communication as "an 'empowering' media that provides increased opportunities for communication, education and online participation, but which at the same time further isolates individuals and aggregates them into masses—more prone to control, and by extension more prone to discipline."[41] Framing media creation this way, via Deleuze, delivers a dark picture of the new stressed world of production indeed.

Scanning other contemporary theories suggests that control and exploitation appear clearly in the eye of the beholder. First, for some cultural institutions and bureaucracies—film festivals, film critics, scholars, creative economies' policy makers, national cinemas' proponents, and artists—deprivation and stress aesthetics pose as novel, exemplary, enabling, or resistant cultural strategies. Second, for many corporate players—executives, producers, bottom-feeding indie companies, reality TV productions, viral marketers, and opportunistic harvesters of user-generated content—deprivation and stress aesthetics serve as cost-effective content development and business strategies in a nasty Darwinian market world. Finally, a third set of stakeholders—increasingly underemployed union professionals, outsourced effects workers, volunteer production workers, unpaid production assistants and interns—experience deprivation and stress aesthetics very differently, as a demoralizing, even if addictive, vocational nightmare.

Despite the sorry quandary of this last sector, a drumbeat of name-dropping and aura-making even by A-listers to mentees can remortar the cultural calculus that undergirds precarity. Look how important (even if ad hoc) the imagined mystical mentorship is between grand master Terry Gilliam and aspirant/initiate Quentin Tarantino as the latter recounts "how I made it." Even more than the name-dropping, trade mythologies like this one (spoken to below-the-line production designers in attendance) show how filmmakers use cultural expressions to make their otherwise disaggregated industry symbolically cohere:

> When I was in preproduction I sent the script to the Sundance Lab, for the director's program, and got accepted to it. . . . I was going to do this wonderful course and then go into production. It was a special, special thing. . . . And the second-week group was Terry Gilliam, at the height of his fame . . . Stanley Donen, director . . . Volker Schlöndorff, director of *The Tin Drum* and the editor of *Badlands,* which was one of my favorite movies. . . . An exciting group. The first day that he was there, they put me together with Terry Gilliam. And we had a little lunch. . . . I was so star-struck. . . . He was probably . . . the greatest visionary director of that particular time. . . . And I was talking to him. And he was giving me advice about this and that, and the other. . . . I even asked him a question about crossing the line. And he took a napkin and drew out this diagram of how, "OK, a guy is looking this way, and a guy is looking that way." And he drew a crazy little Terry Gilliam character that actually looked like a strange Volker Schlöndorff character, to tell you the truth. And he finishes the drawing. And he starts to throw it away. And I said, "Wait a minute! Can I keep that?" (ha ha) . . . You know, I wanted an original Terry Gilliam drawing that I could show to my friends at Video Archives! (Quentin Tarantino, DGA, comments at Design Showcase West, UCLA, June 4, 2016)

The account shows how fully embedded contact zones (Sundance Lab) and semipublic contact zones (Design Showcase West/UCLA) are staged for collective industrial self-reflection. This suggests that contact zones—whether semipublic or embedded—are industrial events that employ habitual or choreographed cultural performance. Tarantino's anecdote about his ancestral trade talisman (a napkin sketch touched by Gilliam) provides a glimpse of how production markets weave cultural capital into a fabric that clothes professional standing.

CONCLUSION

I am arguing that scholars take an institutional approach to acknowledging and understanding these wide and disparate views and manifestations of stress aesthetics. It is important to consider how industry employs stress aesthetics to fold a potentially unruly oversupply of creative labor. It is important to ask how firms use the aesthetic scheme bureaucratically, as a human resource strategy, to manage disruptive or underresourced feeders, subfirms, and affiliates. Instead of explaining stress aesthetics as a one-size-fits-all category or general explanation, I have argued that stress aesthetics functions as an open, malleable cultural regime that can be moved, legitimized, justified, and customized for many different social, economic, and industrial purposes.

Approaching the problem this way allows us to more clearly distinguish between coexistent but divergent interests. One coexistent variant includes those on the outside trying to "break in" to film and media, including the resourceless younger artists enrolled in both Danish and US film schools (like USC, NYU, UCLA), executives and officials branding and marketing "new" national cinemas in Denmark and elsewhere, Scottish cultural policy makers funding Advance Party film productions to revive a cultural economy, and proponents of other "small nations cinemas" by local and marginalized groups. Another group includes the managerial class from "old media" that opportunistically hijacks art-world deprivation aesthetics to justify their flexible, exploitative labor-management practices. The third and final group includes once-established working professionals displaced by the new peer production and outsourcing who betray no ambivalence in critiquing the deleterious human impact of stress aesthetics. All of these views actually coexist in the reflexive digital media chatter that now surrounds contemporary media production in the online era.

The three-level model I have described above—comprising industrial conditions (deprivation as symptomatic), cultural rationalizations (stress as exceptional), and symbolic-economic infrastructure (propping up via deprivation "pay" and exchanges of cultural capital)—follows from my view that stress aesthetics functions as a complex, integrated system. Yet this very interconnectedness between levels raises questions of causality and determination, specifically whether stress aesthetics would be possible without free or unpaid labor and whether the economics are a necessary condition of the aesthetics. The unfortunate brilliance of the stress-aesthetic apparatus is that it functions as a relatively open system of exchange. And this is perhaps a key to its current popularity (and insidiousness). That is, it provides user-friendly terms and benign tropes that even competing or antagonistic parties can agree on and appropriate for very different or divergent ends: production labor and management, Hollywood and small nations cinemas, mainstream and countermedia.

The sobering economic facts, wage and income disparities, and the constrained physical work worlds and accelerated workflows described in this chapter can be unavoidably brutal and resolute. "Art," by contrast, can soothe the frictions between embedded production interests. Media art talk provides a soft, slippery, adaptable, and malleable discourse to corral, buffer, and normalize systemic deprivations. The question should not merely be "Who is sticking it to the workers with these aesthetic lies about deprivation?" Nor is the either/or question sufficient: "are the aspiring media-makers and the unpaid interns that Ross Perlin describes using Disney to get ahead in their careers or being used by the cold conglomerate to increase Disney profit margins?"[42] Both of these motives and many other dynamics can be aligned at these relationship pressure points. Trying to nail down a single culprit behind stressed precarious labor, in definitive, final terms, is less useful than recognizing the odd coalition of interests that keep stressed labor folds from fracturing completely.

My research attempts to better understand something as important yet provisional: why we as cultural subjects and creative workers apparently continue to voluntarily participate in our own subjugation within the new, flexible, neoliberal economies. Arguably, the only way this question can be credibly answered is by deconstructing and better understanding the symbolic economy that "pays" creative labor. The conventionalized exchanges of cultural capital there allow and provide genuine personal gratifications, real benefits, and incentives. Such things increasingly come to us alongside much weaker enabling forms of deferred economic gratification. As such, economic deprivation and cultural self-crediting now seem inextricably linked (fig. 5.11).

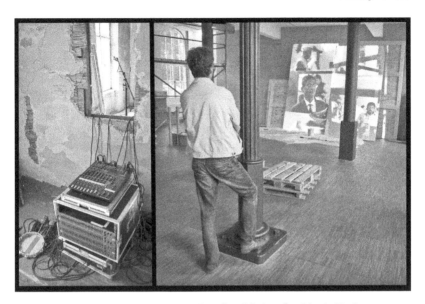

FIGURE 5.11. Self-funded production work as "art." Before "making it," indie creators often self-finance their production work, justifying it as a kind of artistic/political intervention into culture. A video art installation in an abandoned warehouse at Dokumenta-2012 art exhibition offers other aspirants an overrationalized cultural prototype they can try to emulate for success. Photo: Kasel, Germany. © 2012, by J. Caldwell.

In some ways the net effect and logic of stress aesthetics may boil down to which of the three levels one self-identifies with: first, as an "artist" (who endures stress and defers gratification to achieve a longer-term personal vision); second, as a "worker" (who endures stress and provides a service but for an immediate wage); or, third, as an "entre-preneur" (who endures stress and defers gratification as part of a specu-lative investment and long-term financial payoff). Making something creative from nothing, against all odds with few resources, has long been a defining principle and badge of honor in modernist art-making, cubist collage, Dadaist assemblage, neorealism, avant-garde film, "imperfect cinema," "Third Cinema," and indigenous media-making long before Dogme 95. Yet Hollywood also mastered it as a mainstream industrial-management practice long before its current executive hacks now employ the mythos to keep well-trained legions in the production precariat on a very short employment leash.

I hope in this chapter to have added something basic to a discussion of the stressed folding and compliance evident in complex, embedded production systems. That is, the idea that while stress aesthetics may have been preemptively fabricated as an artistic practice or call-to-arms capable of branding an edgy national or Third Cinema in Latin America, Denmark, and Scotland for subsequent distribution in transnational media environments, stress aesthetics in other production cultures (like Hollywood and Mumbai) behaves as a retrospective justification for labor exploitation and cost cutting pure and simple. Sadly, the major transnational corporate conglomerates are as good at rationally monetizing stress aesthetics for economic reasons as film festivals, critics, and auteurs are at critically rationalizing it for cultural reasons and as national brands. One production worker's artistic badge of honor is another worker's admission of consent and compliance under industrial duress. A way to fall into line.

6

Case

Televisioning Aspirant Schemes

This inexact science forces artists . . . to take a more methodical approach. . . . At times he sounds more like a business-
man, speaking about "data-points," and "product." The key
he says is "getting a commodity that not everyone else has,
which is yourself and *your art.*"
—Tai Verde on how she mastered social media content production[1]

The core stark phenomenological differences detailed in chapter 4
between A-list film production poetics (as in *Game of Thrones*) and the
aspirational creator basics of YouTubers (as taught in VidCon creator
workshops) may seem self-evident. Money (or the lack of it) may help
explain each of those antithetical experiential tendencies over issues of
speed, scale, size, speculation, and *scarcity.* At the same time, and
despite such budgetary differences, low and high production also parallel each other with a surprising number of fundamental production
principles that overlap, as this chapter will detail. Each of these additional shared production impulses brings nonformal institutional
schemes that nevertheless structure the "art" of production practice.
Mastering these small-screen administrative skills may indeed prep
aspirants for one kind of career (in TV, marketing, media management).
Yet platform pedagogy about social media administration that poses as
a gate to big-screen cinematic careers behaves more like doublespeak in
the crossover's dilemma.

The parallel production behaviors examined in this chapter include
seriality, sociality, deprivation metrics, subscription, and *sponsorship.*
Unlike the embodied experiences of form and production value outlined
in the earlier differential study, I approach this second set of principles as

managerial, as system-structuring practices. That is, each of the following entails a bureaucratic way of thinking that coordinates, administers, and channels production work practices. These two sets of "basics"—the divergent formal embodied core categories in the chapter 4 pedagogies, and the overlapping managerial systemic behaviors in this chapter—complement each other in functionality. At least within warring creator pedagogies, these two sets of "how-to-succeed" trade norms pose as competing flip sides (the experiential and managerial) of the same "production basics" coin.

Because the five systemic principles that follow were developed and mastered long before the online digital era, in twentieth-century analog *broadcasting,* I characterize these primers from trade pedagogies on production career success as forms of "televisioning." The stripped-down poetics of edgy online production by no-budget aspirants today counterintuitively employ schemes and practices mastered long ago by run-of-the-mill commercial analog TV broadcasters. This business behavior—digital disruptors emulating mercantile bread-and-butter broadcasters—may seem odd. Especially given that start-ups, digital platforms, and venture capitalists (VC) rarely characterize online makers and influencers as bureaucrats. Nor do they promote them as broadcasters or station programmers. Yet, lurking not far below the endless digital overtheorizing, marketing vaporware, and financial speculation that the tech sector uses to define the era of online "creators," contemporary media and tech platforms draw unapologetically (or ignorantly) on something much less disruptive. Tech platforms, that is, reward makers who can leverage the lessons and the tactics of a trusty old media business and industry warhorse: TV.

SERIALITY

One of the most pedestrian (and lucrative) activities in broadcasting and television stations is managed by their "scheduling" departments. Those offices are charged with deciding when *(in time)* media content will be aired. They are therefore also closely tied to what *(in content)* the station chooses to program. Reminiscent of these program-scheduling departments, trade and production discourses today show that *serial time* of broadcast schedulers increasingly rules in both low-end digital production and high-end premium production. This was not always the case. Pre-HBO big-screen *cinema* was once habitually promoted as a marquee, a distinct gateway for one-of-a-kind, event-status viewing—something consumable only when viewers went out to the big screen via the box office. Low-culture television, in contrast, was noted and often mocked for its dull domesticity and clockwork-like regularity. In middlebrow "episodic TV," advertising economics placed a premium on an awareness that another very similar self-contained narrative would unspool at the "same-time, same-station, next-week." This predictable series-thinking during the American postwar period made the phrase "Least Objectionable Programming" (LOP) a mantra for both broadcasters and the FCC. On a weekly basis, broadcasters scheduled familiar story-worlds and unchanging screen characters for viewers to return to (fig. 6.1).

But a "continuing series" form (mastered in early radio soap operas then imported to TV) largely displaced the dull regularity of broadcasting's episodic series TV. By design, continuing series endlessly deferred full resolution of each week's narrative until coming weeks. In so doing, the continuing form built a different kind of anticipation into the viewer's TV ritual. That is, viewers could expect that a series would give them incremental amounts of new narrative revelation each week. Hybrid economic-narrative serial thinking like this, developed by TV, normalized an ideology of deferral and anticipation that creeps into even what is arguably the most "cinematic" media today, premium cable and streaming platforms (e.g., HBO/*Game of Thrones,* Hulu/*9 Perfect Strangers,* Netflix/*Medici,* Amazon Prime/*Jack Ryan*). In effect, broadcasting's seriality has "televisioned" even cinematic premium cable in the streaming era. This is ironic, given that standard-bearer HBO built its brand on denigrating TV: *"It's not TV. It's HBO."* Even discussions among production personnel—whom we might expect to be myopically focused on individual craft specialties—often use seriality and the timed, incremental release of the series to explain it: "On Wednesday, I start scouting for Season 8. And, yes, I know how it ends. . . . So what follows is a quick refresher of what we did in Season 6. . . . And for those of you that haven't seen it, the first trailer for Season 7 appeared a week ago. So this is it."[2] *Game of Thrones'* seasons consisting of seven, eight, or ten episodes, furthermore, are not just distributed over calendar years to frustrate and manage the scarcity of the IP. They are also distributed over the calendar in this way to build audience expectation, to achieve event status, and to reward viewers by meeting the audience at a much-hyped time of the month and year. Even with "view-any-time" HBO-Max, binge-watching, and mobile-device viewing, the serial release over a sequence of time/days keeps

FIGURE 6.1. Marquee events give way to scheduled serial time in distribution. This reverses the humble origins of "TV series" (i.e., programmed monotonous regularity), especially at high contemporary prestige platforms like HBO. Photos: Los Angeles, CA. © 2018, by J. Caldwell.

FIGURE 6.2. "How-to" videos teach YouTube creators to "batch" shoot and stack their content in advance and then to upload/release videos in a predictable clockwork-like schedule over time. Photos: Public displays at panel "A Guide to Not Quitting on YouTube Dreams," VidCon 2017, Anaheim, CA. © 2017, by J. Caldwell.

TV-like seriality at the center of the cinematic phenomenon for both HBO and high production as a whole (fig. 6.2).

As seriality survives the "anytime" impulses now pushing streaming services in big-budget high production, it also prospers increasingly within the "always-on" imperative sold to aspiring creators down in online low production. From one perspective, seriality's expansive *distribution of plot points*—including multiple beginnings and continuing endings—over calendar time would seem in stark contrast to the easy access and impulsive always-online audience engagement marketed on YouTube. Yet this distinction is more apparent than real. Again—as with scarcity—the need to scale up and monetize pushes influencers and online makers to innovate by giving their content greater online seriality. A spokesperson for Crash Course explains to young creators how to fight the continuing threat of losing one's subscribers and audience: "It is important to have consistency in all categories. Tell yourself: 'every other Thursday I will finish a thing.'"[3] Other veterans preach to aspiring makers the value of finding then sticking to weekly, episodic regularity: "and then schedule [your videos] to publish for the appropriate

time on YouTube." Another expert argues that the way to prevent creator burnout means that aspiring online makers need to ensure episodic
serial regularity by shifting to the *disordered shooting but ordered airing* model from television broadcasting: "Consider keeping a few videos
queued up in advance. For that time when you have a crazy week and
you still want to be consistent on your schedule, on your channel, but
you just don't have time to publish something. . . . So work with a
buffer. Don't just go right up until the deadline. Try to stay 2–3 videos
ahead so that you have more wiggle room there."[4] Here, the edgy, fluid
world of lone influencers feels more like the ulcer-inducing world (and
endless content appetites) of broadcast scheduling departments.

The platform system takes a "carrot-and-stick" approach to seriality
with creators. One reason many online makers are obsessed with achieving serialized "microcasting" on their YouTube channels is the awareness that YouTube's algorithms now clearly recognize and reward any
temporal regularity of creator-uploaded videos on individual YouTube
channels. At the same time, online creators share war stories with each
other about how YouTube penalizes makers whose videos are *not*
uploaded at highly regular intervals. Consider this cautionary warning:
"When you hit 'Publish,' and it's 'Public,' that's when the 24hr. clock
hits, when the 'decay rate' or the 'YouTube Death spiral' starts."[5] Many
YouTubers astutely recognized that irregular uploading times can easily
trigger the algorithm's "Death-Spiral," which can dramatically dim
their prospects for success.

These acute time pressures make creator serial thinking circular. The
scheme steers video creators to produce videos that are always perpetually open, iterative, and remakeable at a moment's notice. Consider the
instruction given YouTubers at the in-person workshop entitled "Ultimate Video Content Webinar": "The Secrets?: *Interactive Landing
Page. *Beware of Expiring Content. *Revise Specific Underperforming
Elements, *Instead of the Whole Video*" (Jeremy Pryor, CEO, Epipheo).
Theorist Media echoes and elaborates on this premium now placed on
serial *permutation* (rather than *originality* per video) for aspirant success: "Sustainable content can iterate and optimize. It is important that
content be able to change and improve as information about the success
of individual videos comes in. Sustainability includes the ability to make
a slightly altered, better version of previous videos. . . . A great example
of iteration: *There is a simple set-up. Episodes can be about what the
brand needs or what fans want. *Content can be improved upon for
future videos based on analytics data" (Meredith Levine, Theorist

Media). I found little dissent in fieldwork among creator consultants about this quick-content-iteration-on-demand requirement. Online low-production seriality undercuts the possibility of having a stable or singular production form for low online makers. It militates against having an overarching form or mode of production in any traditional aesthetic sense of the term.

To avoid the ever-present threat of the YouTube Death-Spiral—where a maker's new video uploads and channel aren't recognized and disappear quickly into the YouTube morass—Derral Eves, CEO of Creatus, suggests practical ways by which creators can increase the sheer number of new videos they make and upload. Since most lone online producers are by definition understaffed and unable physically to meet the fast-paced two-to-three "new" creator uploads per week that the platform demands, Eves lays out an alternative. He teaches aspirants how to create the *algorithmic illusion* that "new videos" are apparently being uploaded at this frantic pace—through *automated* high-volume apps that constantly tweak and mechanically reiterate *videos* that already exist on the channel: "For updating your [video] cards, use TubeBuddy. It can change 5 cards on 20 videos [quickly] . . . [and also] try for constant updating of your video end elements" (Eves, "Growth Hacking YouTube"). In this approach, creating new videos means mindlessly creating new "meta-data churn"—a production mode that uses automated means to simply reiterate previously made videos. The maker's goal or ruse: Google's AI robots will *misperceive* this upload churn as a "series" of "new" videos. In this alternative model of video creation, while the substance and pace of the actual videos have not fundamentally changed, the technical platform is tricked into *thinking* they have.

This is just one example of how veterans and creators try to "hack" the algorithm and "game" the system. AI gaming of the platform by makers of this sort betrays the technical pressures that all YouTubers face as they try to achieve regularized seriality to increase their viewers and subscribers. At the same time, using *mindless auto-apps to reiterate* one's existing short videos on an hourly or daily basis renders the aesthetic pretense of the individual "creator" enterprise as a whole absurd. It is difficult to think of video expressions made by robot apps to be art at all. Social media platforms like YouTube make seriality a burden—an obligatory, core task in online maker-production poetics. This pressures individual authors to succeed at the larger task of serial narrative creation and scheduling rather than solely focus their attention "inside-the-frame," as one would do in traditional media aesthetics.

SOCIALITY

The logic of networking significantly impacts contemporary production in the online era, even as it has more broadly altered social relations, markets, and culture in general. Trying to understand the parts of a production poetics that are shared by both the high- and low-creator sectors means taking seriously two practices that reverse or flip some standard views of digital social networks. Sociality serves as a second core part in an online crossover-production core in that it is valued and leveraged in both the low and high creator worlds. Sociality, oddly enough, also has deep roots in TV broadcasting. Digital media theory generally values *network externalities,* with considerable evidence showing how every new outside contact adds value to the collective network or brand as a whole. With roots in broadcasting, televisioning enables us to better understand *network internalities*—that is, how the human social relations *inside* a work world add value to the network or brand as a whole. The following explanation from *Game of Thrones* production designer Deborah Riley lauds the departmental structure in higher production, which promotes a "team" ethos: "As the production designer, I'm the visual guide, but I'm also the champion and the cheer-leader of the art department. Also the protector of the art department, making sure the team has everything that it needs and wants, so that we can progress and move forward as a team." Converting a group of technical workers into a "team" and then into a "family" has a long and proven history in Hollywood and broadcasting. In fact, it represents one of the oldest and most trustworthy traditional "folds" in those classical production systems. Culturally, speaking in "team" rhetoric pushes everyone in the production unit to get on the same page, to pull in the same direction. Invoking "family" symbolism (on a shoot or among a crew) can congeal the diversity, contention, and fractiousness of production into a temporary, falsely unified, consensus that covers over any divergent interests.

In-person workshops and online primers pressure YouTube creators to master network externality thinking. Unlike prepwork-based cinematic production, low production favors preemptively harvesting relationships out in the social world, then quickly bringing that social content onscreen. Jumpwire Media mentors urge aspiring creators who want success to "tag celebrities with large media followings. Hey, you never know." Jumpwire pushes this tactic of hijacking existing social networks to launch one's own channel by showing how established brands hijack UGC the same way: "Disneyland uses UGC for about 95% of their content. We wanted to highlight how they source it as an example for best practice" (Gavin McGarry, Jumpwire Media).

My claim that the go-it-alone world of young YouTubers also show-cases the "team/family" ethos of professional crews may seem counter-intuitive. Yet aspirational creators can also invoke the team and family tropes mastered in the legacy film/TV industries over many decades. Says one online creator about her ceaseless solicitation of affiliates and part-ners: "Top down seems like an old model. They are like my family. . . . Working groups are like teams. . . . Hopefully familial bonds will form. . . . But very firm boundaries have to be put into place: 'Yes, but I am your boss.' Sometimes people lose track."[6] Here, when the creator does not have enough money or pay to control her affiliates as employ-ees, this "successful" YouTuber leverages the soft power of the family trope, even as her trade rhetoric simultaneously tries to keep the "boss" logic alive. Finding evidence of gratifying payoffs from mastering team reciprocity are not difficult to find. They frequent higher-production rhetoric, as well. As she deconstructs and explains a production still from *GoT*, the art director Riley explains: "I am very proud of this big wide/establishing shot. I think this is one of the most effective syntheses of the Art Department and Visual Effects." Creative workers who do not spread the credit for accomplishment around to adjacent colleagues and partner departments on the team often lose the chance for mutual recog-nition in the future. This tacit quid pro quo presupposes an imminent transaction: praise will come back to the one who first acknowledges reciprocating workers in the team/family.

While much has been written about external crowdsourcing as a means to finance media work in hypercompetitive online markets with an oversupply of content, high and low production now both also employ an older tradition mastered in the legacy media of television: inside crowdsourcing. The television writers room, the art department, and now design and visualization software all provide opportunities in production for collective interactions, brainstorming, and negotiation. These interactions can sometimes create liminal spaces enabling corpo-rate discovery. Such spaces seem well-suited as mechanisms for eliciting collective contributions from many workers during production. Most of these workers will return to anonymity once the sharing (and the production) ends. On *GoT*, "the approved concept art . . . was then put into AutoCad [software] so that we could all argue among ourselves, and later agree on exactly how much of that set we were going to build"

(Riley). Here, Deborah Riley underscores the long-term value of internal crowdsourcing as a design-and-set debate floor, a learning effect, and a proven way to innovate: "I've learned a lot about loyalty on *GoT*. Through working with the same crew, year after year, we all know each other so well. So that we are able to push each other, and push the work to create new and interesting images." This is far from the sort of disaggregation of workers typical of many outsourced, nonunion, and gig-economy creator work sectors. Riley provides a map of how one prestige series values long-standing relationships. She does so to clinically negotiate, test, and "source" project strategies together with colleagues and peers from adjacent physical production departments (fig. 6.3).

Granted, this kind of public cheerleading for collective creation and reciprocity in the big-budget world is much scarcer or greatly constrained among aspiring, underresourced online makers. Consider that the lower-budget creator trade shows include many workshops for paying attendees on what I would term "how-to-be-skeptical," "how-to-find-work," and "how-to-survive" panels. Ironically, although these panels and workshops promise helpful hints and routes to career success, they tend (perhaps unintentionally) to underscore and normalize instead a sense of long-odds work precarity. Consider the work-as-love ethos integral to the job criteria promoted by one expert teaching aspiring creators: "We look for people who love learning, a growth mindset. It's the 'no talented assholes rule' in San Francisco. The differences between a 'creative' engineer and great people? . . . Nobody's an expert."[7] This summary principle ignores the alternative possibility that the upstart hiring company simply cannot *afford* real "experts." Instead, by rationalizing passion over expertise, the "expert" symbolically strips costly expertise from his hiring equation (which also lowers budgets). This shows that internalized crowdsourcing (via soft teams and families) has a place in both the trade talk and organization of low- and high-production firms. Team and family talk certainly helps no-budget production labor feel more tolerable.

The TV writers room provides a good example of collective in-sourcing. It shows how industry has mainstreamed specworld impulses with industrial efficiency. How does this differ from UGC and network externalities? In the following interview, the lead creator leverages the room's internal network. This allows her to function as an interactive moderator or story broker who synthesizes all of the possible spec parts:

> A Showrunner tends to run the writers room. So they are guiding the ship in terms of what all of the staff are pitching for an episode. So you might come

FIGURE 6.3. Television mastered inside-crowdsourcing a half-century ago in writers rooms. Author-as-sharer doublespeak now normalized in trade celebrations of the writers room. Photos: Public displays at and still-frames from London Screenwriters' Festival. Photos of video displays: © 2017, by J. Caldwell.

in and say, "Look, this season we start here, we end up here." . . . And I know the first episode, roughly. But I don't know anything about how do we get there. So you just go one by one. And you are all just pitching ideas. And maybe one step toward getting there would be . . . And one story might be about, oh, driver's training, and you get in an accident or something. So you might start pitching all of those ideas. And then they'll break the story (gestures into columns). The showrunner would be with you to say . . . "No, it doesn't feel 100% right. What could it be? Like that—but less young, less teen, more grounded. What do you think?" *And you just keep adjusting. And adjusting the pitches. And you are all just brainstorming. Out loud. To figure out what that story will be.* The showrunner is directing that. (Kelly Fullerton, WGA, TV writer/producer, interview by author, UCLA, April 7, 2016 [italics mine])

The huge content and screen-time demands on TV series producers require the almost factorylike solicitation of story parts and plot options, which writer-producers constantly broach and barter through collective pitching, pushing back on, or adapting.

It is worth stepping back from this paradigm—content sourcing from an internal network—to get a bird's-eye view of where and how industry oversees that mode. For starters, the reciprocal sociality being promoted in the bracketed-off creative-teams trope seems antithetical to the top-down corporate environment that surrounds and ultimately monetizes that very same embedded production unit. The regimented structures of big production corporations and studios are profitable in part because they are proficient at mining and extracting collective creative input from their workers. They then harvest and aggregate that income into consumer screen deliverables. To make this author-as-sharer doublespeak work, companies need to find credible ways to reward workers who share and to incentivize those who share freely. But they must also keep a tight rein on when and where reciprocal sharing takes place and who can see or hear it. Companies can do this by segregating and confining internal crowdsourcing to controlled environments (the writers room, the art department, etc.).

By contrast, the expertise-free improv rhetoric in bare-bones low production forces creators on social media platforms to be more improvisational and generative in their internal crowdsourcing. In the online world, they need to act less corporate, less regimented. In some ways, the impulsive brainstorming promoted publicly in the crowded world of aspirants and YouTubers is really a bet placed on hitting a long-odds "home run" with the maker's ostensibly unique or edgy IP. The bunkered professional sharing-rooms in high production, by contrast, are far more regimented and constrained. To employ the "moneyball" analogy, this makes high-production writers, designers, costumers, and set builders better at tapping out lots of concept "singles" and IP "doubles"—shorter hits, rather than home runs, that producers can aggregate to improve the odds of creating a winning series in a premium media market. The more predictable results of high production's internal creative-labor crowdsourcing conventions expose low production's internal crowdsourcing as mostly aspirational and maddeningly ad hoc. YouTube requires its makers to master sociality in their basic production skill set for "success." But the platform largely does so in a way that forces makers to disclose and share concepts "without a net." That is, without guardrails for their creative ideas, the platform pushes them to freely give away content without a clear or convincing picture of how to harvest or monetize their concepts later.

DEPRIVATION METRICS

Without acknowledging it, TV has long made calculated resource deprivation an unavoidable managerial task to be mastered. Profitability comes only by mastering constricted budgets and schedules. Chapter 4 described how pride about overcoming acute physical limitations often serves as a badge of accomplishment for creators. It detailed how workers convert actual production constraints, stresses, and limits typical of media production into symbolic *fungible self-crediting capital* that can be leveraged vocationally later, by self or others. One might take this symbolic conversion to mean that there is more boasting about hardship in the meager worlds of aspirants than in the well-budgeted worlds of A-listers. But this is not always the case. Celebrating limitations and struggle in production is also evident in the ways premium cable and some television have been lauded as edgier and more prestigious than film or cinema in the twenty-first century.[8] Many of production's limits in both film and TV are always real: not enough budget, too few shooting days, equipment problems, hostile work environment. Yet these physical stresses are also embedded and expressed at another level, in socioprofessional discourses—in war stories about overcoming difficulty or long odds. Creative workers in both high and low production are well-versed in underscoring the physical difficulties against which they create. They often wear those constraints and stresses on their sleeves—offering psychological or cultural rationales of one form or another to explain a physical challenge or cash-in on a given deprivation or stressor (fig. 6.4).

Even big-budget prestige creators often draw attention to their constraints. In one disclosure, the production designer Deborah Riley offers a parable: "I'd start with one of the tiniest sets in the history of set building: Sansa's chambers. . . . The director actually laughed in my face when I described [Sansa's] tiny little space. And yet, I thought it was this restriction of the art department that created some beautiful,

FIGURE 6.4. Pressures to master on-demand pitching and rapid-fire content creating. Adolescent influencers are solicited and bombarded with recreational public stages to rapidly give out their best ideas to the platform harvesting system. Photos: VidCon 2017 "Pitch to Pilot" initiative, Anaheim, CA. Photos: © 2017, by J. Caldwell.

simple, cinematography. Purely because the camera had nowhere else to go!" Here, even on productions that would make creative workers elsewhere green with envy (based on *GoT*'s boast of endless shooting days and globe-spanning locations), its series' professionals echo a core trade litany. Riley invokes the *necessity-as-mother-of-invention* trope. Acute limits are desirable since they somehow enable artistic breakthroughs.

With shooting days and budgets that would make even feature filmmakers jealous, epics like *Game of Thrones* publicize their vast scale in order to dramatize, yes, the difficult limits they overcome: "This is the thing: you have to learn to work a ten-episode season of *Game of Thrones*. . . . We work with five different directing teams at once. Each of those director teams includes the director, the cinematographer, and the first AD. And each directing team is coded with a different color. We also have . . . two different shooting units. And this season, 6, we had a third shooting unit. Because the number of days shot up from 200 to 250" (Riley). The ostensibly sorry "predicament" being described here is less like the stress experienced by manual laborers than like the type of managerial stress Hadrian may have faced when Caesar invaded Britannia. Interestingly, in this high-production variation on stress aesthetics, the lone production designer implies that she knows more about what's going on, overall, than the series' migratory teams of multiple directors. In Riley's mentoring parable, everybody is on a need-to-know basis, and directors apparently do not need to know everything in this serial multiseason prestige production.

Complaining about having to logistically manage transnational creative regiments who "only" get twenty-five shooting days per episode is a bit odd. This is because that long shooting duration dwarfs the normal seven-days-per-episode limits even that A-list big-budget prime-time dramas are given on American television. This month-per-episode formula in high production would also elicit little empathy or pity from aspiring creators in the lower caste of online production. A consultant from Theorist Media clears the air for YouTuber trainees about differences between the time allowed for shooting in budgeted versus nonbudget production: "Take creative burnout. YouTube has weekly and daily content demands that no other media has."[9] Here, lowly YouTube's appetite for large-volume-content uploads dwarfs HBO's appetite for quantity screen content—so much so that it apparently has a psychiatric impact on aspirant makers. Another creator summarizes a common theme when she acknowledges, "I've heard lots of suffering stories." She unpacks that suffering proverb for creator aspirants in a trade workshop that promises to allay anxieties by helping emerging makers "Transition Your Channel into a Full-Fledged Business."[10] Veteran Tim Schmoyer also underscores the psychological threat from online maker stress: "As a YouTube creator it's very easy to feel burned out after a while. Maybe you've just been doing this for so long that the kind of creative passion and juices that kind of energized this whole thing has dissipated."[11] (fig. 6.5).

The early career-threat stresses these maker experts target arise because creators have no viable long-term or even short-term commitment from their platform mothership: "It's how YouTube decides to serve videos. It's the 'Death Spiral' on YouTube. There's a big pop, then the channel dies."[12] The "death spiral" that online makers face daily, discussed earlier, triggers much debate among makers about career futures and survival:

> *Phil Ranta, Studio17.* At what point do you leave your day job?
>
> *Joe Penna, creator.* When you make more money in YouTube than your day job, then you quit. . . . [Back then] I'd go to a soup kitchen if I had to, to steal Wi-Fi. If it doesn't work out, I'll go and work in the film industry.[13]

Setting aside Penna's wishful thinking here that "working in the film industry" would be much easier than working on YouTube, other consultants bring the "tough-love" approach to survive. One advises: "Make videos until you don't want to make them anymore. . . . Focus on motivation. You might say 'I went to film school, now I am stuck editing videos all day. [And] I need to not be a computer.' . . . The heart of all of my advice is to 'get over it!'"[14] Get over it; suck it up; production hardship is the deal we make with the devil from the start. A range of deep texts, and trade talk, in the online era like this suggests that stress aesthetics provides a core function in the contemporary poetics of both aspirational low production and premium high production.

Because of an unforgiving clock from approaching TV episode airdates, former aspirants who've graduated to professional editing often theorize their predicament not as a vanguard badge of honor but as overwhelming, slapdash, and demoralizing:

> It used to be one editor to do the whole episode. I don't know how many people work on one episode of TV by yourself . . . anymore. I mean, it's an assembly line. It's, "You do this piece, you do this piece, you do this piece, you do this piece." Slam it all together. Give it to another editor who's never seen any of the footage [and have it ready] in an hour. . . . "Just clean it up. Just fix it up." That's how they do it. (Anthony Carbone, MPEG, "Reality Check" union organizing meeting, Hollywood, CA, August 30, 2011)

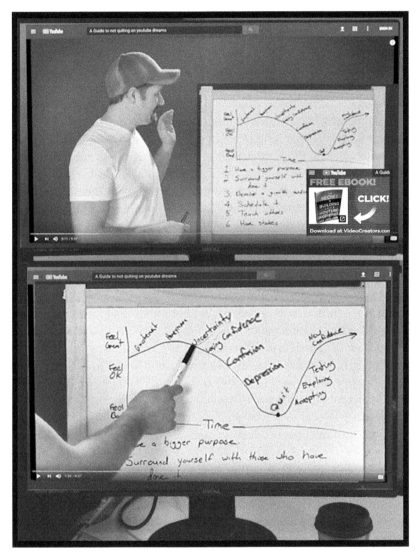

FIGURE 6.5. A peer [psychiatric] "Guide to Not Quitting on YouTube Dreams." This midcareer intervention teaches adolescent makers to prepare emotionally for the psychiatric roller coaster of media production. An X (feeling) Y (time) graph moves from "involvement, happiness, uncertainty, losing confidence, depression, quit[ting], accepting, employing, testing" to "new confidence." The moral? "Have a bigger purpose. Surround yourself with those who have done it." Screenshots, YouTube, 2017.

Carbone's moral about editing—"slam it all together . . . fix it . . . in an hour"—suggests that the psychiatric stress that YouTubers complain about is endemic to professional production, as well. It especially defines temporal pressures in on-air-driven TV production schedules.

Like seriality and sociality, deprivation metrics can also be understood as part of the institutional force that is changing or "televisioning" online making for makers/influencers. This is partly because of a cultural hierarchy that long placed the higher caste of "cinema" above the lower caste of TV. Critics helped form this caste system when they treated TV as cinema's "bad object." Historically, A-list producers from film viewed television as a site that demanded more simplicity and efficiency, ostensibly because that's all it was capable of. These lowered expectations were arguably due to TV's relatively constrained budgets and production infrastructure. Historians praise the golden age of "live anthology drama" on American television, for example. Critics celebrated that format and genre precisely for the way it managed to create great theatrical drama with method actors—but with little or no high-production value visuals. Rhetorically, both high- and low-production creators whine in public about the same *art-without-resources stresses* but for very different ends. For higher production, the stress rhetoric economically adds value to the franchise. For lower production, the stress rhetoric serves as a collective therapeutic discourse, a compensation. Sometimes it is offered as a voluntary delusion.

These are logical distinctions, given the marked institutional differences between the high-production caste (which can pay very well, even as it inflicts regimented stress) and the low-production caste (which makes unpaid stress a conscious talking point for creators). Without meaningful remuneration for the hardships of creating, online low production must concoct and normalize ever more elaborate "symbolic payroll systems" and cultural incentives (of the sort detailed earlier in chapter 5). The degree to which the content produced exceeds available resources provides an inverse metric for cultural capital in this symbolic accounting scheme. Echoing earlier TV producers, aspiring creators try to leverage actual capital by symbolically accounting for how their content productivity trumps their hardship on the platform.

SUBSCRIPTION

It is impossible to unpack creator trade pedagogy today without examining how media economics—not just individuals—help "author" and stylize contemporary screen content. While most media companies envy the ability of HBO (protected inside cable provider monopolies) to make subscribers pay high fees to get premium content, *every* other producing sector today scrambles to find and then lock down a recurring audience or fan base. Unlike historic Hollywood, which underplayed and hid its research behind promotional platitudes about universal entertainment experience, television success has always been research-driven and obsessed with demographics—in public. Television made no secret that its mission was to build content around audiences. This burden of audience management, mastered by television, drives much industry wisdom and pedagogy about production today.

The audience management task assigned to producers in TV and legacy media can also be found pressuring creators in the otherwise "edgy" world of online creators/influencers. In fact, industry now front-loads marketizing fans/subscribers onto Gen-Z makers as a central task, as a core requirement for success in production. This preemptive assignment of audience economics onto aspiring creators gives much of their creative cultural expression a stark bureaucratic profile. Loading market management onto the maker's production palette also helps displace traditional artistic notions. Marketing and sales, that is, seem antithetical to narrative concerns, visual design, and aesthetics that once served to ground production basics. The VidCon 2017 convention launched like a giant introductory or early career "boot camp" for YouTubers. Very few of the hundreds of panels and workshops focused on creator formal concerns or onscreen aesthetics. Instead, the vast majority of workshops taught marketing, financing, fan development, sponsorship, merchandising, and management. Platform pedagogy like this promotes efficient bureaucracy-over-artistry as key to the aspirant creator's skill set. The platform ratchets up its large, ecstatic, refereed contact zone into a bureaucracy with an edgy cultural aura. Pedagogy produces prestige that other culture sectors seldom grant bureaucracies (fig. 6.6).

Aspirational "Production 101" for adolescent creators now looks more like an MBA curriculum than a foundation film aesthetics course. To make room for their new bureaucratic behaviors, some "experts" even urged eager producer aspirants to ditch quality, to *"cut-down on production values."* They were told they could destyle their videos by shifting to a strategy of mass-producing their episodes "in batch" (which would actually make it easier to upload them with clockwork-like series regularity). Attendees were told that this strategy of batch shooting many episodes would provide efficiencies allowing them to get

FIGURE 6.6. Video art as a "membership business" fixated on fan management. *Top:* Public display of Patreon solicitation, Anaheim, CA. The crossover aspirant's multitasking burden intensifies because marketing trumps creation. While high HBO can segregate and leave the nonart task of marketing to its corporate marketing department, the aspirant creator is not so lucky. In the multitasking burden placed on young creators, marketing eclipses creation in the platform's "skill set-for-success." *Bottom:* Viewfinder with "Fans React" public display wooing influencers, Anaheim, CA. Photos: © 2017, by J. Caldwell.

at their true prize: more fans. The message: don't sweat the small stuff, the lighting, framing, sound quality. Just cut back on time-consuming production values and focus on a clear uploading schedule. Trainees were told to spend more time on viewer interactions, *not* content. "Just check back in to your channel to reply to comments, and promote the videos, and do all of those types of things."[15] Redirecting attention from production form and style to subscriptions makes reception metrics a core skill to be mastered by aspiring online makers.

I found one update of this television-like quest to seek and engage viewers odd. Specifically, workshop experts advised aspiring creators to make face-to-face commercial interactions with fans—rather than screen form or content—their underlying goal. Veteran consultants theorized the secret to success to mentees: "Make sure fan experience is your highest priority. . . . The point at which you switched to offline, and tours? My advice? Listen to feedback (from fans), change your video to make it work better." In this proverb, Tom Greenwood-Mears from Endemol-Shine/UK drives home the lesson for aspiring creators that programming for fans remains a priority above all else: "From YouTube to Instagram and Twitter, when fans want to know more about makers, then use Twitter to set up tours, and meet-and-greets."[16] In this scheme, YouTube is merely a portal to the real goal: offline interactions with fans, face-to-face meetings where makers are better able to manage and monetize subscribers and fans outside of the overt control of YouTube.

At first glance, many would distinguish the high-production-value world of HBO from every other level precisely because it is defined and enabled by subscribers paying upfront premiums. But the art of no-budget YouTubers is now based just as much on building a quantifiable subscriber base as HBO's is. The difference is that the aspirant maker must place subscriber sales at the center of their *artistic* task while HBO's A-listers can leave that enormous nonart task to other corporate divisions; that is, they have the luxury of leaving it to departments whose only mission is to shoulder those sales and marketing tasks explicitly. Its network branding to the contrary, HBO *is* television. At the same time, lower-caste YouTube has "televisioned" itself precisely by making audience management a central aesthetic part of the individual creator's task.

SPONSORSHIP

During my fieldwork, the popular names for those who make online screen content shifted from "YouTubers," to "makers," to "influencers," to "creators." For the production system as a whole the logic of this evolving arc of changing names for media artists is worth exploring further. The myth of the "influencer"—the idea that creator "microcelebrities" are the most effective way to engage with committed fans whom they cultivate—now drives both the high-marketing strategies (of prestige production) and the low-creator strategies (of aspirational production). In some ways, this influencer trope helps direct attention away from the advertising agencies who play central roles. The advertising trades laud firms that can capture trending influencers as a revolutionary mode that allows corporations to expand inconspicuously into the new, unruly world of online media. In reality, this gambit of marketing-camouflaged and psychologized influencer campaigns today—where agencies "sponsor" shows to sell consumers products—is precisely the sort of integrated sponsorship mastered long ago by commercial broadcasters. We do not normally think about old media's Madison Avenue or TV history when the celebrity press covers YouTube stars and crossover influencers. Yet broadcast advertising's financial behaviors continue to fuel and drive low-production video making, as well.

To make any sense of "selling out" more tolerable, marketing rhetoric habitually covers-over advertising's deep sponsorship interventions. Advertisers do this by promoting the idea to viewer-consumers that videos by influencers are "authentic" creative expressions and forms of interpersonal community-building rather than hard- or soft-selling marketing. A Weintraub-Tobin executive spells out the logic of his agency's creator-as-influencer focus: "Brands don't profit unless you piggyback on the goodwill the creator has with their audience."[17] One company highlights the degree of influencer sponsorship in its stable of creators, which it contrasts to other forms of monetization and patronage (like Patreon): "About half of our videos have sponsorship [deals], about half do not. We are very selective. We've walked away from 6-figure deals. Because sometimes a brand deal will ruin your audience."[18]

This influencer agent thus reveals that she walks the fine line between cashing in (by taking third-party money) or losing dedicated fans (who might potentially react to the influencer's money train as "too corporate" and self-serving). In 2018, YouTube's online video portal's US net advertising revenues reached nearly US$3.96 billion.[19] By habitually defining YouTube via TV precedents, trade talk underscores how online influencer production apes the TV advertising money mills of earlier broadcasting. Consumer capitalism treats both media (onscreen then, online now) as strategic. This conflation is echoed by online agencies who boast that "online advertising has already overtaken TV advertising in size. . . . The online advertising market outpaced TV in 2016 by roughly $15 billion."[20] To one public sector (popular media and journalism), the aspirant world hypes its ostensibly distinctive cultural innovations (e.g., viral-trending, influencing, disrupting, crowdsourcing, social curating) as antithetical to old TV. To another trade public (the advertising industry), however, creative and managerial figures in low production emulate the time-tested TV sponsorship prototype as a defining metric for online success in the social media economy. Economics becomes their functional aesthetic.

This public rhetorical flip-flop by rising influencers between edgy trade rhetoric (hyped to get buzz) and routine economic trade practice (cloaked to get sponsors) by rising influencers underscores advertising's long tradition of PR sleight of hand. Social media communities often hail trending online videos as signature artistic expressions of influencers (creator communications). Influencers seldom out their content as proficient vehicles for product selling (consumer products for subscribers and fans). This fold benefits corporations because it looks consensual; it shifts awareness away from the overt economic reality of selling and constantly redirects it onto a different metric: the relative "authenticity" of the microcelebrity or his or her signature personality. Far from innovative, this means of spotlighting onstage talent is merely an update and reiteration of "integrated" product placement mastered in mid-twentieth-century commercial broadcasting. In this earlier mode, hard-sell consumer ads also disappeared as broadcasters transformed and collapsed into softer promotions: artistic offerings and cloaked in-scene promotions.

When speaking to peers and colleagues at a media trade gathering, the Weintraub Tobin talent agent cited earlier (who had just lauded influencers as potential financial windfalls) warns other corporate sponsors to watch out for prospective influencer's liability quicksand. Prospects for this downside increase when industry shifts from stable, long-term campaigns (with established companies) to serial speed-dating (with unknown influencers). The executive warns the rising handlers in the room: "The major risks? Is it brand-safe? Do 'content audits.' Do 'lifestyle audits' [of your influencer]. . . . Check every one of their channels. Don't just look at the last 90 days. Do a criminal background check. Google them. In television, we do a background check of everybody in the production, cast and crew."[21] According to this agent's view, faced with the rapid turnover of unpredictable influencers, agencies with influencers need to apply even more due diligence and suspicion to YouTube microcelebrities than they do to traditional "brands" or legacy media talent (fig. 6.7).

One odd outcome of the shift to influencer sponsorship is that such partnerships suggest that the influencer's ideal endgame is to make a version of the creator available who can be approached by fans "off-screen." Although I mostly explore core low-production basics (how to

FIGURE 6.7. One primary goal for aspiring video creators: any success requires sponsorship. *Left:* "Famebit" pavilion offers mixers and workshops on how adolescent influencers can attract corporate sponsors to leverage capital and "build your brand." *Right top:* Offscreen still frame from faux medieval tapestry created as cross-promotion with *GoT* for Irish tourism campaign (Ireland as *"Game of Thrones* Territory"]. *Right bottom:* Teenage influencers taught to hide selling and "marketing" as human "relationships." In effect, consumer sales must be folded into interpersonal "relationships" for both low-content creators and high-content franchises alike. Photos: Famebit public workshop display for "Influence 2.0," Anaheim, CA. Photos: © 2017, by J. Caldwell.

make onscreen creator "content"), low-production trade pedagogies often do just the opposite. They promote diverse ways to get the influencer personality offscreen, out of their studio. Influencers, that is, need to move into the "real world" and into face-to-face contact with fans (and, one gathers, their disposable money). As one YouTube star I witnessed advised his aspiring peers: "For lifestyle creators, there are no rules about how to go from part-time to full-time. *Getting into Target took a LOT of time.*"[22] Meeting fans in person at a Target department store is not like getting into film school or Sundance. Yet it is posed as such in this maker trade talk about creator success. Many successful YouTube creators talk as if their actual YouTube series—their onscreen content—are merely "loss-leaders" that will hopefully push them into the real objective: human interactions with actual fans in retail consumer spaces. One maker/influencer shared her secrets for success using the content *as onscreen loss-leader* strategy: "YouTube ad revenues?

Not really. We go for 'affiliation marketing'; representing services: *'speaker fees'*—we make the most there. Especially if our channels are live performance, [we go for] *'meet-and-greets.'* Since there are lots of *mall openings*. And you might even get paid to come to VidCon."[23] Whereas YouTube might once have been seen as a stepping-stone to professional film and television work, now many see it as a stepping-stone to offscreen celebrity status. They use the virtual online creator platform as a launch point from which to secure actual spaces for retail sales and fee-based fan transactions.

One big surprise during my fieldwork was the degree to which this impulse—overt advertising sponsorship and face-to-face fan and retail interactions—are now justified by both online makers and their (some-times very young) fans as a central mission of YouTubers. One proud mother, who brought and registered her children at the VidCon 2017 trade show, came to a workshop microphone and explained to hundreds of online makers in the room just how early in childhood development the defense and justification of advertising now must be brought to bear. She recounted her young child's righteous advocacy: "My six-year-old defends his (YouTube star) against other kindergartners, by saying that 'he needs those ads to keep his videos on YouTube.'"[24] Apparently, the lowly online maker world does not just turn edgy teen makers into loyal product sponsors and shills; it also turns preschoolers into frontline apologists for neoliberal economics. Social media incessantly normalizes consumer sales in the turnkey cultural skill set needed for childhood development. In these ways, economic practices—including the drive for celebrity status modeled on TV—are not inseparable from core aesthetic concerns and production fundamentals brokered in the aspirational world of low production.

CULTURAL-INDUSTRIAL *BEHAVIORS* NORMALIZED BY TELEVISIONING

If viewed only through the lens of the core creator experiences of speed, scale, size, specwork, and scarcity examined in chapter 4, high and low production differ fundamentally. We have seen in this chapter, however, how high and low creator worlds align with each other. As detailed thus far, these parallel categories—seriality, sociality, stress aesthetics, subscription, and sponsorship—are better understood through institutional systems analysis. These five additional crossover categories for influencers-creators were standardized as pillars of twentieth-century commercial TV broadcasting long before digital. I have argued that we can productively analyze and understand these parallels (even in the disruptive digital social media age) as a kind of "televisioning"—something that has impacted both high and low production. I have used the verb *televisioning* instead of the noun *television* in this way to suggest a *third* and final level for examining production poetics: the recurring industry behaviors that televisioning facilitates and rewards. That is, in this final section of the chapter I will unpack three ways that industry responds to televisioning. These secondary industrial responses promote, first, *"disintermediation and reintermediation";* second, *"gaming the system";* and third, *"administrative production."*

Intermediation (Dis- and Re-)

The genius of late capitalism is that many very profitable companies don't actually make anything. In capital's shortcut scheme, most firms simply "get in the way" of other people's money and ideas, when both move between makers and consumers across media systems. Given the current long odds for financial success that original media content developers face, intercepting or "representing" other people's money and IP as it travels between two existing points is less precarious or risky than actually producing content. Economic risk for content producers was not always as extreme as it is today. During classical Hollywood cinema's half-century and the decades of the American three-television-network oligopoly that overlapped with it in the mid-twentieth century, studios and networks minimized their content-producing risks through vertical integration or outright industry-government collusion. Decades after regulatory government broke up those restraint-of-trade tendencies in "old media," digital and online media promised to "disintermediate" film and television, cutting out the middlemen, so that viewers had limitless choice and direct access to endless channels and content choices.

Online creator-enabler FameBit offers this now-rote talking point to aspiring creators. Their promise: you can now disintermediate to launch your channel/brand, which means that no experience or authority is needed for success: "But now the bar is: *Anyone* can start a YouTube channel, anyone can have an Instagram feed. And become this kind of authority. And this kind of influencer. You don't have to have a million subs or followers to be an influencer. You can have a lot of influence over a community with just a few thousand, or a few hundred subs."[25] Such claims to the contrary, as creator recognition increases, platforms pressure rising YouTubers to pivot from the online "anybody-can-do-it" success formula. Creators who wish to separate from the disintermediated free-for-all peer herd are mentored to *reintermediate*. At least this imperative holds if they ever want to scale up their aspirational content into more traditional "shows and properties":

> *Link.* Suddenly you get put in the same boat with a lot of people who are just . . . "Oh, we're just . . . this person just uploads a Vlog from their bedroom every single day." And that's great. And that works. But that's not really what we are doing. We're trying to create shows and properties that people can incorporate into their lives, in the same way they incorporate other forms of traditional entertainment.[26]

Broadcast TV made this traditional paradigm bankable in the last century: monetizing content requires nimble representation and opportunistic oversight of intermediaries. With 3.7 billion views at the time I listened to him, Link had learned this lesson well.

Admittedly, digital online platforms did disrupt the old media content systems with an aura of on-demand democratization. Yet the old intermediaries the platforms disrupted—advertising agencies, talent agencies, management companies, distribution and sales reps, etc.—were largely just pushed against, threatened, or replaced by all sorts of new intermediary firms and reps with hyphenated titles and hybrid identities. This abrupt shift from the initial promise of digital disintermediation ("get rid of the middleman") to volatile and multidirectional reintermediation ("let *me* now rep you") is dramatically apparent in aspirational creator worlds. Yet this process—a musical chairs of substituted intermediaries—also impacts the ways high production now engages and expands its online audience.

Even long-standing A-list intermediaries, like CAA, try to reinvent and reboot themselves by selling their management skills to rising creators based on their promises to profitably disintermediate the emerging maker they solicit. Says one CAA agent representing makers/influencers: "This is one of the best times to be alive. Because we can find and discover new voices. This is the best time if you are a creator, because former gatekeepers, those barriers are down!"[27] CAA is basically making a disingenuous appeal to aspiring makers, by cheerleading the (laughable) fact that the old "gatekeepers" (like CAA itself) "are no longer in the way." Here, corporate doublespeak sells aspirant creators on a therapeutic scheme in which corporate reps offer themselves as responsive advocates and enablers (not agents) for creators. This conflicted posturing by a powerful agency also shows how competitive the new online fighting pit has become among agency- and representation-wannabes fighting to displace other online intermediaries.

The major agencies now market many competing corporate identities (not just in "representation" but in financing and production as well). This creative agency expansion in scope goes well beyond the classical Hollywood conception that implied a stable of "10 percenters" or "talent agents." The current agency posture of "working both sides of the fence" (agencies as both reps and competitors) has triggered legal conflicts with their longtime partnering unions like the WGA: "I've been at CAA for 4 years. . . . There were half the amount of networks as there are today. And that was just four years ago. As an agency like CAA, we try to be in *everything*. If something is coming, we want to be on it. There are so many departments."[28] Despite the new conflicts of interest, the complex scale and expanded scope the platform enables means that CAA will likely continue to seek new ways to "get in-between" talent and the money, regardless of how digital practices proliferate.

Popular media claims about the lucrative incomes of maker/influencer stars on social media platforms abound. Even so, such headline cases are relative exceptions. From an overall systems perspective, relatively little money is made by the average individual online maker. Yet huge amounts of capital are mined from the proprietary platforms within which they work, extracted from the vast aspirational surge by the platform and its cloaked side-businesses. One consultant pushed for "getting rid of the middlemen" even as he acknowledged that Google and YouTube have simply hijacked the roles of traditional intermediaries. He claimed, with resignation, "YouTube has become more like an ad agency. . . . The more middlemen in the way, the less money you'll get. It's like the telephone game you played as a kid [when you relayed a message from person to person]. By the end, the brand is completely different!"[29] Emerging companies must shape-shift their brands as packagers, aware that a cyclical disintermediation-reintermediation game now helps drive fluid low-production trade practices. One rising creative manager explains: "The monetization model keeps changing. Talent agencies need to keep up. 'MCNs' [multichannel networks]? No one even calls them that anymore. Now we are a 'visual first media company,' building a library of new IP—from online to traditional media platforms"[30] (fig. 6.8).

This model of MCNs and talent agencies attempting to harvest IP from makers is reminiscent of the very old TV *syndication* model developed in

FIGURE 6.8. The industrial creator/influencer "mothership" and influencer "meet-and-greets." *Top:* VidCon 2017 at Anaheim Convention Center brings corporate rationality and harvesting-at-scale to online media's embedded production system. Photo: © 2017, by J. Caldwell. *Bottom:* Epipheo pushes teen influencers to set up "meet-and-greets" and press-the-flesh at shopping mall appearances with fans. Getting direct contact with end users means pushing one's brand away from the various platform intermediaries (who help aspirants launch but then skim off revenues) to the real world, where maker prospects for cashing-in directly are ostensibly greater. Photo: public display by Epipheo, Anaheim, CA. © 2017, by J. Caldwell.

the 1940s and 1950s. TV syndicators taught both studios and networks, their uneasy partners, that the endlessly *reusable library series* was the most valuable asset—not the initial TV "broadcast." More than a half-century later, by promoting novel "business models for online," new intermediary companies like Studio71 suggest that predatory acquisition is the key to their company's business plan and the ideal "long game" to play. Studio71 explains: "[We want to stress] the importance of building original IP with [new] talent. We also think: 'will that IP stand by itself, even without the talent?"[31] This doublespeak suggests unvarnished predatory representation. Studio71 attends VidCon to market, network, find, harvest, and build new "relationships" with unattached, promising young talent. At the very same time, per its own rhetoric, Studio71 secretly calculates whether it can eventually "ditch" that relationship but *keep* the maker's IP. Their appraisal calculation: "is the IP portable?" Yet from a maker's perspective, that IP "jackpot" scenario likely represents an exception. It will come to fruition, that is, only if and when the maker's new IP beats the long odds by trending and starting to make money.

The media trades, the popular press, and eventually Google all marveled at the original YouTube launch, treating it as a much-needed zero-sum regime change in media. This corporate echo chamber cast YouTube as a great global disintermediation event defined by transparency and direct access. The platform and its many affiliates and sub-companies continue to sell online users and creators with this rhetoric of direct access. This fits Google/YouTube's posturing as a benign and enabling "ecosystem." That posturing helped displace traditional media representation and agencies with new intermediaries and forms of media representation, which included the platform as a whole. In effect, the reintermediation cycle functions as a game of musical chairs played with rising makers/influencers. It acts as a circular contest in which the platform or its affiliates almost always win.

Gaming the System

Televisioning also pushes and rewards aspirant creators for mastering a second institutional behavior, something I will term "gaming the system." By this I mean attempts by makers to short-circuit the system, or to find shortcuts in production, or to hack the platform's search and video-ranking algorithms. At first glance, some of the managerial behaviors detailed in this chapter may seem to undercut my stated goal of delineating core production fundamentals, principles that we traditionally associate with cinematic or artistic screen form. This is because the YouTuber space pushes some notions to the vocational background that once defined aesthetics (ideas about creator vision or artistic elements). In their place, makers/influencers are taught to pursue and master secondary forms of production that focus on "meta" behaviors—like shortcutting, hacking, or gaming the system. These metabehaviors include tactics by which online creators tweak, spin, and push the platform's system and its hidden analytics to gain personal advantage.

As the phenomenological traits (speed, scale, stress in production) I described earlier become more intense, the platform pushes aspiring online makers to find and master correspondingly *automated survival tactics*. This pressure to automate some aspect of video creation makes some sense. With too little time and money, makers need to maximize ways to be seen in order to prosper in the host platform's AI-driven ranking system. Individual media-makers in low production simply cannot keep up with (let alone understand) the endless daily and weekly reiterations of the Google/YouTube search and ranking algorithms— upon which the success and visibility (or disappearance and invisibility) of their creator videos depend.

During fieldwork, I observed a sense of resignation among online creators—a growing realization that the platform is their master and that its algorithm is a fickle mistress. The CEO of Creatus lays out the difficult mind-dulling odds faced by all online makers: "Last year alone there were 200 changes to the YouTube algorithm, with ten times that number in experiments [two thousand per year]. You don't ever know how it makes decisions. The algorithm is AI. . . . YouTube will continue to tweak this."[32] While that clockwork-perversity describes the cloaked activities on the platform's inside, public marketing on the outside is sunnier. Outside, the platform solicits and promotes its recommendations to makers and the public as forms of collective "curation." Yet, it employs "curatorial" in ways that undercut the term as traditionally signified. The "exhibition" selections and recommendations are not "signed" by anyone. As such, online creators quickly learn that the best way to respond to the platform's AI is to employ counter-AI semiautomated, formal trigger tactics in their latest videos. Newly learned trade wisdom promotes vigorous anti-AI strategies. Platform workshops and pedagogy promote this gaming-the-system strategy publicly, without subtlety. As one veteran creator and consultant argued to his mentees: "Metadata—thumbnails, titles, topics—matter more than content."[33] This cut-to-the-chase scheme pushes metadata from the background to the front of the stage, treating it as a formal, core property of online production.

Algorithmic anxiety fuels new media production aesthetics, at least according to the creator pedagogies offered by Jukin Media, Monster, and Theorist Media at VidCon 2017: "Keep up with the algorithm! These platforms are constantly changing. Strategies that work today won't always work next week, or next year. Many successful channels adapted to longer content when the algorithm changed from privileging views to privileging watch minutes. Major changes in your content's behavior or success (without major behavioral changes from the channel) can be indications of algorithmic shift." Monster Media took a different approach in its workshop, providing its aspirants with a Rube Goldbergesque diagram of "the recommendation system architecture, demonstrating the funnel where candidate videos are retrieved and ranked, before presenting only a few to the user."

Google/YouTube's automated harvesting of content is demoralizing to aspiring creators who initially thought that their success would depend mostly on the quality of their individual vision and artistic expression. Two creators commiserate about the disorienting impact of being judged mindless by AI: "Being a YouTuber is like being a chameleon. Yes, the algorithm changes everything."[34] Faced with losing control of their video art and IP to algorithmic robots, makers rail against the platform's lack of transparency. Matt Gielen of Little Monster Media protests to his peers: "That's what upsets me most; they don't communicate changes in advance! If it's good for YouTube, it's good for creators. I'd love them to tell that to the creator who's been laid off, or had his health insurance taken away."[35] This cynical sense that creators must countergame the "rigged" YouTube system to survive comes not just from the secretive host platform but from the bad behaviors of fellow makers/influencers.

A cynical fatalism among struggling creators is actually reinforced by corporate efforts to "teach" uploaders how to hack or beat the platform. For example, what video aesthetic makes sense when experts teach aspirants that "61%" of the internet users that creators seek-out are "fake" users? Other firms helpfully deconstruct the "Adpocalypse" that many attending aspirants felt mired within (fig. 6.9). As a result, jaded skepticism about the authenticity of anything online pervades teen influencer pedagogy I observed in workshops and online.

Attempts to artificially game the platform are often justified by creator coaches as a response to evidence that the system already favors online

FIGURE 6.9. "YouTube anxiety disorder" (YTAD). What production approach makes any sense to aspirant creators when they are told that "61%" of the internet users that creators upload for during the Adpocalypse "are fake"? Jaded skepticism about the authenticity of anything online pervades teen influencer pedagogy. Photos: Public displays for workshop audiences by Jumpwire Media and Jukin Media, VidCon 2017, Anaheim, CA. © 2017, by J. Caldwell.

stealth traffic. Specifically, creator automation promises to counter competing videos that are "unfairly" uploaded by "bad actors." This threat comes from companies and influencers who buy views, buy reviews, buy likes, and buy followers to boost their viewer/subscriber numbers. Brian Solis of Altimeter, an online analytics company, draws out *the* lessons for makers: "We talk about "ROI"/return on investment, but have to deal with "ROI/return on ignorance." . . . There's no transparency. Too much shady stuff. Once you lose trust, you're done."[36] This creator cynicism—about both the secretive host platform *and* the ocean of bad-acting content competitors and fakes that dominate it—reinforces a sense that the game may be rigged. An aura of the platform as a rigged game may ultimately prove counterproductive, not just to the lone creator but also to the overall system. Such cynicism can derail or discredit a range of maker-platform synergies that the ecosystem as a whole once presupposed and promised. Pervasive cynicism increases the prospects of "hive collapse" or system decline. This is an especially problematic outcome, from the system's perspective, if it triggers makers/influencers in large numbers to burnout or to jump ship. Exiting the YouTube platform for greener social media creator platforms elsewhere threatens the system as a whole.

A sobering logic underlies the offers that Creatus, another third-party company, sells to makers/influencers as tricks to countergame the rigged YouTube system. The firm's way of thinking goes something like this: Collective online user behavior triggers YouTube-AI. To overcome this, makers/influencers should try to predict what will come up next on the platform's recommendation engine. Informed predictions like this enable makers to quickly alter their video content to match and exploit the platform's fickle AI appetite. The net result of this surveillance/counter-counterintelligence process? Makers/influencers must make incessant changes to their metadata and automated "video-triggers" if they want to survive and be seen. These *maker-produced AI-triggers* come in a range of forms, which are to be added after the video production has been completed and initially uploaded. These post-postproduction "changes" include fine-tuning upload frequency (yours/theirs); making rapid playlist changes; and constantly changing thumbnails, tags, cards, and end titles. All of these semiautomated changes to one's uploaded videos in turn flood the YouTube system and its algorithms with the *appearance of constant change*. This makes the tactic a lazy version of "innovation" in the eyes of machine intelligence (fig. 6.10).

Gaming the system thus represents another distinction between high- and low-production worlds. Traditionally, prestige producers showcased

FIGURE 6.10. Defy the "7 Day Decay Rate" with metadata trigger art for video uploads. From how-to-hack YouTube algorithm workshop at VidCon 2017, Anaheim, CA. Photo of video displays: © 2017, by J. Caldwell.

premium narrative content as their primary focus, even as they relegated a project's metadata to their marketing departments. By contrast, many aspirational low-production creators are urged to make metadata and marketing their primary creative focus. This fold away from artistry is odd in that it overemphasizes metadata in a creator's working method. It thus reduces the narrative content they create to semiautomated, quasi-disinterested reiteration, degrading their media screen expression to a form dictated by or designed around AI triggers. This reflects an ongoing, pitched surveillance counterintelligence tangle between platform host and maker-influencer. Such a standoff between counter-metabehaviors ends up creating a situation that is about as far removed from video production "aesthetics" as one can get. It seems far removed, as well, from the original notion of artistic "making," which served as a framework for traditional poetics.

Administrative Production

After 2017, one recurring complaint among even successful online crea-tors in my fieldwork was "burnout." A growing number were finding it almost impossible for makers/influencers to "keep-up" with the content and pacing demands required by the platform (which skews toward and favors online episodic form). One successful maker sums up this frus-trated relationship: "As much as I loved the creative side, it ultimately became unsustainable for this channel, because I didn't then have the time to develop the business side of the channel that ultimately would make the three videos [per week] sustainable in the first place."[37] The pace and quantity of content demanded by the platform proved impos-sible to sustain. For perspective, the traditional film school education maintained strict boundaries between the art and technique of film pro-duction, on the one hand, and media industry studies and research, on the other. This cleaner boundary between art and business, typical of traditional film school curricula, has collapsed or morphed into much of what passes for creative work on YouTube, Maker Studios, and Patreon today.[38] In effect, these media platforms systematically reward makers who can combine research and analytics in their creative proc-ess. This means that research and analytics become core aspects of the creative focus *and* the responsibility of the maker (not the platform).

To succeed at content production, aspiring creators need to treat ana-lytics as their artform. Workshops and consultants underscore that video artists should learn from analytics to "program," schedule, and crunch research data like a seasoned TV broadcaster. Consider the command-ment for "algorithmic conditioning" by one spokesperson who explained the logic of the tactic in a Theorist Media workshop: "*Pace your content for algorithmic conditioning.* Posting nothing for a while and then releas-ing something major puts a lot of pressure on any single video to suc-ceed. Posting a ton of content, all at once, drowns out any single video's chance of success. Posting regular content over a long period of time on similar subjects is the best way to teach the algorithm [that] you are a reliable source about your subject or brand."[39] For Theorist Media and its creator mentees, the algorithm is a fickle mistress indeed.

Other firms, like Jumpwire Media, take it a step further, instructing creators on how to take proficient "Data-Selfies" that will show exactly how the social media platform algorithms "see" them: "Data Selfie ana-lyzes your Facebook usage to show what companies can learn about you. . . . Chrome Extension . . . lets you see what Facebook tracks on you."[40] The underlying imperative is that online makers must create upload art that performs well on the AI-driven platform's "trackers" stage. To succeed, creators need to learn to see themselves from the outside like an "analytics" robot, if they ever want to respond to fickle unannounced algorithm changes in the future.

This internalization of analytics thinking (including how platforms robotically "see" the creator) represents a third broad industrial behavior that feeds into the televisioning of online ecosystems. I term this core behavior, involving analytic vigilance, *administrative production.* The scheme can be understood as a folding or reorientation of video production away from what is typically understood as "creative production." I am borrowing the term *administration* from a classic account of communication research by the scholar Paul Lazarsfeld, who contrasted "administrative research" to what he termed "critical research."[41] Critical research is relatively more independent for many scholars, since they are free to determine the research question. As such, critical research has the freedom to consider social trends, political economy, and human values questions that go beyond the typically narrow or constricted interests of an external client or funder. By contrast, "administrative research" (i.e., research provided, supported, or funded by external commercial, government, or corporate interests) means that scholars typically give up a degree of intellectual independence in order to produce findings that meet the funder's or administrator's interests. Since Lazarsfeld, many scholars have been critical of administrative research, research that comes with corporate strings attached. This is because it frequently avoids important questions that are not financially relevant to commercial interests (fig. 6.11).

This critical-vs.-administrative distinction in academic research is seldom applied to or used to explain artistic producing practice or media-art "creation"—which I hope to do here. The artistic/economic predicament of aspirants in low production, in particular, make the critical-vs.-administrative analogy fit well as an explanation for cultural production in the online sphere. Online makers/influencers now face considerable pressure to move beyond the "mere" artistic form of the frame or screen in order to master the "bureaucratic" work of media. This dramatizes that a new foundational skill set or norm for video production has been established. The platform has created a collective "Video Production 101" primer that includes programming, scheduling, research, marketing, and financing. Yet these "add-ons"—which were once all considered *management practices* in twentieth-century

FIGURE 6.11. Preuniversity film school: Pedagogy on Neoliberal Marketing Crack. *Top:* The recreational aura of influencer work. "Be the domino." Photo: GenVideo pavilion, VidCon 2017, Anaheim, CA. © 2017, by J. Caldwell. *Bottom left:* The six philosophical pillars of YouTube's preuniversity "1-minute" film school: "YouTube Creator Academy." Image: Offscreen still frame from YouTube "Creator Academy." *Bottom right:* "Data meets Art" exhibit, Slush Helsinki, 2017. Photo: © 2017, by J. Caldwell.

broadcasting—are now front-loaded onto online makers/influencers as part of the makers' creative task and obligation.

Administrative thinking now pervades artistic talk in the maker/influencer sector. The sanction given it may express a strategic turning or fold between two embedded layers in online media platforms. Administrative thinking is a mentored skill set, normalized from one side by corporate handlers and intermediaries and consented to from the other side by aspiring media creators. This means the mentoring or partnering process (between platform and aspirant creator) also provides a mechanism by which commercial media systems and the technical platform can off-load their own bureaucratic tasks. Specifically, it allows the platform to decentralize the time-consuming bureaucratic labor needed for any monetization in the system. Televisioning provides some corporate advantage by persuading makers/influencers to publicly justify and legitimize administrative, bureaucratic work as central to their personal expression, fulfillment, and aesthetic style.

These pressures often produce unapologetic claims by creators that bureaucratic self-management is a valuable, constituent part of their video art, a skill central to the basic poetics they need to master. Endless workshops, panels, online primers, and maker trade publications make this business acumen a "must-have" for online media-making success. Media platforms now posture basic *market research as online "curation."* Trade talk hijacks this attribution from the traditional artworld where the term signifies a "cultural" practice. The curation crossover underscores the general collapse of conventional art-vs.-business distinctions. Pushing curatorship away from the creator side and onto consumers reinforces and goes hand in hand with the folding of artistic media creators into administrative consumer producers.

CONCLUSIONS AND QUALIFICATIONS

Many online, low-production "indies" are essentially forced to chase their tails. Endlessly. Platform pedagogy teaches them to obsess on the management of user info (which they do not ultimately control). The result? User info becomes the life-force that both "authors" and ultimately "critiques" the maker's created and uploaded content. This hanging-by-a-thread posture (i.e., the desperate pursuit of the audience) is how television and broadcasting have always worked, both as industries and in public awareness.[42] Like broadcasting before it, the online creator space has now also mainstreamed and mastered this behavior. Now unashamedly corporatized, social media creator platforms have taught indie makers/influencers that innovation means vigilantly monitoring viewer interaction and triggering the platform/market with ever newer schemes.

To summarize, the process of televisioning creator/influencer production impacts low-production poetics in several fundamental ways:

1. Stance. The location of the low-production maker's creative act tends to shift from behind the camera (invisible but tacit, as in

conventional filmmaking) to a facing-the-camera aesthetic (visible and explicit, a public microcelebrity market as it were). In favoring on-camera creator personalities (over behind-the-scenes directors), the platform rewards makers and aspiring producers who first work to convert themselves into publicly visible "influencers" into celebrity-bait. Good riddance to brooding auteurs who'd rather lurk in a set's shadows. Extroversion rules!

2. Managerial reflexivity. The mission of the media ecosystem, MCNs, and the platform as a whole now often entails bringing industrial rationalities to the vagaries and irrationalities of artistic expression. The online production poetics outlined in chapter 4 and in this chapter offer a road map to these rising aspirant efficiencies. The platform pedagogy examined here incentivizes influencers to perform self-management-as-art in public. The system as a whole rewards managerial self-consciousness in public as a professional behavior that can be monetized onscreen by social media creators.

3. Administration. The platform mentors aspirants to economize basic aesthetic/formal categories. It also rewards aspiring makers who show success as administrative programmers (à la broadcast stations) rather than as individuated artists or auteurs. Channel management, not just producing form or stylizing content, is obligatory in platform aesthetics.

4. Analytics. By converting the artistic task of indie media-makers into bureaucratic tasks (of programming, scheduling, branding, and monetizing), corporate online media ecosystems have transformed what was once the vision-centered, intuition-driven focus of creative production into the outfacing-research-focus of what I have termed "administrative production."

5. Preprofessional value-adding. The task of assembling the *economic value chain* needed for individual creator career-success has been front-loaded onto the shoulders of individual Gen-Z and millennial makers. (This will be detailed further in chapter 8). Makers, that is, now need to pretest, quantify, and prevalue themselves—before firms and platforms will show interest or woo them. Preemptively outsourcing risk to young creators en masse in this way enhances profitability for studios and networks, as well. Those firms essentially leverage all of the crew-earned soft capital that all projects need to aggregate (but erase) when they assemble

crews for any production. This preemptive economic move to make value-adding culture-work a preliminary chore for prepro-fessional aspirants has the aura of a vast shell game by executives and corporations. Platform pedagogy transforms preuniversity aspirants into platform apologists and market ideologues. This preemptive scheme—of getting creative workers to publicly justify their economic predicament—directly benefits industry. Off-loading the value-adding task onto aspirants deflects a lot of unwanted corporate responsibilities and higher costs than one might normally expect in a "partnership."

Finally, I must qualify my arguments in this chapter with some cave-ats about the economizing, bureaucratizing, and preemption practices sanctioned in high- and low-platform pedagogy. Clearly, artists have always had to find day jobs, always had to market themselves (to patrons, dealers, festivals, distributors). Those artists and filmmakers who did not market themselves effectively enough failed or disappeared from the arts scene. Yet the self-marketing normalized today, a 24/7 phenomenon, with ever-moving benchmarks for success, makes auton-omous individual creation even more difficult to pull off. I am the first one to admit to my students that none of us—including universities and research professors like me—exist "outside" the markets. So the argu-ments I make about the predicament creators face in embedded online production systems are actually modest. The collective, analytics-driven, metaproduction promoted in online creator pedagogy is of course valid and valuable. Yet I am ultimately worried about the human cost to my students and younger colleagues. That is, making research-driven administrative production equivalent to vision-focused, frame-centric creative production produces an impossible dual burden for aspirants and independents to work under or prosper within. The out-come? A multitasking double bind for aspirants and rising creators. Indies and aspirants, that is, must excel not just at production artistry but at much more—at marketing, corporate self-management, and research analytics, as well.

One nagging hunch remains. Online systems and platforms that auto-mate the harvesting and monetizing of creative IP from makers/influenc-ers, in the ways I have described, may find the results of those extractive practices counterproductive in the end. Among informants in the maker sector, I found widening cynicism about fickle or perverse ranking algo-rithms, predatory harvesting, and stealthy automated monetization. Yet despite those extractive behaviors, one also hears workshop justifications conflating this bureaucratic work with artistry and self-expression. Yet this double-barrel process—industrial extraction (economics) bundled with wishful self-justifications about bureaucracy-as-art (rhetoric)—may prove counterproductive to the system's "partners" overall. Such divergent behavior brings potential downsides for the corporate partners and host platform, not just for aspiring media creators in the precariat. Whether or not this extractive disposition leads to a platform's hive-collapse, online media predation likely stunts the media "ecosystem" as a whole. It can trigger losses that go well beyond the never-ending line of dashed-hope aspirants and burned-out makers who choose to leave the creator arena.

7

Fracturing

Rifts and Stress Points as System Self-Portraits

Human systems fail where they are already stressed.
—Lucy Jones, seismologist[1]

There were individual shows we would chase down and
organize . . . in different parts of the country. It was a
national campaign. One thing that really hurt them was a
show in New York. The local there, who represents all of the
traditional backlot unions . . . held them up, held up Free-
mantle (UK)! Held them up *good*. They knew we would
probably stop *[X-Factor]*. On several prior shows we did just
that. They didn't negotiate an agreement because we called
and asked, "Gee it would be nice." It was a *fight*.
—Ron Kutak, "Reality Check": MPEG union organizing meeting[2]

FRACTURES AS SELF-DISCLOSURES, FAULT LINES
AS SELF-IDENTIFIERS

Thus far we have explored a complex media industry system comprised
of many embedded production cultures, agents, actors, and firms. This
chapter reflects on a methodological question that such industrial aggregation raises: how can we ensure that production culture research on
that complex configuration is systematic and undertaken with some disciplinary precision? Having established the difficulty or ill fit of scientific
benchmarks for good research (based on probability, causality, prediction, and falsifiability), I have not attempted to encompass or randomly
sample the phenomenon of production embedding. Nor have I tried to
offer a definitive, singular definition of the millions of participants that

make up the embedded creator systems. Instead, I have tried to find other ways to establish transparent, justifiable, and (most important) locatable data frameworks for analyzing cultural phenomena and industrial evidence. My interface ethnographic fieldwork in the preceding chapters focused on contact zones, partnering interactions, workshopping, and sense-making in the workforce. I have framed those practices as social pedagogies, as symptoms of embedded speculation and industrial folding. I shift now to the third dimension of the systems model, to examine what happens when the stability of embedded creator systems is shattered by unanticipated rifts and fractures.

I have proposed that we design research by focusing on the contacts and interactions between adjacent and adjoining layers of production ecosystems. This approach is arguably preferable to isolating exceptional cases (à la humanities) or statistically extracting some imagined correlation or causality (à la social science). Beyond this, I have proposed that we examine and describe more precisely how embedded production cultures are folded (via stressors) or fractured (via unsustainable contradictions and divergent interests), or both. My assumption throughout the book has been that folds and fractures provide abrupt openings through which complex systems reveal and disclose the issues and problems that are most significant to the complex system as a whole. Triggered by structural stresses and contradictions in conflicted production cultures, I take folds and fractures to represent how the system itself reveals or leaks, unintentionally. Acute moments of controversy or debacle often provide unintended snapshots, not just of newsworthy quirks (or aberrant personalities) but of unremarkable yet deep labor routines as well. Fractures often betray the problematic habits that the system seldom acknowledges but *implicitly* deems very significant to the system as a whole (fig. 7.1).

As I wrote this book, the COVID pandemic largely confirmed my general assumptions about folds and fractures as a complex system's self-identifiers. The chaotic failure of the US to meaningfully respond to the pandemic and the resulting widespread fatalities triggered multiple socioeconomic fractures. The crisis ripped clinically through the long-embedded cultural and symbolic layers of US capitalism. More than just a medical catastrophe, the pandemic exposed deeper fault lines, including long-standing racial disparities and structural economic inequalities. Notably, fault lines for these conflicts and disparities had been persistent and evident on the surface for a long time. Stress lines caused by many intermediary folds in public opinion, that is, were visible and

FIGURE 7.1. Strikes and bankruptcies force industry disclosures. *Left:* Periodic union battles open up and expose inside industrial information to scholars. These can trigger a flurry of overproduced disclosures since both management and labor often first mount accusative PR campaigns (precontract) before covering and folding (stabilizing and concealing) that rift (postcontract). *Right:* Bankruptcy auction of Hal Roach Studios. Industry fractures that disclose and expose embedded business and production stresses include studio bankruptcies. Photos: Courtesy of UCLA Library Digital Collections.

available for scholarship long before the pandemic. Yet the pandemic triggered multiple fractures that laid bare otherwise discounted contradictions. In effect, the crisis uncovered evidence that enabled social scientists to represent race and class structures in new ways. Pandemic fallout allowed researchers to create new kinds of statistically valid pictures that clarified the resolute but unjustified disparities in the complex US social fabric as a whole.

Public health epidemiology favors and employs methods of biostatistical analysis. As a quantitative scientific research enterprise, the World Health Organization (WHO) and the Centers for Disease Control and Prevention (CDC) succeed to the extent that they can randomly sample subjects and victims, identify correlations or causalities, and predict trends based on statistical probability. In doing so, epidemiology creates visualized abstract maps and projections to represent both the disease and (in the COVID-19, George Floyd era) graphic representations of the deep structural racial and economic disparities exposed by the fracture. Prepandemic research had long underscored these same vast structural health disparities in the US based on race and class. Yet it was not until the videotaped depiction of the racial murders of Ahmaud

Arbery and George Floyd that Black Lives Matters (BLM) resurged during the pandemic's catastrophic shutdown, and the nation as a whole convulsed over legal reforms. Stressed fractures spur attention in ways that norm-focused stats cannot.

This split between the CDC and BLM (in both outcomes and impacts) parallels the methodological distinctions I am exploring between two alternative approaches to industry research—that is, digital humanities and quantitative media studies, on the one hand, descriptive fold and fracture research of embedded media systems, on the other. Essentially the CDC uses math to bolster its policy argument for any real-world legal or governmental changes. By contrast, Black Lives Matter made the centuries-old fault lines exposed by the 2020 police murder-pandemic undeniable and unavoidable for many local political officials. Data verifies and abstracts the local to make an instrumental case. Fractures expose and amplify the local as they trigger and release system stresses. Yet both frameworks provide methods for actionable, systematic analysis in research. It is worth comparing the CDC's largely botched impact on coherent policy in 2020 (despite its deep statistical proofs) versus the disruptive changes triggered by BLM in the same year. Fox News outed its racism by glibly explaining the live-on-video police killing of Floyd as a profitable stock tip (fig. 7.2). The immediate lower-level Fox employee blowback in public exposed for scholars a charged researchable production fracture of industry's cultural politics.

In this chapter and the next, I consider production industry shifts that occurred in 2020 and 2021 largely as a result of the pandemic and of racial fractures. I explore rifts, that is, as systemic structural phenomena, which I engage through scholarship based on disembedding or unfolding analysis. To do this, the following section surveys precedents for how we might proceed with contact zone ethnographies and fold and fracture research. I begin by surveying disembedding research approaches within a model of three general, commonsense research orientations. I categorize these study methods as "inside," "backdoor," and "outside" research.

NONFRACTURE ALTERNATIVES: FRONT-DOOR VS. BACKDOOR STUDIES

Media industries can act as either willing partners or unwilling subjects for scholarly research. Ideally, media production researchers can find human subjects in the targeted sector that will allow for or welcome

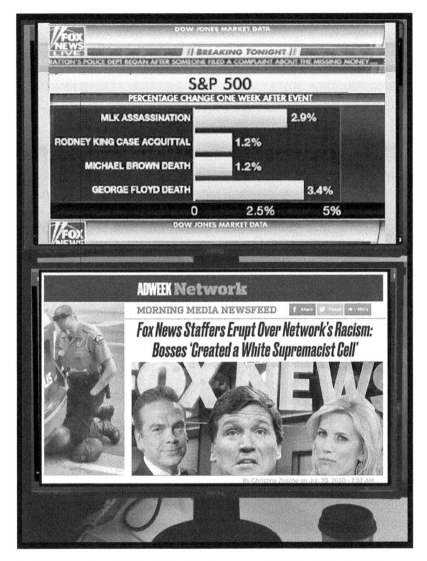

FIGURE 7.2. Fox News' Police-killing-Black-men-as-a-Wall-Street-tip. *Top:* This perverse graphic on Fox News, which correlated police murders of Black men with quick stock-market profits, exemplifies an unforced media industry fracture. Internal production "fails" like these ("Black Lives Matter" as a stock tip) can trigger secondary exposures and leaks from the production community. *Bottom:* This "tip" triggered the Fox News staff uprising that followed the graphic's airing on Fox, which in turn rippled across the trades and press exposing additional interconnections and providing timely context on a specific embedded production community. Images: Composited offscreen still frames from Fox News and the media trade *Adweek,* July 20, 2020.

scholarly observers. But CMS scholars and university IRBs may overestimate how willing proprietary corporations are to let unbridled scholars inside to study in ways that the company cannot then censor or control. Industry's habitual disposition against open access makes some form of noncorporatized research method—like disembedding and fracture research I am proposing—prudent.

Making the case for backdoor fracture methods (following the Fox-race-murder-profit prototype), however, would be remiss without first acknowledging viable precedents for *front-door* scholarship. Several funded research initiatives offer prototypes for front-door corporate-university partnerships that are fully sanctioned and transparent.[3] Redvall's screenwriting research projects at the University of Copenhagen and the Danish Film Institute are built around the shared interests of *both* scholars and national media industry executives in Denmark. Both sides of the partnership use Danish federal funding (for research and production) to systematically explore ways to enhance creative production in Danish television and film. One shared underlying goal is to improve Danish media's standing in world distribution markets. The recent international popularity of Denmark's "small cinema" and national media "brand" in television suggests that positive, lucrative outcomes can follow from sanctioned front-door approaches to industry-university research partnerships.

For scholars in countries that do not provide national federal research funding for creative industries research like Denmark, however, two different precedents for sanctioned front-door research are worth considering. First, the Carsey-Wolf Media Industries Research Center at the University of California, Santa Barbara, underscored how productive corporate-university partnerships could be, even without federal funding. Recent directors Michael Curtin and Jennifer Holt proved particularly good at leveraging industry funds that would allow the center's scholars to pursue independent research questions. They were given this right in return for providing cutting-edge research to their industrial supporters, including Warner Bros. The initiative allowed industry leaders to learn from scholarly conferences, edited volumes, and policy "white papers." In return, the funders agreed to allow the scholars to publish their own articles and research papers without corporate interference. The trick to using corporate money cleanly in this way, as Curtin and Holt demonstrated, was to ensure those terms of independence are included in the initial contract or MOU at the time a partnership agreement is signed.

A similar multiyear initiative—pulled off without federal government or significant university research funding—succeeded as well at UCLA. There, Denise Mann established a university-corporate partnership for contemporary research funded by the French transmedia corporation Havas. Much like UCSB's center, Mann's doctoral researchers undertook original research on digital platforms and social media with two chief outcomes. First, Havas benefited from cutting-edge insights on various adjacent, competitor digital platforms. Like UCSB, UCLA's deliverables came to Havas in the form of symposia presentations and white papers. On the scholarly flip side, Mann and her doctoral researchers were allowed to publish scholarly papers and articles from the research funded by Havas. Both the UCSB and UCLA projects have changed in recent years, yet they provide good prototypes for others to follow. They demonstrate how funding can be secured that supports complex systems research on media industries. Both cases, however, provide one cautionary lesson: industry personnel and corporate funding priorities can change abruptly—sometimes midstream in these crossover front-door partnerships. This prospect of course change is especially real given the organizational and market churn triggered by mergers, bankruptcies, and buyouts that define contemporary film and media industries with which we seek to partner.

"INSIDE" SYSTEM RESEARCH (TYPICALLY OF PRESANCTIONED *HISTORICAL* DATA)

Research from inside production worlds should not be reduced in focus to personal disclosures offered there by industry professionals, or "insiders." Such info tends to be anecdotal, even as it can be contextualized in useful ways. The inside research I am framing here refers instead to (a) research that examines industrial information from within those disclosures and reports; even as it (b) reckons with how that data has been presanctioned. That is, scholars can independently analyze gifted inside info, yet they must contend with the nagging fact that their data bank has been culled and compartmentalized in advance by the industrial system they study. To what end we should ask? Because media industries are corporatized, this kind of preculled data-set scholarship is both possible worldwide and problematic. One exemplary project, an exception that proves the rule, is "Kinomatics: The Industrial Geometry of Culture." This initiative, originally funded by the Australian Research Council, was designed and implemented by a team of scholars from

Australia, Germany, and Canada. Kinomatics' collaborative research center, directed by Deb Verhoeven and Skadi Loist, collects, explores, analyzes, and then publicly disseminates data about the creative industries. Interdisciplinary by design, the current focus of Kinomatics is an analysis of the "spatial and temporal dimensions of international film flow," as well as an attempt to map the new geography of Australian live music performance.[4]

The group self-consciously employs contemporary big data to map international film flows. With a large federal grant, the scholars were able to purchase proprietary industry data about global distribution. This in turn provided the data set used in analysis and visualization. The success of this group raises two issues for industry scholars elsewhere. First, Australia deemed it a national economic priority to develop their nation's "creative industries" sector. Yet prioritizing scholarly-industry partnerships like this is far from the norm in other parts of the world. Second, even with this sanctioned nationalist synergy, the researchers still had to purchase proprietary information from the media industries as a precondition for their scholarship. Scholars seldom explore the preconditioning of their data as problematic. As such, Kinomatics may represent an ideal but difficult-to-replicate partnership arrangement. This especially holds for scholars elsewhere who hope to research cleaner, less prerationed industry information with greater independence (fig. 7.3).

A North American alternative to both fracture research and Kinomatics is "Arclight." Developed by historians Eric Hoyt, David Pierce, and Charles R. Acland, Arclight focuses on machine reading and distant reading to enable analysis of "big data, text-mining, video analytics, databases, [and] networks" within the two-million page "Media History Digital Library."[5] The Arclight project has produced a valuable companion book for historians beginning Digital Humanities research or who want to start research on large, complex legacy media systems computationally. Unfortunately, this kind of archival data mining and distant analysis is only possible up to 1966, the year at which the collection stops. Arclight is extremely valuable for archival film historians. Yet MHDL's policy of primarily "scan[ning] works that are no longer protected by copyright" means that the database is not as suitable for CMS scholars who intend to research or "visualize" current industry trends or *contemporary* production practices from the past half-century.[6]

Another very successful nonfracture precedent for researching large complex industry and production systems is the "Media Ecology

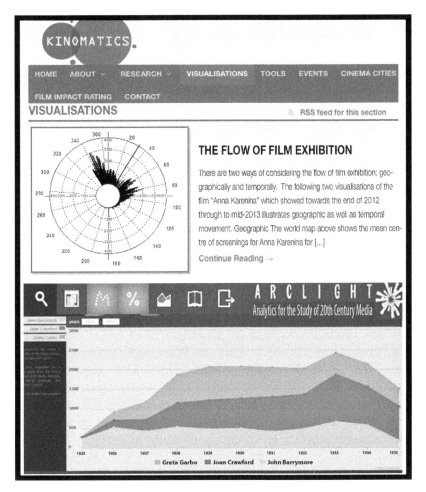

FIGURE 7.3. *Top:* Front-door inside research of presanctioned data at Kinomatics ostensibly provides analysis of media industries that should be valuable to both outside scholars and professional practitioners, who "partner" in sharing data. *Lower:* Inside independent reading of predeposited historical data at Arclight. Charles R. Acland and Eric Hoyt bring digital humanities and the big-data analytics of archives to CMS. Arclight allows scholars to creatively reanimate the dead data available from historical archives. Image: Offscreen still frame from the Kinomatics and Arclight websites, 2016.

Project" (MEP) directed by media historian Mark Williams of Dartmouth.[7] Of the alternatives for inside-industry research discussed in this chapter, the MEP comes closest to the biological conception of ecosystems theory with which I am concerned. This is largely because of how the MEP emphasizes and promotes an interactive, networked process based on feedback and reciprocity. The MEP states that it "enables researchers to digitally access archival moving image collections and contribution of critical analysis to the archival and research communities . . . through the fluid contribution of metadata and other knowledge." This dynamic loop that accrues and modifies metadata breaks free of at least one common inside-research straitjacket. That is, it forces the system to constantly fold-in new metadata, which discourages scholars from misrecognizing industry's predeposited information as somehow stable or clean research data. In effect, the MEP excels at letting *researchers* become part of an expanding feedback network that actively changes the very historical archives the researchers are data-mining. Yet, like Arclight, the MEP is also explicitly geared to *historical* studies and to issues of "memory." As such, it is not entirely suitable for the *contemporary* media industries research and analysis that *Specworld* targets.

FRACTURE RESEARCH PROTOTYPES (BACKDOOR-INSIDE STUDIES)
Breaching, Bots, and Unsanctioned Data

Research inside the Arclight or MEP data bases is necessarily constrained in scope owing to the *historical* boundaries (and deposit agreements) that define almost any preexisting archive. By contrast, Kinomatics does allow for *contemporary* media industry research, yet its data is purchased from proprietary industry sources and thus is preemptively managed and policed. In effect, industry rations its corporate information to scholars, by selectively allocating or selling it. This parsing out inevitably constrains scholarly research questions. Faced with these prospects, some scholars have shifted and become proponents of unsanctioned studies. I next consider these examples of backdoor industry research.

One of the best recent examples of contemporary industry complex systems backdoor research on unsanctioned data is summarized in *Spotify Teardown,* a thoughtfully mixed collection of research approaches authored by Maria Eriksson, Rasmus Fleischer, Anna Johansson, Pelle Snickars, and Patrick Vonderau. This team of social scientists closely examined the company's operations, in part, through front-door means, personal interviews, and trade observations. Yet the team also designed and employed backdoor mechanisms, defining and designing a "backend investigation" approach by creating a fake record label that they set in motion as a "SpotiBot." The researchers uploaded this Trojan horse (a fake musical band) into the platform as if it were a real band.

Their goal: "to peer under the hood" of Spotify's analytics and financial dealings. Once inside, the research bot automatically sent out undetected reports to the scholars that disclosed the platform's internal workings. When the public learned of this breach/research, Spotify threatened the researchers and their funders and warned the team's academic press not to publish their findings. Spotify argued that "unauthorized" entry into the platform was prohibited according to the boilerplate "terms of service" that all users must agree to and sign. This was an odd litigious move, given that the professors and Spotify originally functioned as peers and partners: they were both subsidized in part by the Swedish government. Yet once publication was imminent, Spotify treated their federally-supported peers, the university professors, as consumer criminals.

While Spotify lawyers positioned the scholars as hackers, the scholars posed their method as a "breaching experiment," which is an established research tradition within "ethnomethodology." In the experiment, the research group sought to break into the hidden infrastructures of digital music distribution in order to study the platform's underlying norms and structures. The key idea was to "follow files" (rather than research the people making or using the files) on their distributive journey through the streaming ecosystem. This bot-journey shined a spotlight on the development of music metadata management, even as it suggested links to the field of "big data" knowledge production. In effect, backdoor breaches by the university SpotiBot explored and identified the data-catching mechanisms of the Spotify-owned company The Echo Nest, without securing that company's permission.[8] *Spotify Teardown* offers a viable, alternative model for researching contemporary corporate media ecosystems—at least for CMS scholars who can code (or have a research team that includes capable coders). But this method comes with very real legal, institutional, and economic risks. Spotify's litigious threats and cease-and-desist orders dramatized this downside.

I would argue, however, that Spotify's very overreaction is what makes *Spotify Teardown* a viable scholarly precedent and example of fracture research. The postbreach legal battle against the researchers subsequently triggered the platform to leak/release other proprietary documents. For scholars, this fractured leakage and pushback put all sorts of new corporate information into public circulation. This provided scholars with a fuller, telling snapshot of what Spotify actually is rather than how Spotify typically postures itself to governments and fans (fig. 7.4).

FIGURE 7.4. Two ways in (backdoor, side door). *Top:* Backdoor unsanctioned research of inside host data via breaching bot. Eriksson, Johansson, Fleischer, Snickars, and Vonderau's digital Trojan horse fed scholars the internal behaviors of Spotify's platform. This made the Swedish-funded team's inside scholarship appropriately "independent." Yet Swedish-funded Spotify treated the breach as criminal, with litigious threats. Image: Offscreen still frame of *Rolling Stone* website, 2020. *Lower:* Scaffolding research of independent side data by Andrew deWaard. Image: Visualization of the financial logic of hundreds of onscreen intertexts appearing onscreen in the multiyear series run of *30 Rock*. © 2019, by A. deWaard. Used by permission.

Side-Door Scaffolding Research (Unsanctioned
Independently Aggregated Data)

Both sanctioned front-door and unsanctioned backdoor research have downsides. Some scholars have designed and pursued alternative complex systems media industries research without resorting to either of these options. That is, their research designs have (a) resisted "making a deal with the devil" (at the system's corporate front door) and (b) avoided hacking and entering an automated bot through an unsanctioned "break-in" (at the system's back door). Andrew deWaard's research maps the complex distributions of finance across multimedia systems and connects them to onscreen media texts through big-data analysis. His method in CMS consciously draws on the Digital Humanities. As alternatives to both front and back doors, I conceptualize deWaard's method as "scaffolding research" (from the side) on unsanctioned aggregated data. His research focuses on large industrial data bases that deWaard himself has first identified, collected, and aggregated. The scaffold paradigm resonates, because deWaard has avoided the problem of corporate consent entirely. He undertakes his research adjacent to or along the side of industry. DeWaard's self-aggregating approach to data differs from Kinomatics' approach, which purchases delimited proprietary corporate data to research. DeWaard's contemporary research also differs from that of Arclight and the MEP. They are constrained in historical scope by archive deposit agreements, which necessarily limits the scope and relevance of the archive collection.

DeWaard's data side-scaffolding is by definition neither invented nor industry-gifted. Instead, deWaard builds it by gleaning from a combination of new and reconfigured public data bases (like Twitter, IMDb, etc.). In effect, deWaard cuts across and mines existing public data bases, then reaggregates them with his own data. His goal is to create his own independent modeling of industry's culture-economic system. DeWaard's data hybridizing produces visualizations of the political economy of intertextuality and the use of what he terms "mise-en-synergy" in a media text's construction. Extending his analysis beyond mere formal and thematic relationships between screen texts, deWaard looks at intertextuality as sites for exchanging capital, both economic and cultural (see fig. 7.4, lower). In these examples, the referential capital of the television series *30 Rock* is mapped to discover the variability of references across the episodes, the increasing reliance on intertextuality over the course of the series, and the ecosystem of common references that the series constructs." Surprisingly, deWaard's "distant analysis" approach to "big data" in CMS actually allows him to do the very thing that has been at the heart of the field of traditional film studies. He data-mines to enable the close textual analysis of small (formal) data.

In some ways, deWaard follows Hoyt and Acland's original unrealized pitch for Arclight: "It's Twitter Analytics for film and media history." Acland and Hoyt never followed through fully on that proposal from their platform's launch. Twitter only launched in 2006 and is a very delimited info source. In addition, like Snickars and Vonderau in *Spotify Teardown,* deWaard's research attempts to map the much deeper proprietary space of conglomerate ecosystems. As a complement to *historians* Hoyt, Acland, and Williams, deWaard essentially designs data-mining "workarounds" in order to deconstruct and revisualize corporate media ecosystems. Because those media ecosystems are contemporary, they are otherwise almost always legally inaccessible to CMS scholars (owing to restrictive IP laws, nondisclosure agreements [NDAs], Terms-of-Service [TOS] contracts, and confidentiality agreements).[9]

Unofficial Backdoor (Both-Sides-of-the-Fence)

Sanctioned industry analysis and unsanctioned research (breaching, hacking, and scaffolding data) on embedded production systems are not the only ways to access and research industry. Another research prototype comes from scholar-practitioners who work both sides of the fence in production culture studies. Their professional experience can gain them access via unofficial means. My appreciation for this hybrid may be due to the steady stream of new graduate students I work with at UCLA who come from careers in industry. Sometimes they reenter academia with an air of the walking wounded, often bundled with a sense that the intellectual life may provide spiritual rebirth, career-wise. Others reenter academia while still working professionally, with midstream careers in the often stressful or ill-compensated worlds of professional production. Several individual scholars pursued industry fieldwork at UCLA even as they maintained media or production identities, including Felicia Henderson,[10] Erin Hill,[11] Paul Malcolm,[12] David Craig,[13] and Adam Fish.[14] They provide yet another model and precedent for production culture research. Their relative industry standing arguably helped legitimize their research goals as benign to their industry informants. The production career capital of these scholars, and of many others like them, likely gave their requests for access more legitimacy. A production background can make scholars seem less remarkable or threatening to those guarding the industry's doors.

Yet researchers with crossover professional identities often find that those hybrid orientations can impact the types and degree of disclosure provided by informants in the field.[15] Researchers who are both scholars and practitioners face trade-offs that should be acknowledged as part of the research. These trade-offs include accounting for how fieldwork interactions enable or discourage researchers from maintaining independent critical arguments about their human subjects. At the same time, crossing over can also yield productive insights. An observer's hybrid orientation might facilitate an informant's willingness to disclose "insider" technical knowledge. But it also gives the observer additional insights, allowing them to cut through the industry's carefully maintained layers of promotional flack.[16] Researchers who pursue a reflexive, both-sides-of-the-fence logic in their fieldwork will find an expanding horizon of production practices to research. While unofficial back access may free these hybrid researchers from the straitjackets of sanctioned front-door partnerships, they face less potential for research-ending litigation than the unsanctioned backdoor breachers.

Fracture Research (Unintended Backdoor Research)

Media industries research would benefit if it had more precise descriptive categories to study folds and fractures. The industrial tectonics framework introduced earlier provides a logic for stressed folds and strategic fractures. Chapters 5 and 6 examined fault lines and folding from this media-tectonics perspective. The following section will add two additional categories to that industrial tectonics framework: rifts/scarps and acute fractures. Both of these types expose preexisting stresses, overdetermined interests, and structural contradictions in embedded production systems. The residue of specific interconnections across folds and fractures can provide scholars with locatable, justifiable, and delimited data sets for evidence in production culture research. Industry's self-exposures in unsanctioned fault lines and fissures provide evidence for research that is unscripted and unpackaged by definition. Fractured data leaks can also undercut the corporate ecosystem ethos of intelligent design espoused by large media conglomerates and tech platforms. Table 7.1 provides a schematic of these four dimensions.

This typology of tectonic behaviors in production is geared to a continuum of how relatively disruptive the production stress in question is

222 | Chapter 7

TABLE 7.1   INDUSTRIAL TECTONICS

	System Behaviors	Cases, examples
Fractures	Structural, strategic (industrial biopsies)	Sony hack, AC set death, Paramount Decree, COVID, digital workflow, 12-on/12-off, Fox-race-stock pushback (chapter 7)
Rifts and scarps	Constrained (bad blood memorialized)	Settled strikes, Adpocalypse, 1950s Hollywood vs. TV, 1980s TV-vs.-cable, WGA-vs.-agencies (chapters 7, 8)
Folds	Contained, tactical (turning, consent behaviors)	Nonunion VES & ICG "negotiating," 1980s FCC deregulation, Plandemic blowback, unpaid internships, "dues-paying" ideologies (chapters 5, 6)
Fault lines	Predictive, stored (unsustainable precarity)	WGC, snark, YouTube career burnouts, social media trolling, shadow industries, overleveraged self-funding by aspirants (chapter 4)

to the host industry's environment. These categories run from the most acute (that is, complete or catastrophic industry fractures or breaks) to the least. Less totalizing in disruptive effect, another set of stressors can be understood as major but constrained rifts and scarps. These are followed by a third type: industry's stressed constrained folds that hold and maintain some conflicted production status quo in limbo (even as they show signs of trouble). Finally, researchers will run into a wide range of largely buried yet still visible predictive fault lines. Such latent stresses can flag embedded conflict and potential for future disruption in the system. In the next section, I start with examples of the most extreme fractures and proceed in degrees to offer studyable cases defined by stressors that are more constrained and latent but still visible.

FRACTURES, STRUCTURAL (HACKING, PANDEMICS, AND JURIDICAL DISCLOSURES)

The first category of industry's disruptive self-disclosures involve complete or catastrophic industry fractures or breaks. These are not commonplace but do occur often enough that scholars can take productive advantage in research. Because these fractures are often triggered by legal or prosecutorial actions, litigation, hostile government regulatory action, catastrophe, or hacking, they typically gain public notoriety

FIGURE 7.5. The backdoor Sony hack disclosed mountains of unsanctioned data from the studio. Beyond the resulting international political tension, the unwanted fracture provided scholars with huge amounts of data that Sony legal would never have released for study. Images: Offscreen images from NBC News *(top)* and CBS News *(bottom)*, 2016.

without the willingness or consent of the media companies or networks being fractured. One of the best examples was the Sony hack on November 24, 2014 (fig. 7.5). The press voiced immediate alarm about the unauthorized release of sensitive private employee information from the studio (medical histories, email addresses, intrapersonal takedowns). The celebrity press and real "news" reports alike also emphasized (a) the petty jealousies, enmity, and acrimony being thrown about in Sony's work world, which had long posed as a sunnier organization, and (b) the general threat that hacking poses for the United States' computer infrastructure (a national political perspective). Popular media predictably reduced Sony's crisis to these familiar (person-or-nation) tropes and stereotypes.

Yet the Sony fracture also included another level of evidence less examined by the popular press. The hack, that is, leaked a goldmine of information about midlevel studio practices, including attributable insider quotes, evidence about the work environment, and proprietary financial and market assumptions. Such things are, in fact, relevant to scholarly studies of labor conditions and political economy. Celebrity media covered the hack by marshaling its long-standing appetite for exposing the industry's behind-the-scenes "secrets." With that angle well in hand, I urged my production studies students at the time to think about what was being left out of the coverage. Specifically, I encouraged them to systematically map, data-mine, and analyze everything that both the news media and the celebrity press ignored.

If the hack had fractured preexisting stress lines, then it should also have triggered studyable industry reactions to that fissure downstream. Pent-up frictions now out in the open sparked a flurry of public interactions by the trade press and other production workers, as they reacted to the break and leak. These critical trade interventions could be traced back to different layers of embedding and the interests they represented. Thus, even the trade press coverage, online snark, and real-time worker blowback on social media about the Sony hack could be researched and understood as components and expressions of the bigger industrial system. Specifically they could be taken as an unwilling disclosure and unsanctioned "self-outing" by the host system. Downstream trade debates and analyses merely kickstarted the process and possibility of deeper scholarly production research.

A second, less shadowy, and more managed fracture type results from litigious and prosecutorial disclosures. This is because court cases involving production entities almost always result in the creation and distribution of written descriptions of actual onset practices, attributable quotes, and literal debates that dramatize that studios and networks are nothing like the cohesive monolithic brands they are marketed as. Courts can legally order organizational disclosures that studios would never grant scholars or allow for in employee NDAs and IRBs. The onset death of twenty-seven-year-old AC Sarah Jones in February 20, 2014, on a Jessup, Georgia, shooting location for the film "Midnight

Special," fractured and exposed deep structural problems that had long been normalized and covered over by the production system as a whole.[17] News that a CSX train plowed through the crew on-location, killing Jones and injuring eight other crew members spread through organized labor media. A "We Are All Sarah Jones" movement quickly spread—visibly and symbolically—to other sets and productions across the industry (fig. 7.6). As social media and labor opened up the fissure widely to the trade public, film director Randall Miller was arrested and jailed, and three others were indicted on criminal trespass and voluntary manslaughter charges. This felony prosecution triggered a subsequent lawsuit by the production company Film Allman against its insurer, New York Marine, for refusing to underwrite the financial losses that resulted when the production was terminated.

A clear example of a prosecutorial fracture, this avoidable, tragic death on-set revealed the embedded workings of industry to the public and scholars. The breaching flowed through at least four downstream channels: (1) social media creation and on-set activism by peer workers; (2) a criminal case, which produced eighty-six photos, recreations, and video analyses of the train trestle, along with investigative reports from OSHA and the department of labor (released per a Freedom of Information Act request); (3) the considerable advocacy trade chatter documents that circulated in and around the civil trial by one legal firm or the other; and (4) trade publications. *Variety* and the *Hollywood Reporter* provided timely play-by-play reports on the fallout. Beyond the trades (which are frequently the researcher's first means of accessing any subject), I find the other levels of responses—the ancillary communications, visual artifacts, social media creations, and on-set activism—more compelling as evidence. For they show just how deep below-the-line resentment runs in the broader production industry. The rich array of deep texts and artifacts revealed much about labor conditions (long hours and precarity) and the habit of producers to take unnecessary shortcuts for budgetary reasons.

Systems thinking helps us more effectively triangulate among all these registers. The diversity of evidence dislodged in the Sarah Jones tragedy provides scholars a much more dimensional view of the deep links and webs of labor contestation that make up adjacent strata of embedded production sectors. The case challenges us to consider two alternatives in production research design: an in-the-breach mapping of the aggregated disclosures and a downstream analysis over time of the incident and its aftermath. The first mode entails describing the network's

FIGURE 7.6. The "We Are All Sarah Jones" on-set protests sweep across other productions. AC Jones's tragic on-set death triggers both felony indictments and civil cases against the producers and production company. An apt example of a prosecutorial and litigious fracture that opened to daylight industry debates about dangerous and pernicious production management practices. Photo montage from publicized court documents, OSHA reports, mug shots, location photos, slate solidarity messages, and crew protests on social media.

real-time synchronic ties exposed at the time of the abrupt crisis. Such shutdowns out and then freeze relationships in the public record. In effect, the courts that intervene publicize then embed the shoot's various coproduction relationships in studyable amber. As such, the on-location breach offered researchers both a start-point and a relationship freeze-frame of the many firms and subfirms overseeing the disaster (from insurance companies to state film commissions and tax subsidies).

Second, crises like these also allow scholars to study diachronic inter-actions that subsequently unfold in the public eye downstream from the initial breach. The felony, the prosecution, and the civil trial provide a static synchronic "snapshot" of an industry-stressed fault line laid bare. Yet scholars can also study the impact of the breach through a diachronic lens, as it ripples across adjacent industry sectors. This temporal "ripple effect" enables researchers to systematically trace then study how the overall system reacts to a breach over time. Much as an earthquake spe-cialist uses Richter scale readings to map the digression of disruption over space and time, scholars can trace how the fracture ripples through the trade press, competing production companies, marketing firms, organized labor, and professional craft associations over time. Sarah Jones's death was tragic by any measure. For management and crew alike, it was surely an unplanned exception. Yet it serves as an unin-tended fissure case that underscores how industry systematically pushes limits during location shooting to monetize its flexible, serial, labor force.

The abrupt 2020 shutdown of US film and television production due to the worldwide COVID-19 pandemic offers a third example of a cata-strophic fracture in Hollywood's overall complex embedded produc-tion system. Like the economy in general, US film and television pro-duction had never been unilaterally shut down from the top, this abruptly, ever before. As a result, almost all sectors (except program-ming, management, and streaming) were halted. A months-long freeze of numerous in-progress productions in midstream followed. During the freeze, studios and union reps struggled to come up with "best prac-tices" guidelines for below-the-line work in the postpandemic age. The halt made clear just how much physical production relied on interper-sonal and equipment touch-and-feel, proximity, communal feeding, and a degree of collective work interactions not unlike athletics. Insur-ance underwriters would no longer insure multimillion-dollar shoots if they were halted because of viral outbreaks. In response, studio execu-tives either plotted Byzantine ways to disaggregate crews and schedules, or they moved to tinier modes-of-production on their lots. This was an odd move for majors since the new pandemic crew sizes and budgets were more typical of smaller outsider "indies." This "cheap" mode meant that the studio's vast infrastructure remained acutely underutilized. Foreign travel—the linchpin of transnational coproductions and runaway production—was also halted for months.

Industry's freeze-frame then began to thaw sporadically and irregularly. This protracted thawing exposed numerous, long-standing structural tensions in the industry's complex embedded system. Countries that survived the pandemic sooner—like Iceland, Slovenia, Korea, and the Czech Republic (each of which rejected Trump's COVID-19 management-by-chaos model)—swooped in to lure American companies to relocate their shooting there. What problematic production practices were outed by this systemic rupture? Transnational runaway production was already the union-busting norm, at least from LA media's vantage point. Yet, in the pandemic, even management could not travel to oversee coproductions elsewhere. More alarming still, tens of thousands of contract employees, nonunion, and work-for-hire crew members left in the US were unable to get federal CARES or payroll protection subsidies because the Trump-era IRS considered them neither "employees" nor "corporations."

Of course, Hollywood created that very identity confusion (employee vs. self-employed contractor) by design many decades ago. By treating many contract workers outside of IATSE as "self-employed" Hollywood jettisoned any responsibility for providing medical or retirement benefits or longer-term security. In many ways, Hollywood had arguably invented the "gig economy," which became its production prototype (or addiction) long before Uber and Lyft upscaled and platformed gigging. LA's flexible always-at-the-ready workforce—essentially on-call flex-labor—proved itself to studios as a lean-overhead labor cash cow. Industry took that labor arrangement to the bank for more than a half-century. Yet during COVID-19 industry's labor force was paying an acute price for that once consensual, workable labor mashup confusion. Finally, pandemic production spurred lots of proposals for small crews, small location footprints, and reduced interworker interaction on-set. This, in effect, threatened the narrow craft specialization and technical Taylorism that persists in unionized, A-list production. The executive impulse to switch to an indie mode to reboot Hollywood fits a long history of opportunism that seldom hesitated to add deskilling and multitasking pressures from management onto workers whenever possible. The pandemic fracture in 2020 merely left Hollywood's habitual labor precarity hanging out in public—indirectly exposing it in the wake of the shutdown.

Pandemic Hollywood provides a striking picture of potential cultural outcomes from industry folds and fractures. Acute industry fractures do more than just halt work activity. Those fissures also seem to inject hermeneutic adrenalin into the entire embedded system; that is, fractures spur almost all levels of production to speak out, to self-justify, and to rationalize their very reason that they are, arguably, integral to the complex system. During the pandemic, as physical production ground to a halt, industrial self-theorizing amped up. This theorizing exhibited an inverse logic: the making-halt triggered a theorizing spike. In effect, adjacent production sectors jockeyed to maintain, boost, or reestablish their legitimacy in the system as a whole. So in addition to just exposing problematic structural stresses (e.g., exploitative labor schemes, the gig economy, and precarity), fractures also gift to scholars lots of industrial explanations (trade theorizing) about what went wrong, what needs to change, how the complex system as a whole works. All of this preemptive analysis is researchable and event specific (offering a way to frame and delimit a research sample).

While the Sarah Jones incident was tragic for crews working in physical production, industry's 2020 pandemic fracture went wider. It proved to be a catastrophic scenario for all kinds of crafts, specialties, and trades. The pandemic-triggered economic crisis effectively derailed the status quo (the embedded production hive), reducing the amount of literal physical production, even as it spurred increased cultural speculation about production. Industry fractures like this underscore the imperative for industry scholars to look past predesigned bureaucratic schemes in order to unpack and take seriously the expressive slippery middle term in "production culture studies."

RIFTS AND SCARPS (CONSTRAINED STRESSES, BAD-BLOOD MEMORIALIZED)

A second level in the typology of industrial production tectonics can be likened to geological "rifts" (plates pulled askew in a surface thought to be solid) or "scarps" (vestigial cliffs left by misaligned fissures). These geological tropes resonate with media in part because the history of Hollywood and other film and television industries can be usefully studied as histories of interfirm or intersector conflict and contestation. These contentions include strikes, walkouts, firings, broken deals, and coercion. Yet Hollywood habitually postures as a monolith, often by publicly celebrating its deep 150-year-old linear ancestry. One reason Hollywood can posture as a unity or continuity is because many of its conflicts, strikes, and fissures were ultimately resolved or contractually settled. Those settlements ostensibly corralled untenable management-labor feuds, bringing misaligned strata symbolically back into a functional, inertial film/TV mode of production.

For this reason, I see rifts and scarps as potentially rich sites for tangible evidence of "bad blood" between industry players. They offer evidence of mutual suspicion or conflict that has been buried by industry, left behind. Yet that buried conflict has likely been memorialized in some way (via labor contracts, corporate mergers, hostile takeovers). Like disjointed tectonic plates askew in a rift, or the abrupt ridgeline jutting above a fault in a scarp, descendants of the antagonists in earlier Hollywood blood feuds do not usually forget the contention of a given union war or act of studio malfeasance or coercion. The memories live on even after workers go back to work. The Hollywood Ten and the McCarthy-era blacklist, for example, were technically "resolved" over time in public. Yet they also eventually scarped into their own experiential subgenre of cynical onscreen content. Those two earlier Cold War rifts and boss-labor fissures live on for researchers. It's as if they are buried in onscreen expressions of cynicism: "Yes, we will continue to work together with the studios, but we will never forget what they did."

Without access to examine a cleaner crosscut section exposed by acute fractures, rifts encourage us to pay more attention to how the larger system responds to the disruption. Focusing on reactive behaviors to the stress or fissure in question means paying particular attention to how the stress or conflict was ultimately constrained or mainstreamed by industry. There are many earlier examples of rifts in film and television history. The explosive growth of American TV broadcasting from 1948 to 1952 led to the precipitous collapse of theatrical film box office during the decade that followed as the dominant business model in Hollywood. How did Hollywood constrain the TV beast? It changed itself, its look, color, aspect ratios, and equipment, all in order to redefine and market "cinema." That technology-look provided one key visible scarp left behind from the intermedia rift.

At the same time, less publicly, Hollywood recruited new creators from TV, harvesting a whole generation of film directors in the 1960s who had cut their teeth on the method acting favored in TV's "golden age." Outsider agents like Lou Wasserman from TV introduced the "package system," which dominates film to this day.[18] The "package" can be viewed as another TV-induced scarp researchable "inside" film. For several decades since then, film and TV have cautiously parried and postured around each other as uneasy cultural bedfellows. The posing has been unusual at times—an intermedia odd couple in denial about sharing a deep economic partnership.

Some might see poetic justice in the recent ways that industry since then has again turned the tables on TV's initial industrial ascent and dominance over film. This comeuppance came when prime-time broadcast TV tangled with, and ultimately declined in the face of, its newer multichannel competitor "cable" in the 1980s and 1990s. By the 2000s cable had dethroned and dominated the broadcast networks. Cable accomplished this in part by exploiting a continuing narrative miniseries format that was first developed by broadcast TV in the 1970s and 1980s. That miniseries form can be engaged by scholars as a TV-induced scarp inside of cable. At the same time, TV networks were forced by cable's rise to overhaul themselves with niche branding (another researchable scarp) in the 1980s.

A more recent example of a continuing rift and scarp is the "Adpocalypse" that shuddered through YouTube starting in 2017. In effect, YouTube changed the algorithm by which it ranked and recommended newly uploaded videos to other users. As we saw in chapter 6, most of the ethnographic subjects I talked with in 2017 and 2019 viewed the defunding of their YouTube channels owing to the Adpocalypse as a major threat to their prospects for continued expansion or increased success on the platform. Since YouTube had earlier celebrated that it was "partnering" to share ad revenues with rising and successful YouTubers, the fact that the platform might no longer prioritize one's uploads as highly as it once did felt like an existential threat. "YouTube's Partner Program" only shared ad revenues with YouTuber channels that had one thousand subscribers and four thousand watched hours in the previous twelve months.[19] Many YouTubers were dispirited by the way YouTube had "moved the goalposts" without telling them. The Adpocalypse jeopardized careers.

This ancillary "demonetization" of even good actors/influencers was especially troubling to aspiring creators who had planned to launch and build their careers around a growing subscriber base linked to automated monetization on the platform. Some YouTubers complained that their revenues had been cut to a fraction of their earlier income. Others complained that their new video uploads simply "disappeared" and were now never ranked or seldom liked. What perplexed many was that YouTube never provided an adequate explanation or description with any specifics about how and why it had altered the algorithm. After the change, YouTube did claim that it now had to "flag" and "demonetize" racist and lewd videos uploaded by bad actors. Yet beyond that, YouTube simply posted sunny, vague announcements saying that it would constantly adjust the algorithm in the future to "improve" the ranking and recommendation system.

This unsettled many aspirant creators who felt used and foolish, since they had assumed that they had been building a loyal financial partnership with the platform that was reciprocal. After the Adpocalypse, many remained unpersuaded and resentful. While many jilted YouTubers left the platform, others developed whole channels devoted to critiquing the perverse impulses of their YouTube masters. Some makers created and posted explicit burnout-and-quitting YouTube videos to mark their exit.[20] Other makers/influencers created channels that provided practical psychotherapy for peers who felt betrayed by their host. Surely YouTube therapy could help young creators regain at least some vestige of hope for careers as media artists.

My sense is that the YouTube platform benefits from these kinds of stressed pushback scarps by makers/influencers on their platforms for two reasons. First, having resident critics on the platform stokes the public notion that the platform itself is "agnostic," that it is not a "content producer." Second, the platform's immense size and scale ultimately make it impervious to any localized pushback. I am still troubled as a scholar, however, by the innate perversity of this arrangement. In effect, the long-term partner host implicitly taunts its maker/influencer partners to "guess what is behind the curtain"—if the maker wants to succeed. At the same time that YouTube solicits aspirant creators, however, it warns loyal users that the platform will—continually and without warning—change the "curtain" (the hidden secret of its algorithm). This contradictory platform talk makes the "partnership" feel more like S&M. Its teasing doublespeak ingrains human stress deep within the UGC system, in a way that produces a studyable rift. This conflicted rhetoric produces perverse partnering conditions among the platform's embedded aspiring and rising creators.

FOLDS (TACTICAL, CONTAINED)

Media folds represent a third category of disruption and change evident in embedded production systems that can be framed for research. As we saw in chapters 5 and 6, folds describe industry disruptions that play out when one production entity tries to turn, gain advantage, or survive alongside an adjacent production entity, even ones it is ostensibly partnering with. As the case study of maker/influencer poetics suggested, fold studies pay specific attention to three aspects in the folding process. The first task is to describe the institutional identities of the adjacent production entities engaged or interacting in the fold as partners or competitors. This initial task provides essential foundational perspectives needed to identify the labor systems and political economy in question. The second objective aims to examine the ways that symbolic trade talk "turns," redirects, or reframes one strata or the other. Describing how two or more strata or sectors interact to cocreate a fold is necessary for effective research on targeting cultural politics and practice in production. The third goal aims to analyze the resulting consent behaviors evident in the production entities being folded. Consent behaviors include claims, rationalizations, and behaviors that naturalize or legitimize the fold or change in the embedded production system. This dimension in fold research pays particular attention to discursive rationalizations in firms or trade sectors.

A good historical example of an industrial fold occurred during the Reagan era of media deregulation. Although ABC, CBS, and NBC continue to this day, those TV networks turned or changed as part of a substantive system fold during the 1980s. Although supported by advertising since their launch in the late 1940s and early 1950s, the US television networks also were assigned federal legal standing as "public trustees of the airwaves" since their launch. This meant that even as for-profit corporations, they needed to show publicly that they were not acting in self-interest but in the collective "public interest." This public-interest burden had been specified in the 1934 Radio Act and the 1946 Blue Book. But this earlier big-government-mandated "trusteeship" did not fit the deregulatory ideals of either Reagan or his FCC chief, Mark Fowler. Echoing Reagan's "government is the problem" ethos, Congress, the Whitehouse, and the FCC all moved past the intrusive burden of regulating collective trusteeship to the idea that broadcasters should actually just function as "free market" media voices.[21] Deregulated free markets, according to this view, provide the most "democratic" forms for media. With a big enough and diverse enough market of viewer choice, American citizens could "vote with their remotes" rather than submit to spoon-feeding by some managed, middle-of-the-road "balanced" programing sanctioned by trustees of the "nanny-state."

I have detailed elsewhere the immense formal changes and continuities that US network TV underwent in the 1980s.[22] But even as the networks continued developing and airing the same recognizable genres—sitcoms, hour-long dramas, miniseries, and live sporting events—political and regulatory changes overhauled the self-justifications they made to their affiliates and sponsors. They increasingly shifted from economies of scale to economies of scope—from "mass" to "niche" marketing. At the same time, the FCC, FTC, and DOJ gave the greenlight to corporate conglomeration, multimedia mergers, and vertical reintegration. Those antiregulatory changes left no doubt about the apparent mission of the broadcast networks. They needed to welcome new market competitors to the content smorgasbord now designed to feed the "consumer's" marketplace for onscreen content.

In effect, legal and political-economic frameworks effectively pressured and turned industrial practice and trade discourse. Both now focused on the wonders and profitability of "narrowcasting." In this case, content creators were pushed away from their decades-old embedding in a communications law context. In the 1980s, they were folded and reembedded within a corporate-federal neoliberal market regime. An ideology and rhetoric of narrowcasting at upfronts and affiliates meetings provided effective consent behaviors that publicly normalized this major industry interstrata market fold (from public trustee to niche marketer). Once symbolically folded into this ostensibly more "democratic" media market, Fox, HBO, and then Netflix gradually took over dominant positions in the posttrustee and post–public service world of American TV programming.

The launch of the "ICG" in 2016 provides a more contemporary post-TV example of another almost fully contained fold within an embedded production system. Ambitiously christened the "Internet Creators Guild," the accompanying online call to arms by founder and YouTube star Hank Green raised the possibility of organizing online creator labor in the platform space (fig. 7.7). The WGA- and DGA-aspiring trope of a "guild" evoked questions about whether union organizing might help improve the working conditions of a vast number of aspiring creators on the precarious YouTube platform. Yet the founding ICG charter seemed oblivious or unaware of the actual histories and role of production guilds. That is, while celebrated by many makers/influencers online, the charter somehow managed to strip the ICG of any policy that would guarantee interguild solidarity or rights of YouTubers to collectively bargain for better pay and terms. The ICG gutted the very conditions that define real guilds.

In effect, the new ICG charter disregarded the primary objective of traditional creative unions and "guilds" (DGA, WGA, SAG). Those "old

FIGURE 7.7. YouTubers attempt to regain a foothold of control. *Top:* Offscreen still frame from ICG (2016). Key creators launched an "Internet Creators Guild" (evoking the DGA) yet demanded none of the conditions that unions demand by definition. The ICG functions more like a wishful chamber of commerce than a collective bargaining unit that manages labor expertise through scarcity. *Bottom:* Offscreen still frame from *TubeFilter*, July 10, 2019. "Adpocalypse's" platform pushback against maker anger (cover over and bury the rift). After defunding aspirant creators in their Adpocalypse, YouTube launched an "educational" campaign to teach YouTubers why the robots they used to "take down" creator content was fair. As evermore failed YouTubers transformed "giving up" videos into a platform genre, the ICG itself gave up and closed down by 2019.

media" prototypes require guilds to collectively negotiate and manage the scarcity of the creative labor community. Yet, the new ICG "guild" did just the *opposite*. Rather than managing labor scarcity, it lowered bars to entry—promoting and recruiting others into online creation—thus destroying any scarcity (and higher incomes) for labor specialties. Instead, the ICG launched with a *scarcity-busting* goal. Green marveled at the sunny prospects: "making stuff on the internet is one of the best jobs—and we want that job to be available to more people." In effect, the new ICG embedded within the YouTube ecosystem functioned far less like a union and much more like a promotional chamber of commerce. To be fair, there are parallels and precedents in "old media" for making organized labor act like a chamber of commerce, a promotional entity that has and seeks *no* leverage through labor action or industrial resistance.

The ICG, for example, was not unlike the well-meaning but (in one aspect) toothless Visual Effects Society (VES). Although it acts as an essential educational and socioprofessional resource for its members, the VES has no real contractual or bargaining leverage over the studios that employ its members. As a result, the nonunion VES is stuck begging for the kindness of studios to give its members even simple symbolic mentions or acknowledgments. Actual end-title credits and clips of scenes created by VES workers for personal reels are seldom given to the workers by studios. This reduces an ostensible "labor" organization like the VES into the lobbyist and chamber of commerce promotional functions that prefigured the newer, utopian, and now defunct ICG. Maker/influencer trades like the *Creator Handbook* rationalize the enabling role of the ICG. They thus provide widely circulated consent behaviors that normalize the ways that aspirant makers are folded away from workers' rights and folded into rhetorical promotion. Essentially, both the ICG and VES act like "best-practices" cheerleaders, fenced-off on sidelines away from the structural legal-economic schemes that actually impact them the most.

One final production practice from the social media arena suggests how abrupt folds can reveal themselves to scholars. As deaths from COVID-19 skyrocketed, "veteran" social media creator Mikki Willis reckoned that pandemic-related content would be timely; he surmised that it could generate large numbers of likes and views. The result? On May 4, 2020, Willis uploaded a twenty-six-minute video titled *Plandemic*, which featured a single discredited scientific "expert," Judy Mikovits, who attacked the reported infectious deaths as hysteria. Willis bundled this with damning claims that COVID-19 science and federal medical guidelines were profit-making conspiracies by the CDC, the

NIH, and Bill Gates. Once uploaded, *Plandemic* ricocheted around the social media world at immense speed, fueling right-wing conspiracies and inspiring armed protests at state capitols against government over-reach. On May 6, both YouTube and Facebook pulled down the video. But the damage had been done. *Plandemic* took on a life of its own. It still serves as an armed user's guide for viral media science denial.

How did *Plandemic* serve as a stressed fold? YouTube and Facebook embrace their roles as social media's heavyweight arenas. They protect that dominance with extreme vigilance against any critics or govern-ment regulators that might dare to define or treat them as "content providers." Claiming, instead, to be agnostic "tech platforms" ensures that YouTube and Facebook remain immensely profitable—precisely because they fly under the radar and are not responsible to regulators. Nor are the platforms legally liable for any content violations, racism, sexism, or bad behavior by creators on their platform. By eventually removing *Plandemic* from the platforms on May 6, however, Facebook and YouTube betrayed their true colors—unintentionally acknowledg-ing their roles as content mediators and providers.

In effect, the companies shape-shift when necessary—hand-washers about most bad actors on the platform most of the time but now, appar-ently, responsible for suspect content and standards on their platforms after all. Or maybe this controversy provided only a temporary rift in the platforms' preferred symbolic fold as tech companies. Perhaps *Plan-demic* was a one-off rift triggered by bad actors and exceptional circum-stances, a near-breach controversy that erupted in a month that saw the COVID-19 death toll in the US reach almost one hundred thousand. Notably, after eventually censoring *Plandemic,* YouTube and Facebook went back to their habitual, symbolic tech-platform posturing. Their renewed "just-tech" posture was normalized by rote platform pedagogy explaining that content flagging and takedowns are not, in fact, forms of censorship. They are, rather, merely crowdsourced "community standards" within platform ecosystems defined by mutuality.

Times of industrial crisis and conflict often trigger folds and rifts that reveal much about the system as a whole. Broadcast caretakers for the citizenry became niche-market narrowcasters for consumers in the 1980s. The ICG "guild" channeled an ocean of makers away from man-aged scarcity and actual labor organizing into a community of feel-good boosters who invited newcomers to create content excess as their ticket to a "real" career. The conspiratorial *Plandemic* crisis triggered YouTube and Facebook to briefly unfold and out themselves as content providers, before covering over this brief confession. A spike in cultural trade expressions managed the folding, unfolding, and recontainment in all three of these exemplary cases.

FAULT LINES (PREDICTIVE, STORED)

The fourth level of industrial disruption, fault lines with the lowest stress, can, for a variety of reasons, be both challenging and surprising when examined closely. For starters, even stressed fault lines are sometimes difficult to make out. Locating them can be frustrating because they often appear amorphous and partial when viewed through industry's public facade. The full extent of the frictions or conflicts that cause faults are characteristically buried out of sight within industry's embedded sectors. Production workers during fieldwork often evoke troubled areas and issues tangentially—in comments about inadequate pay, benefits, perks, or conditions, and undue stresses of all sorts. Such issues may feel unresolved, in part because resentment may build up over time, its frictions stored in an unstable limbo required by workplace civility. Like latent earthquake rifts right before they are triggered, production fault lines may be poised to let loose an enormous amount of stored energy. Industry fault lines often issue from conditions of unsustainable occupational precarity. Cases of unsustainability examined in the book include predatory financial partnerships and an overreliance on self-funding by aspiring creative workers. Other practices—online intercraft snark and career burnout videos created by young YouTubers—can be predictive. Buried fault lines like these are cautionary, suggesting the likelihood of some future rift or more acute fissure between production interests.

Self-Exposed Fault Lines

I have found at least three subtypes of fault lines that can be usefully distinguished in embedded production systems: (1) self-exposed fault lines, (2) occluded fault lines, and (3) buried fault lines. As the first term implies, some stress lines in the production world call attention to themselves overtly by design. The infiltration of "new" social media channels in and around "legacy" production communities has made some stress faults and fractures in production difficult to avoid or deny. The aspirational online creators, for example, provide telling examples of angry warnings, cautionary anecdotes, "burnout" videos, and worker pushback. Some are often delivered with the intonation of a jilted lover.

Burned-out makers frequently upload their complaint and protest videos back onto the same problematic platforms that hosted and jilted them in the first place. Self-exposed fault lines issue from stressed participants that still want to be publicly seen.

Even as protests by online creators flag awareness of some industrial fault lines, unfair or predatory contracts (with aspirants and emerging creators by media corporations or MCNs) can also trigger exposed outrage. Maker Studios is an exemplary case. It launched to much acclaim, jumped into the YouTube platform early as a rising MCN, and then was bought out by Disney in 2014 for a $500 million. This astounding price tag ballooned to $675 million once performance related revenue targets "were included in the contract."[23] Makers/influencers, social media platforms, and the media trades all reacted to this flood of corporate money as if a financial "golden age" had suddenly arrived for millennial social media creators. Once Maker scaled-up, however, the terms in the deals Maker had signed with its young creator stars no longer looked like the financial sure bets they had been originally hailed as. Some once highly touted Maker creator-stars, like Ray William Johnson, went public. Johnson uploaded sobering details about the contractual limitations he faced and the problems built into exclusive Maker "partnerships" (fig. 7.8). Others explained the traps that Maker contracts put creators in. Their complaints about the platforms preventing rising makers profiting more fairly from their creations evoked the allegory of beating one's head against the wall.

One established Maker star and a top-ranked video-gamer, "Braindeadly," uploaded a final post for his channel, which carried the air of a vocational suicide note: "I am completely powerless. If this is the last thing I write please don't make the same mistake as I did and always read before you sign something."[24] Although Maker executive Danny Zappin pushed back against accusations by Williams and others, the stream of burnout and "career-over" videos on social media continues unabated. This suggests that deep structural problems persist in the system.[25] One takeaway? Widespread predatory harvesting of rising aspirant makers is likely not sustainable as a default system behavior.

Occluded Fault Lines

A second type of stressor is a bit less obvious, less intentional. This is because the platform or trade rhetoric "occludes" or obscures the extent or depth of some fault lines. Examples of occluded stressors include

FIGURE 7.8. Going down in flames sign-offs often accompany deep fault lines and stresses. In doing so, they expose rich amounts of ethnographic info for researchers, as when these once successful online creators exposed the brutal contract terms that Disney's Maker Studios had used to starve them out. Images: Offscreen still frames from "NewRockstars" and "Braindeadly" websites (2017) over familiar "Quitting YouTube" genre graphic (2021).

online protests by makers who claim they've been stabbed in the back by YouTube's demonetization in the Adpocalypse. More agitated still are makers whose videos have been "flagged" or "taken-down" because YouTube identifies them as stealing or sampling material they didn't create. Or they may have infringed on supposedly copyrighted media content created by others (usually larger corporate owners). Some of these angry pushback uploads provide sophisticated critiques and deconstructions of YouTube's patronizing and naive understanding of copyright "fair use" law and legal precedents.

YouTube's own video uploaded responses to the aspirants' protests posture the platform as a problem-solving referee, a calm mediator "above-the-fray." YouTube's corporate videos patronizingly explain to agitated creators three relevant principles. First, the YouTube "community" (not the corporate platform host) is making those takedown decisions, through crowdsourcing via the "YouTube Heroes" program. YouTube claims the standards used by the "Heroes" crowd are sensitive to the interests of *all* platform members. Second, YouTube offers to help referee any ensuing legal complaint following an appeal by an aggrieved target of flagging or a takedown. Finally, YouTube explains that it is willing to act, as well, as an enabling *financial broker* for both parties. This bridge-building mediation includes both the supposed rights holder and the targeted maker/influencer. In these ways, the platform itself denies that the platform is the problem. Instead, YouTube poses disingenuously as a therapeutic facilitator that can deliver a win-win resolution for other people's problems. YouTube's stated goal is that it can give a fair resolution to, say, both Sony and an aspiring (but flagged) hip-hop artist accused of "stealing" (sampling) Sony's "proprietary" content.

YouTube spurs many creator complaints by robotically taking down any suspect uploads. To do this, the platform preemptively employs its "Content ID" system, a robotic auto-flagging data base comprising *all* of YouTube's previously made, uploaded, and "owned" media. Content ID offers to heal the studio/owner-vs.-artist/sampler split through conspicuous, sunny handwashing. That is, even though YouTube has preemptively taken down (and thus censored) the aspirant creator's upload, the platform bends over backward to convince the aggrieved maker that the takedown process is benign. YouTube's corporate video explains that YouTube is just a "middleman." YouTube, as empathic facilitator, offers to take the financial burden off the lone aspirant (an artist sampling content) by creating a microrevenue sharing scheme with the artist's antagonist (Sony). Through these automated deals, many creators must share monetization with the major studios that knocked them offline in the first place.

The platform thereby acts like it offers a fair win-win fix for both heavyweight Sony and the aspiring hip-hop artist. Yet this boilerplate fix completely covers over the fact that the scheme favors YouTube's major alliance with Sony—not the minor partnership between an aspirant-artist and YouTube. YouTube capably occludes both the depth and extent of its own culpability in the IP-uploader conflict on the platform.

Buried Fault Lines

Stresses that do not draw immediate attention themselves form a third disruptive category for embedded production culture study: buried fault lines. Many troubling, unresolved problems in industry are (obviously) not announced via public claims. They behave, that is, unlike explicit accusations in full-on rifts from antimanagement trolls on social media, hackers, company ship-jumpers, or whistleblowers. In other words, some deep stressors may be vaguely apparent to researchers just under or within otherwise benign workday surfaces or unremarkable industry practices. Yet some production environments feel just enough askance or askew to suggest buried resentments and thus the possibility of eventual disruption. For this reason, buried fault lines can raise useful questions for researchers. Does the ambivalence, subtext, or anxiety I am witnessing suggest that a deeper problem or conflict underlies what I am observing or hearing? Is this a potential rift worth exploring further?

One common stressor among filmmakers during shooting is that department heads have to worry about and manage collective crew feelings alongside their own technical craft specialization. This anxiety over emotional work and employee alienation can spotlight structural conflicts between, say, scheduled work hours and the creativity-draining impact that overwork actually has on productivity and innovation:

> The worst part is people management. That's really hard for me. I'm a social person, but when I'm working I need to retreat. But I also think, that we are stretched when we eat together and work together. And we have to give up so much, of our family life and we go off to another planet when we work on it. And I feel that there's a lot of vulnerability with our own crews. And the responsibility I feel is to keep everyone buoyant. And sometimes it's overwhelming. (Costume designer Arianne Phillips [CDG], "Sketch to Screen" panel, Copley Center for the Study of Costume Design, UCLA, Feb. 8, 2020)

I have to come to regret that researching affective labor, interpersonnel crew mediation, and unit psychotherapeutic cheerleading tasks in film production of the sort Phillips describes was never deemed important enough to include in my own graduate training in cinema and media studies.

Another buried fault line, contradictory production crediting practices, may cover over deeper tensions about the politics and fairness of artistic attribution. As Matt Stahl has detailed, work-for-hire creators in Hollywood, like screenwriters, have long had to settle for "separated rights" of authorship.[26] This means that their studio employers own the copyright and IP for stories the screenwriters create. In return, the writers are compensated with the cultural trappings (but not legal guarantees) of authorship. The WGA long ago sanctioned this doublespeak. To normalize the scheme, the WGA must also work hard to provide cultural capital, awards, critical recognition to make the "separated" authorship predicament sustainable. The fact that the Visual Effects Society, as discussed earlier, has *no* labor bargaining leverage means that its members are stuck begging employers for generosity from studios, hoping they will be kind enough to give VES members even simple symbolic mention (names in end-title credits) and clips (for personal reels). In effect, artistic attribution and crediting is a house of cards in Hollywood, a scheme built on a side marketplace that circulates symbolic capital.

At present, I am trying to understand the informal ways that embedded production workers unfold (or out) their activities in order to claim some vestige of artistic credit—especially when the industry or a firm does *not* acknowledge it. IMDb includes lots of examples of personnel and companies that "jump the credits" of previously made films. For some supporting companies and ancillary individuals, creating a monetizable IMDb production pedigree is a creative production in its own right. Catering companies, rental houses, and consulting firms often pursue credit augmentations after the fact, on IMDb and social media. In this symbolic marketplace, creative credit emendations and augmentations are justified as necessary tasks in personal branding or company marketing. In some ways, this freeform-self-crediting after the fact is just an extension of a long tradition. The postproject crediting that I have observed does not just include caterers and low-level assistants. It includes individuals (including agents and lawyers) who claim in public to have "produced" this or that film when all they did, in fact, was negotiate distribution or package the principals.

My MFA production students in research seminars have translated my characterization of this self-crediting practice: "Oh, you mean the bullshit factor in Hollywood." For them this task entails accepting that for career success in Hollywood, anyone will "need to fake it until you make it." I am less interested in that individual-scale variant of the process than in the other structural ways that creative self-crediting is achieved by production firms, postproduction houses, and other players. For example, the circulation of "breakdown reels" after a production concludes shows that there may be a systematic logic to jumping the credits after the end titles have been locked down for distribution. That is, once the huge coalitions of temporarily contracted subcompanies break-ranks during the feature's long-tail distribution, many of the subcompanies "claim" the feature as their own. Circulating breakdown reels to the trades provides one way to do this. It sustains a production firm's public value long after the bigger film/TV shoot wraps. This tactic is not illogical—especially given the precarity of many contracted production firms and their need to constantly secure short-term business opportunities. Indie subcompanies, post houses, and rental firms have no long-term security with studios or networks. The majors largely keep production subfirms at arm's-length until, of course, they need them again.

Consider the breakdown reel circulated by Rodeo FX for the film *Unbroken* (fig. 7.9).[27] The reel demonstrates to the trades in incremental, technical detail how the VFX firm's staff pulled off and mastered a complicated epic widescreen shot. They did this on a film whose actual distribution revenues were going to a bigger, higher-level firm. Clearly, the creation of "making-ofs" shorts like this circulate far beyond the "behind-the-scenes" videos on the primary marquee screens of HBO, Paramount, or Netflix. Metatexts or breakdown reels like these hijack trade focus to focus attention on the subcontracting VFX firm. They are not paratexts promoting the studio feature mother ship. Significantly, the Rodeo FX breakdown reel proves that technical crafts are also cultural actors. Their firm earns critical accolades when the trade "Below the Line: Voice of the Crew" lauds Rodeo FX with the headline "Video of the Day."

How might this breakdown reel suggest a buried fault line? The huge amount of secondary after-project oblique marketing and metatexts by below-the-line firms like Rodeo FX can provide scholars with a vivid, more holistic picture of the actual economy of Hollywood's densely embedded production system. Taking creative self-crediting seriously (by examining the subproductions produced by firms like Rodeo FX) challenges us to more fully study and map the actual mixed economies

FIGURE 7.9. Jumping the credits becomes a requisite marketing art form for subcompanies that aggregate to make up the paraindustry. Cohorts of specialized contract firms temporarily align on projects, after which many contract firms are buried deeply within the industry and kept out of sight. *Top:* Offscreen still frame of "Rodeo FX's" FX/clip reel from the film on YouTube, 2015. *Bottom:* Still frame from Below-the-Line trade website, April 3, 2015.

of any production sector's complex embedded system. Taking breakdown reels and other deep texts and trade artifacts seriously (that is, considering them as more than the facile singularities of "a" director, "a" studio, or it's box office) opens up a more three-dimensional view of industry. Such a move can also expose the vague or occluded outlines of deeper kinds of structural stress. In this case, a mere breakdown reel provides a window on the economic precarity of the subfirms that comprise the paraindustry as whole.

Unfolding

Considering industrial tectonics in media analysis can change the way we conceptualize production activities and media industry events. The dimensional paradigm may also move us away from focusing on performance exceptions (studios, auteurs, films) and toward working to describe and explain routinization and symptomatic practices in production and industry. Reframing methodology this way might also help scholars new to media industry study—especially if they are suspicious about empiricist and quantitative critiques that deprioritize "small data," "close analysis," or "qualitative research." Industrial rifts, conflicts, and disruptions need not be reduced to, or justified as, mere examples of a "case study." Nor do they need to be scrutinized as particular instances illustrating some broader principle or trend. Folds and fractures appear as acute symptoms that industrial systems leak or lose track of—sometimes unwittingly, sometimes grudgingly. Folds and fractures can, in effect, be defined and understood as unintended self-expressions by the industrial system.

Folds and fractures provide rich opportunities to integrate complex systems thinking in CMS. Each disruption of adjacent production cultures tends to expose numerous, describable nodes in the embedded intertrade strata. Each trade rift can expose many significant links to the overall system that embeds and hosts the fold or fracture, as well. Effectively analyzing the web of connections publicly triggered within those pressure points encourages more holistic (and less monolithic) thinking about media industries. My chapter studies thus far suggest that trade culture does a lot of heavy acting during these intra- and intertrade disruptions, folds, and cover-overs. *Specworld* proposes reverse engineering from stressed or fractured hotspots in order to better see and understand the complex system as a whole. Doing disembedding research like this well and carefully increases the likelihood that we will find answers to important and timely questions other than those industry asks on its own. We would do well, after all, to research areas other than those industry offers up in its well-scripted dominating trade explanations.

Case

Conjuring Microfinance to Overleverage Aspirants

YouTube has paid out $30 billion to creators as the competition for online content intensifies.

—*Fortune* echoes Google's marketing stock trigger[1]

[What happens] when creator funds run dry? Everyone from TikTok and YouTube to Instagram and Snap has proudly announced their multi-million-dollar funds to lure creators to their platforms. But the lessons of the First Punic War still stand: when you buy a mercenary army, you have to keep paying up. Snap, alas, is learning this lesson the hard way.

—Jim Louderback, former GM, VidCon[2]

Fieldwork for the book's three chapters of case studies focused on mentoring, workshopping, and "how-to" discourses. These studies aimed to better understand core differences between high- and low-production worlds by unpacking and deconstructing warring trade pedagogies. Chapter 4 (on specwork and embedding) examined the experiential core of twenty-first-century production that trade groups and consultants now normalize. That study focused on embodied phenomenological dimensions (a microlevel of analysis, involving the conditioning of creators). Industrial mentoring poses those core dimensions as crucial and claims makers need to anticipate and master them in production— if they want to succeed. Chapter 6 (on folding) detailed the new managerial and bureaucratic skills in which industry now mentors aspirant and rising creators, also promoting them as keys to success in the online era. I term these supposedly core skills "administrative production" since each tactic aspires to systematically manage, restructure, and enhance production in some way. This trade rhetoric about what makers will need to managerially succeed (a midlevel analysis, termed "televisioning") incentivizes a tortured MBA-ethos among many young aspirant creators.

The present chapter offers a case study of one stressed rift and pending fracture. I examine a relatively abstract dimension in the idealized skill set being sold to aspirant creators in online trade pedagogy: microfinancing. This scheme requires economic "speculating," which I analyze at the macrolevel of cultural politics. The methods of financing described here show that the earlier manic experiential and stressed administrative levels of production are tightly woven together in aspirant creator cultures. In practice, the micro (formal), mid (administrative), and macro (economic) levels promoted together in production pedagogies combine profitably to benefit the host platforms. Yet the same integrated scheme requires aspirant makers/creators to operate as overleveraged risk systems—an unsustainable predicament for creators over the long haul.

Understanding how aspirant makers become overleveraged requires looking closely at how industry incentivizes or folds them into industry's much larger complex embedded system. Undertaking this task, as I do in the pages that follow, means examining how "affective data work" helps preemptively produce the creator-subject that the industrial system wants. To understand this industrial premaking of creators, I employ a more widely recognized definition of preemptive speculation than those I used in earlier chapters: financial speculation and investment. The analysis that follows attempts to shine some light on the amorphous economic logic of how money interacts with media-makers/influencers and their screens in the online era. My analysis is informed by the important recent work on finance capitalism and media by Patrick Vonderau, Andrew deWaard, Charles Acland, and Aynne Kokas. Their scholarship rightly exposes—in four different geographical regions—large-scale speculation and financial leveraging systems that have transformed the film and television industries. The scale of analysis they employ largely follows macroeconomic models of transnational capital and finance.

But how does finance capital impact or "author" individual creators? Specifically, how does the public staging of microfinance affect the underresourced aspirant producers and the individual creators that toil in online content production? As the comparative fieldwork in the previous chapters shows, I research "speculation work," or specwork, as part of a cultural economy and on a different scale than do Vonderau, deWaard,

Acland, and Kokas. For starters, my earlier work on speculation in production culture framed those economies as creative labor problems. This meant asking how money or its symbolic substitutes incentivize and circulate among workers. Yet specwork also has a higher-level financing and investor logic as well—for both the outside money and the inside creators. At the individual level, corporations teach creator microeconomics as a key to creating one's marketing brand. Media companies self-consciously teach crowdfunding, cobranding, and sponsorship deals as "win-win" strategies on platforms like YouTube. The production trades, popular press, and various online handler firms embedded on the platform (including Indiegogo, GoFundMe, Patreon, and other maker-focused financing start-ups) sell the wonders of crowdsourcing to young and ambitious aspirants. Yet this happy trade talk largely reduces "financial speculation" to a user or crowdsourcing proposition. At the same time, it effectively cloaks the larger investor schemes behind those platforms. Spending any time among online Gen-Z makers and influencers makes clear the presence of a darker side, slightly out-of-frame, as well. Lots of evidence suggests that these creators and microcelebrities in-the-making are integrated within much larger macrofinance systems—ones that are challenging to discern.

MICROFINANCE CONJURING AND DATA WORK

In this chapter, I want to explore how microfinancing works at the level of the ostensibly "lone" online video creator. To do this, I adapt a concept from Patrick Vonderau for my fieldwork as a way to better understand how folding takes place in embedded systems. While I have been using cultural folding to analyze production, Vonderau explicitly targets economic markets. He explores a "company's ability to fold markets into each other: to make disappear an aggressive financial growth strategy and business set-up based on ad tech engineering by creating an aura of Nordic cool."[3] In a system with many "market actors," and on an integrated platform that alternately promotes its shifting identities (as an advertising, technology, music, or finance company), Spotify triggers Vonderau to analyze two things: first, what Spotify tries to "make disappear" and, second, what Spotify ultimately seeks to achieve by marketing its brand or "aura of Nordic cool." I want to employ Vonderau's model of folding markets as a way to understand the cultural folding that converts aspirational maker production culture into something else. For starters, what does YouTube/Google "make disappear"

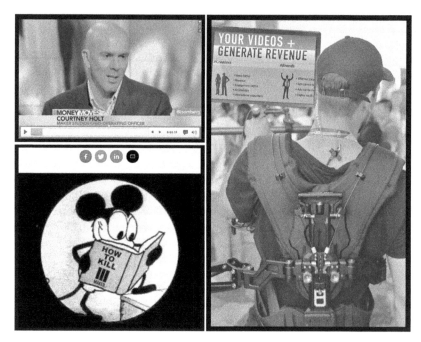

FIGURE 8.1. *Creator* promo trade talk as finance snake oil. *Top left:* Maker Studios promo video still frame. *Bottom left:* Financial Schadenfreude and aspirant blowback. Online makers troll and taunt Disney for multimillion-dollar losses after purchasing once vanguard Maker Studios. *Right:* Lone online creator/videographer "covering" VidCon 2017, with promotion for "Generate Revenue" scheme aimed at aspiring influencers. Composited photo illustration from VidCon 2017, Anaheim, CA. © 2017, by J. Caldwell.

when it converts aspiring filmmakers and creative makers into monetizing influencers? This conversion pressure anchors the "crossover dilemma" at the heart of this book. What happens to film artists who must convert into channel management?

One Maker Studios online promo provides an apt example of how a small-scale creator market is culturally folded and embedded into a larger-scale networked creator market (fig. 8.1, left).

> *Maker promo title.* The World's Largest Multi-channel Network of Online Video Content.
>
> *Courtney Holt, CEO.* We've truly democratized the idea of a creator being able to create what they want, when they want it. We've disrupted the notion of a season, and a format.
>
> *Lisa Donovan, Cofounder.* When we founded Maker, we wanted to be working with content creators who really didn't see it as a stepping stone.

Intertitle. The Most Authentic Way to Reach 13–24 Year Olds.

Maker VO. The company is about four years old. We've built out a production facility. We've got three soundstages. A music studio. And over the last two years we've built out this scaled network behind it.

From a media historical perspective, Maker Studio's punchy claims—to have invented video-on-demand, democratic media, authentic expression—are simply preposterous. Yet those tropes circulate far more broadly among many others in the online creator-world, as well. This chapter drills into precisely this kind of finance snake-oil in promo talk to understand how creator reps and intermediaries seek monetizable beachheads within larger platform economies.

EMBEDDED FOLDING

Vonderau's approach raises two specific questions for my research. First, how are multiple production markets "folded" or "embedded" inside each other within the YouTube/Google "ecosystem"? Second, which production market can we identify as the lead production market? Textual, marketing, and ethnographic research suggests at least three layers of market embedding: (1) The platform system incessantly and publicly foregrounds its social media gift economy. Creators make and upload "free" video content and make it available for access not just to subscribers but to anyone. (2) This social media gift economy is embedded within a second, user-attention market. This attention-market host employs viewer analytics (views, watch-time, etc.) to assign different values to each of the system's millions of created uploads. In addition to making the "look" of the interface different at any given moment, constantly morphing the ever-newer content options, the embedding also allows the system to calculate revenues based on market research (which it sells to cloaked third parties). (3) This user-attention market is embedded within a third, more traditional level: a sponsor/advertiser market.

The question of which of the three levels of embedding cloaks and abstracts to the greatest degree is debatable. The third and highest level is clearly tied to the macroeconomics of corporate consumer capitalism and, thus, to stockholder investment and speculation. But that third (host) level also involves concerted misdirection. Influencers that explicitly hype product placements on their channels also flag or betray that they are part of a much vaster economic enterprise. Yet to self-promote, influencers inevitably disregard or downplay the backstage corporate networks and capital that manufacture and circulate those sponsored products in the first place. As such, of the three embedded markets that make up the maker/influencer ecosystem, the vast corporate and investment capital behind the sponsor/advertiser market is (to use Vonderau's phrase) arguably "made to disappear" the most.

Given this three-level embedded market system constraining online content creators, we need to determine what, fundamentally, is folded, and why? Scale helps us approach this question. Specifically, the third or highest financial level behaves according to a somewhat traditional corporate network economy of scale. That is, this market regime sinks or swims depending on the size of the market available. This level thus favors continual expansion of the creator enterprise—an expansion that can be achieved via the agglomeration, affiliation, and aggregation of content, actors, and firms. This structural economy of scale seems habitually folded—that is, it culturally and rhetorically disappears—into what looks like the individual creator's narrower niche economy of consumer scope.

This creator-niche-market ideology may become a dominant public norm because of what it habitually and symbolically overvalues. Specifically, YouTube's cultural economy appears to be driven explicitly by only two of its principal market actors or levels, not all three; that is, the platform postures as a niche economy that rewards both consumer "choice" and creator "agency." It does not foreground its investors, sponsors, and advertisers in the same way. This is how YouTube translates and embraces the ubiquitous rhetoric about choice and agency as the consent behaviors needed to normalize the folding-in and compliance of aspiring makers. This creator showcasing simultaneously conceals the system's underlying structural financing. What "aggressive growth strategies" does this folding/embedding make disappear" in the YouTube space? The endless hype and incentives surrounding the aggregation and enabling of more and more individual users and lone creators constitutes a vast disappearing act. In the minds of aspiring makers, such platform rhetoric makes big-data mining and big-data selling, alike, fade in importance. The vast scale of the host disappears as a creator concern (fig. 8.2).

Comparing this rhetorical redirection on the platform to an earlier shift in capitalism suggests that the embedded folding under way in YouTube's online system is indeed significant. Changes in the current online system, that is, echo the ways consumer capitalism moved beyond

FIGURE 8.2. "Genius Kitchen" provides a rehearsal area and workable production prototype for teens and preteens to learn the aesthetics of online platform economics (bureaucratic administration) as keys to creator success. Photo: © 2017, by J. Caldwell.

the conditions of industrial capitalism. This earlier transition out of nineteenth-century industrial capitalism succeeded in part by the ways it individuated and psychologized individual buyer choice. In this earlier shift to twentieth-century consumerism, that is, market folding centered on the cultural promotion of personal identities that could be engaged and rewarded under a new system and logic of conspicuous product consumption. By comparison, the folding in the twenty-first-century YouTube cultural market works in a roughly parallel fashion. In the online sphere, something best termed *creator capitalism* leaves behind large-scale, industrial modes of production by psychologizing production into a neater package of personal creativity and individual expression. That is, the widespread promotion in online social media systems of personal brand-building foregrounds not conspicuous consumption but conspicuous production as a benchmark for determining value under creator capitalism in the platform era.

It is important to recognize that complex online production systems do not simply vertically embed different production cultures according to the three levels I have described (embodied, institutionalized, financed). Auxiliary, secondary, and tertiary production markets also pervade each of these levels that make up the system as a whole. The proliferation of side firms at each level occurs because creator capitalism needs auxiliary paramedia and paramarkets to "service" the platform's ever-increasing individual creator numbers and demand. All these side productions, services, and intertextual creations constitute a creator service market and "add value" to the maker/influencer system as a whole. This follows the economic logic of the network effect, where each new connection and node in a network adds value to the network as a whole. This makes the overall creator network more valuable than the sum of its parts. The new manic creator/influencer markets display an appetite for complex, costly ancillary support services. These ancillary production firms solicit and feed aspirant creators with endless candidates for affiliation, aggregation, and representation. Note that this differs from a "user's attention economy." It functions, rather, as an obsessional, affiliation-seeking aspirant economy (or aspirant affiliating economy) for makers. CMS scholars have been better at analyzing the attention economies of fans and consumers than at analyzing the aspirational economies of makers and creators. Yet both economies continue to interact, in monetizable ways, within the YouTube/Google ecosystem.

SPECWORK TRADING FLOOR

Over the years, my research has examined the ways that industrial contexts "author" onscreen texts and, conversely, the ways that onscreen texts "express" or "script" industrial contexts and settings. Swimming upstream in analyses these ways reverses traditional causal explanations in both aesthetics (artists produce cultural objects) and political economy (markets produce culture). The two trajectories also pushed me in this book to better locate and identify the ways soft cultural expressions and symbolic texts help fold and embed production markets. That task requires a credible answer to the question, how and why has this folding, embedding, and converting of production markets worked so smoothly and with relatively little blowback?

To answer this, I draw on the innovative work of Andrew deWaard, who demonstrates that media screen texts now function as "a marketplace ... [where] all of its components [are] for sale." DeWaard's research shows how financialization from "private equity funds" has created "intensified internal markets expressed in a cultural text" (87).[4] To demonstrate the precision of how onscreen media texts serve as investors' markets, he urges us to move beyond the conventional constraints of political-economy and media-industry studies—fields that emphasize ownership, regulation, organization, and policy. As an alternative, deWaard shifts his research sites to the overleveraged domino and pyramid schemes that spurred the Great Recession, urging scholars to think, instead, about media content as expressive and cultural analogues of financial "derivatives." In this "media derivative" scheme, onscreen cultural media texts are conversions, analyzed as investment offerings and bets. This makes film and media screen content "less a factory floor than a trading floor" (89). Films and series are cultural stock markets tied to real economies.

My argument in this book? The maker/influencer world in the YouTube ecosystem actually functions like a stock-market exchange for creative speculation work. Although it poses and promotes itself as a creator's social media site, it also serves as a specwork investment market, a place to bet on promising futures. To adapt deWaard's finance model of onscreen content for online media, we could say that YouTube and its affiliates partner together as a public trading floor for the microfinancing of aspirant creators. The YouTube system succeeds in part because it is an immense and complex risk-distribution system. The ostensible rationality of YouTube's ranking scheme promises to improve the odds for any corporate partners (appraising it from the outside) who wish to put down bets on the trending futures of rising creators and microcelebrities during their process of discovery.

This makes the interface more than just a graphical user interface (GUI), a social media site, or even a recommendation engine. The user interface is a publicly viewable popular site but also a corporately monitored commercial trading floor. In this scheme, AI engines and ranking algorithms function as referees, oddsmakers, and value establishers to help investors and speculators minimize risk. Despite their vast scale, the embedded markets that join to make this media-content trading floor cohere profitably, furthermore, are largely unregulated. This

FIGURE 8.3. Young influencer videos serve as speculative economic "futures." Aspirants upload videos to lure potential investors (bettors on culture trends). Following deWaard, online media content are "cultural stock markets" that are tied to actual economies. A lot of video content (like NYX's and PocketLive's) make no effort to hide their financial logic. Composite photo illustrations from VidCon. *Top:* © 2020, by J. Caldwell; *Bottom:* © 2017, by J. Caldwell.

not-needing-regulation pretense allows the platform to fly largely under the radar of government oversight or media policy (fig. 8.3).

Understanding YouTube as a trading floor and stock exchange that continuously values maker specwork challenges us to reconsider how we do CMS research. The finance/market paradigm, that is, challenges scholars to formulate ways to counter or "unfold" the complex system and to find ways to undertake "disembedding" research. With this approach to more fully analyzing maker/influencer practice, fieldwork for this book underscored several recurring trends. First, most DIY makers are (or may aspire to function as) start-ups seeking capital, not just content creators. Second, many "influencers," when they secure some sponsorship or start-up money, function like "initial offerings" or IPOs. And finally, when corporate sponsors or cobranders engage with young aspirant creators, online platforms behave like low-risk VC or "equity funds"—especially in the ways they find and harvest makers/influencers through speculation.

Silicon Valley is well-versed in such roll-the-dice financial arrangements. In fact, venture capital embraces the high-risk task, because the system allows them to skim-off-the-top select pretested candidates for investment. This willingness to bet on relative unknowns is premised on the fact that everything on YouTube acts as a speculative offering, a prototype, or a series pilot. Plus "home-run" thinking drives much investing in content. Every firm imagines that it is savvy enough to pick an eventual IP-tech-app long-term winner. It is important for us to keep in mind, however, that this logic of maker/influencer value comes from a corporate or finance perspective. This makes the disposition easy for firms that surveil the online aspirant pool for candidates from an initially safe and cloaked distance. From a maker-influencer's perspective, however, YouTubers often feel like they are shadowed by low-risk bottom-feeders. The platform reinforces this anxiety, because aspiring creators only have a vague sense of whether or how, in real time, they are trending as a microcelebrity.

INDUSTRIAL REFLEXIVITY: CONJURING

Production Culture researched "industrial reflexivity" in American film and television. It mapped how and why production communities and organizations constantly reflect back on themselves and critically interrogate the industries and media worlds within which they work. That research showed that self-referencing was far more than simply marketing or self-promotion; it analyzed reflexivity's functions by examining a wide range of embedded texts, tools, technical pedagogy, trade talk, and work habits as forms of grounded "critical practice." Industrial reflexivity involves cultural debates that labor and companies engage in to make sense of themselves and to adapt to change and to disruptions by other intertrade actors. In my research for the present book, I tried

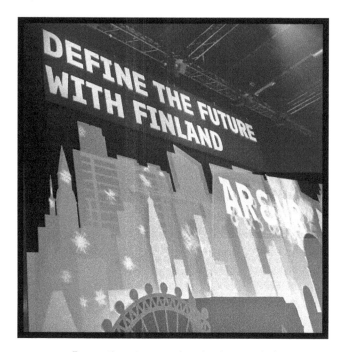

FIGURE 8.4. Even nation-states use imaginative speculation texts to lure financial investors. Here, a trade display in Helsinki brands Finland as a magnet for creator synergies and high-tech innovation. Photo: © 2017, by J. Caldwell.

to understand how industrial reflexivity plays out not just among professionals but also among aspirational makers/influencers in online platforms. In describing how Spotify stages media events "to showcase the prospect of high future income," Vonderau adopts Anna Tsing on the reflexive process by which finance "conjures." Tsing proposes that finance often conjures up scale: "Profit must be imagined before it can be extracted; the possibility of economic performance must be conjured like a spirit to draw an audience of potential investors."[5] Applying Tsing's model to the online maker-world means describing the different entities that conjure and delineating the diverse ways that they conjure or visualize those imagined futures (fig. 8.4).

Embedded production systems by definition mix firms, individuals, and organizations of many different sizes. This raises a question: do firms conjure (or visualize the future) differently depending on their size? From my observations at the aspirational maker/influencer level, the need for investors triggers different types of conjuring. The major firms

TABLE 8.1   FLIPPED FINANCE CONJURING

Scale	Corporate finance	Maker microfinance
Purpose	To heighten profit expectations among possible investors	To lower profit expectations subtly among influencers, while spiking their longshot prestige career aspirations
Conjuring model	Business as a scaled-up, administrative, value-mining discourse	Business as a scaled-down personal, therapeutic discourse

that mine and harvest influencers on YouTube and other social media platforms tend to employ the kind of conjuring typical of the "corporate finance" described by Tsing and Vonderau, the purpose of which is to inflate profit expectations, or heighten investor wagers, among possible investors. Aspiring makers/creators, by contrast, who need "maker microfinancing" to survive, face a veritable flood of conjuring media online that often does just the opposite of corporate finance conjuring. That is, makers are barraged with platform conjuring that aims to lower profit expectations among rising creators. This opposition between inflating investor expectations and lowering creator expectations is logical, given the general principle that investors must "buy low" (from desperate aspirants) in order to "sell high" (to larger corporate entities). This two-sided conjuring model of reflexivity is outlined in table 8.1.

This two-faced conjuring works in part because it appeals to each side of the "partnering" equation in qualitatively different ways. On one side, the corporate/investor conjuring model cultivates the notion that "scaling up" is required to achieve administrative efficiencies, an idea it reinforces through its third-party value-mining rhetoric around the platform. Simultaneously on the same platform, the individual maker and the microfinance conjuring model tend to depict future business as scaled-down and personal. It frequently does this by employing therapeutic rhetoric in its conjuring. The platform often justifies its approach to the precarious individual creator as a way to achieve a loftier goal: a higher ranking based on authenticity in personal expression.

Melissa Gregg provides an apt term to describe this kind of speculative investment conjuring: "the spectacle of 'data work'—mobilizing big data graphs at showcases and tech demos, and betting on the affective properties of data visualization—such growth stories have become

FIGURE 8.5. Constant public pitching becomes a spectator sport at trade gatherings, illustrating Melissa Gregg's notion of "the spectacle of 'data work.'" Photos: Helsinki, © 2017, by J. Caldwell.

an integral part of both finance investments."[6] Trade gatherings for online makers/influencers show that data work is central not just for equity investors and largely anonymous transnational firms but also for emerging creators (and their microfinanciers), who may have only five hundred or even only one hundred subscribers (fig. 8.5).

There are also some general differences in the aspirant-creator world between the data-work done by and for corporate investors and the data work done by and for maker-influencers. This difference is analogous to the administrative-vs.-therapeutic modes of conjuring just considered. This is because speculative data work targeting corporate investors or sponsors or reps tends to seek an "up-affect" impact on those "outsiders." The up-affect goal seems to cultivate and instill the kind of exuberance or confidence needed for investors to take on risk. By contrast, the speculative data work targeting makers/influencers often tends toward what I would term a "down-affect" impact on those "insiders." In the workshops, online tutorials, and how-to sessions I observed, the experiential or affective goal for makers/aspirants seemed to be the production of vigilant fortitude tied to constantly checked anxiety. These antithetical objectives (up-affect vs. down-affect) are summarized in table 8.2.

These divergent strategies are logical, given the different platform pressures each partnering side faces when it enters a platform to cocreate content. Remember, largely singular makers/influencers also need

TABLE 8.2   AFFECT DATA WORK

Type of data work	Up-affect data work	Down-affect data work
Target of data work	Investors (outside)	Makers/Aspirants (inside)
Affective goal	Confidence (for profits)	Anxiety (for productivity)

financing, just at a different scale from the large MCNs or advertising agencies or studios. To make the meager microeconomics of the maker/influencer market optimal, the platform needs to lower the maker's expectations, even as it simultaneously solicits more and more content. Ironically, the anxiety produced by down-affect data work helps fuel evermore content production and uploads by makers (fig. 8.6).

One good way to increase the content uploads of microcreators is to keep creators in a state of unresolved anticipation. The platform facilitates this double bind by ensuring a constant parade of career success-story exceptions on the platform's trade talk and public radar.[7] At the very same time that it symbolically hypes this longshot creator exceptionalism on its marquee, however, the platform features many more modest therapeutic videos (about creator "burnout," financial "survival," and healthier "life-work balance"). This war between up-affect data work and down-affect data work can trigger acute maker anxieties about how to succeed. This cultivation of anxiety and anticipation is analogous (on the maker side) to the anxiety and anticipation that capitalism rolled out in its shift from industrial to consumer capitalism. Cultivated and managed anxiety about what comes next is precisely what makes consumerism so all-encompassing. The parallel creator-stimulating (but demoralizing) magic of down-affect data work spurs upload frequency in creators.

CREATIVE LABOR, MICROFINANCE, AND OVERSIGHT

The world of the platform-hosted aspirant-creator exemplifies the principle that markets generally supplant gift economies (the latter folded into the former), a process detailed in Vonderau's study of Spotify. But parallels and important distinctions can also be made to financialization and to the ways private equity markets work. Andrew deWaard's research calls out the pernicious ways that "private equity firms" have taken over "distressed" Hollywood firms, creating new forms of unrecognizable vertical integration through "leveraged buyouts" (LBOs).

FIGURE 8.6. The trade public "conjuring" needed to "fold" one market into another (per Tsing and Vonderau) often requires effectively leveraging a "spectacle of data work." Photo: Slush Helsinki's tech confab, © 2017, by J. Caldwell.

Two fundamental problems threaten (but mostly fail) to undercut these attempts at financial restructuring through private equity and LBOs: labor pushback and regulatory oversight.

For starters, these leveraged buyouts are short-term arrangements by design. They are premised on creating maximum efficiency through dramatic restructuring of the purchased firm's labor force. This is typically done via rapid layoffs enacted to spur immediate heightened venture capital profits. Spiking profits in this way then requires rapid exit and sale of the company once the firms have been downsized and the immediate profits have been prematurely harvested. In deWaard's account, the new "shadow studios" that have been created by this LBO process face almost no oversight or regulation, in part because they are so difficult for regulators to conceptualize or even locate.

Even though the aspirant-creator world's influencer ecosystem doesn't look flawed in the same ways that private equity and debt-driven LBOs have changed legacy film and television, the YouTube/Google influencer ecosystem also has creative labor and oversight flaws built into its financing. The microfinancing force that spurs and ensures those flaws in the system plays out publicly as an enabling, therapeutic discourse. When economistic models are invoked, the influencer system is only treated as a prediction market. It prices huge amounts of micro-media based on crowdsourcing—taking that as an aggregate belief that determines value and assigns risk.

Why has there been so relatively little concern about these platform schemes? Microfinancing and risk markets are embedded and naturalized as part of the "platform." Whether sponsorship and prices go up or down, whether aspirants become microcelebrities or go bankrupt, "the house wins." YouTube and Google profit from the bipolar nature of this predictive market. The more manic the influencing, partnering, and subsequent abandoning is, the more the platform as a whole profits. This profit-positioning results in part from the platform's corporate identity politics, which are "shape-shifting." Self-identifying only as a "tech platform," YouTube removes any air of vested interest. Alternatively, by self-identifying only as a "media ecosystem," YouTube postures the platform as a natural, holistic world defined by an aura of automated mutual support. Although lone aspirants and influencers are bombarded with imperatives to self-brand and monetize IP—they are not hailed using explicit references to the stock market and trading floor. Yet this entire interactive process and IP auditioning plays out, à la deWaard, on a thinly veiled speculative trading floor.

"Labor" is mostly a missing cognitive category in the aspirant-influencer discourse that makes up platform pedagogy. This is largely because quasi-MBA-style "entrepreneurialism" dominates trade rhetoric, thereby dislocating both labor and class as categories. It favors, instead, the creator's "self" posing as a speculative "start-up." Within this paradigm, aspirant-influencers self-identify as self-management, as corporations of one. In reality, however, the platform ecosystem also functions as a creative labor market and needs to be researched from that perspective (not just via Gen-Z entrepreneurialism).

ASPIRANT INFLUENCING AS OVERLEVERAGING

This chapter has aimed thus far to describe two things: first, that media microfinancing is part of a bigger risk-delegation system; and, second, that the types of risk and value differ widely depending on the size of the firm. By definition, venture capital (VC) and hedge funds risk financial capital, which arrives as disinterested surplus capital extracted from one sector in order to invest and leverage it in another sector. Pain—from hostile takeovers, downsizing, or bankruptcy—is seldom acknowledged in these LBO schemes.

In sharp contrast, while lone makers do risk what little financial capital they have, they primarily risk "social, familial, and vocational capital" to enter the larger market or platform game. For this reason, most online makers/influencers can be usefully understood as "presubsidized offerings (aka start-up investors) who are precariously positioned on the margins of a vast outward-looking market ecosystem. The "buy-in" to the investment market by aspirant creators is largely covered by their families, cultural connections, and social networks. All of these resources function as concrete forms of self-capital, even though they appear (at least initially and disingenuously) as nonfinancial supports. Media scholars need to account for these kinds of soft capital as presubsidized investments, even though (or especially because) Google, TikTok, Instagram, and Facebook will never acknowledge those cloaked forms of domestic, familial, and social subsidies on which their platforms depend. YouTube, that is, will never admit that it is, in effect, taking out low-interest loans—financed by the in-kind and soft-capital predebt of individual YouTubers. Yet that, in fact, is precisely what I am arguing.

Why does microcreator "presubsidizing" matter to the economic health of the Google/YouTube system? Because it creates unsustainable conditions at the microlevel, similar to the overleveraged, derivative-based predicament at the macrolevel that caused the last financial collapse. In the 2007–8 crash, too many firms were owned by VC debt rather than equity (cash or real capital). As a result, and because of the collapse, many funds and lenders ended up owning distressed firms. Previous owners may have owned actual equity and "real" stock in a firm, but the "value" of some postcrash firms was based on the aggregate of the debt that was used to purchase them. This kind of overleveraging is as unsustainable for YouTubers now as it was for earlier cash-short/debt-rich firms that became takeover targets.

FRONT-LOADING THE VALUE-ADDING CAREER TASK

The ways that tech platforms have corporatized adolescent aspirant creators offers a compelling example of a comparable kind of overleveraging at the microeconomic level. My argument is that to achieve this overleverage, film and television have taken traditional bureaucratic aspects of media production from the conventional backend of industry's content-making chain and front-loaded them onto the backs of young aspirational workers who make up a vast online feeder system for media industry. I term this front-loading and folding the "value-adding career task" (VACT). The VACT goes well beyond the venality of either cooking the books or "Hollywood accounting." By VACT I mean the preexisting cultural, reputational, and soft capital earned over a career (or at any given point) that every individual crew member brings to each short-term project or serial shoot they work on. Rather than view individual career arcs just as autonomous personal narratives, or origin myths, I view them as a collective value-adding process in production that feeds industry. These personal arcs, when aggregated, provide immense amounts of unacknowledged, nonfiscal career capital that every production aggregates, monetizes, and leverages for the short lifespan of any film/TV shoot (fig. 8.7).

As described in chapters 3 and 5, studio and network accountants never accurately quantify or account for the vast amounts of aggregated soft capital without which film and TV productions would never be made (at least the way they are today). Film and television management never accurately budgets productions because this aggregating value of the creative-labor system predates their employment as accountants and appears freely and willingly donated. Furthermore, no contractual or fiduciary requirement in industry forces management to ever take responsibility for the bartered, networked, free labor and symbolic capital that enables individual crew members to survive, persist, and live in LA, New York, London, or Mumbai. The ability to be ever-available, and on-call to work, even during lean times (e.g., during serial periods of underemployment or unemployment), always depends directly on huge amounts of donated, but unacknowledged, in-kind capital provided and "banked" by workers. Such conditions sustain and prop up the lazy truism that creative workers must be always available, on-call, always at the ready.

Using my earlier description of specific forms of specwork, precarity, and symbolic capital that production leverages from workers, here I

FIGURE 8.7. The gateway/vortex for managing pre–film school front-loading. Here, sponsor YouTube/Google welcomes legions of adolescent social media creators (and their chaperones!) to VidCon 2019. For a full week they will be mentored day and night on how to corporatize, hijack, brand, and front-load the traditional "Value-Adding Career Task" (VACT) from post–film school adulthood to preuniversity adolescence. This mode is more accurately described as "The Preemptive Film School" for "Influencers." Photo: © 2019, by J. Caldwell.

want to appraise the VACT using a complex-systems framework. I focus specifically on what viewing production as a value-adding hive economy can reveal about production changes in the online era. The vocational flow-chart in figure 8.8 (top) outlines fairly widespread expectations about how one's career should ideally advance in filmmaking. Many aspirants who intend to advance through this trajectory in production's Darwinian system idealize "film school" as an entry point. But vocational skills and critical abilities they acquire elsewhere are valid substitutes for film school, regardless of whether the skill set is received at the university level. After entering the industry, interning, and often a lot of production-assisting, many workers still learn to donate large amounts of their free labor or specwork value to others. Traditionally this meant producing unpaid samples of creative work, much of it disclosed in public, which is freely given to woo producers and win jobs.[8] Although we seldom acknowledge brainstorming and disclosure as a "task," I have done so in this book. The individual creative worker bears the financial

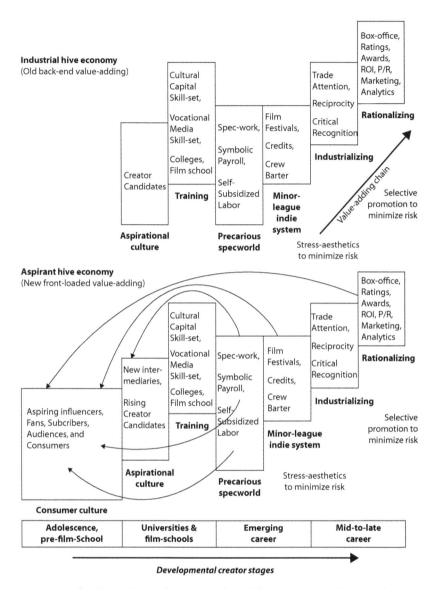

FIGURE 8.8. Overleveraging aspirants: the value-adding creator speculation task. Creator-Influencer Feeder System now front-loads production's traditional bureaucratic chores (the value-adding cultural task, self-analytics research, and financial risk) onto young makers as best-practice requirements in the online platform rhetoric of administrative creation (a.k.a. the Preemptive Film School). Diagram contrasting Aspirant Hive and Industrial Hive Economies. © 2022, by J. Caldwell.

burden for all this paraindustrial cultural creation and preproduction. Yet where this task is assigned in the career arc has changed.

As chapter 5 detailed, elaborate symbolic payroll systems sustain the considerable amounts of spec-labor that result. This symbolic pay includes all forms of "soft capital" with which aspirants and the underemployed are actually paid (buzz, credits, festivals, brand affiliation, creative visibility) or subsidized by (crew bartering, student loans, university credit, spousal support, parents, trust funds, paying-one's-dues, sacrifice, day jobs). Every production leverages massive amounts of this collective symbolic capital—which is never accounted for in studio line-item budgets. If symbolic capital props up the specworld, stress-aesthetic rationales produce the consent behaviors needed to normalize this challenging industrial fold—that is, the trade and cultural rationales that industry uses to justify the long hours, stressful conditions, and precarity of its underemployed, flexible workforce. These include attributions of quality out of struggle, creativity in the face of stress, and profitability from intense collective teamwork. Such tropes regularly surface in "against-all-odds" and "genesis" myths, in below-the-line trades, in union roundtables, and in craft "bake-offs" and "reveals." Stress-aesthetic rationales help negotiate consent and normalize the fold. Creative workers once had to contend with all these oblique forms of labor later in their postgraduate career arcs.

Aspiring filmmakers now must master oblique and ancillary creative work much earlier in the career arcs. Figure 8.8 (lower) shows how the VACT scheme has been adapted from the later stages of conventional career advancement and front-loaded (with some modification) into the aspirational culture of online influencers, YouTubers, and social media creators. In some ways, this front-loading attempts to bring corporate order and rationality to an unpredictable adolescent aspirant surge. This human-feeder supply now dwarfs in size and intensity the much smaller demographic worlds that once fed film schools with applicants. No longer just aspiring, untrained applicants for entry, adolescent creators now constitute a very real and robust precollege aspirant hive economy. As with the traditional value-adding chain for postgraduate "indie" filmmakers that preceded them, online adolescent creators and influencers are now well-versed and trained explicitly in the production of symbolic capital, including its accounting and management. Yet they must master it at a younger age. Undertaking that task feeds the larger industry with vast amounts of starter content, crazy ideas, pilots, and demos. At the same time, it showcases endless candidates for buyable IP. This early tacit recruitment in the aspirant hive economy produces a prospective workforce that is immediately monetizable and, in the optimistic ethos of business investing, infinitely harvestable in the future.

One result? Aspirant creators may be more conscious at an earlier age of media-making as an economic enterprise. Yet like the older generation of indies that precede them, adolescent aspirants also think mostly in personal career arcs. Few of my informants admitted to the value-aggregating logic that their collective hive delivers obliquely to their platform or to the legacy media companies. Young Gen-Z creators prefer instead to tout that their early career work requires them to aggregate bits of reputational and cultural capital into a mobile network that can be leveraged—mostly by others—into "real" capital later. In this way, cultural compensation normalizes deferred financial compensation. This is similar to the older "indies" generation before them. Studios and networks now benefit once the spec-ideas and personalities are strip-mined from the oversupply of self-subsidized workers in the collective, creative aspirant hive.

But how does this widespread transposing of cultural and financial capital entail "overleveraging," as I have proposed? In media microfinancing today, the presubsidies of creators (from familial and social capital) are put at risk in ways that legions of corporate investors—that is, sponsors, branders, marketers, MCNs, agencies, and aggregators—predictably ignore. This is roughly analogous in the maker/influencer sphere to the way firms in the real estate sector ignored the extent of unsustainable debt that was held by their LBO owners in 2007–8. In the current online risk-distribution system, the true value at risk—the aggregate value on which online creation and success depends—is also systematically erased or ignored.

Leveraged buyouts involve a high ratio of debt to equity. LBOs include and incentivize taking out as much debt as possible to finance an acquisition or purchase. In the aspirant-influencer scene, the familial-social-vocational-crowd presubsidies function much like the virtual value of "debt." As such, very little corporate "cosponsor" funding (or cash) is typically needed from the corporate "partner" to leverage huge amounts of soft, informal presubsidies from the creator's informal network. This means that the presubsidies that aspirant makers (unintentionally) bring to the YouTube table function in reality as acute amounts of unacknowledged debt. From this perspective, many platform microcelebrities and creators work unwittingly from "overleveraged" positions. This positions the creators as overleveraged aspirants. In practical terms, this predicament means that rising makers cannot generate enough cash flow to ever "service" their entire de facto (but unacknowledged) start-up "debt." This trap is almost guaranteed by the fact that the high start-up costs for creators are never covered or reimbursed fully by their new corporate sponsors or by the branders or agencies they may be lucky enough to "partner" with once discovered. Aspirant creators carry their debt with them as long as they are on the media platform's trading floor, posing wishfully as clean IP start-ups.

The endless workshops and online fora on how to deal with career burnout in twentysomething makers underscored to me that this over-leveraged predicament may be a widespread structural outcome of the platform. As a result, the "partners" with actual equity (the individual creator, who has risked a lot) ultimately lose ownership to their sup-posed "lenders" (their corporate microsponsors, who have risked little to make the fiduciary partnership happen). The aspirational creator's real value vanishes in favor of an artificially imagined (but greatly con-stricted) ranking value on YouTube's public trading floor.

Beyond social media creator platforms, scholars could improve the accuracy of their economic appraisals of media industries if they recog-nized (and actually accounted for) the veiled ancillary resources that the vast aggregate of aspirant and rising creators bring and collectively con-tribute to the embedded production system as a whole. The overlever-aged-creator predicament detailed in this chapter, that is, does not just apply to aspiring online creators and influencers. For rising screenwrit-ers, for example, the four conventional ways to "break in" (to get one's career started) outlined in my interview below involve placing a signifi-cant bet or prewager on oneself. In the face of long odds, that is, each route to breaking-in requires the self-accumulation of some form of (early career) cultural capital that can later (midcareer) be leveraged into real salaried capital:

> They wanted to option [my script]. To take it for a year to see if they could get some kind of money to make it. But they said they "had no money to pay me." Which is not true for producers. [1.] And I said, "Well what can you give me instead? Instead of cash monies." And they said, "Well, what do you want?" And I said, "Well, I want an agent or a manager or an introduction to an agent or manager." And they said, "Yeah, we know a manager . . . but no guarantees." And they gave the script to her. . . . And I [eventually] got the job. . . . That's a strange way to do it. It's an odd way to break in. It's really random. [2.] But there's also the assistant route. Like being a writ-er's assistant in a writers room. [3.] There's also the contest route. Like if you've won a [scriptwriting] contest of any import. Like that's one way to

get in. [4.] And then internships is another route . . . to get in. (Kelly Fullerton, WGA, TV writer/producer, interview by author, Los Angeles, April 7, 2016)

Consider the four post-SME "gatekeepers" described here that regulate the trajectories of trained screenwriters who want better pro careers. Note that cultural caste systems oversee even these four modest doorways in "introductions," "contests," "internships," and "assisting." That is, each category is highly competitive yet delivers widely varying amounts of institutional prestige to the recipient. The years or calendar time over which aspirants must cover their costs and eat their expenses until they can monetize any of this hard-earned soft cultural capital is key. That duration creates the very early to midcareer predicament under which many rising creative workers overextend and overleverage themselves.

Online maker trade gatherings are loaded with survival and career therapy interventions that try to convince precarious and desperate young creators to stay in the game. The problems of front-loading VACT be damned. Platform pedagogy teaches skills-for-success, but it also needs to sustain the otherwise precarious system. In effect, the platform needs to convince its aspirant creators to keep uploading at all costs, thus subsidizing the platform's ecosystem as a whole. One difference between this current aspirant-creator world and the Great Recession is that in the 2008–9 crash, the banks and VC funds called in their debts and took ownership away from legitimate shareholders of real estate that could in turn be resold (even if at foreclosure prices). Reclaiming ownership was actually possible then, since even the subprime loans involved physical properties with real street addresses. By contrast, in the pending online creator crisis, the hundreds of thousands of online creator-investors, many of whom are adolescents, simply have *no* leverage to "call in" their co-ownership of *any* firm, tangible property, or IP. Media platforms habitually abstract content ownership and risk alike. Risk and ownership are splintered and distributed so widely and informally that the sun never sets on the earnest minions that make up the platform's collective investor-creator crowd.

The perverse genius of the current creator-leveraging system is that it is embedded within a huge proprietary technology platform, with no supposed "outside," with no ostensible "labor" problems, and with no apparent need for regulatory oversight. YouTube/Google's posture as neutral and agnostic enables participants and harvesters alike to psychologize the aspirant-influencer phenomenon. In effect, the platform reserves for itself the role of benign infrastructural enabler and broker for rising aspirant creators. The aspirant's supposed therapeutic interpersonal relationship with platform infrastructure may help take the persistent sting out of the manic pace, overleveraged buyouts, and crash-and-burn careers of young makers/influencers. At the very least, the automated therapeutic management of these creator career and life arcs helps sustain the specworld's vast micromedia speculation stock market.

Methods

Production Culture Research Design

"And then came the grandest idea of all! We actually made a
map of the country, on the scale of a mile to the mile!"

"Have you used it much?" I enquired.

"It has never been spread out, yet," said Mein Herr: "the
farmers objected: they said it would cover over the whole
country, and shut out the sunlight! So we now use the
country itself, as its own map, and I assure you it does nearly
as well."

—Lewis Carroll, *Sylvie and Bruno Concluded*[1]

The thorny mapping problem of accurate scale-vs.-usefulness that Lewis
Carroll mocks applies as well to the vast, diverse, complexity of the
twenty-first-century global film and media industries. My push in the
introduction for ecological or complex systems research on the film and
television industries might seem to celebrate a correspondingly complex
vastness in scholarly accounts and verbiage to match it. Would not
overly detailed accounts that "accurately" echo and map the industry
approximate the 1:1 scale of Carroll's obsessively exact—but completely
useless—same-scale cartography? Practically speaking, how do we simplify the media industry's vast complexity without being reductive?
What specific "part" (of production) will stand for the "whole" (of
media industry) that we hope to generalize about in our research? This
final chapter explores practical problems like these in research design.
One goal is to consider ways that production scholars can reconceptual-
ize research to more effectively unpack embedded production systems.

Yet what could scholars possibly add to the public's knowledge about
film and television production that the media hasn't already disclosed or

hashed out? Critics and the press already habitually announce and end-lessly amplify film and television production's significance. This means media industries pose like anything but a reluctant mentor or shy instruc-tor to those looking into media from the outside. Given this explanatory deluge about production by media companies to the public, surely we do not need more information, or academic theorizing, about film and media production. After all, explaining media production to observers is already an unavoidable, global, 24/7, industry-wide enterprise. And it goes beyond mere marketing. Analysis and explanation are already inextricable, intentional parts of basic business plans and act as baseline behaviors in media production today. In fact, analysis-as-marketing about production (all the behind-the-scenes media stuff) may now be as prominent for viewers as the primary object of industry attention itself, screen content. In many academic disciplines the objects of research are opaque or difficult to see or access by definition (from molecular physics and genetics to psychiatry and agronomy). By contrast, opacity and reluctance to disclose are not initially problems in cinema and media studies, since scholars already face an overload of public explanation and analysis from the industry.

REVERSING THE SIGNIFYING LOGIC OF BEHIND-THE-SCENES INFO

Faced with this ostensibly helpful overload of backstory, media scholars seldom adhere as we should to the cautionary adage "beware of strangers bearing [explanatory] gifts." We should be especially wary of preemp-tively gifted explanations, given their capacity to forestall other kinds of thinking. Students and scholars who want to study production often complain to me about an anxiety: the problem of how to gain "access" to the industry. While access is indeed a task in production studies, I would argue that something more fundamental can derail scholarship before that. Excess (rather than access) can also get in the way of sound research. I would argue that the industry's excessive disclosures and ana-lytical vigilance by publicists are far more likely to skew research inde-pendence than the difficulty of gaining access to study production.

Teaching and supervising film and television production studies over the years have reinforced my requirement that doctoral students must "ask research questions of industry other than industry's own." This, I argue, stands as a prerequisite for meaningful scholarly study. Scholars adopting this goal—trying to identify their industry-independent (and therefore sometimes unwelcomed) questions at the early stages of any research project on film or media production—better their odds of later achieving meaningful research results. Yet formulating industry-independent research questions can sometimes be frustrating, like swimming upstream. If, as I have argued, the voluntary overproduction of knowledge and analysis about film and media production are unavoidable baseline behaviors from our corporate research subjects (the cinema and media industries), then we will need to wade through a lot of flak before getting to our intended scholarly vantage point.

Behind-the-scenes flack about production is problematic for several reasons. First, industry marketing and publicity can serve as powerful forms of misdirection for industry scholars. Industry adroitly uses its vast amounts of secondary behind-the-scenes media content to push viewer/analyst attention back toward its primary showcase for attention (onscreen content, film, star, celebrity, or series) and away from other offscreen industrial practices that may be more relevant and timely for scholars (say, production labor economics, studio sustainability, or racial managerial practices).[2]

Second, behind-the-scenes flack undercuts systematic production culture research because it legitimizes and shores-up an analytical shortcut long-employed by the popular, celebrity, and trade press to direct and manage the public's attention. Specifically, every marketing campaign or promotional buy (no matter how low-budget) asserts, by definition, that its hyped phenom somehow stands out from the crowd; it is exceptional, distinctive, exemplary, notable, must-see, cutting-edge, outfront, or influential in some way. Personnel in PR, advertising, marketing, branding, and public-relations are never trained or paid to undersell or aim low in their claims. They never downgrade their client's industrial status to the level of the formulaic, the predictable, the regular, the symptomatic, or the routine.

The research design and methods proposed here, however, turn the logic of this press-and-trades equation on its head. Contrary to publicists that dismiss industrial routine, the chapters here have aimed to unpack some of that monotonous regularity in industry by backtracking from industrial rifts to find the infrastructures that trigger those rifts. Marketing and the entertainment press, in contrast, reify winners and castigate losers but ignore the regularities of embedded production labor out of habit. *Specworld* aims to unpack the regularity of production through the irregularly appearing portals created by acute controversy, conflict, and unplanned notoriety (rifts). I have tried to systematically trace out creative labor routines (mundane relations), which are often clearest when isolated and viewed via stress points and intertrade rifts. One research takeaway from reversing the signifying logic of exceptions-vs.-routine is clear. Acute rifts signify embedded routines and creative labor stresses. They are much more than just fleeting head-line-worthy one-offs that feed the trades' rapidly changing celebrity news cycle.

EVIDENCE AND STUDY DESIGN

Two goals inform this book. As an industry, media production features no hard boundaries. As such, *Specworld* mines industry's borderlands. As a field, media industry study falters if approached as zero-sum game. *Specworld* merely adds ways-of-thinking to the field's already proven methods. *Specworld*, in short, aims to expand the menu both of what we look at, and how we study it. Yet both goals make practical problems of evidence and scope in research design unavoidable.

Effectively navigating Lewis Carroll's part-vs.-whole mapping dilemma in research, invoked above, usually requires framing and delimiting evidence in more logical, convincing, and productive ways. The next section details the problem of scope in research (i.e., the portion of a wider range of a phenomenon that is deemed sufficient and relevant in scholarship). This discussion challenges production studies scholars to articulate and justify their projects from three different fundamental perspectives: (1) scope of industry, (2) scope of evidence, and (3) rift sampling. This third section in the chapter will summarize the data-framing methods that I employed in this book's ethnographies of high production vs. low. I term the alternative methodology discussed there *rift sampling*.

Scope of Industry

To study production convincingly today requires that researchers must first locate it, frame it as a studyable coherent phenomenon, and clearly state what their study subject will not include. Why should the twenty-first-century abundance of media content and platforms be a problem for scholars? On the one hand, the ease of access to YouTube, Vimeo, Netflix, Apple+, HBO-Go, Amazon-Prime, TikTok, and regional social media creators means that scholars no longer have to travel or pretend that film/TV production only takes place in dense sanctioned cultural and entertainment centers like "Hollywood," London, or Mumbai.

Media production is now undeniably geographically transnational (horizontally dispersed). But production is also immensely stratified (vertically reiterated and diversified) throughout and within most parts of that very same vast geographic spread of production. Evidence of this proliferation and diversification of media is widespread and unavoidable. Those that traffic in this multimedia expansion—tech platforms, social media, and venture capitalism—are not hesitant to publicly promote their media spreading and dimensional upscaling (fig. 9.1).

The industrial scope problem this creates is unavoidable: "500 hours of video uploaded every minute," or 259.2 million new videos per year.[3] How can CMS usefully research 259 million new videos per year? Or research a quarter billion of anything, for that matter? *Forbes* marvels that "today's global Creator Economy is only poised to grow as 50 million people already consider themselves a 'Creator.'"[4] Influencer marketing analysts salivate at the overwhelming scale of the online video-producer community: "2 million global creators make six figures . . . [and] 22 thousand YouTube creators have more than 1 million subscribers."[5] How can scholars add fifty million online video creators to the legacy producers we already struggle to frame, sample, and analyze in production studies? Such numbers make the DGA's eighteen thousand members or the Producers Guild of America's (PGA) seven thousand global members seem quaint. Yet the DGA and PGA were already problematic for researchers, at least if we treated them as somehow representative of global production in general. We need to find ways to frame, sample, and study that go beyond big data analytics in the digital humanities (which often produce outcomes not unlike the analytics of the giant platforms).

Industry Diversification Upsides. In practical terms, I encourage my students to embrace this new horizontal and vertical diversification of production levels because the expansion provides them with a much wider range of options for industry access. Interfaces and access points now range from the recognizable, but highly guarded, old-style "A-list" professionals at the top, to the underemployed lower-budget cadres in the middle zones, to the millions of unemployed "aspirational" online creators at the bottom. The existence and availability of this immense, variable mode-of-production spectrum means, among other things, that a single suspicious or recalcitrant publicist at a major film studio or TV network (aka "gatekeeper") is less likely to derail or stop a production researcher's proposal out of hand. The walls and barriers to entry are not as high when scholars are willing to look lower down in a locale's or region's less prestigious production food-chain.

FIGURE 9.1. Production's expanding footprint makes justifying scope crucial. Location crews move into the material world of viewers and scholars, even as transmedia content and platforms permeate online social worlds. *Top:* Industry's abundant 360-degree offstage disclosure. Here, a building-scale Netflix marketing campaign for *Orange Is the New Black* in Berlin. Photo: © 2016, by J. Caldwell. *Bottom left:* Location crew notice warning neighbors, Los Angeles. Photo: © 2016, by J. Caldwell. *Bottom right:* Giant video mural near Michigan Ave., Chicago. Photo: © 2018, by J. Caldwell.

Media scholars sink or swim today in part by establishing clear but modest boundaries within such vast industries. Can CMS scholars establish a justifiable scope for their research and systematic forms of analysis that meaningfully reflect technical and content diversity? These questions are vexing precisely because there is also so much amorphous content around and so many divergent ways of making media today that we as CMS scholars could potentially analyze. Reckoning with twenty-first-century creator platforms, this book has explored how we might be more systematic in our analyses in ways that enable us to generalize about media and production in credible and convincing ways.

Finally, production research proposals need to include qualifications and caveats about what the research is not. How relatively big, extensive, or small is the practice being researched? Related to this is the imperative that we need to answer the symptomatic-vs.-exceptional cases question. That is, one needs to disclose whether they are studying standard or "symptomatic" conventions or practices that express or reflect (in multiple settings) a bigger system or whether they are analyzing exceptional outliers as a case study (which still might be targeted in order to demonstrate an "exception that proves the rule" of something more general in a system). Regardless, nailing one's positions down on these questions early on can help later in the process, as the researcher shares findings with peers.

Scope of Evidence

One of the worst things that a critic can say about some qualitative research is that a scholar has chosen to cherry-pick evidence. Suspicions that the collection of evidence has been somehow illogical or unsystematic often triggers this criticism. Critics might assume that a humanities scholar has conveniently preselected only those cultural objects and texts that happen to fit the scholar's initial theory and agenda. Even more damning is that the scholar may also have ignored or disregarded evidence that does not fit or that is inconvenient in some way. This takedown of qualitative humanities research often assumes that the researcher knew the results that were needed in advance. Science-informed skeptics of qualitative or critical scholarship typically view the "disinterested" or "randomized" sample (discussed in chapter 2) as a far preferable, firmer foundation to draw general conclusions from in research. Such critics often deem random sampling as far more sound than cherry-picking data to "interpret" or mine for broader principles.

This cross-discipline critique resonates for me as a cautionary prospect. This is because I intentionally include a wide range of different types of production artifacts, media forms, and labor in my research sample. I do so by design. Given the faltering institutional trajectory of the humanities in general, we should take the cherry-picking criticism seriously. We would benefit by better justifying why workable alternatives to randomized data-set "sampling" in production studies research are indeed viable. If using widely varying formats of evidence by design in research makes statistical validity impossible, and vast culture industries prevent our use of single artists or movements to justify oeuvres and canons as delimited samples, then researchers need to demonstrate alternative approaches to framing and delimiting evidence. This requires production scholars to demonstrate why justifiable or justifiably systematic links do indeed exist between the diverse objects being compared in their production study evidence sample.

To justify evidence diversity, for example, how could we hypothetically articulate the logic that connects the various artifacts and habits that make up the following test case? Consider one evidence sample collected during fieldwork on camera crews. What significant links connect all of the following: (1) a cinematographer's comp reel (a collection of short clips edited together of the operator's best shots from the past); (2) a camera equipment company video demo for the DP's gear (an aesthetic trade expression to help potential buyer-users imagine possible uses); (3) edited scenes from the DP's movie (the DP's finished film on Netflix); (4) a trade interview with the DP (on the Variety.com or ASC.com site); (5) the ancillary artistic references made on the DP's social media sites (LinkedIn, Facebook, Instagram); (6) a list of the "in-kind" resources loaned personally to the DP as part of an informal barter-and-trade economy; (7) a strike authorization or budgetary report for the Local-600 camera union; and (8) a tax-incentive policy document from the film commission of the right-to-work state of Georgia?

This diverse group of artifacts is not a collection of mismatched "apples-and-oranges" evidence—as a randomizing, quantitative researcher in the social sciences might argue. Instead, this particular evidence set can—if connected effectively by the scholar—serve as a cohesive research sample. These artifacts all cohere, in fact, precisely because they all have unavoidable direct connections to each other. They all intersect and make contact through the nexus point of a production unit's single human DP. Finding and identifying those nexus contacts in any industrial system provides a networked logic for the diverse evidence sample the scholar chooses to research.

I would counter critics who question the clear (lived and transactional) connections among these diverse artifacts from a single camera-world as missing the mark. The text-artifact-network of evidence from the camera-world outlined above is all threaded together through the DP's labor and life. This contact, intersection, and threading provide a logic for research that is as valid and systematic as a traditional data set, albeit in a different way. The alternative to qualitatively researching mixed-format evidence—that is, reducing the culture of camera practice to a randomized same-type data set (precisely because it is "disinterested")—would ensure that the quantitative research necessarily involves an *irrelevant* form of artificial cherry-picking.

This is because cutting the deck of possible evidence in research strips any evidence culled of its original defining and animating context. "Objective" data sampling disregards the significance of evidence connections, which themselves signal dynamic, lived interactions among different production sectors or strata. Such intersections provide researchers with access to fundamental, locatable dimensions of embedded production systems. As a method, closely describing and analyzing this system connectedness far exceeds the insights one gets from counting objects with false equivalencies and no meaningful connections apart from their randomness in a same-type set. The trick in production culture research is to make a convincing, nonstatistical argument for why the objects in the research sample are justifiable and necessary. The goal is to make a compelling case that the diverse evidence and artifacts in the sample are connected to each other in ways significant to the system as a whole.

One final unavoidable task that scope-of-evidence questions bring to production culture study entails the need to explicitly address up front two interrelated questions in research proposals and design. First, how "representative" can the evidence be that you are starting with and limiting yourself to? Second, how "generalizable" beyond your sample can your final conclusions potentially be? The two questions are linked. Establishing how representative your sample is (accounting for what it can potentially stand-for) will impact how broad your final conclusions about "production" or "industry" can be. Responding to these two questions early on, as you design and propose production research, can help a researcher preemptively address potential criticisms of the logic and methods of study later on.

Translocalism and Rift-Trace Sampling

Throughout this book, I have adapted for production studies two methods from ethnography in response to the problems of scope (relative to range and representativeness) in both media industries and evidence sampling. First, translocal fieldwork methods (i.e., to study how the actions or circumstances in one place have a reciprocal or immediate impact on other connected places) helped free anthropology of one premodern straitjacket. The participant-observation mode that launched modern anthropology provided rich insights about local cultures that moved the field well beyond folklore studies. The field succeeded in part because extended observation and interaction with Indigenous peoples produced complex insights about the systematic nature and organization of those non-Western cultures that social survey instruments and quantitative distant analysis never could. Even though geographically bounded, ethnography's early influence followed in part from the richness of its deep and narrow scope and focus. But this deep narrowness and rich description also frustrated or angered those who claimed the local cannot be credibly isolated from broader systems—neocolonial, imperial, capitalist, neoliberal—within which the local is always bounded. To get beyond this scale and scope problem, poststructuralist anthropologists proposed and pursued translocal ethnographies. This method allowed ethnographers to systematically connect multiple local cultures (sometimes across vast distances) to broader social systems like neocolonialism and neoliberal political economies.

For example, while the structural racism or political economy of the coffee trade might not be fully realizable within any single "village" setting, it might be better understood through a different kind of ethnographic and geographic arc. That is, instead of limiting one's research to observation of a single village of growers, for example, the "translocal" ethnographer could closely follow the coffee production through its entire global supply chain. This might result in a series of individual chapters on a succession of local communities involved in growing, processing, shipping, and marketing. Yet each chapter in this workflow would still require the same anthropological method—ethnographic participant observation and deep description—even though the chapter studies would now be geographically "distributed," sometimes vastly, across different countries and locales.

The genius of the translocal innovation was that it uncovered new forms of systematic connectedness (in this case, the route coffee travels before it gets to US or German markets). The translocal paradigm substitutes for another, older, simpler—and now academically suspect—form of connectedness (the village). Translocalism provides an apt prototype for production culture research. The trope helps solve the vexing problem of what kinds of industrial location and evidence to include in the data sample and what kinds of evidence to leave out. In short, we might ask how a production practice "travels" through various embedded systems. In some ways, the "life cycle" of a film/TV production practice as it travels provides an elegant way to cut the deck and delimit industry's evidence. With translocalism we would study only the connections that are justified by the route or travel of the production practice through the industrial system.

Specworld also adapts a second methodology from anthropology: the chain-referral sampling approach to collecting human research subjects. Sometimes termed "snowball sampling" or "referral sampling," chain referral offers a slightly different model for establishing credible connections and boundaries for the research sample. If the translocal allows a researcher to describe a production practice as it travels across the borders of a complex industrial system, in some ways, the snowball method does just the opposite. It describes instead how the production researcher travels across that same system. In this method, the analyst approaches and solicits first contacts as informants in the production sector. These initial subjects are later used for referrals to recruit future subjects from among their acquaintances. This chain referral continues until an appropriate sample size is achieved. Chain-referral sampling does not seek to establish "probability" in the research (a requisite in science and quantitative research), since this "predictive" task from science is largely irrelevant when studying aesthetic and cultural phenomena.[6]

This evidence-delimiting framing logic works because chain referrals provide an elegant internal picture of what the system itself thinks is significant. That is, chain referral betrays what the system thinks (at least tacitly) should be included in the outsider-scholar's research sample. The method provides an internal snapshot of an actual active social network. The burden of selecting which evidence to include in the data set is thus taken off the shoulders of the scholar and becomes largely the industry's or the informants' task. One upside of shifting the sampling burden onto the system is that the chain-referral method shows how the system itself thinks about what to leave in (who to talk to next) and who to leave out (names normally never disclosed from the informant's rolodex). In effect, a researcher's industry subjects are now tasked with creating the sample based on their own "insider" logic, not the scholar's.

For this book, the 2016 Adpocalypse rift discussed in chapters 6 and 8 offers a fitting prototype for how translocalism and chain-referral sampling can be productive in research. In response to widespread blowback from YouTubers after YouTube demonetized their channels, YouTube/Google/Alphabet helped host a single hybrid in-person trans-media event that exposed for research a deep traceable cross section within a complex political-economic ecosystem. An in-person show and Q&A onstage at VidCon 2017 by Link and Rhett of *Good Mythical Morning* (for their fans and other influencers) was strategic in YouTube's attempt at an Adpocalypse "fix." The show's place within the larger rift allows us to isolate a clear research starting point. Evidence tracing from this point allows a sampling alternative to either "random sampling" or "cherry-picking" data.

The schematic in figure 9.2 provides a researchable snapshot, a key that further details the odd network triggered when YouTube attempted to cover and contain its snowballing controversy. Furthermore, the platform exposed its complex roots for scholarly analysis on a single day (June 22, 2017). This diagram exemplifies "contact trace sampling" and disembedding analysis on one overhyped corporate attempt to "fold" and contain a rift between the YouTube platform and its vast numbers of precarious, cynical online creator "partners." Tracing from this single nexus point exposes potentially vast interconnections across firms and intermediaries.

In this snapshot, researchers can trace the ripple effect of embedded, multidirectional creator-platform engagement across at least four different corporate conglomerates: (1) the YouTube/Google/Alphabet system that hosts the creators (upper left); (2) the Amazon system and manufacturers that merchandize and monetize the creator's spin-off products (lower left); (3) the CNBC/NBC-Universal/Nasdaq financial trades system that covered and valued the event as a financial market in real-time (upper right); and (4) the Vice/HBO/Warner Media/AT&T conglomerate that makes its own spin-off content, starting with a ViceNews feature (lower left) on the show hosts featured on the convention hall stage. Within this fleeting corporate web, frozen here in time, the self-dealing by YouTube/Google/Alphabet comes as no surprise. Yet the cross-conglomerate linkages triggered by the event exposed a researchable but more unorthodox network comprising content-harvesting competitors, angry YouTubers, wannabe reps, and bottom-feeding opportunists.[7]

For production study, I have modified the chain-referral method for building-out the research sample to go beyond just interviews and referrals from informants. I do this to trace nonhuman interactions and organizational relationships, in addition to human connections. Since I use industrial fault lines and fractures as starting points in the sample, I term the method *rift-trace sampling* rather than chain referral. Every crew habit and piece of gear comes with its own footnotes, de facto referrals, and interfirm relations. Even if they are not disclosed in written or verbal form, all technology and labor behaviors come packaged with their own specific technical genealogies, origins, instigators, and outcomes. As such, tech and operators form parts of significant networks (nonhuman and human) that can and should be productively tracked down and mapped by the scholar. Rift-trace sampling thus echoes Bruno Latour's actor-network theory, which distributes agency across nonhuman subjects in mixed systems.[8] Good research can show how the object or practice in question connects directly to a specific, nonrandomized but delimited network of other practices, institutions, and contexts.

Employed carefully, the rift-trace sampling method can preempt the potential criticism of cherry-picking evidence. That is, faced with an industry that is opaque and dissembling out of habit, rift-trace (like snowball) sampling selects only subjects via self-defined relationships that the local system itself deems significant.[9]

ANALYSIS, THEORY BUILDING, AND CROSS-DISCIPLINARY RESEARCH QUESTIONS

Each of these basic evidence-framing, scope, and research-design problems affects the relative persuasiveness of the researcher's observations and descriptions in the early stages of a project. After first addressing those questions, research-design proposals should also articulate how that gathered data will be inductively analyzed, and then generalized from, as part of a midlevel theorizing process. In contrast to top-down prescriptive theory (with its preselected data sets and explanatory schemes), grounded theory building is self-adjusting and incremental. The method, that is, requires the researcher to sequentially switch attention from (1) initial observation and data collection to preliminary analysis; (2) additional observation and data collection (refocused per the initial analysis) to secondary analysis (reframed per the additional data); (3) subsequent data (further refocused per the secondary analysis) to

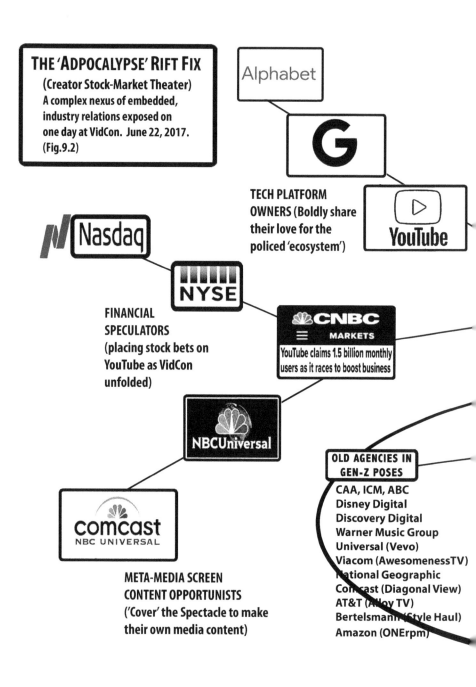

THE 'ADPOCALYPSE' RIFT FIX
(Creator Stock-Market Theater)
A complex nexus of embedded,
industry relations exposed on
one day at VidCon. June 22, 2017.
(Fig.9.2)

Alphabet

TECH PLATFORM
OWNERS (Boldly share
their love for the
policed 'ecosystem')

YouTube

Nasdaq

NYSE

FINANCIAL
SPECULATORS
(placing stock bets on
YouTube as VidCon
unfolded)

CNBC MARKETS
YouTube claims 1.5 billion monthly
users as it races to boost business

NBCUniversal

OLD AGENCIES IN
GEN-Z POSES

CAA, ICM, ABC
Disney Digital
Discovery Digital
Warner Music Group
Universal (Vevo)
Viacom (AwesomenessTV)
National Geographic
Comcast (Diagonal View)
AT&T (Alloy TV)
Bertelsmann (Style Haul)
Amazon (ONErpm)

comcast
NBC UNIVERSAL

META-MEDIA SCREEN
CONTENT OPPORTUNISTS
('Cover' the Spectacle to make
their own media content)

FIGURE 9.2. Rift trace sampling to research a vast interfirm nexus point. A research snapshot from a single day. Illustration: Original drawing and photos from VidCon 2017, Anaheim, CA. © 2017, by J. Caldwell.

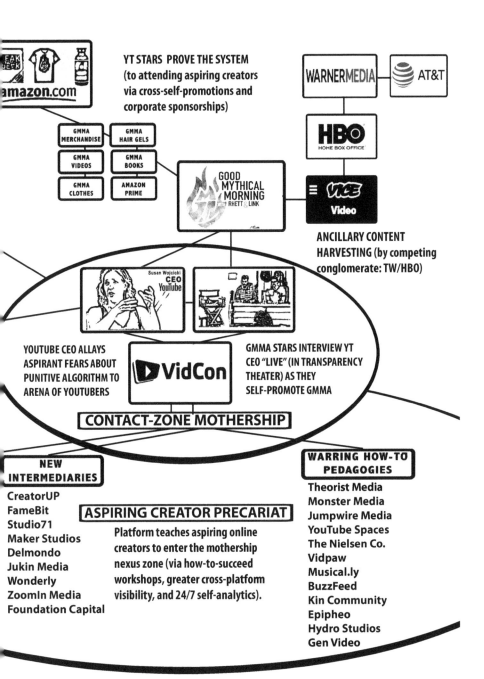

amazon.com

YT STARS PROVE THE SYSTEM
(to attending aspiring creators
via cross-self-promotions and
corporate sponsorships)

WARNERMEDIA — AT&T

HBO
HOME BOX OFFICE

GMMA MERCHANDISE	GMMA HAIR GELS
GMMA VIDEOS	GMMA BOOKS
GMMA CLOTHES	AMAZON PRIME

GOOD MYTHICAL MORNING
WITH RHETT & LINK

VICE
Video

ANCILLARY CONTENT
HARVESTING (by competing
conglomerate: TW/HBO)

Susan Wojcicki
CEO
YouTube

VidCon

YOUTUBE CEO ALLAYS
ASPIRANT FEARS ABOUT
PUNITIVE ALGORITHM TO
ARENA OF YOUTUBERS

GMMA STARS INTERVIEW YT
CEO "LIVE" (IN TRANSPARENCY
THEATER) AS THEY
SELF-PROMOTE GMMA

CONTACT-ZONE MOTHERSHIP

NEW
INTERMEDIARIES

CreatorUP
FameBit
Studio71
Maker Studios
Delmondo
Jukin Media
Wonderly
ZoomIn Media
Foundation Capital

ASPIRING CREATOR PRECARIAT

Platform teaches aspiring online
creators to enter the mothership
nexus zone (via how-to-succeed
workshops, greater cross-platform
visibility, and 24/7 self-analytics).

WARRING HOW-TO
PEDAGOGIES

Theorist Media
Monster Media
Jumpwire Media
YouTube Spaces
The Nielsen Co.
Vidpaw
Musical.ly
BuzzFeed
Kin Community
Epipheo
Hydro Studios
Gen Video

subsequent analysis (per the subsequent data), and so forth. In this paradigm, any general theory in a production study ideally emerges over time, and any theorizing should always remain grounded in fieldwork observations.

Grounded theory building requires concurrent critical self-reflection by the scholar alongside the data gathering and analysis process as it unfolds. This parallel self-reflexive dimension will likely require the scholar to address two midlevel decisions early in the process. First, even at the proposal stage, scholars should articulate where their research questions and methods come from and provide some indication of their cross-disciplinary scope (and thus relevance). They should ask what kinds of added conceptual leverage can methods from adjacent disciplines bring to media industry studies in CMS? Second, scholars should disclose and reflect on the impact of their own scholar-informant interactions during the research. What etic-vs.-emic (scholar/informant) predicament have the research findings been filtered through? The final discussion below will underscore the ethnographic importance of acknowledging the impact that local knowledge (from informants, professional knowledge regimes, and trade communities) have had on the scholarly researcher's findings.

Production studies have benefited by employing and integrating methods from across adjacent and traditional disciplinary boundaries. Those undertaking production research should explore and describe the relative range of research methods to be integrated into the scholar's tool kit. This task pivots on a principal question: what additional conceptual leverage might disciplinary questions or perspectives from other fields bring to the scholar's CMS research on production and industries? Especially for those entering production study from the humanities and arts, the following section outlines ways to broaden the conceptual tools and disciplinary frameworks in their research skill sets.

The three ethnographic chapter studies in this book (chapters 4, 6, and 8) featured a range of ethnographic observations that compared maker-influencer production pedagogies in the online space with traditional professional production norms. That comparative fieldwork employed cross-disciplinary perspectives to unpack warring pedagogies over what production "sells" to aspirants as "core" principles for success in production today. Addressing this question required integrating some basic conceptualizing questions from nine areas that we use to brainstorm our research designs in the UCLA Production Culture seminars. I briefly outline those disciplinary areas and frameworks next.

Each framework includes a bibliographic endnote listing relevant publications that students can consult for more in-depth coverage or elaboration of each subfield or disciplinary area. Each is paired with specific evidence from fieldwork to provoke further discussion on methodology.

While established scholars in other fields will find the next section remedial, I offer the following foundational questions primarily to assist CMS students, and arts-and-humanities scholars new to media industries research as they conceptualize, design, and operationalize new production culture research projects. These questions can help researchers unpack embedded systems and identify and examine key folds where one production practice abuts with or is subsumed by another system or sector. Each of the ten disciplinary frameworks below includes examples gleaned from my fieldnotes (ethnographic transcripts) and relevant photographs (visual documentation). I begin any research project inductively, by collecting and puzzling over this very sort of spoken and visual evidence from fieldwork. I offer these evidence puzzles as discussion starters, as exemplary cases that may inspire readers to consider expanding how they frame (or reframe) the production phenomenon they plan to study.

1. *Who established the media market that your object of research is located within, and why? How is this media market embedded or interconnected with other markets? What policies, laws, social norms, or constraints (overt/explicit or tacit/implicit) oversee, regulate, or manage your media practice, within that market?* (Political Economic Practice)[10]

Such questions are crucial today in media-industry studies given how explicitly media creation is showcased as a monetizable, financial art form. Yet in selling aspirant creators on financializing their brands (neoliberalism as film school), platform creator workshopping intermediaries almost always ignore the political dimensions (including ownership, control, and regulation) on which political economy is based (fig. 9.3).

The fieldwork photographs in figure 9.3 show a rising maker-filmmaker as he is enjoined or folded into the vast consumer-products system of an immense host platform. Ethnography can expose the embodied cross-cultural stresses of these collisions in logic between maker and host. To make disembedding research more systematic, scholars need to map this cultural evidence and financial connections in actual contact zones within the embedded system.

2. *Who is given credit for authorship, artistic responsibility, or innovation in the production sector or community that you are researching?*

FIGURE 9.3. The aspirant cinematographer/creator's low-to-high crossover dilemma: filming VidCon's influencer merchandizing ecstasies. Photos: VidCon, Anaheim, CA. © 2017 and 2019, by J. Caldwell.

How and why? How do these attributions relate to actual intellectual property (IP) ownership? Who else is partly responsible for authorship, artistic responsibility, or innovation in that sector but does not get credit? Why and how is their real or relative artistic agency explained, ignored, covered over, or justified? What social, legal, or institutional practices are used to normalize this system of attribution? (Institutional Authorship and Attribution)[11]

I formulated these questions during fieldwork as I observed one director theorizing his authorship to lower-level personnel as akin to that of a creator-as-midwife giving birth. In speaking to craftworkers embedded below himself, Quentin Tarantino lauds bodily tactility as the secret to successful cinematic midwifery. In effect, the director leverages costumes and props to help actors make their characters "crown" narratively during their preproduction delivery:

> The minute Robert DeNiro has figured out the shoes, that's 75 percent of him figuring out who the character is. . . . Every time you have a costume fitting, you, the director, need to be in that fitting . . . because the character

is being born, right there. When they put on the costume. When they put on the shoes. When they put on the pants. This one versus that one. Yes, the costume designer could do it and then send you pictures. But [that way] an important part of the creative process is happening without you. And if you are a writer-director, you need to be there as your characters are crowning. (Quentin Tarantino, DGA, comments at production design workshop, UCLA, June 4, 2016)

What research methods (and adjacent disciplines) could best explain this production posturing: creation as gestation, preproduction as pregnancy, and birth as managerial and industrial analogies? Certainly, this kind of thick symbolizing would frustrate political economics, organizational sociology, and even digital humanities in production culture research. Narratology or feminist theory from CMS and the humanities is likely far more suited to deconstruct this kind of industrial embodiment and back-channel trade-myth telling than social science paradigms in fieldwork.

3. *Does your media research subject or community employ "symbolic" trade expressions, or secondary artistic expressions, trade or sociopro-fessional rituals? Why and how? Can you find any examples of "focused gatherings" or Geertzian subjects "thinking out loud" about themselves? Whose shoulders can you look over as those insiders try to make sense of their own communities and tasks?* (Ethnography, Anthropology)[12]

Consider how self-theorizing takes place in the postproduction edit suite. Reflexive chatter among editors makes describing and analyzing the etic-emic problem an unavoidable opportunity in production studies. In a sales demo (fig. 9.4), an editor works on a "Sample Scene" for the firm "Pro-Reels," which sells demo-making services to aspiring filmmakers and underemployed creators. This metaproduction sector (this one in editing) floods industry trade shows with abundant content ideas, often brainstormed-out unremarkably in trade meetings and promotions.

How can the humanities better engage with the hierarchies and embedding within this kind of complex production system involving creative worker self-reflection? Symbolic and interpretive anthropology provides a helpful bridge for emerging arts and humanities scholars trying to cross the disciplinary divide that still largely separates the methods of close textual analysis and observational fieldwork. The work of Clifford Geertz and Victor Turner, as well as cultural ethnographies in general, provides precedents for bridging this divide, especially given Geertz and Turner's textual studies of human subjects and

FIGURE 9.4. Metaproduction video editors flood embedded specworld with sample, clip, and demo reels. Documentary photo-illustration from Creatasphere, Burbank, CA. © 2013, by J. Caldwell.

social communities as cultural expressions. A fuller discussion of their insights can be found later in the notes. Apart from some differences, Geertz and Turner excel at accounting for the expressive and symbolic dimensions of social collectives. Together they provide alternatives to the "positivism" that some humanities scholars may prematurely conflate with the "empiricism" of "fieldwork." In some ways, *Specworld* has explored the prospects of hermeneutic and critical dimensions that persist (and are studyable) in fieldwork after scholars add and integrate observation and ethnographic methods to cinema and media studies.

4. *What role do "intermediaries" or "contact persons" play in your media phenomenon? How is flexibility established and maintained? What kinds of interorganizational relations exist, and how are they maintained? How is "consensus" developed or "dissensus" managed?* (Organizational Sociology)[13]

Archival film historians have been good at detailing the modes of production, guiding personalities, and the managerial organization of the classical-era film studios. Until recently, they have paid less atten-

tion to the interdepartmental politics, cultural dimensions, and emotional labor that animated and stressed those bureaucratic studio hierarchies. Organizational sociology provides media historians with
additional ways of understanding and researching production organizations and their personnel. During one interview, I was struck by a resonant comment about "not being chained to a desk." The junior development executive I interviewed elaborated on how intermediaries make
hierarchies work and cohere and on how physical proximity can steer
the management, sharing, and policing of production knowledge:

> As you age up, your relationships age up. So my boss might know all the
> heads of these networks, but he doesn't know all of the junior people. So,
> yes, they have this upper-level understanding. And I have this level of under-
> standing. So together we can kind of figure out what needs to be done. As a
> junior executive you don't get all that much credit. But you learn a lot. You
> get to go to meetings. [But] as an assistant, you don't get to go to meetings.
> You are chained to a desk. (Michael Masukawa, Piller/Segan Agency, inter-
> view by author, UCLA, April 7, 2016)

Agency staffers like Masukawa are seldom credited. In exchange for
access, they are allowed to shadow and learn from their executive agents
and (unbeknownst to the executive) allowed to develop mutually supportive side relationships with junior personnel at other firms. By contrast, even the nearby office assistants to executives and producers are
sometimes not allowed to leave their desks, at will, to take restroom
breaks. This split (related to proximity) effectively segregates who gets
to learn production. It is analogous to an earlier industrial change in
postproduction: the shift from videotape footage to recording on digital
cards. Assistant editors, who traditionally logged incoming footage,
once worked alongside their editors and supervisors. This created at
least the possibility of eventual upward career advancement. But when
logging digital recordings was sent out to specialty and contract firms,
the remote digital sweatshops that resulted effectively cut logger/aspir-
ants off from the physical proximity that even low-level PAs (on an
actual set) still might have to higher-ups who could potentially mentor
and help their careers. Theories of organizational sociology in fieldwork
allow CMS scholars to expand their understanding of things like physical proximity and micronetworking as knowledge tactics.

*5. What forms of "social capital" or "cultural capital" are employed in
your research sector? How are these forms "learned" or "gained"?
How are they subsequently "leveraged" or converted into forms of*

FIGURE 9.5. Main film screen in public square, Locarno International Film Festival. Venues like this symbolize the quality big-screen goal that online administrative platform pedagogy clouds, undercuts, or derails for many aspirants. Composite documentary photo illustration of aggregating cultural capital, with typical award-season ad projected onto prestige big screen at film festival. Locarno, Switzerland. © 2017, by J. Caldwell.

"financial capital" distinction or legitimacy? (Sociology of Taste Cultures, Cultural Capital)[14]

Production scholars should pay attention to any interrelations between the economics of the physical production they are studying and the circulation of trade, artistic, and cultural distinctions around and within that sector. As discussed in chapter 4 on "stress aesthetics and symbolic pay systems," film festivals, awards, competitions, and cultural capital help move even highly segregated below-the-line craft labor into a higher culture cinematic public sphere (fig. 9.5).

Consider how one costume designer describes even preproduction hiring, not as a bureaucratic task but as a creative production involving cultural capital. Arianne Phillips describes a film director who is looking to find and hire a cultural cinephile—not just a mere craftsperson. Creative labor often employs an artistic cultural skill set in the workplace, long before production, even in prework meetings, as in this case:

And before the [pitch] meeting, I got to read the script. I had to go to Quentin's office to read it. And they took it out of a safe. I was sitting at his desk. I could see the "Hollywood" sign outside. [The set-up] felt quite art directed! [laughter] Well I felt like it was. Like the stars were just aligning. (Costume designer Arianne Phillips, CDG, "Sketch to Screen" panel, UCLA, Feb. 8, 2020)

In this case, the film director of *Once upon a Time in Hollywood* (2019) has "art directed" a workday meeting in advance, trying to "stage" his understanding of his script to see how the prospective costume designer responds. The designer's takeaway? Phillips conjectures that the director wants her to think and feel the cultural weight of the imagined world of Hollywood distinction, before their actual contract negotiation begins. This suggests that creative workers aren't just paid in cultural capital; they are often hired based on their appraisal of it.

6. *Where is your media research subject actually or materially located? Where is it symbolically located, and why? What is the "cultural geography" of your research subject? Can you draw it, diagram it, or map it? What "clusters" or resource "agglomerations" enable your research object/subject? What forces are "centrifugal" or push to decentralize your media phenomenon (to the peripheries)? What forces are "centripetal" or push your phenomenon to cohere in media "centers?"* (Economic Geography, Cultural Geography)[15]

Asking how closed (anchored) or how open (borderless) the production practice being researched is can give the production scholar insights about whether the material geography or symbolic geography is more important to chosen production sector (see fig. 9.6). How does industry behave—both materially and conceptually—in terms of access, transparency, or opacity? Does this industry posturing (or cultural geography) skew or problematize your evidence in any way? The traditional security of a soundstage at Paramount, for example, makes high production opaque (upper left). AC ducts outside a bunkered film-production stage signify severely restricted backstage access and disclosure (lower). By contrast, giddy over-the-top invitations to enter the digital production industry—from anywhere in the world—promise transparency to online aspirant creators (upper right). Ideally, production researchers should first account for these geographic access-vs.-bordered behaviors before analysis.

7. *What "media rituals" are central to your research subject or community? What are the everyday "habitual" and "liminoid" rituals, and*

FIGURE 9.6. Gatekeeping and the art of disclosure. *Top left:* Paramount Studios security. Photo © 2016, by J. Caldwell. *Top right:* Offscreen still frame of "Easy" Famebit sponsorship solicitation. 2018. *Bottom:* One of countless, bunkered LA soundstages. Photo: © 2016, by J. Caldwell.

are there any collective "liminal rituals" involved in your media phenomenon? What self-interpretations of these trade rituals exist inside your trade community? (Symbolic and Sociological Anthropology)[16]

Early in a research project, scholars should map out the yearly calendar of trade summits, expos, panel discussions, Q&As, and throwdowns in their trade or production sector (fig.9.7). These events offer ideal field sites for ethnographies of trade rituals and socioprofessional

FIGURE 9.7. Aca-Industry trade confabs spur ancillary metaproductions for specworld. Photo of filmed trade interview between panels at "Transforming Hollywood," moderated by Denise Mann and Henry Jenkins, UCLA. © 2015, by J. Caldwell.

interactions. This is because intertrade haggling, self-reflexive trade coverage, marketing, and industry's own research congeal in such interface sites. These emic contact zones (for speculation and negotiation) enable and fuel critical industrial practice in the collective specworld.

8. *What forms of "embedded texts," "metatexts," "paratexts," or "intertexts" exist or circulate within your media phenomenon? To what ends? In what direction do they "travel"? Are these communications or expressions back-channeled, oblique, tangential, interpretive, promotional, or critical? What value or logic do they have in the system as a whole?* (Industrial Textual Practice)[17]

The intimate dimensions of hand-holdable production merch in specworld can provide CMS scholars with thick cultural insights that are germane even to political economics. Material artifacts, that is, are embedded with industrial significance and with cultural dimensions that go well beyond close textual analysis or aesthetics. Consider the "personal touch" PR undersell in the "Prevue" record of a stunt song.

 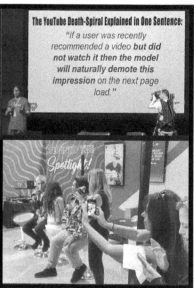

FIGURE 9.8. Reflexive metatexts proliferate well before and long after the primary onscreen content. How and why does this take place within your research sector? *Top left:* Cross-promotional "Prevue" record produced by Sid Caesar and Carl Reiner (collection of the author). *Bottom left:* Black-and-white photo by Dorothea Lange of *Grapes of Wrath* billboard, FSA/OWI Collection, Library of Congress. *Top right:* Creator "expert" publicly triggers anxiety attacks in teen influencers with visual warnings about the coming "YouTube Death-Spiral." *Bottom right:* A "Step into the Spotlight" multimedia workshop cheerleads the same teens to help fold them into the same YouTube ecosystem. Photos: © 2017, by J. Caldwell.

This vinyl LP (fig. 9.8, upper left) was produced by Cid Cesar and Karl Reiner to cross-promote their live TV show. Yet there are also examples of PR overkill, including the *Grapes of Wrath* publicity billboard dominating an impoverished Oakie shack in California's Central Valley (fig. 9.8, lower left). Finding ways to make sense of pregnant artifacts like these can help the researcher avoid being misdirected by industry's overdone rhetorical trade hype.

Rather than look at all these metatextual permutations as an apples-and-oranges data set, production researchers should work to keep conflicting evidence in check or in productive tension. Stressed industrial faults can trigger immense amounts of cultural rhetoric, trade texts, and artifacts, much of it contradictory. Explore whether those contradictions and oblique back-channel messaging are outcomes or expressions of unresolved negotiation. The barrage of metatexts being researched may offer keys that help explain the embedded production system's creative labor or broader industrial logic.

9. *How is work performed within your sector? What are the barriers to entering this field, and who manages those entry points? How do workers self-identify (crafts, technician, creator, professional, specialist, consultant)? How is your craft or specialization learned, acquired, or mastered? How are your workers "paid" (financially, culturally, socially)? Do hierarchies define your labor system, and, if so, how are those hierarchies maintained institutionally? Who "organizes" these workers? How do your workers/creators interact with adjacent workers?* (Labor Studies)[18]

At the same time that industry allows flexibility "upstairs," at the corporate management level, it often employs command-and-control to lock down worker knowledge "downstairs," in physical production. One truism—"the project is on a need-to-know basis, and you don't need to know"—encourages many craftspersons to disconnect (at least publicly) from any pretense of having an overall, holistic understanding of the film project. This disaggregation (allowing system thinking above the line vs. preventing system thinking below the line) is perpetuated within crews both through signed NDAs and almost universal prohibitions against unauthorized copying or printing script pages:

> I'm on a film right now and I'm not allowed to use a script. You have to go through this torturous process to even get to the script. You can't even print it out. I get in a panic about the amount—about the number of things you COULD look at. You really just need a few good [visual references] and you work from there. And you can imagine the rest. I think there's almost too much. . . . I don't really like technology very much. I find it difficult to use. (Costume designer Jacqueline Durran, CDG, "Sketch to Screen" panel, UCLA, Feb. 8, 2020)

Compare this info-choke-hold frustration, voiced by one department head (a costume designer being kept in the dark), with an approach to production-info sharing and disclosure voiced by another department head (a cinematographer). DP John Bailey describes how an excessive amount of speculative info-sharing and overdisclosure in preproduction (aimed at control) triggered the firing of a second director on a troubled film shoot that Bailey was lensing:

> We thought it was going to be a three- or four-hour session. We were there for, like, thirteen hours. [New director Michael] Cimino had his script, and a very fine, hard-point pencil, where you could barely see it. Every margin, every piece of the script, was filled with the most microscopic notes he had

made. He just spent twelve hours interrogating us about locations. He hadn't even seen where trucks were going to be parked, what sight lines . . . it was unbelievable. I had never seen anything like it. It kind of gave me a real window into what, say, his earlier films might have been like in terms of the level of hyperfocused attention. I think the producers realized that this was probably not the right director for this film because this film is kind of a loosey-goosey thing. (John Bailey, ASC, Kodak Cinematographer in Residence, Workshop no. 2, directed by Bill McDonald, UCLA, April 19, 2010)

Bailey sketches a vivid picture of a production dystopia: one director's specwork on steroids gushed in front of the crew on set. In this case, too much previsualization and directorial bird's-eye-view sharing proved to be a breaking point on a film that had neither the ample budget nor enough time available for any meticulous rendering of an obsessive auteur's grand, overly detailed, speculation plan. The practical outcome was that a third director was hired the next day to "save" the shoot and finish the film.

Remember also that industry's reproduction of knowledge is always necessarily embodied, always a part of some person's work. At the same time, trade reflection is also always collective, always an expression of a broader socioprofessional network. Faced with this individual-vs.-collective tension, I have argued that another goal in research should be to unpack the fuller range of habits and practices that constitute media-making—to put "work" more fully back into our conception of artwork. I am, of course, building on and reinforcing the important recent work in this area by Michael Curtin, Kevin Sanson, David Hesmondhalgh, Andrew Ross, Sarah Baker, Toby Miller, Vicki Mayer, Erin Hill, and Miranda Banks (see works cited). These influential scholars have countered the general disregard that greets labor or making into two adjacent scholarly areas in the humanities. I join them, first, in challenging the lip service paid to labor in film philosophy and aesthetics and, second, in pushing back against the impulse to de-aestheticize creative work into social scientific abstractions in media economics and political economy.

10. *What kinds of "network effects" drive or are impacted by your media practice? What kinds of "externalities" create value in your network? How have digital technologies impacted this system? How does your network impact creative labor or "precarity"? Have social media practices impacted your phenomenon, and if so, how?* (Digital Culture Theory)[19]

My doctoral students in production studies are digital natives, so they seldom have trouble thinking through the impact social media net-

FIGURE 9.9. Factor in the living part of any "network effect" in production. The "El Cazador" Mexican restaurant in the small town of McFarland, California, used as a shooting location for Disney Studio's feature film *McFarland, USA*. Photo: © 2018, by J. Caldwell.

works have on creative media (film and television) within digital platforms. The notion that each new connection in a network increases the value of that network provides a convincing logic for exploring how media content travels and how it finds synergies with other media forms, producers, and fans. I do, however, caution these researchers not to overlook the more modest ways that social networks may affect media content and creative production. Networks, that is, are not simply the aggregate IP addresses, connections, comments, subscriptions, and viral trends that YouTube, Facebook, Instagram, or TikTok host. They also include the upstream networks of real-world human subjects, material resources, technical infrastructure, real estate, and interpersonal partnering that underresourced creators needed to produce media in the first place, along with the networks of human subjects in real communities much further downstream.

During one of my ethnographic projects in California's Central Valley (the film *Land Hacks*), I documented the ways that small rural communities memorialized Hollywood feature shoots that had used physical film locations in their town. Disney Studios, for example, filmed its feature biopic "McFarland, USA" in the small farm town of McFarland. One of its scenes was shot at the El Cazador Mexican restaurant (fig. 9.9). I was taken with the fact that long after the film's release, the owners proudly displayed evidence to show (a) that the café is certified by both a government safety "grade" from the Kern County Health Department and (b) that it is culturally certified by an entrance poster of the Disney movie filmed at the same café. This reminded me to explore how local communities also keep film production lore memorialized and (thus) alive in their own, remote social spaces, long after the film crews from LA have departed.

THE EMIC-VS.-ETIC FACE-OFF

Industry's effusive disclosures and churn of self-analysis challenge production culture researchers just starting fieldwork to reckon with the problem that they are not alone as either holders or brokers of critical knowledge about the industry sector that they are researching. Far from it. A knowledge economy and critical understanding exists within and for that sector long before the scholar ever arrives. Production cultures themselves can be thought of as knowledge brokerages, where specialized knowledge is bought, sold, traded, and normalized. As such, when trying to justify scholarly parameters for a field or research project, a researcher should first identify the types of organizations and institutions that already produce and manage knowledge about that sector within that sector and for outside publics, as well. Reflexive knowledge in production includes conventionalized, collective behaviors that force the scholar to account for the cultural aspects and functions of the production practice being researched. In these ways production practice includes far more than just technique, labor, screen content, or workflow. A conceptual apparatus already exists before study, and it must be identified and accounted for. How does that conceptual apparatus blocking the researcher behave, where does it come from, and why? (fig. 9.10).

Answering those questions favors a fifth and benchmark for good production research. For the humanities and CMS scholars I supervise, I appraise the extent to which they have explicitly engaged a very basic anthropology framework: the emic-vs.-etic distinction in fieldwork. This paradigm is remedial for ethnographers and anthropologists, yet it can sometimes throw text-and-theory-trained arts/humanities graduate students for a loop, as they head into fieldwork. These terms refer to the very basic tension in ethnography between my own understanding of media and culture as a scholarly observer (an "etic" perspective, from the "outside") and the explanations of my research subjects and informants (an "emic" perspective, from the "inside").

My early research pushed TV studies to factor in an emic perspective even as my later studies aimed to complicate any simple deference to the

FIGURE 9.10. Ethnographic face-off (the emic-vs.-etic predicament). Anthropologist Vanessa Diaz observes, interviews, and documents Latino paparazzi as they in turn observe and document film and TV celebrities in LA. UCLA's Chicano Studies Research Center provides an exemplary "contact zone" for scholars and paparazzi to make sense of their embedded predicament, as they jointly discuss race and divisions of labor. Photo: © 2017, by J. Caldwell.

ethnographic subject in industry by employing the Geertzian precedent and insight that culture is always first textualized.[20] In the latter, I explored how production communities are never directly accessible or observable by the scholar because they are scripted and pretextualized cultures.[21] Beyond that, such cultures and texts—if we are willing to look closely enough—always include their own embedded critical interpretations. Channeling Geertz, I urged scholars to try to "look over the shoulder" of production personnel (especially below-the-line workers), as they tried to make sense of themselves to themselves. Industry has its own built-in critical theories. As scholars, we just have to learn how to read and decipher them.

One practical suggestion I now offer researchers is that the emic interpretation spoken by an "insider" is not simply that professional's individual concept or personal evaluation of some media practice in question. I ask them to examine how wider economic and labor systems industrially produce emic interpretations collectively over time, often turning them into historical convention. Hollywood's creative agencies, for example, represent one inside site whose very mission is to systematically understand industry's embedded complex production system as a whole. Consider, in the following interview, how one agency requires a junior development executive's emic fingers to always be on the pulse of what is going on in the industry:

> So we have a number of projects in development. Some are scripts, some are books we are trying to find a writer for, some are articles we are trying to find a writer for. Those are the projects we are developing. Someone needs to go through and make Excel docs tracking everything. Someone needs to come up with ideas for . . . Once a script gets to a certain point they say, "Oh, what directors can we attach to this project"? So I come up with directors lists. Or my boss comes up with a question like: "has anybody tried to remake *Dead Poet's Society*?" And I go look it up. And "are the rights available for this book?" Someone who does the more grunt work with development stuff. Someone needs to meet with lower level writers. Someone needs to meet in B-meetings with other companies. To keep their fingers on the pulse of what's going on in town. (Michael Masukawa, Junior Development Executive, Piller/Segan Agency, interview by author, UCLA, April 7, 2020)

Work sites like these—where industry trackers, overseers, and packagers use their workaday radar to monitor the complex embedded system as a whole—offer ideal Geertzian sites for analysis. They enable us to look over the shoulders of industry workers, intermediaries, and assistants who themselves are "looking over the shoulders" of everyone else as they try to make sense of the systemwide trends within which they are embedded. In some ways, the fieldwork informant struggles to keep up with the field in tandem with the ethnographer, who attempts to do the same.

Production researchers also need to address the relative degree to which the researcher defers to informants in the knowledge regime being studied. This is because, otherwise, media industries research today can easily carry the aura of explanations of the media professions dictated from a commercial script or transcribed from a corporate playbook. Transcribing industry discourse "faithfully" in this way can, admittedly, serve as a useful scholarly check on theoretical or "ivory-tower" overspeculation. Yet scholarly amplification (and thus reinforcement) of industry's perspectives like this can also hand over too much intellectual authority to institutions whose vested interests are not necessarily those of either scholars or graduate researchers. Beware of being used by industry as a ventriloquist in research. Or vice versa. No one gains when universities become industry's echo chambers.

Describing how the origins and behaviors of knowledge regimes have impacted the production sector being studied, helps researchers appraise the outcomes and validity of their own scholarly interactions with industry practitioners. An honest appraisal of the interaction of inside and outside information can help steer research projects toward greater transparency and reflexivity in scholarship. Those disclosures, when published, will also move the project closer toward the dimensions examined in chapter 1. That is, accounting for the production-of-the-scholarly analysis—not just the scholarly analysis-of-production—helps move research in the ethical directions that Vonderau proposed for media industry studies as a field.

DIMENSIONAL PRODUCTION INDUSTRIES

Specworld has explored practical and systematic ways to research complex embedded production systems. It has undertaken this task from two perspectives. The first entailed fieldwork observations of high- and low-production workshops and warring aspirant creator-vs.-A-list production pedagogies. This industrial doublespeak triggers the aspirant creator's crossover dilemma. The critical framework built from this fieldwork on trade rhetoric was then brought to bear in a second area of analysis—specifically, in institutional managerial research focusing on production's systemic stress points: industrial folds, fault lines, rifts, and fractures. Such fractures—like the tragic killing on the *Rust* film set in October 2021—continue to provide scholars not with sensational *exceptions* but with exposed, researchable cross-sections of industry's *routine* conditions. The trade and celebrity presses, by contrast, immediately short-circuit discussion of deeper systemic labor problems (like those between *Rust* producers and labor unions) in order to headline more reader-friendly culprits and one-off exceptions to industry's stressed systems (fig. 9.11). I have tried to avoid short-circuiting industry by rethinking the questions we ask about deeper, systemic, routine fractures like these. My hope has been to explore ways to make cinema and media studies more connective, behavioral, dimensional.

The book has explored whether integrating a set and sequence of complementary research approaches might help us better disembed folds and rifts that make the lives of both pro and aspirant creators excessively precarious. A set of recurring arguments and commitments have informed the methods and analyses in each of *Specworld*'s chapters: find ways to observe greater diversity of production practices, deep texts, and artifacts. Increase descriptive precision. Find more systematic ways to frame and delimit evidence. Locate and sample data based on unintended system self-disclosures at stress points. Frame and analyze evidence based on what coheres in intersections and contact zones after

ACCESS HOLLYWOOD
NEWS EXCLUSIVE
On-Set *Rust* Fracture:
10/18/21- 60,000 IATSE union members vote to authorize strike.
10/20/21- Union crew protests *Rust's* set safety, and working conditions
10/21/21- Producers fire union camera crew, hire nonunion replacements
10/21/21- On same-day an on-set shooting kills DP Halyna Hutchins
10/22/21- Young armorer among first suspects
10/23/21-to-12/1/21- Press looks past system-wide labor dysfunctions to track-down singular individual culprits
12/2/21- Baldwin gives 'unscripted' ABC interview to deflect blame in causal finger-pointing PR frenzy
HALYNA HUTCHINS ASC
1979 2021
S.O.S.
SHE DESERVED A SAFE WORKPLACE!
FIGHT
SAFETY
RUST
AMPTP
new mexico FILM OFFICE
FIGHTING FOR MEAL BREAKS
WE HAVE A RIGHT TO GOOD JO
AND
FILM INDUSTRY IS BROKEN
IATSE MEMBERS DEMAND

FIGURE 9.11. The celebrity press, news, and most trades refused to look deeply into the routine and underlying labor conditions that led to the tragic killing in 2021 on the *Rust* set. The press habitually reduces deep systems to isolated exceptions (culprits, victims, individuals). This paves over the complex structural stresses that scholars can capably research and explain as systems of some importance. Photo montage: © 2021, by J. Caldwell.

industrial rifts and fractures. Integrate disciplinary perspectives and triangulate questions, in order to unpack the fold or labor rift in question from multiple angles. Build theory inductively, and incrementally, from this intersecting evidence and multimodal analysis. Finally, make system connections to the broader social, economic trends and financial systems within which creative workers and trade communities are embedded, monetized, and managed.

Industries are far more than organizational schemes, managerial enterprises, markets, networks, or showcases for exceptional artists. Studio claims to the contrary, industries do not have clean boundaries. "The" film and television industries are false unities, formed and armored by entrenched collective posturing. All of the folding and embedding of production labor required to make those systems appear cohesive, to seem like a unified enterprise, require huge amounts of cultural work by parafirms, trade workers, and production communities. This cultural labor required to make the complexity cohere—from the ground up—is provided by creative workers who are otherwise flexibly disaggregated within the trade monolith and hidden well under Hollywood's official marketing marquee.

Making all of those precarious system fragments cohere in the twenty-first century also requires huge amounts of new preemptive, getting-out-in-front transactions from the top, by media companies. Industry incentivizes speculative and preemptive media work to keep those flexible creative workers manageable and in line. *Specworld* has explored ways to more patiently excavate, map, and detail this industrial-cultural work across production communities, proposing ways to locate, trace, and disembed industry's stressed fault lines; to research consent and pushback behaviors by workers; and to flag preemption and front-loading schemes leveraged by industry. Engaging those tactics more methodically, with reimagined tools, may enable media industries research to breathe more, to unpack more that matters. It may allow scholars to ask additional relevant research questions in the platform era.

I confess that by further adapting complex systems thinking for cinema and media studies, I risk the prospect Lewis Carroll warned of. That is, his maps describing minute detail with the same obsessive complexity as the earth they represent would be absurdly unworkable—even if perfectly "accurate." This is because their achieved one-to-one scale would dwarf, obscure, or smother any human user actually trying to chart a course through the world using such a map. Complex system thinking only works if it provides some reliable and practical mechanism for inference and generalization. Attempting to extrapolate from production's complex systems for this book, I have narrowly analyzed warring trade pedagogies through ethnographic fieldwork (2011–20) in order to locate and describe the industry's behaviors of folding, embedding, and fracturing. I hope that my exploration of the cultural dimensions of industry's stressed tectonic and connective frameworks might make production study more timely and resonant than many scholars have already proven it to be. Production doublespeak continues to matter, especially to aspiring creators tangled up in it.

Acknowledgments

I have benefited from a number of individuals who have been kind enough to invite, allow, answer, tolerate, or join me as I have tried to think out loud about media and culture over the years. Some did not know me well, and my ideas were characteristically in-progress and provisional. As such, these were kind invitations, generous gifts of time and attention from students, peers, and colleagues that I very much appreciate and want to acknowledge here.

A few decades of teaching and mentoring have reinforced my belief in the productive dimensions of collective intelligence. I have long believed that each of us comprises expressions of the communities we come from. That certainly describes me. It also means that this book necessarily reflects the many graduate students I have been fortunate to work with on PhD dissertations and in the rooms where this book originated: my "FTV201 Cultures of Production" seminar and in the courses that led to it. For this reason I want to acknowledge and thank the many talented rising scholars that I was able to work with and learn from in those capacities: Lindsay Affleck, Erica Aguero-Bochanty, Michael Albright, Miranda Banks, Jaimie Baron, Rebecca Baron, Daniel Bernardi, Heather Birdsall, Gilberto Blasini, Lauren Boumaroun, Vincent Brook, Emily Carman, Stephen Charbonneau, Cynthia Chris, Hye Jean Chung, Michael Clarke, Jonathan Cohn, Heather Collette-Vanderaa, Bernard Cook, David Craig, Karrmen Crey, Dante d'Ambrosio, Layla Danley, Manohla Dargis, Joe Davis, Jess DePrest, Andrew deWaard, Aruna Ekanayake, Chiara Ferrari, Adam Fish, James Fleury, Kwanda Ford, Jessica Fowler, Dawn Fratini, Jason Gendler, Mohannad Ghawanmeh, Lindsay Giggey, Tarleton Gillespie, Harrison Gish, Shaina Goel, Devora Gomez, Brandon Green, Suryansu Guha, Colin Gunckel, Bambi Haggins, T. S. Hale, Ben Harris, Kylie Harris, Bryan Hikari Hartzheim, Kristen Hatch, Felicia Henderson, Erin Truesdell Hill, Clifford Hilo, Jennifer Holt, Samuel Hunter, Veronica Zevala Jacobo, Kris Jones, Grace

Jung, Lahn S. Kim, Aynne Kokas, Todd Kushigemachi, Zizi Li, Dennis Hwa Lo, Brian MacDonald, Paul Malcolm, Maja Manolovich, Katie Marpe, Mark Matich, Vicki Mayer, Ross Melnick, Slaveya Minkova, Candace Moore, Jen Moorman, Drew Morton, Jerry Mosher, Maria Munoz, Hector Negrete, David O'Grady, Deron Overpeck, Hana Peoples, Matt Perkins, Alisa Perren, Jennifer Porst, John Pudaite, Mark Quigley, Justice Robinson, Ben Sampson, Mary Samuelson, Monica Sandler, Dahlia Schwartz, Adrien Sebro, Sudeep Sharma, Sharon Karleskint Sharp, Ben Sher, Beretta Smith-Shomade, Maya Smukler, Nicole Spagnola, Daniel Steinhart, Ariel Stevenson, Matthias Stork, Saundarya Thapa, Josias Troyer, Ethan Tussey, Eric Vanstrom, Phil Wagner, Qi Wang, Dan Westergren, Tom Westergren, Laurel Westrup, Bryan Wuest, Andrew Young, Mila Zuo, and Daniel Zweifach.

I was also fortunate that scholars with more standing than I were kind enough to invite me to visit and speak to their students and colleagues about the research that went into this book. I am particularly grateful to several who provided fellowships for two extended residencies where early drafts of the chapters were developed, including John Jackson, Barbie Zelizer, and Joe Turow (Annenberg School, University of Pennsylvania) and Lorenz Engell and Bernhard Siegert (IKKM, Bauhaus University, Weimar). Other generous hosts and scholars included Kirsi Rinne (Aalto University, Helsinki), Peppino Ortoleva (Turin), Dennis Göttel (University of Cologne), Eva Novrup Redvall (Copenhagen, Aarhus), Heidi Philipsen (Odense, Denmark), Patrick Kelly (RMIT, Melbourne), Patrick Vonderau (Stockholm and Halle), Petr Szczepanik (Masryk, Prague), Paul Grainge (Nottingham), Andrew Spicer and Steve Presence (UWE, Bristol), Haidee Wasson, Charles Acland (Concordia, Montreal), Jane Gaines and Rob King (Columbia University), Josh Glick, John MacKay, Charles Musser, and Francesco Cassetti (Yale), Michael Curtin, Jen Holt, Kevin Sanson, Anna Everett (UC, Santa Barbara), Michael Renov, Nitin Govil, and Tara McPherson (USC), and Vicki Johnson, Bambi L. Haggins, Peter Krapp, and Fatimah Tobing-Rony (UC, Irvine).

As someone who early on never imagined being able to work with graduate and doctoral students, I appreciate the faculty colleagues that allowed me to join their university departments and communities. I am especially grateful for these supportive neighbors: Steve Anderson, Janet Bergstrom, Barbara Boyle, Nick Browne, Kristy Guevara-Flanagan, Shelleen M. Green, Erkki Huhtamo, Gina Kim, Arnie Lund, Liza Johnson, Deborah Landis, Stephen Mamber, Purnima Mankekar, Denise Mann, Bill McDonald, Kathleen McHugh, Chon Noriega, Sherry Ortner, Veronica Paredes, Nancy Richardson, Ellen Scott, Chuck Sheetz, Becky Smith, and Jasmine Nadua Trice (at UCLA); and Phil Agre, Susan Davis, Daniel Hallin, George Lipsitz, Chandra Mukerji, Ellen Seiter, Dan Schiller, Herb Schiller, and Michael Schudson (at UC, San Diego). I give special thanks for the observations and insights enabled by my colleague DP Bill McDonald, who organized and directed the annual Kodak Cinematographer-in-Residence Workshops at UCLA over two decades.

Special thanks to the two UC Press external readers, whose names were anonymous until late in the publishing process. I owe a debt, that is, to Lynn Spigel and Victoria Johnson, for their systematic help in corralling early drafts featuring mind-gush into chapters with greater focus and clarity. Three previously published essays fed into this book project but were greatly revised as I applied and adapted them for the research in this book: "Para-industries, Shadow Academies," from *Cultural Studies* (2015); "Stress Aesthetics," from Vonderau and Szczepanik, *Behind the Screen* (2012); and "Spec World, Craft World, Brand World," from Curtin and Sanson, *Precarious Creativity* (2017). My "Ethics" chapter began in Germany as a public lecture at the University of Cologne in June 2019, and so shares DNA with a parallel article edited by Dennis Göttel and Stefan Udelhofen in a volume published by Springer (forthcoming). I thank those editors and publishers for allowing me to change, update, and adapt those papers for this book. I am especially grateful to the exceptional editorial group at UC Press—Raina Polivka, Jessica Moll, Lia Tjandra, Joe Abbott, and PJ Heim—for the way they shepherded and fine-tuned this book into a reality that I can share with others.

I will always be thankful for the kind mentorship over my career provided by Mimi White, Joel Sheesley, Robert Finney, Chuck Kleinhans, Dave Johnson, John Baldessari, Peter Wollen, and Teshome Gabriel. I very much regret that I can no longer offer that thanks in person to Chuck, Dave, John, Peter, and Teshome.

Finally, I dedicate this book with affection to Thekla E. Joiner, the best ally, force, and sage anyone could ever have on a journey like *Specworld*.

Select Field Sites

Observations, Interviews, Transcriptions

Research locations and trade events cited and referenced in the chapters.

2002, January 10–20. Sundance Film Festival. Discussions with distributors and network buyers, observations and panel participation, author/filmmaker Q&As, and workshops. Park City, Utah.

2003, February 22–23. Twenty-Sixth CineFestival, San Antonio International Film Festival. Author/filmmaker Q&A. San Antonio, Texas.

2003, October 3. Author interviews with producers, directors, editors, and cinematographers from *The Shield* (F/X) and 24 (Fox). "The Normal Rules Do Not Apply: The Impact of MTV on Primetime Television," Academy of Television Arts and Sciences (ATAS), North Hollywood, CA.

2004, March 3–5. Tenth Sedona International Film Festival. Author/filmmaker Q&A. Sedona, Arizona.

2004, April 19. Lazlo Kovacs, ASC, cinematography and lighting workshop. Kodak Cinematographer-in-Residence, Department of Film, Television and Digital Media, UCLA. Soundstage 3. Los Angeles, CA.

2005, March 3. Los Angeles Center Studios Soundstages, HD Expo. Equipment demonstrations and production workshops. Los Angeles, CA.

2005, June 11–12. Raleigh Film Studios, Below-the-Line Expo. Equipment demonstrations and production workshops. Hollywood, CA.

2005, November 5. Twenty-First Annual San Francisco Film Arts Festival, author/filmmaker Q&A, Roxie Theater, San Francisco, CA.

2007, October 9. Vittorio Storaro, ASC, AIC. Workshop, Q&A, and lecture on Caravaggio as cinematographer. James Bridges Theater. School of Theater, Film and Television, UCLA. Los Angeles, CA.

2009, June 1. Lighting workshop with Vilmos Zsigmond, ASC. Kodak Cinematographer-in-Residence at UCLA. Department of Film, Television and Digital Media, Soundstage 3. Los Angeles, CA.

2010, February. Chiat-Day Advertising Agency. Branding workgroup and breakout sessions. Venice, CA.

2010, April 26. John Bailey, ASC, with Rob Hummel and Ray Zone, Kodak Cinematographer-in-Residence Workshop #3, Department of Film, Television and Digital Media, UCLA, Los Angeles, CA, Tape 1 of 3.

2011, August 30. "Reality Check": Motion Picture Editors Guild union organizing meeting (for nonunion editors working in "unscripted" reality TV). Hollywood, CA. Participants included Anthony Carbone, MPEG; Mary DeChambres, MPEG; Charlie Kramer, MPEG; Rob Kraut, MPEG; Twigger Moul, MPEG; Richard Sanchez, MPEG; and the guild's executive director, Ron Kutak.

2011, September 19–22. "Prix Italia." "The Art of Television and Radio Testimonies and Collective Memory." Museum of Radio Via Verdi 16. Torino, Italy.

2011, November 2–3. "Creatasphere: Entertainment Technology Expo." Production and postproduction workshops and equipment demos. Burbank, CA.

2012, July. Cinecittà Film Studios. Rome, Italy.

2013, April 12. "Transmedia Hollywood 4: Spreading Change." James Bridges Theater, UCLA. Los Angeles, CA.

2014, June 6–7. Paramount Studios. Cine Gear Expo. Equipment demonstrations and production workshops.

2015, May 8. "Transforming Hollywood 6: Alternative Realities, World Building, and Immersive Entertainment." Panels and technical demonstrations. James Bridges Theater, UCLA. Los Angeles, CA.

2015, June 5–6. Paramount Studios. Cine Gear Expo. Equipment demonstrations and technical workshops.

2016, April 7. Author interview with David Gauch, UX and Interaction Designer, Icon-Mobile. "The New 'New Hollywood': Careers in TV, Cable, and Digital Media." Panel 1: "Digital Media." UCLA Career Center. Los Angeles, CA.

2016, April 7. Author interviews with Kelly Fullerton, screenwriter; Amanda Lie, TV Talent Coordinator, CAA; and Michael Masukawa, Junior Development Executive, Piller/Segan Agency. "The New 'New Hollywood': Careers in TV, Cable, and Digital Media." Panel 2: "Television." UCLA Career Center. Los Angeles, CA.

2016, June 3–4. Paramount Studios. Cine Gear Expo. Equipment demonstrations and technical workshops.

2016, June 4. Panel discussion on union and labor issues in production design, with presentations by representatives from the Art Directors Guild Local 800, Costume Designers Guild Local 892, United Scenic Artists Local 829, Set Decorators Society of America, Motion Picture Costumers Local 705. Freud Theater, UCLA. Los Angeles, CA.

2016, June 4. Quentin Tarantino, DGA, presentation. Following production designer portfolio review. Fourteenth Annual Design Showcase West, UCLA. Los Angeles, CA.

2016, June 26–28. Barrandov Film Studios. Prague, The Czech Republic.

2016, June 29. Babelsberg Film Studios. Potsdam-Babelsberg, Germany.

2016, August 9–13. Locarno International Film Festival and Market. Author/filmmaker workshops and lectures. Locarno, Italy.

2017, June 10. Deborah Riley, production designer, *Game of Thrones*/HBO. Master class in production design. Design Showcase West. Los Angeles, CA.

2017, June 21–25, VidCon 2017. Creator/influencer industry convention. Anaheim Convention Center. Interviews, workshops, panel presentations, discussions. Anaheim, CA.

2017, December 1–6. "Slush." International Digital Technology Convention. Helsinki, Finland.

2019, July 10–13. VidCon 2019. Creator/influencer industry convention. Anaheim Convention Center. Interviews, workshops, panel presentations, discussions. Anaheim, CA.

2019, December 2–4. "Sightlines: 3rd Film Festival and Conference." Production industry-academy research collaborations. Author/filmmaker Q&A. RMIT University, Melbourne, Australia.

2020, February 3. "Screenwriting: Breaking into the Industry." Presentations and discussions with Felischa Marye, WGA; Michelle Amor, WGA; Steven Canals, WGA; and Bo Yeon Kim, WGA. James Bridges Theater, UCLA. Los Angeles, CA.

2020, February 8. Presentations, including clips and discussions, with Mark Bridges, CDG, costume designer, *Joker;* Jacqueline Durran, costume designer, *1917* and *Little Women;* Christopher Peterson, CDG, *The Irishman;* Arianne Phillips, CDG, *Once upon a Time in Hollywood;* Sandy Powell, CDG, costume designer, *The Irishman;* and Nora Sopkova, costume designer, *Jojo Rabbit.* "Sketch to Screen: Oscar Nominees, Costume Design Panel and Celebration." Panel hosted by the Copley Center for the Study of Costume Design, UCLA.

Notes

PREFACE

1. Vittorio Storaro, ASC, AIC, "An Introduction to Caravaggio," copresented with the film's director, Angelo Longoni, Kodak Cinematography Workshop, Oct. 9, 2007, UCLA.

2. Bill Hines, SOC, "Rules of Professional Conduct," in *Setiquette: A Guide to Working Effectively on the Set for Each Classification in the Cinematographers Guild* (ICG/IATSE Local 600, 2011), [15].

3. Kraut was complaining about postproduction workflow instabilities caused by clueless professional camera crews. The meeting at which he made these remarks took place in Hollywood, CA, on August 30, 2011.

4. After a stint at MIT, Buckminster Fuller began his professorship at Southern Illinois University, Carbondale, in the 1950s, and his affiliation with SIU and other universities continued until his death in 1983. Fuller lived in an iconic geodesic home during his tenure in Carbondale, the lone university town in a vast rural region. I was raised in the nearby Illinois coal town of Carterville, in what was widely referred to as "Bloody Williamson County," named that way because of the violent union-busting wars against coal workers by law enforcement and company "gun thugs" who brought in scabs to fight the unionizing coal miners in the 1920s and 1930s.

5. For a better sense of the terms quoted here, and how Buckminster Fuller's theories live on, see the Buckminster Fuller Institute website, www.bfi.org/about-fuller/big-ideas/design-science/design-science-primer/eight-strategies-for-comprehensive-anticipatory-design-science. Here, the Buckminster Fuller Institute works to individuate Fuller's legacies apart from the parallel but ostensibly separate fields of "ecology" and "cybernetics" that developed in roughly the same quarter century. Fuller's book *Synergetics: Explorations in the Geometry of Thinking* (New York: MacMillan, 1975)—an eight-hundred-page condensation

of Fuller's fifty-year investigations into geometry, mathematics, physics, and metaphysics—is widely regarded as a magnum opus of his comprehensive thinking.

6. On "vaporware" in the "dotcom era," see my "Introduction: Theorizing the Digital Landrush," in *Electronic Media and Technoculture* (New Brunswick, NJ: Rutgers University Press, 2000), 1–31. For my first description of network "re-branding" in the "post-network" era, see *Televisuality: Style, Crisis, and Authority in American Television* (New Brunswick, NJ: Rutgers University Press, 1995, 2020). For my account of "viral marketing," see *Production Culture: Industrial Reflexivity and Critical Practice in Film and Television* (Durham, NC: Duke University Press, 2008), esp. chap. 7.

7. For innovative recent scholarship on digital, online, and social media, see especially Maria Eriksson, Rasmus Fleischer, Anna Johansson, Pelle Snickars, and Patrick Vonderau, *Spotify Teardown* (2019); Lisa Parks, *Rethinking Media Coverage: Vertical Mediation and the War on Terror* (2018); Michael Curtin and Kevin Sanson, *Precarious Creativity* (2016); Lisa Parks and Nicole Starosielski, *Signal Traffic: Critical Studies of Media Infrastructures* (2018); Charles Acland, *Swift Viewing* (2011); Jennifer Holt and Kevin Sanson, *Connected Viewing* (2016); Haidee Wasson and Lee Grieveson, *Cinema's Military Industrial Complex* (2018); Denise Mann, *Wired TV* (2014); Derek Johnson, *From Networks to Netflix* (2017); Amanda Lotz, *We Now Disrupt This Broadcast* (2018); Stuart Cunningham and David Craig, *Social Media Entertainment* (2019); and Andrew deWaard, "Derivative Media: The Financialization of Film, Television, and Popular Music, 2004–2016" (2018).

8. For research that has pushed the boundaries of media industry studies, see especially Petr Szczepanik and Patrick Vonderau, *Behind-the-Screen: European Production Studies* (2013); Mark Deuze, *Making Media* (2018); Sherry Ortner, *Not Hollywood: Independent Film at the Twilight of the American Dream* (2013); Jennifer Holt and Alisa Perren, *Media Industries* (2010); Charles Acland, *Residual Media* (2007); Jaroslev Andel and Petr Szczepanik, *Cinema All the Time* (2008); Vicki Mayer, *Below-the-Line* (2011); Miranda Banks, *The Writers* (2016); Erin Hill, *Never Done* (2017); Miranda Banks, Bridget Connor, and Vicki Mayer, *Production Studies: The Sequel!* (2014); and Eric W. Rothenbuhler and Mihai Coman, *Media Anthropology* (2005).

9. For deep localized research, see Vicki Mayer, *Below-the-Line* (Durham, NC: Duke University Press, 2011); Eva Novrup Redvall, *Writing and Producing Television Drama in Denmark* (New York: Springer, 2013); Kristen Warner, *The Cultural Politics of Colorblind TV Casting* (New York: Routledge, 2018); Petr Szczepanik, *Film Industries in East-Central Europe* (London: BFI, 2021); and James Fleury, "Space-Invaders: Warner Bros. and the History of Hollywood in the Video Game Industry" (PhD diss. UCLA, 2019).

1. ETHICS?

1. "OnlyFans Turns Its Back on Sex Workers and They Are Pissed," *Daily Beast,* July 24, 2021, www.thedailybeast.com/onlyfans-turns-its-back-on-sex-workers-and-they-are-pissed?ref=author.

2. This book avoids explaining injurious interactions by reducing industry's bad behaviors to the mythic singularities of personality, celebrity, career hubris, or out-of-touch exceptionalism. Instead, I hope to gain a clearer picture of racism, sexism, classism, labor exploitation, and precarity as industrially produced; as commonsensical (even if unintended) outcomes from managerial systems designed ostensibly to bring order, rationality, and efficiency to the otherwise irrational, disordered inefficiency of creative screen content production in film and television. How are the cultural controversies and blowback just described systemic rather than exceptions, routine rather than acute?

3. Patrick Vonderau, "Ethics in Media Industries Research," opens with this statement: "Do ethics matter? . . . Introductory [media industries] textbooks often all but ignore ethical considerations." See Vonderau's essay in *The Routledge Companion to Media Industries,* ed. Paul McDonald (New York: Routledge, 2022), 518–26.

4. Akiva Goldsman, quoted in Mike Fleming, "Akiva Goldsman Explains 'Transformers' Writers Room as Paramount Adds Scribe Pair," *Deadline.com,* June 4, 2015, https://deadline.com/2015/06/transformers-akiva-goldsman-writers-room-paramount-1201438017 (italics mine).

5. This sequence of quotes is drawn from the online reader replies attached to Fleming.

6. Goldsman, quoted in Fleming (italics mine); "Wga Writer," from the reader replies.

7. Vonderau, "Ethics in Media Industries Research," 522–23. Vonderau draws in part from ideas of "covert research": "At the same time, however, research cannot be routinized completely and must always allow some space for exploratory work and the unpredictable, as it remains a dynamic process that works against 'compulsive tidiness in methodology' (Calvey 2017: 456)" (Vonderau 518–19). See David Calvey, *Covert Research: The Art, Politics and Ethics of Undercover Fieldwork* (London: Sage, 2017).

2. FRAMEWORK

1. Content creator Joseph Melles is describing getting stiffed by Snapchat's Spotlight feature fund, designed to "share" revenues with its creators. Alongside his sobering quote, CNBC provides a breathless summary of how the "social media giant [Snapchat] minted a new class of millionaires, changing hundreds of lives." See Salvador Rodriguez and Jessica Bursztynsky, "Snap Creators Say They're Leaving the App's Spotlight Feature as Payments Dry Up," CNBC.com, August 11, 2021, www.cnbc.com/2021/08/11/snap-creators-say-theyre-leaving-the-apps-spotlight-feature-as-payments-dry-up.html.

2. During that time a series of observations in industry settings triggered inductive hunches that became less and less provisional as the project advanced. In this chapter I want to flag and introduce in advance some of these working hunches, given that the reader will encounter these underlying themes as they recur in the chapters that follow. These notions evolved as I started and moved from one location and form of evidence to the next. This hypotheses trajectory

spurred supplemental research questions that I held alongside my initial questions, even as I observed and analyzed various forms of evidence.

3. Researching production as a complex embedded system requires mixing different scales of analysis. This multiscalar approach may seem odd in film studies, which has traditionally taken an exemplary extractive approach to evidence. As a humanities field, CMS has a long tradition of immensely productive scholarship based on isolating distinctive, exceptional, exemplary, rationalized, and (industrially) foreordained cases for research and analysis. I offer this book to supplement and complement that tradition, intending to fill-in and describe some nagging gaps between those cleaned-up cinema studies distinctions.

4. Industry often echoes the academy on the intellectual quandary over whether we should isolate and study exemplary patterns (order) or routine contingencies (disorder) in media production systems.

5. Capitalism rewards executives who can bring rationality to unpredictable supply-chain or market conditions. Giant media platforms depend on these rationality incentives (many of which are now AI-driven). Big tech's transformation of scale and time confounds anyone trying to make sense of film and media today. The new transnational media platforms—Netflix, Amazon, Apple, Hulu, Google—hawk "downstream" screen-content-abundance marketing to consumers. Yet this stance is linked to troubling digital shifts that also disrupt the creative labor "upstream" that makes the screen content. Making profitable media in a world of content abundance today now apparently spurs corporations to find better ways to manage upstream creator unruliness as well. Faced with ever more risky returns on investment (ROIs) for content production, companies must find new ways to bring managerial rationality and control to the upstream volatility of creators as well.

6. Costume designer Arianne Phillips gave this lengthy explanation of her successful use of specwork as a process for professionals in her public comments at "Sketch to Screen: Oscar Nominees, Costume Design Panel and Celebration," a panel hosted by the Copley Center for the Study of Costume Design at UCLA, Feb. 8, 2020.

7. My previous account of the "collapsing workflows" in traditional film/TV, detailed in *Production Culture,* argued that media was intentionally "getting the cart before the horse," primarily as an industrial efficiency measure. Producers bragged to me in 2008 about their flexibility to totally "recreate" film production scenes in downstream post. Yet digital postproduction activities, and their fixation with "metadata," encroached in the other direction, upstream. In the 2000s, tasks that had long defined "editing," that is, invaded sets that had once been cleanly segregated off from "post" into a bounded work-phase termed "production." This workflow confusion, as filming shifted to digital, triggered labor conflicts and new job descriptions. My intent is to examine trends that go beyond these technical disruptions to labor and "workflows."

8. Yet those studies appeared right before the full force of the online vortex had confused production flows and disrupted creative labor. Even though I mapped local collapses of workflows in *Production Culture* (e.g., between production and postproduction owing to digital cameras, DITs, and data wran-

glers), I underestimated the extent of workflow collapse that was about to engulf the earlier stages in media-making as well: development and preproduction.

9. This gambit by industry to remove and isolate creation from the industrial sediment is not unlike scholars who, when they establish A-lists, genres, auteurs, or canons, isolate those exceptions outside of the systemic mess that necessarily defines and produces them.

10. This is especially true since studio and agency management (unlike the craft world) takes surveillance and monitoring of the overall industry-wide system as their raison d'être. In some ways, this midlevel shadow networking by assistants comprises a silent insurgency that undercuts the top-down strip-mining that defines agencies and studios.

11. A decade later, as chapter 7 will show, mock mutuality like this would spark accusations of platform exploitation rather than mutual benefit. Overt content predation often triggers a flood of back-channel and online critique that can be researched as a case study—precisely because it can be localized within a rift. Folds often break open because the hosts oversell the actual contradiction underlying their scheme. How platforms have altered the ways aspiring media creators are rewarded provides one example. In effect, corporate immersion in social media—using innovation metrics geared to the extent and intensity of crowdsourcing—seems to feed into a robust but largely symbolic payroll system for aspiring makers. The symbolic and cultural capital in play among YouTubers is eventually converted into financial capital—by someone, somewhere. But this monetization takes place largely outside the aspirant's control. This creates an alienating predicament for aspiring creators that can become untenable and lead to rifts.

12. See the "down-in-flames" video posts by overleveraged online creators exposed in the chapter 8 examples of fractures.

13. See Ryan Faughnder, "Hollywood Isn't So Easy to Crack," *Los Angeles Times,* May 26, 2021, E1, E3.

14. Wendy Lee, "Talent Agency Is Accused of a Hostile Culture," *Los Angeles Times,* May 9, 2021, E1, E12–13.

15. See Madhavi Sunder, "Tik Tok's Bad Dance Moves," *Los Angeles Times,* July 7, 2021, A13.

16. See especially my essays: "Corporate and Worker Ephemera: The Industrial Promotional Surround," in *Ephemeral Media,* ed. Paul Grainge (London: BFI, 2011), 175–94 ; "Worker Blowback: User-Generated, Worker-Generated, and Producer-Generated Content," in *Television as Digital Media,* ed. James Bennett and Niki Strange (Durham, NC: Duke University Press, 2011), 283–311; and "Hive-Sourcing Is the New Out-Sourcing," *Cinema Journal* 49, no.1 (Fall 2009): 160–67.

17. Drawing from "standpoint theory," which has origins in feminist theory and cultural studies, Vincent Mosco has proposed "labor standpoint theory," which adds workers' points of view to critical, economic, and industrial analysis. See Vincent Mosco, *The Political Economy of Communication,* 2nd ed. (London: Sage, 2009), 113–19.

18. In sociology, the neologism *precariat* is formed by mixing the terms *precarious* with *proletariat* to describe anxious class conditions in advanced capitalist

creative economies. See Guy Standing, *The Precariat* (New York: Bloomsbury Academic, 2011).

19. Competition for work has long spurred unrest and public condemnation in overcrowded labor markets. A genre of trolling online snark videos have been created and uploaded by anonymous professional craft employees castigating the destructive implications of aspirants and wannabes. Scholars can value and appraise the "standpoint theory" implicit in animated video missives, like the following one.

20. The videos function instead as acutely oblique communications and trade confrontations meant to flag, if not intervene, in bad production behaviors off-set and on.

21. The quote of this Twitter broadcast and the quotes in the following paragraph are from Anthony Ocasio, "FX Signs 'Sons of Anarchy' Creator for Seasons 6 & 7," ScreenRant, Jan. 31, 2012, http://screenrant.com/sons-anarchy-season-5-6-7-kurt-sutter-aco-149044.

22. This final trade account from ScreenRant.com also explained the series as "continuously referencing (as well as mirroring) elements from William Shakespeare's famed tragedy *Hamlet*." It is not clear whether this analysis applied literary theory to the fictional narratives of *Sons of Anarchy* or to the exposés and trade narratives about the constant fighting among the real producers, studios, and networks that made *Sons of Anarchy*.

23. See, e.g., Lance Strate, *Media Ecology: An Approach to Understanding the Human Condition* (London: Peter Lang, 2017); and Matthew Fuller, *Media Ecologies: Material Energies in Art and Technoculture* (Cambridge, MA: MIT Press, 2005).

3. REGIMES

An earlier version of this chapter was published in Michael Curtin and Kevin Sanson, eds., *Precarious Creativity* (Berkeley: University of California Press, 2016).

1. Chapter 5 will drill deeper into an interrelated foundational perspective, describing a broad preemptive scheme employed by industry to manage production cultures. Specifically, that chapter details a conventionalized industry scheme that employs "art thinking" to legitimize a profitable cultural-economic labor regime. Such an arrangement I term *stress aesthetics*. That account will detail how the strategic allocation of symbolic, social, and cultural capital constitute a "deprivation payroll system." Stress aesthetics provides a way of thinking and working that is habitually used to normalize long hours, low budgets, and difficult shooting conditions. The adept allocation of *cultural deprivation as incentives* to workers helps in justifying and scripting precarious worker conditions and in folding workers into the system as a whole.

2. Allen Scott, *On Hollywood* (Princeton, NJ: Princeton University Press, 2005); and Toby Miller, Nitin Govil, John McMurria, and Richard Maxwell, *Global Hollywood* (London: BFI, 2001).

3. Media scholars have paid considerable attention to the unstable world of unruly fans, digital media, and remix and gift economies. I am arguing that we need to attend to the unruliness of the creative labor pipeline with equal care.

4. Vicki Mayer, *Below the Line* (Durham, NC: Duke University Press, 2011); Matt Stahl, *Unfree Masters* (Durham, NC: Duke University Press, 2013).

5. Tech and labor were contexts that critical TV scholars, in many cases, largely overlooked or disregarded in the 1980s.

6. Henry Jenkins, *Convergence Culture* (New York: New York University Press, 2006).

7. I am riffing here on Jenkins's notion of spreadable media; see Henry Jenkins, *Spreadable Media* (New York: New York University Press, 2013).

8. See John Caldwell, "Para-industry," *Cinema Journal* 52, no. 3 (Spring 2013): 157–65.

9. Scott, *On Hollywood;* Michael Curtin, *Playing to the World's Biggest Audience* (Berkeley: University of California Press, 2007).

10. See John Thornton Caldwell, *Televisuality: Style, Crisis, and Authority in American Television* (New Brunswick, NJ: Rutgers University Press, 1995); and John Thornton Caldwell, *Production Culture: Industrial Reflexivity and Critical Practice in Film and Television* (Durham, NC: Duke University Press, 2008).

11. By contrast, screenwriters still write spec scripts for film without promise of payment, maintaining "long-odds" hope that someone might buy their script to make a movie. See Erin Hill, "Women's Work: Feminized Labor in Hollywood, 1930–1948" (PhD diss., UCLA, 2014).

12. See Erin Hill, *Never Done* (New Brunswick, NJ: Rutgers University Press, 2016).

13. One of the best explorations of cross-cultural spec-mediation is Aynne Kokas, *Hollywood Made in China* (Berkeley: University of California Press, 2017); and Aynne Kokas, "Shot in Shanghai: Western Film Co-production in Post-WTO Mainland China" (PhD diss., UCLA, 2012).

14. See, for example, the crowd-sourced online-to-feature film project *Life in a Day.* YouTube solicited thousands of user-shot videos to make its feature project. When the resulting aggregate project was screened online, then shown as a feature film in festivals, the project was boldly hyped as a "Ridley Scott Production," clearly erasing its utopian collectivity.

15. See Caldwell, *Televisuality;* Anna Everett and John Caldwell, eds., *New Media* (New York: Routledge, 2003); and Caldwell, *Production Culture.*

4. CASE

1. The basic categories I was trained with in the late twentieth century for both conventional film/video aesthetics (spatial continuity, psychological realism, linear narrative, seamless editing) and avant-garde practice (countercinema, reflexivity, assemblage, pastiche, distancing, deconstruction as a radical tactic) appear to have little resonance today as the fundamental media production categories promoted in the corporatized online space. Millennial media-makers today, in the age of effusive social media, are being trained, disciplined, and rewarded differently than they were forty years ago in an age of production scarcity.

2. Surprisingly, the ideal of core production principles as a quasi-stable category persists whether or not one is making an infomercial, a crowd-sourced online video, or a transnational 8K feature shot on mechanized camera mounts.

On top of the physical conditions of a shoot, production also includes what we say, out loud, repeatedly, to convince ourselves that we know what we are doing or talking about. Beyond describing work, perhaps production talk provides a cultural mechanism we use to make sense of ourselves to ourselves—making it a utilitarian self-organization scheme. But where does this tactical assumption about production as self-evident category come from, and why do we continue to use it?

3. The full quote: "I came from film school. [For them] that is a problem. 'No viewer is ever going to pay you.' To them, the world of online video was invalid." Fellow attendee at the "Alternate Careers in Online Video" workshop, VidCon 2017, Anaheim, CA, June 23, 2017.

4. Stephanie Patrick, Theorist Media, "Alternate Careers in Online Video," workshop, VidCon 2017, Anaheim, CA, June 23, 2017.

5. Joe Penna (creator), "Transitioning Your Channel into a Full-Fledged Business," panel discussion, VidCon 2017, Anaheim, CA.

6. One much-copied example by YouTubers of the genuine desire for big-screen careers (but with little prep) is the oft-emulated shortcut genre (be-a-film-director-but-don't-bother-to-go-to-film-school aesthetic) prototyped in "The Robert Rodriguez: 10 minute Film School" YouTube video (www.youtube.com/watch?v=nMEAMHlulRo). Creator Ahsante Bean and other panelists on the "Alternate Careers in Online Video" workshop at VidCon 2017 praised the quick-and-painless bootstrapping-as-career-training being offered there and by PBS Digital Studios via Craig Benzine's less snarky but still expedited "Crash Course in Film History" (www.youtube.com/watch?v=vsnB4iBb780).

7. This enabled Singh to become the first bisexual woman of color to host a late-night talk show on a US network.

8. Aymar Jean Christian, *Open TV: Innovation beyond Hollywood and the Rise of Web Television* (New York: NYU Press, 2018).

9. This, and quotes in the following paragraph by Christian, are from Liz Shannon Miller, "Can an Online Star Make It in Hollywood?," Vox, Jan. 3, 2020, www.vox.com/the-highlight/2019/12/27/21031780/youtube-star-make-it-hollywood-lilly-singh-issa-rae-michael-buckley-hannah-hart.

10. David Gauch, digital interaction designer, interview by author, UCLA, April 7, 2016.

11. I observed and recorded these creators, arguing about making-it in film/TV, in the panel discussion "Transitioning Your Channel into a Full-Fledged Business," VidCon 2017, Anaheim, CA.

12. Deborah Riley, "Production Design in *Game of Thrones*," master class at Design Showcase West (DSW), UCLA, June 10, 2017.

13. Tom Greenwood-Mears, "From Online to Offline: How to Engage with Audiences beyond the Screen," VidCon 2017, Anaheim, CA. June 22, 2017.

14. Matt Gielen, CEO, Little Monster Media Co., "Reverse Engineering the YouTube Algorithm," workshop, VidCon 2017, Anaheim, CA, June 22, 2017.

15. Derral Eves, CEO-Creatus, "Growth Hacking YouTube: Triggering Algorithm-Driven Views," workshop, VidCon 2017, Anaheim, CA, June 22, 2017.

16. Patrick, "Alternate Careers in Online Video."

17. Gielen, "Reverse Engineering the YouTube Algorithm."

18. Another graphic from an online creator mentoring site echoes the same short-shrift approach: "SECRETS: (1) Mirror Your Target Audience. (2) Clear, Compelling, and Brief. (3) Weave Multiple Stories Together Into One Compelling Story About Your Company." Text from publicly displayed promo by Epipheo in its "Ultimate Content Webinar," VidCon 2017, Anaheim, CA, June, 23, 2017.

19. Nick Jenkins, Senior Producer at Crash Course, for example, tells aspirants that "one of the first things they teach you in film school is to make something very early [quickly]." Nick Jenkins, "How to YouTube 101," workshop, VidCon 2017, Anaheim, CA, June 23, 2017.

20. "Theorist Media," text from public display, VidCon 2017, Anaheim, CA, June, 23, 2017.

21. Matthew Patrick, Theorist Media, "MatPat: Sustainability in Digital: How to Build a Programming Strategy That Won't Burn You Out." VidCon 2017, Anaheim, CA, June 23, 2017.

22. Benji Travis (creator), "Transitioning Your Channel into a Full-Fledged Business," panel discussion, VidCon 2017, Anaheim, CA, July 22, 2017.

23. Nicole Sweeney, "Workshop: How to YouTube 101," VidCon 2017, Anaheim, CA, June 23, 2017.

24. Tim Schmoyer, "Turning YouTube into a Career," workshop, VidCon 2017, Anaheim, CA, June 23, 2017.

25. Schmoyer, "Turning YouTube into a Career."

26. One possible lesson from this practice linking low production and high production? Realizing actual profits online may eventually require scaling-up in some form. Schmoyer uses crowdfunded Patreon to upscale the microeconomy of his content to some degree. But the transnational scale of the platform's "ecosystem" as a whole suggests that the monetary benefits of geographically scaling up are mostly reserved for the YouTube/Google regime in which Schmoyer and Patreon are very deeply embedded. This means that the disaggregated reach of remote online makers—even after successfully expanding their subscriber base—could realize little of the monetization that HBO's geographic scaling-up strategy brings to its big-budget *GoT* screen content.

27. Riley, "Production Design in *Game of Thrones*."

28. Riley.

29. Riley.

30. Riley.

31. Sweeney, "How to YouTube 101."

32. Schmoyer, "Turning YouTube into a Career."

33. Riley, "Production Design in *Game of Thrones*."

34. Riley continues: "So, the shooting schedule Chris shepherds through production looks like this: . . . I'll teach you how to read it. First of all, the dates are all down on the left. . . . This document tells the art department . . . first, in what order the producers expect the sets to be built and then how many days they expect each set to shoot for. This gives us some idea of where the money will be spent."

35. Riley shows an illustration: "This is the approved concept art for the House of Faces." She then explains how stages of approval can alter design: "This photo was taken during the lighting test. It was here that we decided that

the color palette would not be warm, as in the concept art. But that we'd move to a cooler palette."

36. This unionized system typically brings to a production company high barriers to entry for aspirants.

37. This low-production variant employs specwork as its primary onscreen content, whereas the collective writers room typical of premium production remains behind-the-scenes. Curly Velasquez, "Alternate Careers in Online Video," VidCon 2017, Anaheim, CA, June 23, 2017.

38. Patrick, "Alternate Careers in Online Video."

39. "Cue the proof-of-concept video. Simply stated, a proof-of-concept is a scene from your feature film script, shot and fashioned into a short. Its purpose is to provide an example of the writing, directing, and cinematography that will go into the feature, as well as demonstrate the film's viability on the big-screen." William Dickerson, "A Script Is No Longer Enough," *MovieMaker.com,* April 19, 2016, www.moviemaker.com/why-first-time-directors-must-make-proof-of-concept.

40. Caitlin Hofmeister, producer, SciShow, "Building Teams: People Management 101 for Creators," workshop, VidCon 2017, Anaheim, CA, June22, 2017.

41. Penna, "Transitioning Your Channel."

42. Schmoyer, "Turning YouTube into a Career."

43. Deborah Riley notes: "Our co-creators, writers, and showrunners issue an outline, which tells the producers and myself very, very clearly what will be contained within each episode." Deborah Riley, "Production Design in *Game of Thrones.*"

44. Schmoyer, "Turning YouTube into a Career."

45. Vice News highlighted these immense metrics about Rhett and Link's channel; see "How Good Mythical Morning Became the Biggest Daily Show on YouTube," Vice News (HBO), August 30, 2018, www.youtube.com/watch?v=u9pbRBJu3PU. For the print version see Dexter Thomas, "Fans Are Worried the Internet's Biggest Daily Show Is Getting Too Big," Vice News, Nov. 20, 2017, www.vice.com/en/article/pazzxb/fans-are-worried-the-internets-biggest-daily-show-is-getting-too-big.

5. FOLDING

This chapter was adapted from an earlier essay published in *Behind the Screen: European Production Cultures* (2013) and from a keynote lecture given at University of the West of England (2014).

1. For a good elaboration of this research paradigm, see Howard Becker, "The Epistemology of Qualitative Research," in *Ethnography and Human Development: Context and Meaning in Social Inquiry,* ed. Richard Jessor, Anne Colby, and Richard A. Shweder, 53–71 (Chicago: University of Chicago Press, 1996). Perhaps the most influential example of this kind of study is Bruno Latour and Steve Woolgar, *Laboratory Life: The Construction of Scientific Facts* (Princeton, NJ: Princeton University Press, 1987).

2. Interestingly, Latour used the "shop-floor" paradigm not to study some practice from industrial capitalism but to research the construction of scientific knowledge, which in effect was research on the practice of epistemology. Whereas Latour invoked the low-industry metaphor to study high science, I am employing high theory to understand working epistemologies in low, or below-the-line, labor sectors.

3. I employ a more straightforward view of folding (informed by computer science and geology) than Deleuze's version of the term. In his book *The Fold: Leibniz and the Baroque* (Minneapolis: University of Minnesota Press, 1993), Deleuze derives his concept from the Baroque period, as a process that transformed European garden art. He adapts Baroque folding for contemporary culture by theorizing how formal objects transmutate into time-based phenomena. Deleuze influenced other time-based film philosophers and theorists who now mine the term to describe cinema's mostly scopic, cognitive, and experiential effects. A good example of this Deleuzian turn in film philosophy is Saige Walton, *Cinema's Baroque Flesh: Film, Phenomenology and the Art of Entanglement* (Amsterdam: University of Amsterdam Press, 2016).

4. I use *recursive* and *recursion* (terms that suggest a repeated feedback loop) because they underscore the centrality and general function that reflexivity or circular reflection plays in cultural production. Production cultures emerge, build, and reiterate over time through recursion, when a trade community reflects on itself, and incrementally changes based on the repetitive process. Recursion is often understood as a repeating process whose output at each stage is applied as input in the succeeding stage. But the computer programmer's understanding of the term—a way to use the least amount of code to perform a necessary function—also resonates with the discursive efficiencies and cultural simplifications that cover over and normalize potentially disruptive "folds" in production.

5. Amanda Lie, TV talent coordinator, interview by author, UCLA, April 7, 2016.

6. See David Bordwell, Janet Staiger, and Kristin Thompson, *The Classical Hollywood Cinema* (New York: Columbia University Press, 1985); and Thomas Schatz, *Hollywood Genres* (Philadelphia: Temple University Press, 1981).

7. See Jason Hellerman, "This Guy Used Free Software to De-age 'The Irishman' and . . . It Looks Great," No Film School, Jan. 7, 2020, https://nofilmschool .com/irishman-done-at-home. Hellerman has embedded the remarkable video "Beating Netflix AI De-Aging," which was originally uploaded to YouTube (and still available as of this writing) as "The Irishman De-Aging: Netflix Millions VS. Free Software!," YouTube, Dec. 23, 2019, www.youtube.com/watch?v= dyRvbFhknRc.

8. The balance of this chapter expands and provides a more systematic account of the stress aesthetics behaviors detailed in the fieldwork/case study on online Maker/Influencer poetics in chapters 7 through 9.

9. For an extended foundational discussion of these principles, see John Caldwell, "Hive-Sourcing Is the New Out-Sourcing: Studying Old (Industrial) Labor Habits in New (Consumer) Labor Clothes," *Cinema Journal* 49, no. 1

(Fall 2009): 160–67; for a different context, see my conclusion to *Production Culture: Industrial Reflexivity and Critical Practice in Film and Television* (Durham, NC: Duke University Press, 2008).

10. This assertion is taken from an online discussion by an anonymous (cited as "redacted" to protect identity from backlash) Indian VFX artist. The original post is no longer available, but the quote survives at several online venues, its ubiquity a testament to the artist's complaint. See, e.g., David S. Cohen, "Is the VFX Biz in India Tricking Artists into Working for Free?," *Variety,* March 6, 2013, https://variety.com/2013/film/news/is-the-vfx-biz-in-india-tricking-artists-into-working-for-free-1200004302.

11. This segmentation and distribution of VFX work into international sub-units aligns perfectly with the model of NICL (or "new international cultural division of labor") outlined in Toby Miller et al., *Global Hollywood* (London: BFI, 2001).

12. These locations include Mumbai, Hyderabad, Bangalore, Chandigarh, and Chennai in India, as well as Florida in the United States.

13. Pete Tomkies, "How to Compete with Filmmakers Who Work for Free," Videomaker.com, Oct.13, 2014, www.videomaker.com/how-to/profitmaking/how-to-compete-with-filmmakers-who-work-for-free.

14. For an example of a deprivation aesthetics championed by radical academic critics, see Julio Espinosa, "For an Imperfect Cinema," trans. Julianne Burton, *Jump Cut,* no. 20 (1979): 24–26. For a later iteration of this against-all-odds deprivation stance (production ascetics but without the Marxist politics), see Mette Hjort and Scott MacKenzie, eds., *Purity and Provocation: Dogma 95* (London: BFI, 2003).

15. On this point, see especially Mette Hjort, *Small Nation, Global Cinema* (Minneapolis: University of Minnesota Press, 2005); and Mette Hjort, "Small Cinemas: How They Thrive and Why They Matter," *Mediascape* (Winter 2011): www.academia.edu/24378049/Small_Cinemas_How_They_Thrive_and_Why_They_Matter.

16. Petr Szczepanik, personal communications, Jan. 20, 2013. I thank Petr for generously suggesting how the stress aesthetics I researched in contemporary mainstream Hollywood aligns with certain film practices elsewhere in Europe.

17. Scott Willingham *(X-Files, 24),* interview by the author, Academy of Television Arts and Sciences (ATAS), Los Angeles, CA, Oct. 30, 2003.

18. See John Caldwell, "Stress Aesthetics and Deprivation Payroll Systems," in *Behind the Screen: European Production Cultures,* ed. Petr Szczepanik and Patrick Vonderau (New York: Palgrave Macmillan, 2013), 91–111.

19. For a more detailed discussion of this, see my article from which the next two paragraphs were adapted: "Breaking Ranks: Backdoor Workforces, Messy Workflows, and Craft Disaggregation," *Journal of Popular Communication* 8, no. 3 (2010): 221–26.

20. For example, as Hollywood TV shifted from film mags and videotape recording to removable digital hard drives and solid-state computer cards as recording devices on the set, who would now handle and organize the footage in preparation for post? The traditional AC/loader, the video-assist operator, or the newly defined "data wranglers" or "DITs"? Production now feels more like

digital "IT management" than traditional "photography," and this unsettles many workers. In both of these workflow examples, a single new digital function threatens two existing job descriptions.

21. A-list production still distributes graphics, effects, sound, and timing tasks out to contracted specialists in those areas. But producers in middle- and low-budget production inevitably create pressures on their workers to use and incorporate the bells and whistles, even if they lie outside the worker's specializations. To wit, reality TV and dating shows are largely created in postproduction by interns and production assistants using FCP and Adobe Premiere. Again, the shortcut. As in any sector, multitasking stresses workers and undercuts control and focused fine-tuning. In addition, the boundary-crossing inherent in multitasking creates intercraft contention, which combines with disruptive changes in economy and technology to impact what viewers see on the screen.

22. To take but one example: no longer limited to their original editing task, AVID, Final Cut Pro, and Adobe Premiere software now boast capabilities in almost every area of production and postproduction, save actual shooting. This makes the software a far cry from the hardware that it obsoletes. Any apprentice editor could learn to operate an upright Moviola in a week or two.

23. "12 On/12 Off" was a grassroots practitioner movement aimed at compelling studios, producers, and unit production managers (UPMs) to limit workdays to twelve hours maximum, with twelve hours off, for turnaround, and no more than six hours of work before or between meals. The goal of the campaign was to reduce workplace dangers that come from unrealistic managerial and scheduling demands intended as production "shortcuts." The campaign involved wearing cautionary T-shirts during shoots with the "12 On/12 Off" message, websites with instructions to workers about how and how not to wear and use the shirts on sets and on locations, and compilations of stories compiled to underscore the hostile conditions that workers face across the industry.

24. This statement, from producer/director Scott Brazil, and the excerpts that follow from producer/director Jon Cassar, editor Scott Willingham, and cinematographer Scott Palazzo are excerpted from interviews I conducted at the Academy of Television Arts and Sciences (ATAS), located in North Hollywood, CA, as part of a project titled "The Normal Rules Do Not Apply: The Impact of MTV on Primetime Television," Oct. 30, 2003.

25. Jon Cassar, interview by author, Academy of Television Arts and Sciences (ATAS), Los Angeles, CA, Oct. 30, 2003. Cassar was paraphrasing actor Kiefer Sutherland's account of his experience shooting a feature film.

26. See Mark Andrejevic, "Estrangement 2.0," *World Picture* 6 (winter 2011): www.worldpicturejournal.com/WP_6/Andrejevic.html#_ednref50.

27. In addition to the Andrejevic article cited above, see Nicholas Carr, *The Shallows: What the Internet Is Doing to Our Brains* (London: Norton, 2011); and Carr's website: www.nicholasgcarr.com. For a discussion of "prosumption" and "prosumerism," see George Ritzer and Nathan Jurgenson, "Production, Consumption, Prosumption: The Nature of Capitalism in the Age of the Digital 'Prosumer,'" *Journal of Consumer Culture* 10, no. 1 (March 2010): 13–36; and Axel Bruns, *Blogs, Wikipedia, Second Life, and Beyond: From Production to Produsage* (New York: Peter Lang, 2008).

28. Caldwell, "Hive-Sourcing."

29. See, in particular, my chapter "Authorship Below-the-Line," in *Companion to Media Authorship,* ed. Jonathan Gray and Derek Johnson (Oxford: Wiley-Blackwell, 2013), 349–69.

30. See my chapter "Industrial Geography Lessons: Socio-professional Rituals and the Borderlands of Production Culture," in *MediaSpace: Place, Scale, and Culture in a Media Age,* ed. Nick Couldry and Anna McCarthy (London: Routledge, 2004), 163–89.

31. The four paragraphs that follow in this section are adapted and summarized from a longer and more extensive study in my chapter "Authorship Below-the-Line."

32. Although nepotism is a standard Hollywood trope for above-the-line figures, family connections also regularly benefit aspirants to below-the-line jobs, giving them an edge in highly contested and overcrowded craft and union job markets, if for no other reason than greater proximity to rapidly changing job opportunities.

33. Such claims from an online posting by an Indian VFX artist, along with defensive pushback by offshore Hollywood sweatshop managers, can be found at Cohen, "Is the VFX Biz in India Tricking Artists?" (see note 9 above). One Indian apologist quoted in Cohen's article defends the requirement to prepay cash deposits in order to start work: "The amazing thing is, thanks to living with your parents, etc., you can survive on this wage comfortably. The official international benchmark for people below the poverty line is those who have purchasing power of $1.25 or less per day." Another endorses indentured outsourcing: "The deposit is not only to keep them but also to encourage them to stay as they don't want to lose employees to competitors after they've trained them."

34. Production designer Jackson De Govia makes this statement in an interview in a retrospective documentary produced in the United States for the Art Directors Guild (ADG) entitled *The Hidden Art of Hollywood* (Timeline Films, 2002).

35. See Caldwell, "Hive-Sourcing." Carr discusses "leveling up," "unsourcing," and "sharecropping" in Nicholas Carr, "Workers of the World, Level Up!," *Rough Type* (blog), May 28, 2012, https://roughtype.com/?p=1607. Chris Webb promotes the idea that these practices are merely a form of "business socializing" in the comments to the original blog post.

36. See Vicki Mayer, *Below the Line* (Durham, NC: Duke University Press, 2011); and Matt Stahl, *Unfree Masters: Recording Artists and the Politics of Work* (Durham, NC: Duke University Press, 2012).

37. See https://twitter.com/specwatch?lang=en. SpecWatch (@Twitter) is not to be confused with SpecWatch (see "SpecWatch: A Framework for Adversarial Spectrum Monitoring with Unknown Statistics," *Computer Networks* 143 [2018]: 176–90, www.sciencedirect.com/science/article/abs/pii/S1389128618305255), which does "adversarial spectrum monitoring" to keep on top of misuses of the channel spectrum by broadcasters and wireless companies.

38. Fiona Graham, "Crowdsourcing Work: Labour on Demand or Digital Sweatshop?," BBC News, Oct. 22, 2010, www.bbc.com/news/business-11600902.

39. See Gilles Deleuze, *Negotiations, 1972–1990* (New York: Columbia University Press, 1995), 174; and Gilles Deleuze, "Postscript on the Societies of Control," *October* 59 (Winter 1992): 3–7.

40. For fuller treatment of my alignment with Deleuze and my take on "worker-generated snark," see my two chapters "The Industrial Promotional Surround," in *Ephemeral Media,* ed. Paul Grainge (London: BFI, 2011); and "Worker Blowback: User-Generated, Worker Generated, and Producer-Generated Content within Collapsing Workflows," in *Television as Digital Media,* ed. James Bennett and Niki Strange (Durham, NC: Duke University Press, 2011), 283–311. I am especially thankful to Thomas Elsaesser for suggesting that my research on the media worker's industrial promotional surround aligns very closely with Deleuze's theory of the "control society."

41. Ulises Mejias, "Confinement, Education and the Control Society," blog entry, http://blog.ulisesmejias.com/2006/08/25/confinement-education-and-the-control-society, accessed August 25, 2006. Mejias's blog is no longer active, but interested readers can find this essay archived on the WayBackMachine at https://web.archive.org/web/20210505205251/https://blog.ulisesmejias.com/2006/08/25/confinement-education-and-the-control-society. From Deleuze's theory of "control" originally outlined on that blog, Mejias worked out a broader more systematic critique of the limits of social media networks in general. See Ulises A. Mejias, "The Limits of Networks as Models for Organizing the Social," *New Media & Society* 12, no. 4 (2010): 603–17.

42. See Ross Perlin, *Intern Nation: How to Earn Nothing and Learn Little in the Brave New Economy* (London: Verso, 2012).

6. CASE

1. Quoted in Rachel Yang, "TikTok . . . Boom," EW.com, https://ew.com/music/tiktok-music-influence, August 18, 2021 (italics mine).

2. Deborah Riley, "Production Design in *Game of Thrones,*" master class at Design Showcase West (DSW), UCLA, June 10, 2017.

3. Nicole Sweeney, "How to YouTube 101," Crash Course workshop, VidCon 2017, Anaheim, CA, June 23, 2017. The full quote is "It is important to have consistency in all categories. Tell yourself: 'every other Thursday I will finish a thing.' If you don't enjoy the work, you don't enjoy the results."

4. This is "recommendation #5" in the seminar lesson by Tim Schmoyer, "Turning YouTube into a Career," workshop, VidCon 2017, Anaheim, CA, June 23, 2017.

5. Derral Eves (CEO, Creatus), "Growth Hacking YouTube: Triggering Algorithm-Driven Views," VidCon 2017, Anaheim, CA, June 22, 2017. Unless otherwise indicated (by reference to DSW, MPEG, ASC, UCLA, etc.), any quotes cited below were recorded at the VidCon 2017 trade convention in Anaheim, California, June 22–25, 2017, and are cited parenthetically in the text.

6. Caitlin Hofmeister, SciShow, panel discussant at "Building Teams: People Management 101 for Creators," VidCon 2017, Anaheim, CA, June 22, 2017.

7. Jack Conte, Patreon, panel discussant at "Building Teams: People Management 101 for Creators," VidCon 2017, Anaheim, CA, June 22, 2017.

8. See Caldwell, *Production Culture*, esp. 37–59, 150–67.

9. Matthew Patrick, Theorist Media, "MatPat: Sustainability in Digital: How to Build a Programming Strategy That Won't Burn You Out," VidCon 2017, Anaheim, CA, June 23, 2017.

10. Megan Batoon, spoken comments at "Transitioning Your Channel into a Full-Fledged Business," VidCon 2017, Anaheim, CA, June 22, 2017.

11. Schmoyer, "Turning YouTube into a Career" (see note 4 above). Schmoyer also visualizes this psychological crash-and-burn profile on a whiteboard at "A Guide to Not Quitting on YouTube Dreams," www.youtube.com/watch?v=xBsrNFxnnuY.

12. Matt Gielen (CEO, Little Monster Media), "Reverse Engineering the YouTube Algorithm Expanded," VidCon 2017, Anaheim, CA, June 22, 2017.

13. Debate between YouTubers recorded on June 22, 2017 at VidCon 2017, Anaheim, CA.

14. Sweeney, "How to YouTube 101."

15. Schmoyer, "Turning YouTube into a Career" (see note 4 above).

16. Tom Greenwood-Mears, Endemol/Shine-UK, "From Online to Offline: How to Engage with Your Audiences beyond the Screen," VidCon 2017, Anaheim, CA, June 22, 2017.

17. Scott Hervey, Weintraub-Tobin, spoken comments at "Navigating Risk in the Brand/Influencer Relationship," VidCon 2017, Anaheim, CA, June 22, 2017.

18. Mindy McKnight, spoken comments at "Transitioning Your Channel into a Full-Fledged Business," VidCon 2017, Anaheim, CA, June 22, 2017.

19. "Net Advertising Revenues of YouTube in the United States from 2018 to 2022," Statista, www.statista.com/statistics/289660/youtube-us-net-advertising-revenues.

20. "US Online and Traditional Media Advertising Outlook, 2017–2021," Marketing Charts, www.marketingcharts.com/television-79007.

21. Hervey, "Navigating Risk."

22. Benji Travis, spoken comments at "Transitioning Your Channel into a Full-Fledged Business," VidCon 2017, Anaheim, CA, June 22, 2017 (italics mine).

23. McKnight, "Transitioning Your Channel."

24. This statement justifying the economic neoliberalism governing the online video ecosystem that is taught to preschoolers was provided by an impassioned mother and was directed at panelists in a session titled "Alternate Careers in Online Video," VidCon 2017, Anaheim, CA, June 23, 2017.

25. FameBit promo video, Famebit.com, accessed March 2, 2016, at Famebit.com. FameBit was rebranded as "YouTube BrandConnect" on June 16, 2020. The original URL is no longer viable, but the re-uploaded FameBit promo video can again be viewed at https://youtu.be/rxTIqypUHk4.

26. This quote and video clip from GoodMythicalMorning.com are from "How Good Mythical Morning Became the Biggest Daily Show on YouTube," ViceNews(HBO), August 30, 2018, www.youtube.com/watch?v=u9pbRBJu3PU.

For the print version see Dexter Thomas, "Fans Are Worried the Internet's Biggest Daily Show Is Getting Too Big," Vice News, Nov. 20, 2017, www.vice.com/en/article/pazzxb/fans-are-worried-the-internets-biggest-daily-show-is-getting-too-big.

27. Arleta Fowler, CAA, spoken comments at "New Business Models for Online Video," workshop, VidCon 2017, Anaheim, CA, June 23, 2017.

28. Amanda Lie, TV talent coordinator, interview by author, UCLA, April 7, 2016.

29. A YouTube consultant made this statement at an open-mic in a workshop optimistically titled "Creators Tell Brands and Agencies What THEY Want," VidCon 2017, Anaheim, CA, June 23, 2017.

30. Peter Csathy, CREATV Media, spoken comments at "New Business Models for Online Video," workshop, VidCon 2017, Anaheim, CA, June 23, 2017.

31. Naomi Lennon, Studio71, spoken comments at "New Business Models for Online Video," workshop, VidCon 2017, Anaheim, CA, June 23, 2017.

32. Derral Eves, Creatus, spoken comments at "Growth Hacking YouTube: Triggering Algorithm-Driven Views," VidCon 2017, Anaheim, CA, June 22, 2017.

33. Matt Gielen, Little Monster Media, spoken comments at "Reverse Engineering the YouTube Algorithm," VidCon 2017, Anaheim, CA, June 22, 2017.

34. This public debate took place between Mindy McKnight and Phil Ranta in the workshop "Transitioning Your Channel into a Full-Fledged Business," VidCon 2017, Anaheim, CA, June 22, 2017.

35. Gielen, "Reverse Engineering the YouTube Algorithm."

36. Brian Solis, Altimeter Group, spoken comments at "Return on Relationships: Influence vs. Influencer Marketing," VidCon 2017, Anaheim, CA, June 23, 2017.

37. Schmoyer, "Turning YouTube into a Career" (see note 4 above).

38. Jack Conte founded Patreon in May 2013 as a way to make a living from his popular YouTube videos. With Sam Yam, Conte developed a platform that allowed patrons to pay money over time to artists, which gave them extended periods to produce art in quantity. Patreon raised $2.1 million in August 2013 from a group of angel investors and venture capitalists. In January 2016, the company raised more investors, which pushed the total raised for Patreon to $47.1 million. Patreon marveled that it had signed up more than 125,000 "patrons" in its first eighteen months. The website stated that patrons were sending over $1 million per month to the site's content creators in 2014. Patreon eventually took over Subbable in March 2015, a competing subscription service founded by John and Hank Green. This takeover brought in a stable of notable new creators and content from Subbable, including Destin Sandlin's *Smarter Every Day* and CGP Grey, along with the Green brothers' own *Crash Course* and *SciShow* channels. The trades noted in May 2017 that Patreon had more than fifty thousand active creators, one million monthly patrons, and was on track to send over $150 million to creators in 2017. For more detailed backstory on the corporate trajectory of Patreon see https://en.wikipedia.org/wiki/Patreon.

39. Panelist recommendation, "What Brands and Media Companies Need to Learn about Fandom—From Today's Digital Creators," workshop moderated

by Meredith Levine of Theorist Media, VidCon 2017, Anaheim, CA, June 23, 2017 (italics mine).

40. Gavin McGarry, Jumpwire Media, "Hacking the Facebook Algorithm: Facebook's Secret Promotional Code," VidCon 2017, Anaheim, CA June 22, 2017.

41. According to Lazarsfeld, administrative research is undertaken on behalf of administrative bodies to achieve well-defined purposes. Much sponsored research fits this definition. By contrast, critical research questions do not follow from or serve the regime of the sponsor; rather, they have an evaluative dimension that stands apart from narrow institutional interests and are informed by an understanding of social trends, including political economic factors and basic human values. On Paul Lazarsfeld see Robert E. Babe, *Canadian Communication Thought* (Toronto: University of Toronto Press, 2000), 15–16.

42. See, e.g., Ien Ang, *Desperately Seeking the Audience* (London: Routledge, 1991).

7. FRACTURING

1. Jones elaborates on this principle in her "Commentary: What Earthquakes Can Teach Us about the Coronavirus Pandemic," *Los Angeles Times,* May 6, 2020; reprinted in the *Daily World,* www.thedailyworld.com/opinion/commentary-what-earthquakes-can-teach-us-about-the-coronavirus-pandemic.

2. Kutak served as executive director of the Motion Picture Editors Guild Local 700, IATSE Los Angeles, from 1985 to 2016. The meeting at which he made these remarks took place in Hollywood, CA, on August 30, 2011.

3. Along with Denmark, the UK has set an enviable standard for successfully funding highly productive front-door research partnerships. A more comprehensive survey of sanctioned partnerships would go well beyond the spare taxonomy of research methods sketched in this chapter to preface fracture research. It would include the scholar-industry alliances underway at a wide range of UK universities. These influential research directors and partnerships include: James Bennett (StoryFutures, Royal Holloway University); John Ellis (ADAPT: Hands-on History of TV Technology, Royal Holloway University); Paul Grainge (Digital Nottingham, University of Nottingham); David Hesmondhalgh (Digital Futures at Work Research Center, University of Leeds); Catherine Johnson (Centre for Participatory Culture, University of Huddersfield); Paul McDonald (Culture, Media, and Creative Industries, Kings College); and Andrew Spicer and Steve Presence (UK Feature Docs, University of the West of England).

4. See "Kinomatics: The Industrial Geometry of Culture," https://kinomatics.com.

5. An accompanying book lists these terms (all of which are nontraditional approaches in film studies) as the research methods enabled in Arclight research. See *The Arclight Guidebook to Media History and the Digital Humanities,* ed. Charles R. Acland and Eric Hoyt (University of Sussex: Reframe, 2016), https://projectarclight.org/book. The broader "Media History Digital Library" is directed by David Pierce and Eric Hoyt and can be found at http://mediahisto-

ryproject.org. To access Arclight's big-data-mining search engine (named "Lantern") see http://search.projectarclight.org.

6. For the Media History Digital Library's scanning protocols see https://mediahistoryproject.org/about.html.

7. Media Ecology Project, https://mediaecology.dartmouth.edu/wp.

8. The research project was entitled "Streaming Heritage: 'Following Files' in Digital Music Distribution," and it received multiyear funding from the Swedish Research Council. The project was based on a set of tools provided by Selenium. These allowed the SpotiBot engine to automate the Spotify web client by simulating user interaction within the web interface. The research team's principal investigator explains the logic behind the research:

> From a computational perspective the Spotify web client appeared as [a] black box; the logics that the Spotify application was governed by was, for example, not known in advance, and the web page structure (in HTML) and client side scripting quite complex. It was not doable within the experiment to gain a fuller understanding of the dialogue between the client and the server. As a consequence, the development of the SpotiBot-experiment was (to some extent) based on "trial and error," how the client behaved, and what kind of data was sent from the server for different user actions. Using a single virtual machine—hidden behind only one proxy IP—the results nevertheless indicate that it is possible to automatically play tracks for thousands of repetitions that exceeds the royalty rule. (Pelle Snickars, "Our 'Spotify-Project'—an Update," Nov. 13, 2015, http://pellesnickars.se/2015/11/our-spotify-project-an-update)

9. For examples of deWaard's visualizations of big-data intertextual analysis, see Andrew deWaard, "Financialized Hollywood: Institutional Investment, Venture Capital, and Private Equity in the Film and Television Industry," *Journal of Cinema and Media Studies* 59, no. 4 (2020): 54–84; and "Derivative Media: The Financialization of Film, Television, and Popular Music, 2004–2016" (PhD diss., UCLA, 2018).

10. Felicia Henderson is a prime-time screenwriter, executive producer, and now a media studies scholar pursuing fieldwork and dissertation research at UCLA on the television "writers room." Her credits include *The Fresh Prince of Bel Air* (writer), *Moesha* (writer/producer), *Sister, Sister* (writer/producer), *Gossip Girl* (writer/coexecutive producer), *Everybody Hates Chris* (consulting producer), and J. J. Abrams's series *Fringe* (writer/coexecutive producer). Felicia was the creator/executive producer of the long-running, critically acclaimed, award-winning Showtime series *Soul Food*. She was recently an assistant professor in the Radio-Television-Film Department at the University of Texas at Austin.

11. Erin Hill worked as an assistant to writers, directors, and producers at various film and television companies, including Jerry Bruckheimer Films *(Pirates of the Caribbean, Pearl)*, Hofflund/Polone *(Curb Your Enthusiasm, Panic Room, and Gilmore Girls)*, and Shukovsky English Entertainment *(Murphy Brown, The Women)*, and as a freelance story analyst for studios and production companies. She completed her PhD dissertation in Cinema and Media Studies at UCLA and continues her work as a story analyst, film industry blogger, and participant in the channel 101 underground filmmaking community.

Dr. Hill is presently an assistant professor in the Communication Department at the University of California, San Diego.

12. Paul Malcolm worked as a journalist and associate film editor for *LA Weekly* for ten years, where he contributed regular reviews, interviews, and "on the set" pieces. He has since worked as the Membership and Special Projects Coordinator for the Visual Effects Society (VES) in Los Angeles. This enabled him to pursue his fieldwork and serves as the basis for his UCLA dissertation, "World of Effects: The Craft and Culture of Visual Effects Production in the Digital Age." He currently programs films for the Los Angeles Film Festival and the UCLA Film and Television Archive.

13. A former network television executive and producer, David Craig completed his dissertation, "Out of the TV: The Cultural History and Pedagogy of LGBT-Themed TV Movies," in 2014 at UCLA. He is perhaps best known for the definitive book *Social Media Entertainment: The New Intersection of Hollywood and Silicon Valley* (New York: NYU Press, 2019), which he coauthored with Stuart Cunningham. Craig is currently a clinical associate professor at the USC Annenberg School for Communication and Journalism.

14. Adam Fish has a PhD from the University of California, Los Angeles. His dissertation, "Reforming the American Public Sphere: The Media Reform Models of Progressive Television Journalists," was completed in 2012. Fish is the author of *Technoliberalism and the End of Participatory Culture in the United States* (New York: Palgrave Macmillan, 2017), an ethnography of the politics of internet and television convergence in Hollywood and Silicon Valley. He is currently an associate professor and Scientia Fellow in the Faculty of Arts and Social Sciences, School of Arts and Media, at the University of New South Wales. He is a cultural anthropologist, documentary video producer, and interdisciplinary scholar who works across the fields of social science, computer engineering, environmental science, and the visual arts.

15. The next two paragraphs are adapted from my chapter "Both Sides of the Fence: Blurred Distinctions in Scholarship and Production (A Portfolio of Interviews)," in *Production Studies,* ed. Vicki Mayer, Miranda J. Banks, and John T. Caldwell (London: Routledge, 2009), 214–30.

16. I provide a fuller discussion of these issues in chapter 9.

17. See Ted Johnson, "'Midnight Rider' Filmmakers Raise Doubts about Trespass Charges with New Evidence," *Variety,* Oct. 7, 2016, https://variety.com/2016/biz/news/midnight-rider-randall-miller-new-york-marine-1201881733.

18. One of the best books on the history of the new "package" era is Denise Mann's *Hollywood Independents* (Minneapolis: University of Minnesota Press, 2007).

19. These numbers are from Marc Johnson, "The Adpocalypse Aftermath," *Creator Handbook*, Dec. 2, 2019, www.creatorhandbook.net/the-adpocalyse-aftermath.

20. For those brave enough to start down the rabbit hole of YouTuber burnout, see, e.g., "Inside the Weird World of YouTuber Burnout," BBC News, Jan. 11, 2019, www.youtube.com/watch?v=QUrNbl1lNV4; and "YouTube Burnout Is Real. Here's How to Avoid It," Think Media, March 12, 2020, www.youtube.com/watch?v=wDRnmhnfnh8.

21. For the best, meticulously researched book on this period and phenomenon (i.e., on this "fold"), see Jennifer Holt, *Empires of Entertainment: Media Industries and the Politics of Deregulation, 1980–1996* (New Brunswick, NJ: Rutgers University Press, 2011).

22. See John Thornton Caldwell, *Televisuality: Style, Crisis, and Authority in American Television* (New Brunswick, NJ: Rutgers University Press, 1995, 2020).

23. See Sahil Patel, "Inside Disney's Troubled $675 Mil. Maker Studios Acquisition," *DigiDay,* Feb. 22, 2017, https://digiday.com/future-of-tv/disney-maker-studios.

24. For an account of top-ranked video-gamer Ben Vacas's and Braindeadly's crash-and-burn, see Anita Hamilton, "Cashing in on YouTube Fame Not Easy: Reaping Income with Ads Tougher as the Competition Keeps Growing," SFGATE, April 23, 2013, www.sfgate.com/technology/article/Cashing-in-on-YouTube-fame-not-easy-4458192.php. For an example of Vacas's online presence before he left YouTube, see Ben Vacas, "Hunter PvP introduction—Ben 'Braindeadly' Vacas—LearnWoW Episode 3—Razer Academy," Sept. 19, 2012, www.youtube.com/watch?v=n5Hi-7VorMs

25. See Ray William Johnson, "Why I Left Maker Studios [Exclusive]," in New Rockstars: What the Internet Cares About Right Now," Dec. 12, 2012, https://newmediarockstars.com/2012/12/why-i-left-maker-studios.

26. See Matthew Stahl, *Unfree Masters* (Durham, NC: Duke University Press, 2013).

27. See "Video of the Day: *Unbroken* VFX Breakdown," Below the Line, April 3, 2015, www.btlnews.com/crafts/visual-fx/video-of-the-day-unbroken-vfx-breakdown.

8. CASE

1. Mark Bergen, Lucas Shaw, and Bloomberg, "YouTube Has Paid Out $30 Billion to Creators as the Competition for Online Content Intensifies," *Fortune,* August 23, 2021, https://apple.news/A2pfmRMgoQ_essmt-w8oSsQ.

2. Jim Louderback "The Thumbnail's Days Are Numbered—Here's What Comes Next," LinkedIn, August 23, 2021, www.linkedin.com/pulse/thumbnails-days-numbered-heres-what-comes-next-jim-louderback.

3. Patrick Vonderau, "The Spotify Effect: Digital Distribution and Financial Growth," *Television and New Media,* Nov. 21, 2017, https://doi.org/10.1177/1527476417741200.

4. Andrew deWaard, "Derivative Media: The Financialization of Film, Television, and Popular Music, 2004–2016" (PhD diss., UCLA, 2017), 84, 87, https://escholarship.org/content/qt69wov6n3/qt69wov6n3_noSplash_of1d9a8f56obae86ea05131e8f457efb.pdf.

5. Anna Lowenhaupt Tsing, *Friction: An Ethnography of Global Connection* (Princeton, NJ: Princeton University Press, 2005), 57.

6. Gregg is quoted in Vonderau, "The Spotify Effect."

7. For a parade of YouTube success stories, see "Creators Going Pro," Tubefilter, www.tubefilter.com/category/creators-going-pro.

8. As discussed in chapters 1–3, examples of this include demos, pilot-creating, treatments, leave-behinds, public pitches, scripts, workshops, table-reads, shootouts, prototyping, brainstorming, thinking-out-loud, and growth-hacking workshops.

9. METHODS

1. Lewis Carroll, *Sylvie and Bruno Concluded,* illustrations by Harry Furniss (London: Macmillan, 1893), 169. This edition has been digitized and made available at https://ia800206.us.archive.org/8/items/sylviebrunoconcloocarriala/sylviebrunoconcloocarriala.pdf.

2. In effect, industry can push attention away from deeper practices that it hopes to keep unseen. This compulsion (even in making-ofs) to point toward the "primary" phenomenon—the "onscreen" film or TV show—is far from a difficult pill for many scholars to swallow. In fact, in terms of onscreen-vs.-offscreen hierarchies, many scholars align with industry by emphasizing one side of that binary that they value. This is because traditional film studies also habitually pushed the discipline's attention over to what it considers the main staged event, the film form, the screen.

3. "YouTube by the Numbers: Stats, Demographics, and Fun Facts," Omnicore, March 14, 2022, www.omnicoreagency.com/youtube-statistic. This upload rate results in thirty thousand new videos per hour; 720 thousand new videos per day; 21.6 million new videos per month; and 259.2 million new videos per year.

4. Matt Klein, "50 Million Join the 'Creator Economy' Thanks to Platforms," *Forbes,* Sept. 23, 2020, www.forbes.com/sites/mattklein/2020/09/23/50m-join-the-creator-economy-as-new-platforms-emerge-to-help-anyone-produce-content--money/?sh=5ce83c433165.

5. Werner Geyser, "22 Creator Economy Statistics That Will Blow You Away," Influencer Marketing Hub, March 15, 2022, https://influencermarketinghub.com/creator-economy-stats.

6. By definition, and experientially, culture is far more than the sum of its ostensibly atomized parts. For many industry researchers, the attempt to "excise" a discrete "trait" to count statistically borders on a fool's errand. But snowball sampling can provide something different: a credible logic for delimiting the evidence studied (i.e., a data-delimiting logic) in what are otherwise potentially massive media industry systems.

7. This transmedia fold and nexus point rippled through four different conglomerates, ad agencies, the financial markets, and thousands of makers angry at YouTube's punitive "Adpocalypse," providing a framework for the ethnographic observations of aspirant online creators in chapters 4, 6, and 8.

8. See Bruno Latour. *Reassembling the Social: An Introduction to Actor-Network Theory* (Oxford: Oxford University Press, 2005).

9. This extends the book's earlier argument that contact zones provide optimal sites for examining embedded systems. That is, the chain-referral approach allows production researchers to find and describe both interfaces and hierarchies within embedded production systems that can be historically documented. This interface/hierarchy framework encourages researchers to look for and try to bet-

ter understand the points of contact, pressure-points, and fault lines between one production sector or systems and another system within which it is embedded.

10. Several of my respondents in the field have suggested that my research and approach may have a dark undertone or fatalism to it. Given that I study corporate economics, it probably does, at least compared to important recent wide-ranging accounts of "social media entertainment" by Cunningham and Craig (see, e.g., their *Social Media Entertainment* [New York: New York University Press, 2019]). Yet I hope this volume mitigates any overpessimism about totalizing, global, neoliberal economic "enclosure," in ways that point to local openings for human participants in media industries and organizations. I continue to underscore that even production "markets" are always sites of collective negotiation and disruption. The architects of corporate schemes and industrial strategies simply cannot control the human agents inside their organizations. My view is that it is better to acknowledge and address this than to paper-over the reality. Indeed, corporate media theory (branding, marketing) vigilantly pursues ideological "house-cleaning" and dissonant "noise-reduction," all in the search to find working efficiencies needed to bring "rationality" to the cultural chaos that pervades the industrial predicament. For this very reason, production poetics and production culture research attempts to provide a sober accounting of the inevitable irrationalities that define media organizations. As always, I am particularly drawn in this book to the "wrenches thrown into machines"—some intentional, some out of habit—by human agents who must coexist within production units.

11. For more scholarship on issues of authorship, artistic attribution, and IP, see Miranda J. Banks, *The Writers* (New Brunswick, NJ: Rutgers University Press, 2016); and Vicki Mayer, *Below-the-Line* (Durham, NC: Duke University Press, 2011).

12. I want to emphasize the importance of Geertz's argument that cultures can only be accessed in textualized form. This culture-as-text holds even if an informant in the field claims to offer a disclosure as "the truth about what is really going on." For Geertz, culture represents a social group "thinking out loud about itself." Both positions show how the object of our research, a production group or practice, also embeds critical analysis inside itself. In some ways, this embedded analysis shadows and mirrors the scholar's. Early on, a production researcher should identify the conventions by which a trade group "thinks out loud about itself." This provides another opportunity: reflect on and articulate how the scholar's analysis relates to the trade group's own workaday, embedded critical analysis. Ethnography requires precisely this form of parallel reflexivity from the observing scholar. Both Geertz and Victor Turner provide insights germane to "industrial reflexivity" and suggest how and why media production groups may obsessively reflect back on themselves as part of their professional activities. See Clifford Geertz, "Deep Play: Notes on the Balinese Cockfight," in *The Interpretation of Cultures* (New York: Basic Books, 1973); and Victor Turner, *The Anthropology of Experience* (Urbana: University of Illinois Press, 1986, 2001). The pervasiveness of this industrial critical reflexivity is precisely why scholars trained in the humanities are so well suited to study production. Industry's layers of embedded reflexivity are not things that empiricists can easily reduce, aggregate, or sample into a research "data

set." Industrial reflexivity is critical and recursive in precisely the ways that scholars have mastered in literary theory and the digital humanities.

13. See Paul Dimaggio, "Cultural Entrepreneurship in Nineteenth-Century Boston," *Media, Culture and Society* 4 (1982): 33–50; and Paul Hirsch, "Processing Fads and Fashions: An Organization-Set Analysis of Cultural Industry Systems," *American Journal of Sociology* 77, no. 4 (Jan. 1972): 639–59. See also an insightful later collection of research: Derek Johnson, Derek Kompare, and Avi Santo, eds., *Making Media Work: Cultures of Management in the Entertainment Industries* (New York: New York University Press, 2014).

14. See Pierre Bourdieu, *Distinction: A Social Critique of the Judgement of Taste,* trans. Richard Nice (Cambridge, MA: Harvard University Press, 1984); and Herbert Gans, *Popular Culture and High Culture: An Analysis and Evaluation of Taste* (New York: Basic Books, 1999).

15. See Allen Scott, *On Hollywood* (Princeton, NJ: Princeton University Press, 2005); Michael Curtin, *Playing to the World's Biggest Audience* (Berkeley: University of California Press, 2007); and Allen Storper and Robert Salais, *Worlds of Production* (Cambridge, MA: Harvard University Press, 1997).

16. Victor Turner also undercuts the naive empiricism often assumed when scholars imagine they are observing and explaining the "real world." Turner's research on social rituals enables production researchers to think about the habitual and liminal rituals as collective cognitive expressions through which the identities of industry groups are made, sanctioned, and remade. For Turner, industry's trade rituals can be viewed as mirrors in front of which groups of production workers imagine themselves and make and remake themselves. Culture is not just an expression or "signifier" of something more real. Neither Turner's or Geertz's paradigms are static. Both provide models for observing and understanding production culture as a collective of dynamic imaginative systems built around reiteration.

17. These kinds of "secondary" media texts can provide researchers with insights into a sector or trade's "industrial epistemologies." Several additional concerns guide this research: epistemology, labor, and complex systems theory. Although poetics (my etic analysis) may seem to disrupt ethnography (my emic observation), taken together they can show in an integrated way how knowledge is produced (and, more important, reproduced). Embedded texts may seem antithetical to the "empirical" impulses in fieldwork, yet this is far from true. I have tried to analyze embedded industry texts in order to move beyond instrumental, a priori, or top-down views of production (a deep collective habit in professional craft/film-school traditions) and to move toward and explore emergent/recursive/collective models of production. For a very good account of this, see Jonathan Gray, *Show Sold Separately* (New York: New York University Press, 2010). The case studies of online creators earlier in this book raise a set of recurring themes and questions applicable to other production studies as well: where does knowledge about production come from, and why? What alternative sources or sites of this production knowledge might we usefully consider? How has "authority" about production knowledge shifted, and why?

18. See Mark Deuze and Mirjam Prenger, eds., *Making Media* (Amsterdam: Amsterdam University Press, 2019); Arlie Hochschild, *The Managed Heart*

(Berkeley: University of California Press, 2012); Andrew Ross, *No Collar* (Philadelphia: Temple University Press, 2004); and Michael L. Siciliano, *Creative Control* (New York: Columbia University Press, forthcoming). See also the insightful book by David Hesmondhalgh and Sarah Baker, *Creative Labour* (London: Routledge, 2013).

19. See Jeremy Rifkin, *The End of Work* (New York: Putnam, 1995); and Jeremy Rifkin, *The Age of Access* (New York: Putnam, 2000).

20. In *Televisuality* (New Brunswick, NJ: Rutgers University Press, 1995), I argued against the "etic" theoretical overreach of textualism and postmodernism in film studies. To circumvent high theory in the field, I attempted to better describe the emic dimensions of television production by listening more closely to practitioners. In effect, I researched media aesthetics by factoring into stylistic analysis the industry's own workaday interpretations. I referred to these sometimes modest industrial self-interpretations as "low theory." I argued that low theory included industry's sense-making conceptualizations, which emerged from reflexive programming strategies, technology interfaces, workforce trends, and marketing practice. The bias for the first term in the text-vs.-context binary favored in the humanities and CMS no longer seemed tenable to me as a useful explanation for media—especially mass-market multichannel TV at that time—on any level.

21. Later, *Production Culture* (Durham, NC: Duke University Press, 2008) steered the theory-vs.-research argument in the opposite direction. That book pushed back against the facile but problematic "go to the industry for answers" impulse. That book did more fully underscore the value of systematically understanding the emic perspectives of film/video practitioners (through interviews, observation, and the textual analysis of industry's "deep texts"). At the same time, however, the book also cautioned against reducing analysis to naive empiricism and to grateful overdeference to that "insider's" or industry's perspective.

Works Cited

Acland, Charles R. *American Blockbuster: Movies, Technology, and Wonder.* Durham, NC: Duke University Press, 2020.

———, ed. *Residual Media.* Minneapolis: University of Minnesota Press, 2007.

———. *Swift Viewing: The Popular Life of Subliminal Influence.* Durham, NC: Duke University Press, 2011.

Acland, Charles R., and Eric Hoyt, eds. *The Arclight Guidebook to Media History and the Digital Humanities.* University of Sussex: Reframe, 2016. https://projectarclight.org/book.

Andel, Jaroslev, and Petr Szczepanik, eds. *Cinema All the Time: An Anthology of Czech Film Theory and Criticism, 1908–1939.* Prague: National Film Archive, 2008.

Andrejevic, Mark. "Estrangement 2.0." *World Picture* 6 (Winter 2011): www .worldpicturejournal.com/WP_6/Andrejevic.html#_ednref50.

Ang, Ien. *Desperately Seeking the Audience.* London: Routledge, 1991.

Aristotle. *The Poetics.* Oxford: Oxford University Press, 2013.

Babe, Robert E. *Canadian Communication Thought: Ten Foundational Writers.* Toronto: University of Toronto Press, 2000.

Banks, Miranda, Bridget Conor, and Vicki Mayer, eds. *Production Studies, the Sequel! Cultural Studies of Global Media Industries.* London: Routledge, 2014.

Banks, Miranda J. *The Writers: A History of American Screenwriters and Their Guild.* New Brunswick, NJ: Rutgers University Press, 2016.

Becker, Howard. "The Epistemology of Qualitative Research." In *Ethnography and Human Development: Context and Meaning in Social Inquiry,* edited by Richard Jessor, Anne Colby, and Richard A. Shweder, 53–71. Chicago: University of Chicago Press, 1996.

Bennett, James, and Niki Strange, eds. *Media Independence: Working with Freedom or Working for Free?* London: Routledge, 2014.

Bordwell, David, Janet Staiger, and Kristin Thompson. *The Classical Hollywood Cinema: Film Style & Mode of Production to 1960.* New York: Columbia University Press, 1985.

Bourdieu, Pierre. *Distinction: A Social Critique of the Judgement of Taste.* Translated by Richard Nice. Cambridge, MA: Harvard University Press, 1984.

Brook, Vincent. *Driven to Darkness: Jewish Émigré Directors and the Rise of Film Noir.* New Brunswick, NJ: Rutgers University Press, 2009.

Browne, Nick. "The Political Economy of the Television (Super)Text." In *Television: The Critical View,* 4th ed., edited by Horace Newcomb, 585–99. New York: Oxford University Press, 1987.

Buckminster Fuller Institute. "Eight Strategies for Comprehensive Anticipatory Design Science." Buckminster Fuller Institute. www.bfi.org/about-fuller/big-ideas/design-science/design-science-primer/eight-strategies-for-comprehensive-anticipatory-design-science.

Caldwell, John Thornton. "Authorship Below-the-Line." In *Companion to Media Authorship,* edited by Jonathan Gray and Derek Johnson, 349–69. Oxford: Wiley-Blackwell, 2013.

———. "Breaking Ranks: Backdoor Workforces, Messy Workflows, and Craft Disaggregation." *Journal of Popular Communication* 8, no. 3 (2010): 221–26.

———. "Convergence Television." In *Television after TV: Essays on a Medium in Transition,* edited by Lynn Spigel, 41–74. Durham, NC: Duke University Press, 2003.

———, ed. *Electronic Media and Technoculture.* New Brunswick, NJ: Rutgers University Press, 2000.

———. "Hive-Sourcing Is the New Out-Sourcing." *Cinema Journal* 49, no.1 (Fall 2009): 160–67.

———. "Industrial Geography Lessons: Socio-professional Rituals and the Borderlands of Production Culture." In *MediaSpace: Place, Scale, and Culture in a Media Age,* edited by Nick Couldry and Anna McCarthy, 163–89. London: Routledge, 2004.

———. "Corporate and Worker Ephemera: The Industrial Promotional Surround, Paratexts and Worker Blowback." In *Ephemeral Media: Transitory Screen Culture from Television to YouTube,* edited by Paul Grainge, 175–94. London: BFI, 2011.

———. "Para-industry: Researching Hollywood's Blackwaters." *Cinema Journal* 52, no. 3 (Spring 2013): 157–65.

———. "Para-industry, Shadow Academy." *Cultural Studies* 28, no. 4 (2014): 720–40. http://dx.doi.org/10.1080/09502386.2014.888922.

———. *Production Culture: Industrial Reflexivity and Critical Practice in Film and Television.* Durham, NC: Duke University Press, 2008.

———. "Stress Aesthetics and Deprivation Payroll Systems." In *Behind the Screen: Inside European Production Cultures,* edited by Petr Szczepanik and Patrick Vonderau, 91–111. New York: Palgrave Macmillan, 2013.

———. *Televisuality: Style, Crisis, and Authority in American Television.* New Brunswick, NJ: Rutgers University Press, 1995.

———. "Worker Blowback: User-Generated, Worker-Generated, and Producer-Generated Content." In *Television as Digital Media,* edited by

James Bennett and Niki Strange, 283–311. Durham, NC: Duke University Press, 2011.

Calvey, David. *Covert Research: The Art, Politics and Ethics of Undercover Fieldwork.* London: Sage, 2017.

Carr, Nicholas. *The Shallows: What the Internet Is Doing to Our Brains.* London: Norton, 2011.

———. "Workers of the World, Level Up." *Rough Type* (blog), May 28, 2012, 1–8. http://roughtype.com/?p=1607.

Carroll, Lewis. *The Complete Illustrated Works.* New York: Gramercy, 1982.

Casetti, Francesco. *The Lumière Galaxy: Seven Key Words for the Cinema to Come.* New York: Columbia University Press, 2015.

Christian, Aymar Jean. *Open TV: Innovation beyond Hollywood and the Rise of Web Television.* New York: New York University Press, 2018.

Chung, Hye Jean. *Heterotopias: Digital Effects and Material Labor in Global Film Production.* Durham, NC: Duke University Press, 2018.

Clarke, Michael J. *Transmedia Television: New Trends in Network Serial Production.* New York: Bloomsbury, 2012.

Cohen, David S. "Is the VFX Biz in India Tricking Artists into Working for Free?" *Variety,* March 6, 2013. https://variety.com/2013/film/news/is-the-vfx-biz-in-india-tricking-artists-into-working-for-free-1200004302.

Cohn, Jonathan. *The Burden of Choice: Recommendations, Subversion, and Algorithmic Culture.* New Brunswick, NJ: Rutgers University Press, 2019.

Craig, David. "Out of the TV: The Cultural History and Pedagogy of LGBT-Themed TV Movies." PhD diss., UCLA, 2014.

Cunningham, Stuart, and David Craig. *Social Media Entertainment.* New York: New York University Press, 2019.

Curtin, Michael. "On Edge: Culture Industries in the Neo-network Era." In *Making and Selling Culture,* edited by Richard Ohmann, 181–202. Hanover, NH: University Press of New England / Wesleyan University Press, 1996.

———. *Playing to the World's Biggest Audience: The Globalization of Chinese Film and TV.* Berkeley: University of California Press, 2007.

Curtin, Michael, and Kevin Sanson. *Precarious Creativity: Global Media, Local Labor.* Berkeley: University of California Press, 2016.

Deleuze, Gilles. *The Fold: Leibniz and the Baroque.* Minneapolis: University of Minnesota Press, 1993.

———. *Negotiations, 1972–1990.* New York: Columbia University Press, 1995.

———. "Postscript on the Societies of Control." *October* 59 (Winter 1992): 3–7.

Deleuze, Gilles, and Félix Guattari. *A Thousand Plateaus: Capitalism and Schizophrenia.* Translated by Brian Massumi. London: Continuum, 2004.

Densham, Pen. "A Filmmaker's 'Positive' Thoughts on Stress, Part Two: The Struggle That Led to an Oscar Nom." Originally published in *SSN Insider,* April 22, 2015. Reprinted by *Final Draft* (blog), www.finaldraft.com/blog/2015/04/22/filmmakers-positive-thoughts-stress-part-2.

Deuze, Mark, and Mirjam Prenger, eds. *Making Media: Production, Practices, and Professions.* Amsterdam: Amsterdam University Press, 2019.

deWaard, Andrew. "Derivative Media: The Financialization of Film, Television, and Popular Music, 2004–2016." PhD diss., UCLA, 2017.

———. "Financialized Hollywood: Institutional Investment, Venture Capital, and Private Equity in the Film and Television Industry." *Journal of Cinema and Media Studies* 59, no. 4 (2020): 54–84.

Dimaggio, Paul. "Cultural Entrepreneurship in Nineteenth-Century Boston." *Media, Culture and Society* 4 (1982): 33–50.

Dornfeld, Barry. *Producing Public Television.* Princeton, NJ: Princeton University Press, 1998.

Douglas, Susan J. "Does Textual Analysis Tell Us Anything about Past Audiences?" In *Explorations in Communications and History*, edited by Barbie Zelizer, 66–76. New York: Routledge, 2008.

Egri, Lajos. *The Art of Dramatic Writing.* New York: Wildside, 2007.

Eriksson, Maria, Rasmus Fleischer, Anna Johansson, Pelle Snickars, and Patrick Vonderau. *Spotify Teardown: Inside the Black Box of Streaming Music.* Cambridge, MA: MIT Press, 2019.

Espinosa, Julio. "For an Imperfect Cinema." Translated by Julianne Burton. *Jump Cut,* no. 20 (1979): 24–26.

Ferrari, Chiara Francesca. *Since When Is Fran Drescher Jewish? Dubbing Stereotypes in "The Nanny," "The Simpsons," and "The Sopranos."* Austin: University of Texas Press, 2010.

Field, Syd. *Screenplay: The Foundations of Screenwriting.* New York: Delta, 1979, 2005.

Fish, Adam. "Reforming the American Public Sphere: The Media Reform Models of Progressive Television Journalists in the Era of Internet Convergence and Neoliberalism." PhD diss., UCLA, 2012.

———. *Technoliberalism.* London: Palgrave Macmillan, 2017.

Fleming, Mike. "Akiva Goldsman Explains 'Transformers' Writers Room as Paramount Adds Scribe Pair." Deadline.com, June 4, 2015. https://deadline.com/2015/06/transformers-akiva-goldsman-writers-room-paramount-1201438017.

Foucault, Michel. "Authorship: What Is an Author?" *Screen* 20, no. 1 (Spring 1979): 13–34.

Fuller, Buckminster. *Synergetics: Explorations in the Geometry of Thinking.* New York: Macmillan, 1975.

Fuller, Matthew. *Media Ecologies: Material Energies in Art and Technoculture.* Cambridge, MA: MIT Press, 2005.

Gans, Herbert. *Popular Culture and High Culture: An Analysis and Evaluation of Taste.* New York: Basic Books, 1999.

Geertz, Clifford. "Deep Play: Notes on the Balinese Cockfight." In *The Interpretation of Cultures,* 412–53. New York: Basic Books, 1973.

Giddens, Anthony. *The Consequences of Modernity.* Stanford, CA: Stanford University Press, 1990.

———. *Modernity and Self-Identity.* Cambridge: Polity Press, 1991.

Gillespie, Tarleton. *Guardians of the Internet: Platforms, Content Moderation, and Hidden Decisions That Shape Social Media.* New Haven, CT: Yale University Press, 2018.

Grainge, Paul. *Brand Hollywood: Selling Entertainment in a Global Media Age*. London: Routledge, 2007.

Grainge, Paul, and Catherine Johnson. *Promotional Screen Industries*. London: Routledge, 2015.

Gray, Jonathan. *Show Sold Separately: Promos, Spoilers, and Other Media Paratexts*. New York: New York University Press, 2010.

Grindstaff, Laura. *The Money Shot: Trash, Class, and the Making of TV Talk Shows*. Chicago: University of Chicago Press, 2002.

Haggins, Bambi. *Laughing Mad: The Black Comic Persona in Post-Soul America*. New Brunswick, NJ: Rutgers University Press, 2007.

Hamilton, Anita. "Cashing in on YouTube Fame Not Easy." *SFGATE*, April 23, 2013. www.sfgate.com/technology/article/Cashing-in-on-YouTube-fame-not-easy-4458192.php.

Hesmondhalgh, David. *The Cultural Industries*. 4th ed. London: Sage, 2018.

Hesmondhalgh, David, and Sarah Baker. *Creative Labour: Media Work in Three Cultural Industries*. London: Routledge, 2013.

Hill, Erin. *Never Done: A History of Women's Work in Media Production*. New Brunswick, NJ: Rutgers University Press, 2017.

———. "Women's Work: Feminized Labor in Hollywood, 1930–1948." PhD diss., UCLA, 2014.

Hirsch, Paul. "Processing Fads and Fashions: An Organization-Set Analysis of Cultural Industry Systems." *American Journal of Sociology* 77, no. 4 (Jan. 1972): 639–59.

Hjort, Mette. "Small Cinemas: How They Thrive and Why They Matter," *Mediascape* (Winter 2011): www.academia.edu/24378049/Small_Cinemas_How_They_Thrive_and_Why_They_Matter.

———. *Small Nation, Global Cinema*. Minneapolis: University of Minnesota Press, 2005.

Hjort, Mette, and Scott MacKenzie, eds. *Purity and Provocation: Dogma 95*. London: BFI, 2003.

Hochschild, Arlie. *The Managed Heart: The Commercialization of Human Feeling*. 3rd ed. Berkeley: University of California Press, 2012.

Holt, Jennifer. *Empires of Entertainment: Media Industries and the Politics of Deregulation, 1980–1996*. New Brunswick, NJ: Rutgers University Press, 2011.

Holt, Jennifer, and Kevin Sanson. *Connected Viewing*. Berkeley: University of California Press, 2016.

Holt, Jennifer, and Alisa Perren, eds. *Media Industries: History, Theory, and Method*. London: Blackwell, 2010.

Howe, Jeff. "The Rise of Crowdsourcing." *Wired*, June 1, 2006. www.wired.com/wired/archive/14.06/crowds.

Jenkins, Henry. *Convergence Culture: Where Old and New Media Collide*. New York: New York University Press, 2006.

———. *Spreadable Media: Creating Value and Meaning in a Networked Culture*. New York: New York University Press, 2013.

Johnson, Derek. *From Networks to Netflix: A Guide to Changing Channels*. London: Routledge, 2018.

Johnson, Derek, Derek Kompare, and Avi Santo, eds. *Making Media Work: Cultures of Management in the Entertainment Industries.* New York: New York University Press, 2014.

Johnson, Marc. "The Adpocalypse Aftermath." *Creator Handbook.* www.creatorhandbook.net/the-adpocalyse-aftermath.

Johnson, Ray William. "Ray William Johnson: Why I Left Maker Studios [Exclusive]." New Rockstars, Dec. 12, 2012. https://newmediarockstars.com/2012/12/why-i-left-maker-studios.

Johnson, Ted. "'Midnight Rider' Filmmakers Raise Doubts about Trespass Charges with New Evidence." *Variety,* Oct. 7, 2016. https://variety.com/2016/biz/news/midnight-rider-randall-miller-new-york-marine-1201881733.

Jones, Lucy. "Commentary: What Earthquakes Can Teach Us about the Coronavirus Pandemic." *Los Angeles Times,* May 6, 2020. Reprinted in *Daily World,* www.thedailyworld.com/opinion/commentary-what-earthquakes-can-teach-us-about-the-coronavirus-pandemic.

"Kinomatics: The Industrial Geometry of Culture." Kinomatics.com. https://kinomatics.com.

Kokas, Aynne. *Hollywood Made in China.* Berkeley: University of California Press, 2017.

———. "Shot in Shanghai: Western Film Co-production in Post-WTO Mainland China." PhD diss., UCLA, 2012.

Latour, Bruno. *Reassembling the Social: An Introduction to Actor-Network Theory.* Oxford: Oxford University Press, 2005.

Latour, Bruno, and Steve Woolgar. *Laboratory Life: The Construction of Scientific Facts.* Princeton, NJ: Princeton University Press, 1987.

Lo, Dennis. *The Authorship of Place: A Cultural Geography of the New Chinese Cinemas.* Hong Kong: Hong Kong University Press, 2020.

Lotz, Amanda. *We Now Disrupt This Broadcast.* Cambridge, MA: MIT Press, 2018.

Mann, Denise. *Hollywood Independents: The Postwar Talent Takeover.* Minneapolis: University of Minnesota Press, 2007.

———, ed. *Wired TV: Laboring over an Interactive Future.* New Brunswick, NJ: Rutgers University Press, 2014.

Marx, Karl. *Kapital.* London: Penguin Classics, 1992.

Mayer, Vicki. *Below-the-Line: Producers and Production Studies in the New Television Economy.* Durham, NC: Duke University Press, 2011.

———. *Producing Dreams, Consuming Youth: Mexican Americans and Mass Media.* New Brunswick, NJ: Rutgers University Press, 2003.

Mayer, Vicki, Miranda J. Banks, and John T. Caldwell, eds. *Production Studies: Cultural Studies of Media Industries.* London: Routledge, 2009.

McKee, Robert. *Story: Style, Structure, Substance and the Principles of Screenwriting.* New York: Harper Collins, 2010.

McRobbie, Angela. "Clubs to Companies." *Cultural Studies* 16, no. 4 (2002): 517–31.

Mejias, Ulises. "Confinement, Education and the Control Society." Blog entry. Accessed August 25, 2006. http://blog.ulisesmejias.com/2006/08/25/confinement-education-and-the-control-society (discontinued). Archived on the Internet Archive's WayBackMachine at https://web.archive.org/web/20210505205251/https://blog.ulisesmejias.com/2006/08/25/confinement-education-and-the-control-society.

———. "The Limits of Networks as Models for Organizing the Social." *New Media & Society* 12, no. 4 (2010): 603–17.

Melnick, Ross. *American Showman: Samuel "Roxy" Rothafel and the Birth of the Entertainment Industry, 1908–1935*. New York: Columbia University Press, 2012.

———. *Hollywood's Embassies: How Movie Theaters Projected American Power around the World*. New York: Columbia University Press, 2021.

Miller, Liz Shannon. "Can an Online Star Really Make It in Hollywood?" Vox, Jan. 3, 2020. www.vox.com/the-highlight/2019/12/27/21031780/youtube-star-make-it-hollywood-lilly-singh-issa-rae-michael-buckley-hannah-hart.

Miller, Toby, Nitin Govil, John McMurria, and Richard Maxwell. *Global Hollywood*. London: BFI, 2001.

Mittell, Jason. *Complex TV: The Poetics of Contemporary Storytelling*. New York: New York University Press, 2015.

Moore, Candace. "Liminal Spaces and Places." In Mayer, Banks, and Caldwell, *Production Studies,* 125–39.

Mosco, Vincent. *The Political Economy of Communication*. 2nd ed. London: Sage, 2009.

Netburn, Deborah, and Karen Kaplan. "UCLA Scientist Shares Nobel." *Los Angeles Times,* Oct. 7, 2020, A1, A12.

Ocasio, Anthony. "FX Signs 'Sons of Anarchy' Creator for Seasons 6 & 7." ScreenRant, Jan. 31, 2012. http://screenrant.com/sons-anarchy-season-5-6-7-kurt-sutter-aco-149044.

Ortner, Sherry. *Not Hollywood: Independent Film at the Twilight of the American Dream*. Durham, NC: Duke University Press, 2013.

Parks, Lisa. *Rethinking Media Coverage: Vertical Mediation and the War on Terror*. London: Routledge, 2018.

Parks, Lisa, and Nicole Starosielski. *Signal Traffic: Critical Studies of Media Infrastructures*. Urbana: University of Illinois Press, 2018.

Patel, Sahil. "Inside Disney's Troubled $675 Mil. Maker Studios Acquisition." *DigiDay,* Feb. 22, 2017. https://digiday.com/future-of-tv/disney-maker-studios.

Perlin, Ross. *Intern Nation: How to Earn Nothing and Learn Little in the Brave New Economy*. London: Verso, 2012.

Perren, Alisa. *Indie, Inc.: Miramax and the Transformation of Hollywood in the 1990s*. Austin: University of Texas Press, 2012.

Peterson, R., and Anand, N. "The Production of Culture Perspective." *Annual Review of Sociology* 30 (2004): 311–44.

Phillips, W.D. "'A Maze of Intricate Relationships': Mae D. Huettig and Early Forays into Film Industry Studies." *Film History* 27, no. 1 (2015): 135–63.

Pierce, David, and Eric Hoyt. "A Resource for Film, TV & Radio History." http://mediahistoryproject.org.

Plattner, Stuart. *Economic Anthropology*. Stanford, CA: Stanford University Press, 1989.

Polanyi, K. "The Economy as Instituted Process." In *Economic Anthropology,* edited by E. LeClair and H. Schneider, 122–43. New York: Holt, Rinehart and Winston, 1968.

Porst, Jennifer. *Broadcasting Hollywood: The Struggle over Feature Films on Early TV.* New Brunswick, NJ: Rutgers University Press, 2021.

Redvall, Eva Novrup. *Writing and Producing Television Drama in Denmark.* London: Palgrave-Macmillan, 2013.

Rifkin, Jeremy. *The Age of Access: The New Culture of Hypercapitalism.* New York: Putnam, 2000.

———. *The End of Work: The Decline of the Global Labor Force and the Dawn of the Post-Market Era.* New York: Putnam, 1995.

Riley, Deborah. "Production Design in *Game of Thrones.*" Master class at Design Showcase West, UCLA, June 10, 2017.

Ritzer, George, and Nathan Jurgenson. "Production, Consumption, Prosumption." *Journal of Consumer Culture* 10, no. 1 (March 2010): 13–36.

Rodriguez, Salvador, and Jessica Bursztynsky. "Snap Creators Say They're Leaving the App's Spotlight Feature as Payments Dry Up." CNBC.com, Aug. 11, 2021. www.cnbc.com/2021/08/11/snap-creators-say-theyre-leaving-the-apps-spotlight-feature-as-payments-dry-up.html.

Rogers, Adam. "The Superspreading Presidency of Donald Trump." *Wired,* Oct. 7, 2020. www.wired.com/story/the-superspreading-presidency-of-donald-trump.

Ross, Andrew. *No Collar: The Humane Workplace and Its Hidden Costs.* Philadelphia: Temple University Press, 2004.

Rothenbuhler, Eric W., and Mihai Coman, eds. *Media Anthropology.* Thousand Oaks: Sage, 2005.

Schatz, Thomas. *Hollywood Genres: Formulas, Filmmaking, and the Studio System.* Philadelphia: Temple University Press, 1981.

Schlesinger, P. *Putting Reality Together: The BBC Newsroom.* London: Constable, 1978.

Schmoyer, Tim. "How to Avoid Burnout on Your YouTube Channel." YouTube video. Sept 8, 2016. www.youtube.com/watch?v=6JFeccVJoyo.

Schwoch, James. *Global TV: New Media and the Cold War, 1945–69.* Urbana: University of Illinois Press, 2009.

Scott, Allen. *On Hollywood.* Princeton, NJ: Princeton University Press, 2005.

Siciliano, Michael L. *Creative Control: The Ambivalence of Work in the Culture Industries.* New York: Columbia University Press, 2020.

Smith-Shomade, Beretta. *Pimpin' Ain't Easy: Selling Black Entertainment Television.* New York: Routledge, 2007.

Smukler, Maya Montanez. *Liberating Hollywood: Women Directors and the Feminist Reform of 1970s American Cinema.* New Brunswick, NJ: Rutgers University Press, 2018.

Snickars, Pelle. "Our 'Spotify-Project'—an Update." Pelle Snickars (blog), Nov. 13, 2015. http://pellesnickars.se/2015/11/our-spotify-project-an-update.

Spigel, Lynn, ed. *Television after TV.* Durham, NC: Duke University Press, 2003.

Staff. "Video of the Day: Unbroken VFX Breakdown." *Below the Line,* April 3, 2015. https://www.btlnews.com/crafts/visual-fx/video-of-the-day-unbroken-vfx-breakdown.

Stahl, Matthew. *Unfree Masters.* Durham, NC: Duke University Press, 2013.

Standing, Guy. *The Precariat.* New York: Bloomsbury Academic, 2011.

Steinhart, Daniel. *Runaway Hollywood: Internationalizing Postwar Production and Location Shooting.* Berkeley: University of California Press, 2019.

Storper, Allen, and Robert Salais. *Worlds of Production: The Action Frameworks of the Economy.* Cambridge, MA: Harvard University Press, 1997.

Strate, Lance. *Media Ecology: An Approach to Understanding the Human Condition.* London: Peter Lang, 2017.

Szczepanik, Petr, and Patrick Vonderau, eds. *Behind the Screen: Inside European Production Cultures.* New York: Palgrave Macmillan, 2013.

Tsing, Anna Lowenhaupt. *Friction: An Ethnography of Global Connection.* Princeton, NJ: Princeton University Press, 2005.

Tsing, Anna, and Elizabeth Pollman. "Global Futures: The Game." In *Histories of the Future,* edited by Daniel Rosenberg and Susan Harding, 105–22. Durham, NC: Duke University Press, 2005.

Turner, Victor. *The Anthropology of Experience.* Urbana: University of Illinois Press, 1986, 2001.

Tussey, Ethan. *The Procrastination Economy: The Big Business of Downtime.* New York: New York University Press, 2018.

Vonderau, Patrick. "Ethics in Media Industries Research." In T*he Routledge Companion to Media Industries,* edited by Paul McDonald, 518–26. New York: Routledge, 2022.

———. "The Spotify Effect: Digital Distribution and Financial Growth." *TelevisionandNewMedia,*Nov.21,2017.https://doi.org/10.1177/1527476417741200.

Walton, Saige. *Cinema's Baroque Flesh: Film, Phenomenology and the Art of Entanglement.* Amsterdam: University of Amsterdam Press, 2016.

Wasson, Haidee. *Everyday Movies: Portable Film Projectors and the Transformation of American Culture.* Berkeley: University of California Press, 2020.

———. *Museum Movies: The Museum of Modern Art and the Birth of Art Cinema.* Berkeley: University of California Press, 2005.

Wasson, Haidee, and Lee Grieveson. *Cinema's Military Industrial Complex.* Berkeley: University of California Press, 2018.

Whang, Victor W. "The Next Big Business Buzzword: Ecosystem?" *Forbes,* April 16, 2016. www.forbes.com/sites/victorhwang/2014/04/16/the-next-big-business-buzzword-ecosystem/#17481a496e12.

White, Mimi. *Tele-Advising: Therapeutic Discourse in American Television.* Chapel Hill: University of North Carolina Press, 1992.

Williams, Mark. "What Is the Media Ecology Project?" Media Ecology Project. https://mediaecology.dartmouth.edu/wp/about.

Williams, Raymond. *Television: Technology and Cultural Form.* New York: Schocken, 1974.

Wollen, Peter. "Godard, and Counter-Cinema." *Afterimage* 4 (Autumn 1972): 6–17.

Index

Milton Keynes UK
Ingram Content Group UK Ltd.
UKHW022000050524
442194UK00004B/229